Taking Sides: Clashing Views
on Political Issues, 21/e

William J. Miller

http://create.mheducation.com

ISBN-10: 1260494195   ISBN-13: 9781260494198

2 3 4 5 6 7 QVS 24 23 22 21 20

Contents

i. Detailed Table of Contents by Miller   1

ii. Preface by Miller   5

iii. Introduction by Miller   8

Unit 1   15

1. Democracy and the American Political Process by Miller   16
   1.1. Is Bigger Government Better Government? by Miller   17
   1.2. Is the Current Presidential Nomination System Actually Democratic? by Miller   29
   1.3. Are Entitlement Programs Creating a Culture of Dependency? by Miller   38
   1.4. Should Free Tade Remain the Backbone of American Trade Policy? by Miller   50

Unit 2   61

2. The Institutions of Government by Miller   62
   2.1. Does the President Have Unilateral War Powers? by Miller   63
   2.2. Is President Trump's Relationship with Vladimir Putin Detrimental for the United States? by Miller   75
   2.3. Is Congress a Dysfunctional Institution? by Miller   84
   2.4. Should Supreme Court Justices have Term Limits? by Miller   93
   2.5. Should the Senate Be Able to Delay Hearings on Nominations While Waiting for an Investigation to Conclude? by Miller   103

Unit 3   113

3. Social Change and Public Policy by Miller   114
   3.1. Should Access to Abortions Be Restricted? by Miller   115
   3.2. Is Lethal Injection as a Method of Execution Still Constitutional? by Miller   126
   3.3. Should Colleges and Universities Consider an Applicant's Race When Deciding Whether to Accept a Student? by Miller   143
   3.4. Does the NRA Hold Too Much Power in the Gun Control Debate? by Miller   152
   3.5. Should "Recreational" Drugs Be Legalized? by Miller   161
   3.6. Should Business Owners Be Able to Refuse Clients Based on Religious Beliefs? by Miller   171

Unit 4   183

4. America and the World by Miller   184
   4.1. Should the President Have the Power to Limit Immigrants and Refugees from Specific Countries? by Miller   185
   4.2. Should the United States Build a Border Wall with Mexico? by Miller   200
   4.3. Should the United States Expect North Korea to Denuclearize? by Miller   210
   4.4. Is the United States Too Tied to Israel when Deciding Policy in the Middle East? by Miller   220

Detailed Table of Contents

Unit 1: Democracy and the American Political Process

Issue: Is Bigger Government Better Government?
YES: Jeff Madrick, from "The Case for Big Government," Princeton University Press (2008)
NO: David Boaz, from "The Return of Big Government," *Cato Policy Report* (2009)

Humanities professor Jeff Madrick surveys the numerous government interventions in the economy since the end of World War II and concludes that they have been essential to America's growth and well-being. Executive Vice President of the Cato Institute David Boaz traces America's libertarian traditions and reminds readers that there are times where government's best course of action is simply deciding to do nothing.

Issue: Is the Current Presidential Nomination System Actually Democratic?
YES: Jamelle Bouie, from "The Process Worked," *Slate* (2016)
NO: William Saletan, from "The Primaries Aren't Democratic? They're Not Supposed to Be Democratic," *Slate* (2016)

Journalist Jamelle Bouie argues that the current presidential nomination system is in fact quite democratic by allowing states to determine how best to conduct elections within their borders. He notes that even outside of elections, American government has always flourished under a blend of majoritarian, non-majoritarian, and counter-majoritarian elements. William Saletan, also a journalist, acknowledges that the nomination process is not particularly democratic but reminds readers that the goals of primaries and caucuses are to select candidates that best represent party interests.

Issue: Are Entitlement Programs Creating a Culture of Dependency?
YES: Nicholas Eberstadt, from "The Rise of Entitlements in Modern America, 1960-2010," Templeton Press (2012)
NO: William A. Galston, from "Have We Become 'A Nation of Takers'?" Templeton Press (2012)

Social scientist Nicholas Eberstadt argues that the increase in entitlement programs is unprecedented in American history and has created a large dependency class that has lost the will to work. Political theorist William A. Galston sees the growth of American entitlement programs as an appropriate response to the needs of an aging population and rising costs of higher education and medicine; he sees them not as evidence of dependency but of "interdependence."

Issue: Should Free Trade Remain the Backbone of American Trade Policy?
YES: Samuel Gregg, from "Trump's Tariffs and Why America Needs a Patriotic Case for Free Trade," *Public Discourse* (2018)
NO: Daniel McCarthy, from "The Case for Trump's Tariffs and 'America First' Economics," *The New York Times* (2018)

Researcher Samuel Gregg argues that free trade supporters need to more actively explain to Americans how free trade serves the nation's long-term national interests and represents the ideals of patriotism more than isolationism. On the counter, conservative news editor Daniel McCarthy describes how economic nationalism can best serve America's political and economic needs in the current era. Only by building up our domestic economy can the country hope to regain strengths it has seen eroded by foreign nations in recent years.

Unit 2: The Institutions of Government

Issue: Does the President Have Unilateral War Powers?
YES: John C. Yoo, from "The President's Constitutional Authority to Conduct Military Operations Against Terrorists and Nations Supporting Them: Memorandum Opinion for the Deputy Counsel to the President," *Memorandum Opinion for the Deputy Counsel to the President* (2001)
NO: Kurt Couchman, from "The War Powers Resolution Doesn't Let the President Start Wars," *The Hill* (2018)

John C. Yoo, a Law Professor at the University of California, Berkeley, argues that the language of the Constitution, long-accepted precedents, and the practical need for speedy action in emergencies all support broad executive power during war. Kurt Couchman, on the other hand, delineates how the War Powers Resolution positions Congress to be the definitive decider of when the American military is sent into action.

Issue: Is President Trump's Relationship with Vladimir Putin Detrimental for the United States?
YES: Elena Chernenko, from "An Easy Win for Vladimir Putin," *The New York Times* (2018)
NO: Paris Dennard, from "Trump Meeting with Putin Is the Right Thing for America," *The Hill* (2018)

Elena Chernenko—foreign editor at *Kommersant*—writes that Russia is holding the power in their relationship with the United States today because President Putin has nothing to lose at home while President Trump has everything at stake. As a result, Trump's perceived ties to Russia seem to be harmful to the United States' larger interests. Paris Dennard, on the other hand, argues that Trump's bold approach to international diplomacy is reviving America's clout on the global stage. By requesting action, he can get Putin to listen and respond in kind.

Issue: Is Congress a Dysfunctional Institution?
YES: Sheryl Gay Stolberg and Nicholas Fandos, from "As Gridlock Deepens in Congress, Only Gloom Is Bipartisan," *The New York Times* (2018)
NO: Thomas Petri, from "Our Government Is Messy—But That Doesn't Mean It Isn't Working," *Washington Post* (2016)

Congressional correspondent Sheryl Gay Stolberg and Nicholas Fandos discuss how gridlock in Congress has reached an all-time low and both parties seem to only agree on how poorly performing Congress is to the American people today. On the other hand, Thomas Petri, a former member of the U.S. House from Wisconsin, argues that Congress is actually operating exactly how the Framers intended despite public perceptions of dysfunction.

Issue: Should Supreme Court Justices Have Term Limits?
YES: Norm Ornstein, from "Why the Supreme Court Needs Term Limits," *The Atlantic* (2014)
NO: Alexander Hamilton, from "Federalist No.78," *The Federalist Papers* (1788)

Writer Norm Ornstein argues that the most effective way to address the problems created by an increasingly politicized Supreme Court is to limit all justices to 18-year terms. Founding Father Alexander Hamilton, on the other hand, argues that the judiciary will be the weakest branch of government and life terms protect judges from political pressures while preventing the invasion of their powers by either the president or Congress.

Issue: Should the Senate Be Able to Delay Hearings on Nominations While Waiting for an Investigation to Conclude?
YES: Paul Schiff Berman, from "A Better Reason to Delay Kennedy's Replacement," *The New York Times* (2018)
NO: Jonathan Turley, from "No One Can Use Mueller Probe to Hold Up Supreme Court Nominee," *The Hill* (2018)

Law Professor Paul Schiff Berman argues that people under the cloud of investigation do not get to pick the judges who may preside over their cases. Consequently, he believes presidents under any type of investigation should not be able to appoint judges who may ultimately be involved in deciding their legal fate. Jonathan Turley—also a public law academic—instead points to a complete lack of historical precedent or statue for holding such a view. Instead, he argues such arguments are typically politically opportunistic and not rooted in substantive law.

Unit 3: Social Change and Public Policy

Issue: Should Access to Abortions Be Restricted?
YES: Berny Belvedere, from "Abortion Is Wrong Even If the Fetus Is Not a Person," *National Review* (2017)
NO: Julie Hirschfield Davis, from "How New Abortion Restrictions Would Affect Women's Health Care," *The New York Times* (2018)

Philosopher and writer Berny Belvedere argues that debates between pro-life and pro-choice groups are rooted too much in rhetoric and not enough in reality. Regardless, he examines how moral arguments suggest abortion should not be legalized in any way. On the other hand, Julie Hirschfield Davis—a reporter and political analyst—examines how increased restrictions regarding abortion access would negatively affect women's health care, which directly counters arguments made by some anti-abortion advocates.

Issue: Is Lethal Injection as a Method of Execution Still Constitutional?
YES: Samuel Alito, from "*Glossip v. Gross*," United States Supreme Court (2015)
NO: Sonia Sotomayor, from "*Glossip v. Gross*," United States Supreme Court (2015)

Supreme Court Justice Samuel Alito argues that lethal injection remains a viable and constitutional method of execution despite some states experimenting with different protocols given the inability to acquire sodium thiopental or pentobarbital. Writing for the minority, Justice Sonia Sotomayor argued that she believes capital punishment, in any form, likely violates the Eighth

Amendment protection against cruel and unusual punishment. As such, too much responsibility is being placed on petitioners to demonstrate certain drugs are not available, leading to a slippery slope of possible execution methods.

Issue: Should Colleges and Universities Consider an Applicant's Race When Deciding Whether to Accept a Student?
YES: Maureen Downey, from "Trump Doesn't Think College Admissions Should Consider Race. Do You?" *The Atlanta Journal-Constitution* (2018)
NO: Shane Croucher, from "Campus Diversity: Will Trump End Affirmative Action in College Admissions?" *Newsweek* (2018)

Reporter Maureen Downey argues that not considering affirmative action as part of college admissions will have negative—and potentially unanticipated—consequences on the composition of campuses across the country. Shane Croucher, on the other hand, describes the changes being administered by the Trump administration and why they believe they assure federal guidelines better align with the prevailing sentiment of recent Supreme Court decisions.

Issue: Does the NRA Hold Too Much Power in the Gun Control Debate?
YES: Bill Scher, from "Why the NRA Will Always Win," *Politico* (2018)
NO: Mel Robbins, from "The Real Gun Problem Is Mental Health, Not the NRA," CNN (2014)

Author and editor Bill Scher argues that the National Rifle Association's power as a lobbying group is not rooted in the money it has been able to raise but instead in the permeation of a culture that believe gun ownership is a way of life, central to one's freedom, and deserving of defence on a daily basis. Either way, the influence of the organization is vast. Mel Robbins—a legal analyst—argues that the NRA is not the main problem with gun violence in the United States. Instead, she points to concrete examples that demonstrate how and increased focused on mental health could better alleviate current issues.

Issue: Should "Recreational" Drugs Be Legalized?
YES: Alex Suskind, from "Cory Booker Explains Why He's Making Legal Weed His Signature Issue," *Vice* (2017)
NO: David Brooks, from "Weed: Been There. Done That," *The New York Times* (2014)

Writer and interviewer Alex Suskind interviews New Jersey Democratic Senator Cory Booker about his proposed legislation to legalize marijuana at the federal level. Through the interview Booker explains why he wants to see marijuana legalized and how he sees government being able to repair the egregious harm the War on Drugs has causes to targeted communities. David Brooks—*New York Times* columnist—argues that making marijuana more accessible raises important moral and ethical questions that must be considered as part of the larger policy argument.

Issue: Should Business Owners Be Able to Refuse Clients Based on Religious Beliefs?
YES: Anthony Kennedy, from "*Masterpiece Cakeshop, Ltd., et al., v. Colorado Civil Rights Commission, et al.*," United States Supreme Court (2018)
NO: Ruth Bader Ginsburg, from "*Masterpiece Cakeshop, Ltd., et al., v. Colorado Civil Rights Commission, et al.*," United States Supreme Court (2018)

Supreme Court Justice Anthony Kennedy, writing for the Court, identifies the fundamental conflict between freedom of religion and civil rights. In the matter of a businessman's decision on whether to serve a gay couple, Kennedy acknowledges how imperative it is to balance religious sincerity with the rights of a group to be served. In this case, however, he sides with the business. Justice Ruth Bader Ginsburg agrees with much of Kennedy's argument but believes at a fundamental level it is not right that a business provides services to one group that it wouldn't provide to another.

Unit 4: America and the World

Issue: Should the President Have the Power to Limit Immigrants and Refugees from Specific Countries?
YES: John Roberts, from "*Majority Opinion: Trump v. Hawaii*," United States Supreme Court (2018)
NO: Sonia Sotomayor, from "*Dissenting Opinion: Trump v. Hawaii*," United States Supreme Court (2018)

Writing for the Court, Chief Justice John Roberts argues that the Trump Administration based its immigration policy on a sufficient national security justification to survive a rational basis review. Regardless of politicized statements made, the president's broad power over immigration matters trumps potential concerns that are not in direct violation of any Constitutional provisions. Writing for the minority, Justice Sonia Sotomayor points to both Trump's statements about Muslims and the Establishment Clause to argue that the president should not have the power to ban immigrants from specific countries—especially when there is a strong religious correlation.

<u>**Issue: Should the United States Build a Border Wall with Mexico?**</u>
YES: Reece Jones, from "Why Build a Border Wall?" *North American Congress on Latin America* (2012)
NO: Vanda Felbab-Brown, from "The Wall: The Real Costs of a Barrier between the United States and Mexico," *Brookings Institute* (2017)

Geographer Reece Jones writes that a possible border wall would serve a greater purpose than responding to immigration and drug problems. Instead, it can help establish sovereignty, protect the wealth of impacted states, and limit the possible dilution of cultural practices by immigrants. On the other side, Vanda Felbab-Brown—a senior fellow at the Brookings Institute— demonstrates the true costs of building a wall between the United States and Mexico. Her argument focuses on real costs and potential negative externalities of such a decision.

<u>**Issue: Should the United States Expect North Korea to Denuclearize?**</u>
YES: Eleanor Albert, from "What Would Denuclearization Look Like in North Korea?" *Council on Foreign Relations* (2018)
NO: Aaron David Miller and Richard Sokolsky, from "Trump Should Learn to Live with a Nuclear North Korea," *Washington Post* (2018)

Eleanor Albert—a writer for the Council on Foreign Relations—interviews Melissa Hanham (a Senior Research Associate in the East Asia Non-proliferation Program) about how denuclearization could happen in North Korea. Through the interview, she emphasizes ways the United States could help encourage and assure a denuclearized North Korea in the future. On the other hand, Aaron David Miller (a vice-president at the Woodrow Wilson Center) and Richard Sokolsky (a fellow at the Carnegie Endowment for International Peace) argue denuclearization is an unreachable dream and instead the United States should identify more achievable outcomes from continuing talks with the once rogue nation.

<u>**Issue: Is the United States Too Tied to Israel When Deciding Policy in the Middle East?**</u>
YES: Ramzy Baroud, from "The Uneven Alliance: How America Became Pro-Israel," *Al-Jazeera* (2017)
NO: Tamara Cofman Wittes and Daniel B. Shapiro, from "How Not to Measure Americans' Support for Israel," *Brookings Institute* (2018)

Ramzy Baroud—an author and media consultant—examines how and why Israel's influence on the United States has grown over time. He believes this has had a direct impact on American policy choices within the Middle East and negatively impacted many Arab nations. Tamara Cofman Wittes, a senior fellow at Brookings, and Daniel Shapiro, a former ambassador to Israel, argue that

Americans continue to support their country's relationship with Israel even as attitudes regarding the Israeli-Palestinian conflict continue to demonstrate increased polarization.

Preface

As I write this, Christine Blasey Ford has accused Brett Kavanaugh—President Donald Trump's nominee to the United States Supreme Court—of sexual harassment 30 years ago, when they were both in high school. Already facing a contested confirmation based on its timing near midterm elections and the continuance of the Mueller probe, the sheer volume of protected documents, and uncharacteristic infighting among members of the Senate Judiciary System, Kavanaugh has become symbolic of American politics today: Divisive, Raw, Emotional. And perhaps most importantly, evolving. If I flip on news coverage at this moment, I'd hear about response to Hurricane Florence (and likely about the lack of response to Puerto Rico's plight a year ago), the upcoming midterm elections (and how Ted Cruz is in trouble along with many of his peers in typically assume safe states), Barack Obama and Joe Biden's reemergence in politics, how professional and amateur football players are being removed from games over issues of safety, and whatever President Trump has opted to tweet in the past 30 seconds. Beyond what is being covered, the FDA is inspecting food I'll consume next week, my Homeowner's Association is measuring my grass, a parent is lamenting the loss of their child to gun violence, the FCC is monitoring the National Football League game on television, the Social Security bathtub is ebbing and flowing, a young African female is being taught how to pull the detonating device on a suicide vest, the NSA is watching my text messages, my employer is screening my e-mails, and I am unable to kick the urge to pull the tag off of my mattress. In short, public policy is happening around me. And I cannot possibly imagine in all the ways it is doing so.

In recent years, the world has seen how important political issues truly are. From the impact of retirements on the Supreme Court to international reactions to terrorism and immigrants alike, we have witnessed enough chasing of views on political issues to fill volumes, let alone a single reader. At the end of the day, we work to frame issues in macrolevel terms when possible to assure applicability and continued relevancy, even after the initial moment of interest has passed. We strive to encourage dialogue on these ever-important issues occurring around us in our daily lives. And we hope to hearten a more meaningful debate than the one Americans witness among talking heads every evening. Rather than simply observing two ships as they pass in the night, this volume aims to provide a groundwork that allows all readers to critically assess the political world around them.

If Americans are forced to rely on talking heads, they will likely fail to ever grasp the complexities of government and policy in the democratic context. Talking heads, after all, have both an audience and an agenda. Consequently, it is highly unlikely that they will provide the necessary context and clarity for a given issue so that the average viewer can formulate their own opinion. As debate continues, everyone involved will typically utilize vague, emotion-laden language and tend to speak past many viewers, in some cases intentionally. If the conversation gets too heated, they may rely on epithets or simply spewing party-based rhetoric meant to win over viewers with an impressive dose of partisanship. For example, when the discussion of affirmative action comes down to both sides accusing the other of "racism," or when the controversy over abortion degenerates into taunts and name-calling, then no one really listens and learns from the other side.

I still believe there is value in learning from an opponent. No matter how diametrically opposed two sides may be, there is knowledge to be gained from fully comprehending the arguments made against you. Your own case, after all, can be made significantly stronger if you account for your own potential weaknesses. Sometimes, after listening to others, we change our view entirely. But in most cases, we either incorporate some elements of the opposing view—thus making our own richer—or else learn how to answer the objections to our viewpoint. Either way, we gain from the experience. For these reasons, I believe that encouraging dialogue between opposed positions is the most certain way of enhancing public understanding.

The purpose of this 21st edition of *Taking Sides* is to continue to work toward the revival of political dialogue in America while encouraging the development of a sense of relevancy. As has occurred in the past 20 editions, I examine leading issues in American politics from the perspective of sharply opposed points of view. I have tried to select authors who argue their points vigorously but in such a way as to enhance comprehension of the issue. In short, I have aimed to include works that will stimulate interest and encourage understanding of multiple angles in any given issue.

I hope that readers who confront lively and thoughtful statements on vital issues will be stimulated to ask some of the critical questions about American politics. What are the highest priority issues with which government must deal today? What positions should be taken on these issues? What should be the attitude of Americans toward their government? I firmly believe that in order to be a truly great, stable democracy, citizens must be willing to consider such questions, even if they are unsure of where they stand. Acknowledging a need to become more informed will forever be favored as opposed to apathy, passivity, or misunderstood resentment.

Book Organization

The text is divided into four units, each addressing a different aspect of politics. At the beginning of each unit is a unit opener that briefly identifies the specific issues in the section. Next are the issues themselves, each of which starts with an introduction that sets the stage for the debate as it is argued in the YES and NO selections. An "Exploring the Issue" section follows the selections and provides some final observations and comments about the topic. The "Exploring the Issue" section contains "Critical Thinking and Reflection Questions," the common ground between the two viewpoints, and print and Internet suggestions for further reading.

William J. Miller
Campus Labs®

Editor of This Volume

William J. Miller, an unabashed data wonk, indulges his fascination for analytics and political science, whether analyzing public opinion data from central Asian nations for the U.S. Department of State or assessing the role of the Tea Party in recent U.S. elections. As assistant vice president, Campus Adoption, he leverages data best practices to help campuses make strategic decisions. As a teacher, he draws on his perspective as a public intellectual to engage students in courses on political science, public policy, program evaluation, and organizational behavior.

Will joined the Campus Labs team in late 2016, after serving for four years as both a faculty member and senior administrator at Flagler College in Florida. There, as Executive Director of Institutional Analytics, Effectiveness, and Planning, he helped transform the campus-wide outcomes assessment process. He also served as the college's Accreditation Liaison to the Commission on Colleges of the Southern Association of Colleges and Schools (SACSCOC). Before joining Flagler, he held faculty positions at Southeast Missouri State University, Notre Dame College, and Ohio University.

As a prolific author and dynamic speaker, Will regularly presents at professional conferences for both higher education and political science. He has also advised elected officials, agency administrators, and social service agencies. His scholarly pursuits focus on assessment, campaigns and elections, polling, political psychology, and the pedagogy of political science and public administration. He received a Master of Applied Politics from the Ray C. Bliss Institute at The University of Akron, where he also earned his Doctor of Philosophy in Urban Studies and Public Affairs. He holds both a Master of Arts in Political Science and Bachelor of Arts from Ohio University.

Acknowledgments

I am thrilled to be able to draft another edition of this important volume. I want to start by thanking a few of my mentors who have helped me through my career. Michael John Burton, Karl Kaltenthaler, Lysa Burnier, Bill Cunion, Brian Smentkowski, and Jeremy Walling have been a constant sounding board for research ideas and thoughts. I'm also always thankful for Jill Meloy for her confidence and never-ending assistance throughout the process. I look forward to hearing from readers—instructors and especially students—about their thoughts on the issues and materials selected. Feel free to reach out at any time via e-mail: wmiller@ campuslabs.com. It goes without saying that anything found to be incorrect throughout the book is of no one's fault but my own.

Academic Advisory Board Members

Members of the Academic Advisory Board are instrumental in the final selection of articles for *Taking Sides* books. Their review of the articles for content, level, and appropriateness provides critical direction to the editor and staff. We think that you will find their careful consideration reflected in this book.

James Hite
Clackamas Community College

Elizabeth Hull
Rutgers University—Newark

Jean-Gabriel Jolivet
Ashford University

Orin Kirshner
Florida Atlantic University

Lisa Krasner
University of Phoenix

Anne Thrower Leonard
Embry-Riddle Aeronautical University

Nancy Lind
Illinois State University

Ed Miller
University of Wisconsin-Stevens Point

Mark Miller
Clark University

Allyn Milojevich
University of Tennessee

Patrick Moore
Richland College

Derek Mosley
Meridian Community College

Lynn Paredes-Manfredi
Seminole State College

Joseph Romance
Fort Hays State University

David Smith
Texas A&M University Corpus Christi

Howard W. Starks Jr.
Wayne State University

Ron Vardy
University of Houston

Lowell F. Wolf
Farmingdale State College

Introduction

Labels and Alignments in American Politics

As I write this, we are less than two months from midterm elections. While the president's party historically fares poorly during the initial midterm, this year's election has an entirely different feeling to it. President Trump has been as polarizing a figure as anyone historically encountered in the United States—even within his own party. As a result, what occurs in November will be an indicator of what the next two years hold—along with predicting the potential for Trump to successfully win a second term in 2020. From the Mueller probe to the Kavanaugh confirmation to Bob Woodward's book, this isn't the White House political scientists are used to studying. For the electorate at large, it appears as if the democratic bargain is little more than an afterthought. There was a time in our country's history where parties put candidates up for election and accepted the election results, win or lose. Yet today both Democrats and Republicans alike take electoral losses and throw them aside while determining ways to be obstructive. And few seem willing to mention that the country loses as a whole when this happens. We often talk about right and left, red and blue. But such simple dichotomies unfortunately over simplify the political realities facing the United States today. All the while, talking heads continue to throw around ideological labels designed to help simplify our understanding and allow us to better categorize ourselves. Unfortunately, the opposite often occurs.

Liberal, conservative, moderate, pluralist, radical, right wing, left wing, "classical" economics, "progressive"—what do these terms mean? Or do they have any meaning? Some political analysts regard them as arbitrary labels slapped on by commentators seeking quick ways to sum up candidates (or in some cases to demonize them). The reaction against the ideological labels is understandable, not only because they are often used too loosely but, as we shall see, because the terms themselves can evolve over time. Nevertheless, we think there are some core meanings left, so if they are used carefully, they can help us locate positions on the political stage and the actors who occupy them. In this Introduction, we shall try to spell out the meanings of these terms, at least as they are used in American politics.

Liberals versus Conservatives: An Overview

Let us examine, very briefly, the historical evolution of the terms *liberalism* and *conservatism*. By examining the roots of these terms, we can see how these philosophies have adapted themselves to changing times. In that way, we can avoid using the terms rigidly, without reference to the particular contexts in which liberalism and conservatism have operated over the past two centuries.

Classical Liberalism

The classical root of the term *liberalism* is the Latin word *libertas,* meaning "liberty" or "freedom." In the early nineteenth century, liberals dedicated themselves to freeing individuals from all unnecessary and oppressive obligations to authority—whether the authority came from the church or the state. They opposed the licensing and censorship of the press, the punishment of heresy, the establishment of religion, and any attempt to dictate orthodoxy in matters of opinion. In economics, liberals opposed state monopolies and other constraints upon competition between private businesses. At this point in its development, liberalism defined freedom primarily in terms of freedom *from.* It appropriated the French term *laissez-faire,* which literally means "leave to be." Leave people alone! That was the spirit of liberalism in its early days. It wanted government to stay out of people's lives and to play a modest role in general. Thomas Jefferson summed up this concept when he said, "I am no friend of energetic government. It is always oppressive."

Despite their suspicion of government, classical liberals invested high hopes in the political process. By and large, they were great believers in democracy. They believed in widening suffrage to include every white male, and some of them were prepared to enfranchise women and blacks as well. Although liberals occasionally worried about "the tyranny of the majority," they were more prepared to trust the masses than to trust a permanent, entrenched elite. Liberal social policy was dedicated to fulfilling human potential and was based on the assumption that this often-hidden potential is enormous. Human beings, liberals argued, were basically good and reasonable. Evil and irrationality were believed to be caused by "outside" influences; they were the result of a bad social environment.

A liberal commonwealth, therefore, was one that would remove the hindrances to the full flowering of the human personality. The basic vision of liberalism has not changed since the nineteenth century. What has changed is the way it is applied to modern society. In that respect, liberalism has changed dramatically. Today, instead of regarding government with suspicion, liberals welcome government as an instrument to serve the people. The change in philosophy began in the latter years of the nineteenth century, when businesses—once small, independent operations—began to grow into giant structures that overwhelmed individuals and sometimes even overshadowed the state in power and wealth. At that time, liberals began reconsidering their commitment to the *laissez-faire* philosophy. If the state can be an oppressor, asked liberals, can't big business also oppress people? By then, many were convinced that commercial and industrial monopolies were crushing the souls and bodies of the working classes. The state, formerly the villain, now was viewed by liberals as a potential savior. The concept of freedom was transformed into something more than a negative freedom *from*; the term began to take on a positive meaning. It meant "realizing one's full potential." Toward this end, liberals believed, the state could prove to be a valuable instrument. It could educate children, protect the health and safety of workers, help people through hard times, promote a healthy economy, and—when necessary—force business to act more humanely and responsibly. Thus was born the movement that culminated in New Deal liberalism.

New Deal Liberalism

In the United States, the argument in favor of state intervention did not win an enduring majority constituency until after the Great Depression of the 1930s began to be felt deeply. The disastrous effects of a depression that left a quarter of the workforce unemployed opened the way to a new administration—and a promise. "I pledge you, I pledge myself," Franklin D. Roosevelt said when accepting the Democratic nomination in 1932, "to a new deal for the American people." Roosevelt's New Deal was an attempt to effect relief and recovery from the Depression; it employed a variety of means, including welfare programs, public works, and business regulation—most of which involved government intervention in the economy. The New Deal liberalism relied on government to liberate people from poverty, oppression, and economic exploitation. At the same time, the New Dealers claimed

to be as zealous as the classical liberals in defending political and civil liberties.

The common element in *laissez-faire* liberalism and welfare-state liberalism is their dedication to the goal of realizing the full potential of each individual. Some still questioned whether this is best done by minimizing state involvement or whether it sometimes requires an activist state. The New Dealers took the latter view, although they prided themselves on being pragmatic and experimental about their activism. During the heyday of the New Deal, a wide variety of programs were tried and—if found wanting—abandoned. All decent means should be tried, they believed, even if it meant dilution of ideological purity. The Roosevelt administration, for example, denounced bankers and businessmen in campaign rhetoric but worked very closely with them while trying to extricate the nation from the Depression. This set a pattern of pragmatism that New Dealers from Harry Truman to Lyndon Johnson emulated.

Progressive Liberalism

Progressive liberalism emerged in the late 1960s and early 1970s as a more militant and uncompromising movement than the New Deal had ever been. Its roots go back to the New Left student movement of the early 1960s. New Left students went to the South to participate in civil rights demonstrations, and many of them were bloodied in confrontations with southern police; by the mid-1960s they were confronting the authorities in the North over issues like poverty and the Vietnam War. By the end of the decade, the New Left had fragmented into a variety of factions and had lost much of its vitality, but a somewhat more respectable version of it appeared as the New Politics movement. Many New Politics crusaders were former New Leftists who had traded their jeans for coats and ties; they tried to work within the system instead of always confronting it.

Even so, they retained some of the spirit of the New Left. The civil rights slogan "Freedom Now" expressed the mood of the New Politics. The young university graduates who filled its ranks had come from an environment where "nonnegotiable" demands were issued to college deans by leaders of sit-in protests. There was more than youthful arrogance in the New Politics movement; however, there was a pervasive belief that America had lost, had compromised away, much of its idealism. The New Politics liberals sought to recover some of that spirit by linking up with an older tradition of militant reform, which went back to the time of the Revolution. These new liberals saw themselves as the authentic heirs of Thomas Paine and Henry David

Thoreau, of the abolitionists, the radical populists, the suffragettes, and the great progressive reformers of the early twentieth century.

While New Deal liberals concentrated almost exclusively on bread-and-butter issues such as unemployment and poverty, the New Politics liberals introduced what came to be known as social issues into the political arena. These included the repeal of laws against abortion, the liberalization of laws against homosexuality and pornography, the establishment of affirmative action programs to ensure increased hiring of minorities and women, and the passage of the Equal Rights Amendment.

In foreign policy, too, New Politics liberals departed from the New Deal agenda. Because they had keener memories of the unpopular and (for them) unjustified war in Vietnam than of World War II, they became doves, in contrast to the general hawkishness of the New Dealers. They were skeptical of any claim that the United States must be the leader of the free world or, indeed, that it had any special mission in the world; some were convinced that America was already in decline and must learn to adjust accordingly. The real danger, they argued, came not from the Soviet Union but from the mad pace of America's arms race with the Soviets, which, as they saw it, could bankrupt the country, starve its social programs, and culminate in a nuclear Armageddon. New Politics liberals were heavily represented at the 1972 Democratic national convention, which nominated South Dakota senator George McGovern for president. By the 1980s, the New Politics movement was no longer new, and many of its adherents preferred to be called progressives.

By this time, their critics had another name for them: radicals. The critics saw their positions as inimical to the interests of the United States, destructive of the family, and fundamentally at odds with the views of most Americans. The adversaries of the progressives were not only conservatives but many New Deal liberals, who openly scorned the McGovernites. This split still exists within the Democratic Party, although it is now more skillfully managed by party leaders. In 1988, the Democrats paired Michael Dukakis, whose Massachusetts supporters were generally on the progressive side of the party, with New Dealer Lloyd Bentsen as the presidential and vice presidential candidates, respectively.

In 1992, the Democrats won the presidency with Arkansas governor Bill Clinton, whose record as governor seemed to put him in the moderate-to-conservative camp, and Tennessee senator Albert Gore, whose position on environmental issues could probably be considered quite liberal, but whose general image was middle-of-the-road. Both candidates had moved toward liberal positions on the issues of gay rights and abortion. By 1994, Clinton was perceived by many Americans as being "too liberal," which some speculate may have been a factor in the defeat of Democrats in the congressional elections that year. Clinton immediately sought to shake off that perception, positioning himself as a "moderate" between extremes and casting the Republicans as an "extremist" party. (These two terms will be examined presently.)

President Obama comes from the progressive liberal wing of the Democratic Party; although in his campaign for office, he attempted to appeal to moderates and even some conservatives by stressing his determination to regard the country not in terms of red (Republican) states and blue (Democratic) states but as a nation united. Once in office, however, his agenda, which included an $830-billion "stimulus" expenditure to jump-start the economy and an ambitious social insurance program, came from the playbook of progressive liberalism; by 2010, it faced unanimous resistance from the Republican minority in Congress. In the 2010 congressional races, its unpopularity in the so-called "swing" districts and states, that had swung Democrat in the 2008 election, costs many moderate Democrats their seats in Congress. Yet by 2012, the Democrats seemed to be recovering. With the surprise election of Donald Trump in 2016, the recovery seemed to be short-lived, however. Hillary Clinton was supposed to move the party forward, but now Democrats instead wait to see how voters respond to two years of Trump rule in 2018.

Conservatism

Like liberalism, conservatism has undergone historical transformation in America. Just as early liberals (represented by Thomas Jefferson) espoused less government, early conservatives (whose earliest leaders were Alexander Hamilton and John Adams) urged government support of economic enterprise and government intervention on behalf of certain groups. But today, in reaction to the growth of the welfare state, conservatives argue strongly that more government means more unjustified interference in citizens' lives, more bureaucratic regulation of private conduct, more inhibiting control of economic enterprise, more material advantage for the less energetic and less able at the expense of those who are prepared to work harder and better, and, of course, more taxes—taxes that will be taken from those who have earned money and given to those who have not.

Contemporary conservatives are not always opposed to state intervention. They may support larger military expenditures in order to protect society against foreign enemies. They may also allow for some intrusion into private life in order to protect society against internal subversion and would pursue criminal prosecution zealously in order to protect society against domestic violence. The fact is that few conservatives, and perhaps fewer liberals, are absolute with respect to their views about the power of the state. Both are quite prepared to use the state in order to further *their* purposes. It is true that activist presidents such as Franklin Roosevelt and John Kennedy were likely to be classified as liberals. However, Richard Nixon was also an activist, and, although he does not easily fit any classification, he was far closer to conservatism than to liberalism. It is too easy to identify liberalism with statism and conservatism with antistatism: it is important to remember that it was liberal Jefferson who counseled against "energetic government" and conservative Alexander Hamilton who designed bold powers for the new central government and wrote "Energy in the executive is a leading character in the definition of good government."

In today's political environment, many are left wondering what it means to be a conservative. While President Trump won office as a Republican, he does not fit all of the typical expectations of conservatives. Thus, beyond attempting to examine the interplay between conservatives and liberals, we find ourselves gauging the reactions of conservatives to Trump supporters.

The Religious Right

The terms "right" and "left," as in "right wing of the Republican Party" and "leftist Democrats," came from an accident of seating in the French National Assembly during the Revolution of the early 1790s. It just happened that the liberals flocked to the left side of the assembly hall, while conservatives went to the right. "Left" and "right," then, are almost synonyms for liberals and conservatives, the main difference being that they give a sense of continuum and degree—someone can be "center-left" or "center-right" instead of at the extremes.

Even so, the terms have a certain hard edge. To call someone a "leftist" or a "right-winger" is to give an impression that they are strident or excessively zealous. That impression is conveyed in the term "religious right," a term few of its adherents would use to describe themselves, preferring softer terms like "religious conservatives" or "cultural conservatives."

For better or worse, although, the term "religious right" has entered the media mainstream, so we shall use it here to designate observant Christians or Jews whose concerns are not so much high taxes and government spending as the decline of traditional Judeo-Christian morality, a decline they attribute in part to wrongheaded government policies and judicial decisions. They oppose many of the recent judicial decisions on sociocultural issues, such as abortion, school prayer, pornography, and gay rights, and they were outspoken critics of the Clinton administration, citing everything from President Clinton's views on gays in the military to his sexual behavior while in the White House.

Spokesmen for progressive liberalism and the religious right stand as polar opposites: the former regard abortion as a woman's right; the latter see it as legalized murder. The former tend to regard homosexuality as a lifestyle that needs protection against discrimination; the latter are more likely to see it as a perversion. The list of issues could go on. The religious right and the progressive liberals are like positive and negative photographs of America's moral landscape. Sociologist James Davison Hunter uses the term *culture wars* to characterize the struggles between these contrary visions of America. For all the differences between progressive liberalism and the religious right, however, their styles are very similar. They are heavily laced with moralistic prose, they tend to equate compromise with selling out, and they claim to represent the best and most authentic traditions of America.

This is not to denigrate either movement, for the kinds of issues they address are indeed moral issues, which do not generally admit much compromise. These issues cannot simply be finessed or ignored, despite the efforts of conventional politicians to do so

Neoconservatism

The term *neoconservatism* came into use in the early 1970s as a designation for former New Deal Democrats who had become alarmed by what they saw as the drift of their party's foreign policy toward appeasing Communists. When Senator George McGovern, the party's presidential nominee in 1972, stated that he would "crawl to Hanoi on my knees" to secure peace in Vietnam, he seemed to them to exemplify this new tendency. They were, then, "hawks" in foreign policy, which they insisted was the historic stance of their party; they regarded themselves as the true heirs of liberal presidents such as Truman and Kennedy and liberal senators such as Henry (Scoop) Jackson of Washington State. On domestic policy, they were still largely liberal, except for their reactions to three new liberal planks added by the "progressives": gay rights, which neoconservatives tended to regard as a distortion of civil rights; abortion, which to some degree or another went against the grain of their moral sensibilities; and affirmative action, which some compared to the "quota system" once used to keep down the number of Jews admitted to elite universities. In fact, a number of prominent neoconservatives were Jews, including Norman Podhoretz, Midge Decter, Gertrude Himmelfarb, and Irving Kristol (although others, such as Michael Novak and Daniel Patrick Moynihan, were Roman Catholics, and one, Richard John Neuhaus, was a Lutheran pastor who later converted to Catholicism and became a priest).

The term *neoconservative* seemed headed for oblivion in the 1980s, when some leading neoconservatives dropped the "neo" part and classified themselves as conservatives. By the time the Soviet Union collapsed in 1991, it appeared that the term was no longer needed—the Cold War with "world communism" was over. But the rise of Islamic terrorism in the 1990s, aimed at the West in general and the United States in particular, brought back alarms analogous to those of the Cold War period, with global terrorism now taking the place of world communism. So, too, was the concern that liberal foreign policy might not be tough enough for the fight against these new, ruthless enemies of Western democracy. The concern was ratcheted up considerably after the events of 9/11, and now a new generation of neoconservatives was in the spotlight—some of its members literally the children of an earlier "neo" generation. They included Bill Kristol, John Podhoretz, Douglas Feith, Paul Wolfowitz, Richard Perle, David Brooks, and (although he was old enough to overlap with the previous generation) Bill Bennett.

Radicals, Reactionaries, and Moderates

The label *reactionary* is almost an insult, and the label *radical* is worn with pride by only a few zealots on the banks of the political mainstream. A reactionary is not a conserver but a backward-mover, dedicated to turning the clock back to better times. Most people suspect that reactionaries would restore us to a time that never was, except in political myth. For most Americans, the repeal of industrialism or universal education (or the entire twentieth century itself) is not a practical, let alone desirable, political program.

Radicalism (literally meaning "from the roots" or "going to the foundation") implies a fundamental reconstruction of the social order. Taken in that sense, it is possible to speak of right-wing radicalism as well as left-wing radicalism—radicalism that would restore or inaugurate a new hierarchical society as well as radicalism that calls for nothing less than an egalitarian society. The term is sometimes used in both of these senses, but most often the word *radicalism* is reserved to characterize more liberal change. While the liberal would affect change through conventional democratic processes, the radical is likely to be skeptical about the ability of the established machinery to bring about the needed change and might be prepared to sacrifice "a little" liberty to bring about a great deal more equality.

Moderate is a highly coveted label in America. Its meaning is not precise, but it carries the connotations of sensible, balanced, and practical. A moderate person is not without principles, but he or she does not allow principles to harden into dogma. The opposite of moderate is *extremist*, a label most American political leaders eschew. Yet there have been notable exceptions. When Arizona senator Barry Goldwater, a conservative Republican, was nominated for president in 1964, he declared "Extremism in defense of liberty is no vice! . . . Moderation in the pursuit of justice is no virtue!" This open embrace of extremism did not help his electoral chances; Goldwater was overwhelmingly defeated. At about the same time, however, another American political leader also embraced a kind of extremism, and with better results. In a famous letter written from a jail cell in Birmingham, Alabama, the Reverend Martin Luther King, Jr., replied to the charge that he was an extremist not by denying it but by distinguishing between different kinds of extremists. The question, he wrote, "is not whether we will be extremist but what kind of extremist will we be. Will we be extremists for hate, or will we be extremists for love?" King aligned himself with the love extremists, in which category he also placed Jesus, St. Paul, and Thomas Jefferson, among others. It was an adroit use of a label that is usually anathema in America.

Pluralism

The principle of pluralism espouses diversity in a society containing many interest groups and in a government containing competing units of power. This implies the widest expression of competing ideas, and in this way, pluralism is in sympathy with an important element of liberalism. However, as James Madison and Alexander Hamilton pointed out when they analyzed the sources of pluralism in their *Federalist* commentaries on the Constitution, this philosophy springs from a profoundly pessimistic view of human nature, and in this respect it more closely resembles conservatism. Madison, possibly the single most influential member of the convention that wrote the Constitution, hoped that in a large and varied nation, no single interest group could control the government. Even if there were a majority interest, it would be unlikely to capture all of the national agencies of government—the House of Representatives, the Senate, the presidency, and the federal judiciary—each of which was chosen in a different way by a different constituency for a different term of office. Moreover, to make certain that no one branch exercised excessive power, each was equipped with "checks and balances" that enabled any agency of national government to curb the powers of the others. The clearest statement of Madison's, and the Constitution's, theory can be found in the 51st paper of the *Federalist:* it may be a reflection on human nature that such devices should be necessary to control the abuses of government. But what is government itself, but the greatest of all reflections on human nature? If men were angels, no government would be necessary.

This pluralist position may be analyzed from different perspectives. It is conservative insofar as it rejects simple majority rule; yet it is liberal insofar as it rejects rule by a single elite. It is conservative in its pessimistic appraisal of human nature; yet pluralism's pessimism is also a kind of egalitarianism, holding as it does that no one can be trusted with power and that majority interests no less than minority interests will use power for selfish ends. It is possible to suggest that in America pluralism represents an alternative to both liberalism and conservatism. Pluralism is anti-majoritarian and anti-elitist and combines some elements of both.

Synthesis

Despite our effort to define the principal alignments in American politics, some policy decisions do not fit neatly into these categories. Suffice it to say that through the following pages, readers will be able to pull nuggets of the labels and alignments introduced above. Yet some will be far more obvious than others. Obviously, one's position on the issues in this book will be directed by circumstances. However, we would like to think that the essays in this book are durable enough to last through several seasons of events and controversies. We can be certain that the issues will survive. The search for coherence and consistency in the use of political labels underlines the options open to us and reveals their consequences. The result must be more mature judgments about what is best for America. That, of course, is the ultimate aim of public debate and decision-making, and it transcends all labels and categories.

Unit 1

UNIT

Democracy and the American Political Process

Democratic societies are known for allowing individuals to freely participate in the political process. Democracy is derived from two Greek words, demos and kratia, which mean, respectively, "people" and "rule." While there are clear differentiations between varying types of democracies, citizens have access and opportunities not present in other forms of government. For example, while a citizen in a representative democracy, such as the United States, may not get to individually vote on every issue that comes up for debate (like a citizen living in a direct democracy), they do have substantially more influence than a citizen living under a totalitarian dictator. And with the advent of new technologies, involvement is possible in ways never imagined before.

Regardless of the type of democracy being considered—or how citizens are seeking to actively engage—questions still remain. Who are "the people," and how much "rule" should there be? Does big government mean better government? Do the people need more, or fewer, "rules"? Are citizens equally able to participate in politics or strive in American society? Does "special interest" money in elections undermine the general interest? Are elections in America truly democratic? Some analysts of democracy believe that a viable democratic system requires widespread belief in their country's unique mission. But is that necessary? And economically, should free trade still dominate all economic discussions?

ISSUE

Selected, Edited, and with Issue Framing Material by:
William J. Miller, *Campus Labs*®

Is Bigger Government Better Government?

YES: Jeff Madrick, from "The Case for Big Government," Princeton University Press (2008)

NO: David Boaz, from "The Return of Big Government," *Cato Policy Report* (2009)

Learning Outcomes
After reading this issue, you will be able to:
• Discuss the benefits of government expansion.
• Assess the weaknesses of limited government.
• Describe the economic benefits of government.
• Discuss the role of libertarian ideals in American society.
• Analyze how the size of government has impacted the current economic crisis.

ISSUE SUMMARY

YES: Humanities professor Jeff Madrick surveys the numerous government interventions in the economy since the end of World War II and concludes that they have been essential to America's growth and well-being.

NO: : Executive Vice President of the Cato Institute David Boaz traces America's libertarian traditions and reminds readers that there are times where government's best course of action is simply deciding to do nothing.

A continuing debate about government runs through the course of American history. The debate is between those who see government as an instrument for doing good versus those who see it as a potentially oppressive institution. Those who take the latter view usually concede that, yes, we do need government for strictly limited purposes—but, in the words of Thomas Paine, government "even in its best state, is but a necessary evil."

Paine wrote those words in 1776, when America was still governed by a foreign nation. Does the situation change when a nation becomes self-governed? Alexander Hamilton thought so. Hamilton fought fiercely against the imperial government of Great Britain, but once American independence was achieved he became a champion of what he called "energetic" government, a term that included the pursuit of public programs aimed at increasing the nation's prosperity. He helped create the first federally owned Bank of the United States, encouraged the government to subsidize domestic industries,

and even experimented with government-owned mills in New Jersey. Opposing him was Secretary of State Thomas Jefferson. Jefferson wanted government to stay out of the domestic economy.

Despite the protestations of Jefferson and those who followed him, government became increasingly energetic during the nineteenth century. Though Andrew Jackson killed the rechartering of the Bank of the United States with his presidential veto, the federal government passed tariffs and financed the building of roads, canals, and railroads; during and after the Civil War federal power expanded into areas such as civil rights and higher education, areas once reserved to the states. By the close of the nineteenth century, government began tentatively moving into the areas of social welfare and business regulation—though not without resistance.

In the twentieth century, government growth expanded during World War I, contracted in the 1920s, and exploded during the years of President Franklin Roosevelt, 1933–1945. A host of "alphabet" bureaucracies (e.g., WPA, PWA, NLRB, NRA, and so on) were created, government spending increased to unprecedented levels, and new entitlement programs such as Social Security and Aid to the Families of Dependent Children (AFDC) were created. During this period the terms "liberal" and "conservative" crystallized into descriptions of the two sides in the debate: liberals were those who championed government activism and conservatives were those resisting it. Today, almost 70 years later, "liberal" and "conservative" still work reasonably well, at least in the economic sphere, as thumbnail labels for those who favor government and those who don't.

Liberals and conservatives have won some and lost some since the end of the 1940s. President Dwight Eisenhower was a moderate conservative, yet it was under his administration that the Federal-Aid Highway Act was passed, which put the federal government into the business of financing the construction of 41,000 miles of instate highways throughout the nation; Eisenhower also established a new cabinet department, Health, Education and Welfare (later renamed the Department of Health and Human Services).

During President Lyndon Johnson's term, 1964–1968, the largest expansion of the federal government since the Roosevelt administration took place. Johnson boldly declared an "unconditional war on poverty." He created a variety of new federal agencies to teach job skills, stimulate community action, and dispense welfare. He pushed Medicaid and Medicare through Congress, and led Congress in passing new civil rights laws.

During Ronald Reagan's administration there was a serious challenge in the White House to liberal economic programs. The number of pages added to the *Federal Register*, which records the rules and regulations issued by federal agencies, declined each year of Reagan's presidency, breaking a sharp increase since 1960. The centerpiece of his economic program was his tax cuts, enacted in 1981, which lowered the top personal tax bracket from 70 to 28 percent in seven years. Reagan failed, however, to lower government expenditures, and the deficit soared.

What many conservative Americans today seem to be clamoring for is right-sized government. This type of government performs all functions necessary to protect life, liberty, and property of citizens. The word necessary is the key. Only those things that individuals are incapable of doing themselves should government step in to perform. Government should be practicing concerted constraint to not become an aggressor against its citizens or compel them to do things that they either would not choose to do or would prefer not to do.

Yet conservatives who strongly disagree with Barack Obama's alleged government expansion seem to not realize how many layers of government President George W. Bush brought to the federal government through the creation of the Department of Homeland Security. Going directly against the ideals of Reagan, Bush chose to increase spending and employment in the name of security. While everything was on the table in the aftermath of September 11, the new Cabinet-level department will continue to require significant federal investments for as long as it exists.

Today's conservatives have made Reagan's approach their model, while liberals seek to build on Franklin Roosevelt's legacy. The Obama administration's decision to mandate individuals to have health insurance, first proposed as a form of universal health care by President Harry Truman in 1945, rests on assumptions about government broadly shared by liberals since Roosevelt's time but whose philosophical roots can be traced to Alexander Hamilton. Yet again, whether one believes government is inherently good or bad seemingly follows Miles' Law. Those who see the benefit of government (or who personally benefit) will be the most likely to stand up and call for expansion. Perhaps this is the great irony of American politics today. The Tea Party movement has been shown to have a significant number of elderly support. The same folks who are clamoring for government to cease to exist would also like government to keep its hands off of their Medicare. And with the Trump Administration now in office, pundits and citizens alike are attempting to determine how conservative ideals match with efforts to protect our nation at a high cost from perceived threats. Who ever said that citizens must be consistent?

Professor Jeff Madrick takes the liberal view that activist government has done much to enhance the quality of life and increase American prosperity. However, David Boaz, of the Cato Institute, traces America's libertarian traditions and reminds readers that there are times where government's best course of action is simply deciding to do nothing—no matter how difficult this can be to admit.

YES

Jeff Madrick

The Case for Big Government

After World War II, almost all economists feared a reprise of the Depression. It was hard to imagine what could replace all the lost military demand. But the opposite occurred. After a pause in 1947, the economy grew as rapidly on average as it ever did before, and the incomes of most working Americans grew faster than ever before. The progressive turn of policy, despite a resurgence of antigovernment sensibility, did not deter growth. Nor did higher income tax rates, which were raised by Roosevelt during the Depression and were raised again to record levels during World War II, where they remained for more than a decade. The highest tax bracket reached approximately 90 percent, where it remained until 1964. To the contrary, bigger government seemed to go along with ever faster growth. Roosevelt had proposed a G.I. Bill of Rights in 1943, among other things, to provide aid for veterans to go to college and to buy a house. Congress raised objections, but in 1944 the G.I. Bill was passed. By the late 1950s, half of the returning sixteen million soldiers financed college or other training programs as a result. Millions of mortgages were guaranteed. The nation was thus directed in a particular way. The Marshall Plan under President Truman, and named after the secretary of state who strongly advocated it, provided billion of dollars of aid to rebuild Europe.

Dwight Eisenhower, as a former president, incurred the ire of the Republican right wing by proposing to expand Social Security coverage to another ten million workers—to include farm workers and professionals such as teachers, accountants, and dentists. He also increased benefits. Eisenhower said that it was simply clear that not all could save enough for retirement. Eisenhower also advocated the development and federal financing of a national highway system. He had strong support from the major auto companies, of course, and the bill passed in 1956. By the late 1950s, 90 percent of all homes in America were reachable by road, and often by highway. It was an explicit case of national government coordination and investment that deeply influenced the development of the

nation into a new geography of suburbs, based on cheap gas, cheap property, and mostly free roads.

In these decades, the federal government financed and administered the antipolio vaccines. In the wake of the Soviet launch of the first space satellite, Sputnik, Congress passed the National Defense Education Act, providing billions of dollars of annual grants and loans to support higher education, technical training, and other educational programs. Young people were further spurred to go to college. The National Institutes of Health, as an extension of late nineteenth-century government investment in health research, were expanded dramatically after World War II, and accounted for a high proportion of medical breakthroughs. Research and development (R&D) was undertaken in many federal agencies, not least the Defense Department, where the Internet had its origins. The federal government accounted for most of America's R&D, in fact, through the 1960s, topping out at 67 percent of all such research in 1963. Many economists contend that such intense research efforts account for greater American economic superiority in these years than any other single factor. The Supreme Court under Eisenhower, led by Johnson's appointee as chief justice, Earl Warren, ordered that public schools be integrated.

In the 1960s, President Johnson passed Medicare and implemented his War on Poverty, including health care for the poor under Medicaid. Regulatory changes were significant, and included landmark civil rights legislation, which protected voting rights for blacks, ended Jim Crow laws once and for all, and forbade gender and racial discrimination in labor markets. Other regulatory reforms involved cigarettes, packaging, motor vehicle safety, consumer credit, and the expansion of the authority of the Food and Drug Administration.

Between 1948 and 1970, the share of spending in GDP by the federal, state, and local governments rose from 16.5 percent to 27.5 percent, nearly eleven percentage points. Most of this increase was in social expenditures. Yet productivity, wages, and overall GDP grew very rapidly, as noted. What is the complaint then in light of all this success? It is hard to escape the conclusion as noted earlier in this section that government did not hurt but significantly helped economies to grow.

The Economic Benefits of Government

. . . Few economists disagree with the theory that some measure of public investment in infrastructure, education, and health care is necessary. Because public goods such as roads and schools benefit society overall more than any individual or business, such investment would not have been adequately undertaken by private firms. . . . Government support is required for primary education, roads, and the poor.

Far less frequently discussed is the fact that government can be the focus of needed and useful coordination. When railroads used different size track (gauge), government was needed to standardize them. By organizing communities to use a single public water system, government creates economies of scale for such a public good. The highway system was an immense act of coordination that probably couldn't have been attained through a private network; there is no example of one in the world, in any case. The system of international trade and currency valuation is a government-led example of coordination.

Similarly, regulations can and often do make economies work better. They can make information about products and services more open. They can reduce corruption, monopolistic pricing, and anticompetitive policies regarding research, innovation, and new products. They can temper financial speculation, which distorts the flow of capital toward inefficient uses and can often lead to costly corrections and serious recessions, as occurred yet again in 2008.

Some regulations can be poorly administered and reduce economic efficiency. Others will outlive their usefullness; they should be pruned and streamlined over time. But other regulations will be a short-term cost to business that the nation chooses to bear for quality of life and even a better economy. Maintaining the safety of products that consumers cannot judge for themselves is an example; but the safety and effectiveness of products also makes consumers more confident buyers of products. Environmental regulations adopted in the early 1970s have probably been costly to all of us, but they are a cost we bear for cleaner air and water and the diminution of global warming. It is no cause for alarm that regulations have multiplied as the economy supplies so many more goods and services to the people. As economies change and grow more complex, it is only natural that more oversight is needed.

At the still more liberal end of the political spectrum, some economists will argue—though not the American mainstream—that programs that help raise and make wages more equal, such as laws that facilitate union organizing, minimum wages, and equal rights, may well aid economic growth, not undermine productivity, by creating demand for goods and services, and also reinforcing faith in workers that they will be fairly rewarded for their effort. . . .

One of the key benefits of the larger post–World War II government, if in some quarters still a controversial one, is also that it makes the economy more stable. Well before Keynes's work during the Depression there were calls for government spending to create jobs and support incomes. Massive public works projects that reignited economic growth, such as Baron Hausmann's rebuilding of Paris, are common in history. But in the post–World War II era, such activities gained new theoretical justification from Keynes's theories. Both Keynesian liberals and some Friedmanite conservatives accepted, to one degree or another, that fiscal and monetary policy—deficit spending by the treasury or the adjustment of interest rates by the central bank—could help avoid or ameliorate recessions and thereby raise the rate of growth over time. A large government is itself, despite conservative arguments cited earlier, a bulwark against rapidly declining spending. Unemployment insurance, Social Security, and government employment itself are stabilizing factors.

If the size of government truly and directly caused the inflation of the 1970s and contributed demonstrably to slower economic growth, it would be reason for concern. But we have seen that it did not in the United States, and nations with far larger governments have produced neither more rapid inflation nor substandard levels of income for their citizens. The public goods and social programs of many countries—from Sweden and Norway to France and Germany—are significantly more generous than America's. . . .

In fact, enlightened regulation has been imperative for economic growth at least since Jefferson's policies for governing the distribution of land. When done well, regulation keeps competition honest and free, enables customers to know and understand the products they receive, and fosters new ideas. When neglected, abuse becomes easy, information in markets is suppressed, capital investment is channeled to wasteful and inefficient uses, and dangerous excesses occur. The open flow of products and services information is critical to a free-market economy. The conditions for healthy competition have simply not been maintained under a free-market ideology of minimal government that professes great faith in competition. Competition requires government oversight; the wool has been pulled over our eyes.

We now know the following. If federal, state, and local governments absorb roughly 35 percent of GDP in America, rather than the current roughly 30 percent, it will not inhibit growth and undermine entrepreneurial spirits, productivity, or prosperity if the spending is well-channeled. Government absorbs much more of national income in other nations whose prosperity is the equivalent of or perhaps superior to America's. In European nations, government spending absorbs approximately 40 percent of all spending, and standards of living are high. If government programs are managed well, they will on balance enhance productivity. A rise to 35 percent will raise approximately $700 billion a year to the federal, state, and local governments to provide protections to workers, finance social programs, maintain an adequate regulatory presence, and raise significantly the level of investment in transportation, energy, education, and health care. Part and perhaps all of this $700 billion can be paid for with higher taxes. . . .

. . . The most productive way to address rising global competition is not trade restrictions per se but for the government to invest in the nation. Consumer spending leaks to foreign imports and business investment leaks across borders. But potential returns to the economy from spending on transportation projects are at this point significant, partly due to years of neglect, and the jobs created to implement them largely stay at home. The proportion of the federal budget spent on investment in the nation—including transportation, science, technology, and energy—are well down from the levels of the 1970s. Federal spending on education as a proportion of GDP fell under Clinton but was raised under his successor, George Bush, and it remains slightly higher as a proportion of GDP than it was in the 1970s. Overall, public investment equaled nearly 3 percent of GDP in the 1970s, which would come to more than $400 billion today. Under Clinton it fell to half of that proportion, and under Bush it rose but remains at less than 2 percent of GDP. Merely raising it to 1970s levels would produce $140 billion more a year to spend. To reemphasize, such spending usually creates domestic jobs and builds future productivity at the same time.

To take one estimate, a House Transportation Committee report cites a Federal Highway Administration model that claims that a $75 billion investment will create more than 3.5 million jobs and $464 billion in additional nationwide sales. Every $1 billion, in other words, yields 47,500 jobs and an other $6 billion in sales. Spending has been so inadequate that such estimates can be accepted confidently. The Society of Civil Engineers suggest that much of America's infrastructure should get a grade of D. While these studies are hardly definitive, they are suggestive of the possibilities.

The most exciting potential returns are for high-quality pre-K education. A wide range of studies has been undertaken on several high-quality programs that have long been underway in the United States. The benefits of such programs include not only improving the ability of children to learn, but also long-term reduction in crime rates, reduced need for special education and repeating grades, and lower welfare enrollment rates. A conventional conservative economist such as James Heckman, a Nobel laureate who opposes college subsidies, nevertheless favors significant funding of preschool programs. Some estimate these programs create benefits that exceed costs by five to ten times. A highly sophisticated recent analysis by two economists estimates that if a high-quality program was instituted nationwide, the federal moneys spent would be fully paid for in increased tax revenues due to improved incomes and would reduce welfare, crime, and special education expenses. In other words, it would pay for itself. . . .

As a consequence of neglect and change, an adequate agenda for America is a lengthy one, but it is not an anti-growth agenda. It favors growth. Growing personal income is more necessary to a full life than is recognized, in part because the cost of some key needs rise very fast, in part because a wealthy society can finance innovation, and in part because a wealthy populace will find it easier and more congenial to pay for communal needs through taxes. But for too long, mainstream economists have accepted the notion that more savings and technology will alone lead to faster growth. The agenda for government is therefore inappropriately limited; government spending, for example, will allegedly erode savings. America has been able to test this economic philosophy for a full generation and it has failed. Years of below-par productivity growth, low and stagnating wages, inattention to basic needs, persistent poverty, and the undermining of assets necessary to future growth, including education, health care, energy alternatives, and transportation infrastructure are the consequences.

The gap between a growing economy and falling wages is the major contemporary mystery. Global competition and off-shoring may explain part of the gap, but the trend began decades ago. Research shows that a gap in worker compensation and productivity began to open up slowly in the late 1980s: typical workers got less than their historical share, while capital (profits) and high-income workers got more. This gap widened explosively in the 2000s.

Furthermore, there was little explanation as to why male incomes in particular fared especially poorly over this long period we have described. A major reason is the withdrawal of government from its traditional purposes.

JEFF MADRICK is the editor of *Challenge* magazine, the author of *The End of Affluence* (1995) and other books, a frequent contributor to *The New York Review of Books*, and a Visiting Professor of Humanities at The Cooper Union in New York.

David Boaz    **NO**

The Return of Big Government

It's been a long time since a U.S. election generated feelings of actual joy beyond the ranks of partisan activists. If Barack Obama hasn't yet ushered in a new "era of good feelings," all Americans can take pride in the demise of yet another glass ceiling in a nation conceived in liberty and dedicated to the proposition that all of us are created equal, entitled to the inalienable rights of life, liberty, and the pursuit of happiness.

Indeed, we can take some satisfaction in observing that something normal happened: A party that had given Americans a long war and an economic crisis, led by a strikingly unpopular president, was defeated. Republican government requires that failed parties be turned out of office. The American Founders believed firmly in the principle of rotation in office. They thought that even successful officeholders should go back home to live under the laws after a short period in office. No doubt more members of the 110th Congress would have been given that privilege were it not for the vast incumbent protection complex of laws and regulations and subsidies.

George W. Bush and the Republicans promised choice, freedom, reform, and a restrained federal government. As far back as the Contract with America in 1994, congressional Republicans pledged "the end of government that is too big, too intrusive, and too easy with the public's money." But over the past eight years they delivered massive overspending, the biggest expansion of entitlements in 40 years, centralization of education, a war that has lasted longer than World War II, an imperial presidency, civil liberties abuses, the intrusion of the federal government into social issues and personal freedoms, and finally a $700 billion bailout of Wall Street that just kept on growing in the last month of the campaign. Voters who believe in limited government had every reason to reject that record.

At the Cato Institute we stand firmly on the principles of the Declaration of Independence and the Constitution, and on the bedrock American values of individual liberty, limited government, free markets, and peace. And throughout our 32 years we have been willing to criticize officials of both parties when they sought to take the country in another direction. We published papers critical of President Clinton's abuse of executive authority, his administration's misguided antitrust policies, his nation-building experiments, and his unwillingness to take on corporate welfare. Our analysts were among the first to point out the Bush administration's profligate spending, as well as the administration's policies on executive power, habeas corpus, privacy, expansion of entitlements, the federal marriage amendment, and the misbegotten war in Iraq.

But we have also been pleased to work with administrations of both parties when they seek to expand freedom or limit government—with the Clinton administration on free trade, welfare reform, and a few tentative steps toward Social Security reform; with the Bush administration on tax cuts, the initial response to the 9/11 attacks, health savings accounts, immigration reform, and Social Security accounts. We look forward to opportunities to work with the Obama administration when it moves to reverse the worst mistakes of the Bush years or otherwise to advance policies that would enhance peace, freedom, and prosperity.

The Current Crisis

In the current economic crisis, our first task is to understand it and its causes. This was a crisis caused by regulation, subsidization, and intervention, and it won't be cured by more of the same. Christopher Hitchens had a point when he wrote, "There are many causes of the subprime and derivative horror show that has destroyed our trust in the idea of credit, but one way of defining it would be to say that everybody was promised everything, and almost everybody fell for the populist bait."

The backdrop is central banking and implicit federal guarantees for risky behavior. The Federal Reserve Board creates money and adjusts interest rates, so any notion that our financial system was an example of laissez-faire fails at the start. Meanwhile, Congress and regulators pushed Fannie Mae and Freddie Mac to become a vast duopoly in the mortgage finance industry. Their debt was implicitly backed by the U.S. Treasury, and they were able to expand their debt and engage in risky transactions. As Lawrence Summers wrote, "Little wonder with gains privatized and losses socialized that the enterprises have gambled their way into financial catastrophe."

There was substantial agreement in Washington that home ownership was a good thing and that more home-ownership would be even better. Thus Congress and regulators encouraged Fannie, Freddie, and mortgage lenders to extend credit to underqualified borrowers. To generate more mortgage lending to low- and moderate-income people, the federal government loosened down-payment standards, pressured lenders to increase their percentages of "affordable" loans, and implicitly guaranteed Fannie and Freddie's dramatic expansion. All that hard work paid off: The share of mortgages classified as nonprime soared, and the quality of those loans declined. And Federal Reserve credit expansion helped to make all of this lending possible, as Lawrence H. White wrote in his Cato Briefing Paper, "How Did We Get into This Financial Mess?"

"Everybody was promised everything"—cheap money, easy lending, and rising home prices. All that money and all those buyers pushed housing prices up sharply. But all good things—at least all good things based on unsustainable policies—must come to an end. When housing prices started to fall, many borrowers ran into trouble. Financial companies threatened to fall like dominos, and an ever-expanding series of bailouts began issuing from the Treasury department. And instead of the usual response to businesses that make bad decisions—let them go into bankruptcy or reorganization and let their workers and assets go to more effective companies—the federal government stepped in to keep every existing enterprise operating.

At this point it is important that the recent emergency measures be recognized as just that: emergency—if not panic—measures and not long-term policy. Congress should turn its attention to extricating the government from financial firms and basing long-term policies on a clear diagnosis of what went wrong. Congress should repeal the Community Reinvestment Act and stop pressuring lenders to make loans to underqualified borrowers. The Treasury should use its authority as conservator to liquidate Fannie Mae and Freddie Mac. The federal government should refrain from using its equity investments in companies to exercise power over their operations and should move with all deliberate speed to withdraw from corporate ownership.

One lesson of the credit crisis is that politicians prefer to "promise everybody everything"—low interest rates, affordable mortgages, higher housing prices, lower gas prices, a chicken in every pot. That's why it's important to keep politics out of such matters.

The End of Libertarianism—or a New Beginning?

Various pundits and public figures have claimed that the credit crisis means "the end of libertarianism" or even more dramatically "the end of American capitalism." As noted above, the crisis can hardly be considered a failure of laissez-faire, deregulation, libertarianism, or capitalism, since it was caused by multiple misguided government interventions into the workings of the financial system. It was and is precisely a failure of interventionism.

But could capitalism or libertarianism come to an end despite the facts? After all, the Great Depression was primarily caused by poor Federal Reserve policy and high tariffs. But a false impression that it was somehow caused by laissez-faire led to New Deal policies (pursued first by Herbert Hoover and then by Franklin D. Roosevelt) that turned a contraction into the Great Depression. What policies? Restrictive banking regulations, increases in top marginal tax rates, interventions to keep wages and prices from adjusting, and government rhetoric and activism that created (in the words of historian Robert Higgs) "pervasive uncertainty among investors about the security of their property rights in their capital and its prospective returns." That set of policies lengthened the Great Depression by eight years or more and is uncomfortably similar to recent and proposed policy responses to the 2008 credit crisis.

In *Newsweek*, Jacob Weisberg declared that the financial crisis is "the end of libertarianism." But it was in fact "progressive" interventionism that caused the crisis—just the economic philosophy that Weisberg supports. So if one big failure can kill an ideology, then let's hear it for "the end of interventionism."

If this crisis leads us to question the "American-style capitalism" in which a central monetary authority manipulates money and credit, the central government taxes and redistributes $3 trillion a year, huge government-sponsored enterprises create a taxpayer-backed duopoly in the mortgage business, tax laws encourage excessive use of debt financing, and government pressures banks to make bad loans—well, it might be a good thing to reconsider that "American-style capitalism." Or indeed, as a *Washington Post* editorial put it in October, "Government sponsored, upside-only capitalism is the kind that's in crisis today, and we say: Good riddance."

Libertarianism calls for freedom and responsibility, free markets and civil liberties, a minimal government that stays out of both boardrooms and bedrooms. Obviously libertarianism wasn't in the driver's seat in either the Clinton or the Bush administration.

Even if there are misperceptions about the causes of the crisis, both the system of capitalism and the idea of libertarianism are going to have more staying power than pundits such as Weisberg would like. There was a time when half the world rejected capitalism, and leading intellectuals in the "free world" worried that the centrally planned economies would obviously out compete the capitalist countries and that "convergence" on some sort of half-capitalist, half-socialist model was the wave of the future. But after the world got a look at the results of the two systems in East and West Germany, North and South Korea, Hong Kong and Taiwan and China, the United States and the Soviet Union, it became clear that socialism is a clumsy, backward looking prescription for stagnation at best and tyranny at worst.

Meanwhile, the half-planned economies of the West—Great Britain, New Zealand, the United States, and more—developed a milder version of economic sclerosis. Starting in the 1970s many of those countries began eliminating price controls, removing restrictions on market competition, opening up the economy, cutting tax rates, and reducing trade barriers. It came to be widely recognized—eventually on both sides of the Iron Curtain—that private property and markets are indispensable in organizing a modern economy. A nearly simultaneous cultural revolution opened up society. Women, racial minorities, and gays and lesbians entered the mainstream of society throughout the Western world. Art, literature, and lifestyles became more diverse and more individualized. The Sixties and the Eighties both led us to what Brink Lindsey in *The Age of Abundance* called "the implicit libertarian synthesis" of the United States today.

Some people see a future of ever more powerful government. Others see a future of greater freedom. *Reason* editors Nick Gillespie and Matt Welch write: "We are in fact living at the cusp of what should be called the Libertarian Moment, the dawning of . . . a time of increasingly hyper-individualized, hyper-expanded choice over every aspect of our lives. . . . This is now a world where it's more possible than ever to live your life on your own terms; it's an early rough draft version of the libertarian philosopher Robert Nozick's 'utopia of utopias. . . . This new century of the individual, which makes the Me Decade look positively communitarian in comparison, will have far-reaching implications wherever individuals swarm together in commerce, culture, or politics."

Is it possible that Congress will choose to pursue policies—tax increases, yet higher spending, continued subsidies for risky decisions, intrusion into corporate decision making—that would slow down U.S. economic growth, perhaps make us more like France, with its supposedly kinder, gentler capitalism and its GDP per capita of about 75 percent of ours? Yes, it's possible, and clearly there are proposals for such policies. But if we want economic growth—which means better health care, scientific advance, better pharmaceuticals, more leisure opportunities, a cleaner environment, better technology; in short, more well being for more people—there is no alternative to market capitalism. And if we want more growth, for more people, with wider scope for personal choice and decision making, libertarian policy prescriptions are the roadmap.

A Libertarian Agenda

Beyond the immediate financial crisis, there are many more issues confronting us. Fiscal reform, for instance. Federal spending increased by more than a trillion dollars during the Bush years, or more than 70 percent (even before the budget busting bailout and stimulus packages). The national debt rose even more sharply, from $5.727 trillion to more than $10.6 trillion, or an increase of more than 85 percent. The 2009 budget deficit may exceed $1 trillion. Trends like this are unsustainable, yet elected officials continue to promise more spending on everything from new weaponry to college tuitions. Congress and the administration must find a way to rein in this profligacy.

The current rates of spending don't yet reflect the acceleration of entitlement spending as the baby boomers start retiring. Entitlements are already about 40 percent of the federal budget. In 20 years they may double as a share of national income. The unfunded liability of Social Security and Medicare is now over $100 trillion, an unfathomably large number. Within barely a decade, the two programs will require more than 25 percent of income tax revenues, in addition to the payroll taxes that currently fund them. Congress needs to think seriously about this problem. Are members prepared to impose the tax burden necessary to fund such levels of transfer payments? Do we want that many Americans dependent on a check from the federal government? Eventually, the projected level of entitlements will not be feasible. It would be best to start now to make changes rationally rather than in a panic a few years from now.

Private property, free markets, and fiscal restraint are important foundations for liberty, and the party that claims to uphold those values has done a poor job of it lately. But there are restrictions on liberty beyond the realm of taxes and regulations. We hope that elected officials of both parties will recognize the dangers of censorship, drug prohibition, entanglement of church and state, warrantless wiretapping, indefinite detention, government interference with lifestyle and end-of-life choices, and other such policies. Americans declared in 1776 that life, liberty, and the pursuit of happiness are inalienable rights, and in 1787 they wrote a Constitution that empowers a limited government to protect those rights.

Fidelity to those founding principles of respect for civil liberties and limited government may be easy when times are easy. The true test of our faith in those principles comes when we are beset by diabolical assaults from without and economic turmoil within, when public anxiety may temporarily make it seem expedient to put those principles aside. The importance of paying scrupulous deference to the Constitution's limits on federal power, of respecting its careful system of checks and balances, is greatest precisely when the temptation to flout them is strongest.

For those who go into government to improve the lives of their fellow citizens, the hardest lesson to accept may be that Congress should often do nothing about a problem—such as education, crime, or the cost of prescription drugs. Critics will object, "Do you want the government to just stand there and do nothing while this problem continues?" Sometimes that is exactly what Congress should do. Remember the ancient wisdom imparted to physicians: First, do no harm. And have confidence that free people, left to their own devices, will address issues of concern to them more effectively outside a political environment.

David Boaz is the Executive Vice President of the Cato Institute and has played a key role in the development of the Cato Institute and the libertarian movement. He is a provocative commentator and a leading authority on domestic issues such as education choice, drug legalization, the growth of government, and the rise of libertarianism.

EXPLORING THE ISSUE

Is Bigger Government Better Government?

Critical Thinking and Reflection

1. Madrick argues that the federal government's expansion since World War II has been good for the country. Why does he reach that conclusion? What sort of evidence does he cite?
2. Madrick often refers to the success of big government in Western Europe and cites it as a model for this country. Do you think the European model fits the United States? Why, or why not?
3. How does Boaz categorize libertarianism in the United States? Does it appear that libertarian ideals are gaining momentum today? Why or why not?
4. Why is it difficult for politicians to choose not to act on a problem facing society?
5. How do we assess whether government is working in the United States? Do different individuals utilize different metrics? Why does it matter?

Is There Common Ground?

There might be common ground between Madrick and Boaz if the latter could convince the former to limit government to (a) protecting people from other people or countries that want to harm them and (b) guaranteeing that all citizens be treated equally and fairly. But it does not seem likely that Madrick would consent to these limited functions of government, unless of course terms like "fairness" and "equality" were given very expansive definitions—which is what Boaz and other conservatives seem to complain that liberals always do!

Ultimately, America will never find agreement on the size of government. Those who need government will likely always favor expanding its power and reach, while those who do not need assistance will wonder why they are paying taxes. Unless citizens begin to look past their own self-interest and realize the larger societal goals of government, we will be faced with constant clamoring for government to both expand and condense. For elected officials and government workers, this means being stuck in a never-ending tug-of-war in which nothing that is done is pleasing to half of Americans.

Additional Resources

Timothy P. Carney, *The Big Ripoff: How Big Business and Big Government Steal Your Money* (Wiley, 2006).

Milton Friedman, *Capitalism and Freedom* (University of Chicago Press, 1962).

John K. Galbraith, *The Affluent Society* (Houghton Mifflin, 1960).

Max Neiman, *Defending Government: Why Big Government Works* (Prentice Hall, 2009).

Amity Shales, *The Forgotten Man* (Harper Perennial, 2007).

Internet References . . .

Brookings Institute

www.brookings.edu

Cato Institute

www.cato.org

Center for American Progress

www.americanprogress.org

Center for Small Government

www.centerforsmallgovernment.org

Foundation for Economic Education

www.fee.org

Selected, Edited, and with Issue Framing Material by:
William J. Miller, *Campus Labs*®

ISSUE

Is the Current Presidential Nomination System Actually Democratic?

YES: Jamelle Bouie, from "The Process Worked," *Slate* (2016)

NO: William Saletan, from "The Primaries Aren't Democratic? They're Not Supposed to Be Democratic," *Slate* (2016)

Learning Outcomes
After reading this issue, you will be able to:
• Assess the democratic values currently embedded in the American electoral system. • Explain the deficiencies within the American electoral system. • Discuss electoral controversies in American presidential elections. • Explain ways the system could be made democratic. • List reasons why any changes to the presidential electoral system will be difficult to achieve.

ISSUE SUMMARY

YES: Journalist Jamelle Bouie argues that the current presidential nomination system is in fact quite democratic by allowing states to determine how best to conduct elections within their borders. He notes that even outside of elections, American government has always flourished under a blend of majoritarian, nonmajoritarian, and countermajoritarian elements.

NO: William Saletan, also a journalist, acknowledges that the nomination process is not particularly democratic but reminds readers that the goals of primaries and caucuses are to select candidates that best represent party interests.

The 2016 presidential nomination system for the Democratic and Republican parties in the United States produced Hillary Clinton and Donald Trump as the two candidates to vie for the nation's highest office. In August 2016, they solidified their positions as the two most unpopular presidential candidates going back more than 30 years. Among all adults, 56 percent viewed Clinton unfavorably compared with 63 percent for Trump. While with registered voters, it is 59 percent unfavorable for Clinton and 60 percent for Trump. And it's not like there were not other options: Clinton faced five other legitimate challengers while Trump shared the stage with roughly a dozen other Republican hopefuls. So how did a nomination system produce two candidates that more Americans dislike than like? And what does this suggest for future nomination cycles?

As if Democrats and Republicans do not have enough differences, they also select their presidential nominees in different ways. Both parties choose delegates to represent them. And those delegates vote for presidential nominees at their party conventions. This is an important key to remember about nominations: they are conducted by political parties for members to select nominees for general elections. They are not controlled by any national office or regulations. And the Supreme Court has supported their right to be viewed as party-specific activities.

The Democrats prefer to allocate delegates by percentage of votes won in each state's primary—a method called proportionality. Republicans lean generally, but far from exclusively, toward winner-take-all outcomes. Even so, there are many variations in different states, each of which sets its own primary voting rules. In Iowa, for example, Republican delegates were awarded proportionally, rounded to the nearest delegate. Nevada was divvied up proportionally as well.

There is a rich and convoluted history to these formulas, most of which stem from states' efforts to build up their political clout on the national scene. Politicos have always wanted an early say on who will be a presidential contender so they can ultimately shape the final outcome. And presidential candidates like it, at least usually, because they get an early start on amassing delegates and can then build momentum to lay claim to a political coronation. But when more states began to schedule their contests earlier and earlier to shore up their importance, the parties adopted changes in 2008 that required most states—with exceptions like Iowa, Nevada, New Hampshire, and South Carolina—to hold their contests after February. The rest have to follow in March or even later.

Tinkering over the years has made each party's presidential nomination process anything but simple. In a Democratic primary, candidates are awarded delegates in proportion to their share of votes in a state primary or caucus, but a candidate must first win at least 15 percent of the vote in any given state. Once that threshold is crossed, then the candidate racks up the delegates. The Republicans lack a uniform approach. Some states still stick to the traditional winner-take-all approach, but others have introduced variations. So now, some states give out delegates proportionally and—just to make things thoroughly confusing—some states mix the proportional and winner-takes-all formulas.

Before diving for the nearest spreadsheet, it is also good to know that in many states, but not all, the Republican Party requires that a candidate win at least 20 percent of the vote before actually earning delegates. But others, like Iowa, do not set a limit. So Iowa, an early voting state, parceled out its delegates to several presidential hopefuls. Setting such minimum thresholds means that fewer presidential candidates can amass many delegates. That's a surer way to abbreviate drawn-out contests and knock out those who do not latch on early to the voting public's imagination.

If that weren't complicated enough, Republicans also take into account both statewide and congressional district results. A Republican candidate could lose a statewide vote but salvage some delegates if she or he wins at least one congressional district in that state. The Democrats' proportional approach makes it harder for the party to narrow its field, as voters are seeing in the contest between Hillary Clinton and Bernie Sanders. The large number of Republican presidential contenders this cycle has also resisted winnowing.

Even so, that doesn't guarantee that they will. All kinds of variations are in play. For example, Democrats have super delegates (mostly party leaders) among their 4,765 delegates. They are free to make their own candidate choice regardless of who wins the primaries or caucus contests. Meanwhile, the 2,470 Republican delegates are bound to support their state's choice only for the first vote at the upcoming July 18 Cleveland convention. If no one achieves the 1,237 votes necessary to nail down the presidential nomination, then delegates are, at least theoretically, free to follow their personal political allegiances. Those allegiances can vary considerably.

Both parties have both primaries and caucuses throughout their nomination calendar with states choosing which method to use. Caucuses were once the most common way of choosing presidential nominees. Today, Alaska, Colorado, Hawaii, Kansas, Maine, Minnesota, Nevada, North Dakota, Wyoming, and Iowa are the only states to rely solely on the caucus, according to the Federal Election Commission. The territories of American Samoa, Guam, and the Virgin Islands use the caucus also. All other states and Puerto Rico use primary elections or a combination of the voting formats. Caucus meetings are arranged by either the state or political party to take place at a certain place and time. Caucuses are unique in that they allow participants to openly show support for candidates. Voting is often done by raising hands or breaking into groups according to the candidate participants support. The results of the caucus are used to determine the delegates present at county, state, and national nominating conventions of each political party. Most often, only registered voters can participate in a caucus, and they are limited to the caucus of the party with which they are affiliated.

Primaries are a direct, statewide process of selecting candidates and delegates. Similar to the general election process, primary voters cast secret ballots for the candidates of their choosing. The results are used to determine the configuration of delegates at the national convention of each party. Primaries come in two basic forms: In an open primary, all registered voters can vote for any candidate, regardless of their political affiliation. Registered

Democrats may vote for a Republican candidate, and Republican voters may cast ballots for a Democrat, for instance. And registered Independents can participate in either party's primary. But in a closed primary, voters may vote only for candidates of the party with which they are registered.

Since the parties are permitted to control the nomination system used for picking presidential nominees, there is already a clear argument to be made that the process is not truly democratic since you have to belong to a party to vote in their primary or participate in their caucus. Unless you live in an open primary state (where you can simply request a ballot for a particular party on Election Day), you have to legally declare a party preference to participate in their primary. What becomes interesting about this scenario is that if Donald Trump and Hillary Clinton are so unpopular with voters yet still managed to win crowded primaries, it suggests there are bigger problems related to voter turnout than the actual rules in place presently.

While the nomination system itself will be questioned for its own merits, many also wonder about how the primary selection process impacts general elections. In short, was the primary system part of how Trump was able to win the presidency despite losing the popular vote by nearly three million voters? If so, why? If not, how are the two separated?

In the following selections, journalist Jamelle Bouie argues that the current presidential nomination system is in fact quite democratic by allowing states to determine how best to conduct elections within their borders. He notes that even outside of elections, American government has always flourished under a blend of majoritarian, nonmajoritarian, and countermajoritarian elements. However, William Saletan, also a journalist, acknowledges that the nomination process is not particularly democratic but reminds readers that the goals of primaries and caucuses are to select candidates that best represent party interests.

YES

Jamelle Bouie

The Process Worked

On Monday night, the Associated Press broke news. Tallying its survey of Democratic superdelegates—the cadre of party members and elected officials who help select the nominee—the AP found that Hillary Clinton had met the threshold needed for nomination. Regardless of Tuesday's outcomes in California, New Jersey, and elsewhere, Clinton will be the Democratic Party's nominee for president and the first woman to win a major party nomination.

Team Clinton was restrained at the announcement, telling an audience in California that "we are on the brink of a historic, historic, unprecedented moment, but we still have work to do.... We have six elections tomorrow, and we're going to fight hard for every single vote, especially right here in California." Team Sanders, understandably, was defiant. "It is unfortunate that the media, in a rush to judgement, are ignoring the Democratic National Committee's clear statement that it is wrong to count the votes of super delegates before they actually vote at the convention this summer," said campaign spokesman Michael Briggs in a statement.

The reactions fit the campaigns' respective attitudes toward the primary. Team Clinton wants to avoid any sense that her win was unfair or illegitimate, while Team Sanders has criticized the process as suspect and, at worst, deeply unfair to his candidacy. "What is really dumb is that you have closed primaries, like in New York state, where 3 million people who were not Democrats or Republicans could not participate," said Sanders in a recent interview with CBS News' John Dickerson. "You have a situation where over 400 superdelegates came on board Clinton's campaign before anybody else was in the race, eight months before the first vote was cast."

To this point, Sanders has offered a few reforms for the Democratic primary process, aimed at smoothing the path for future ideological candidates like himself. "In those states where it's applicable," he said, "we need same-day registration, we need open primaries." This is echoed elsewhere, from supporters who see closed primaries and superdelegates as obstacles to a candidacy like Sanders', to surrogates who slam the Democratic National Committee as an unfair lever for the Democratic "establishment." And in general, this primary season has convinced a number of observers that the Democratic Party's process for selecting a presidential nominee is broken and ripe for reform.

I'm skeptical. To say that the process is "broken" presupposes both an idea of what it's supposed to do in the first place and a general consensus that it didn't accomplish the goal. We have the former: The aim of the Democratic primary process is for the party to choose a nominee who is acceptable to all of its parts, from dedicated supporters and casual voters to elites and activists, and who could plausibly lead the party to victory in the general election. But a close look at the conversation over the nomination process shows that we don't have much of the latter—there's no consensus over the efficacy of the process. Instead, we have an argument from the losing candidate and his backers that borders on special pleading.

To wit, Sanders' supporters say the process is flawed because it harmed their candidate in critical ways: Closed primaries kept out pro-Sanders independents; superdelegates gave his opponent an appearance of inevitability; and the order of the calendar gave her an early advantage.

The problem is that these aren't flaws in the process so much as they are contingent disadvantages. Yes, Bernie Sanders flailed with stalwart Democratic voters, lacked elite party support, and couldn't win in the South. But it's a trivial task to imagine a candidate who *could* have done some combination of three, or pulled a hat trick, full stop. (In fact, we have one: Barack Obama.) That Sanders was a poor fit for some aspects of the Democratic primary doesn't mean those parts were *bad*. To make that call, we have to see if these parts are out of alignment with our stated goal.

They aren't. Well before Clinton announced her bid for the White House, she held broad support across the Democratic Party. And going into the general election, she's the clear favorite, with a modest but growing lead over her likely opponent, Donald Trump. It's possible that—per his recent argument—Sanders is the better choice for the fall, but that doesn't make Clinton a bad or unacceptable one.

If there's a stronger case for reform beyond "my preferred candidate lost," it's that the processes of the *Democratic* Party aren't especially democratic, that, together, caucuses, closed primaries, and superdelegates either preclude participation or actively subvert the "will of the people." This isn't wrong. Caucuses, which require long hours from participants, are notoriously inhospitable to voters with tough schedules or attachments. Closed primaries and strict registration deadlines are designed to remove independent voters from consideration. And in theory, superdelegates could overturn the decision of voters. (For weeks, in fact, Sanders was asking them to do just that.) These are real problems and dangers in the primary process as it stands. But there are virtues, too.

Closed primaries force candidates to appeal directly to loyal Democratic voters in the same way that open ones force them to win over moderates and independents. Given the degree to which this is a party selection process, that's not only fair—it's desirable. Likewise, caucuses are a proving ground for the organizational capabilities of the candidates, as well as an opportunity both for smaller constituencies to make their mark on the process and for underdog candidates to pick up momentum. Barack Obama couldn't have made ground without winning the Iowa caucus, and this year's Sanders insurgency was fueled by grass-roots activity as channeled through caucuses. They aren't the most democratic method for selecting delegates, but they serve a vital purpose nonetheless.

The same goes for superdelegates, who represent important party stakeholders and elected officials. They force candidates—who are vying to lead the party—to take another constituency into account. Yes, the fact that they always back the pledged delegate winner undermines the extent to which they're "unbound" (as we saw in 2008,

when Clinton superdelegates switched sides to bring Obama to the threshold after he finished the contest with a lead). But this year's Republican presidential contest is a testament to the value of an anchor in the case of a candidate who violates core party principles; an emergency brake, to use in potentially catastrophic situations like the rise of a Trump-style figure.

That the process may benefit from "undemocratic" elements gets to a larger point. Majoritarian procedures are a necessary part of democracy, but they're not synonymous with it. And most democratic systems—including our own—are a blend of majoritarian, nonmajoritarian, and even countermajoritarian elements that translate, temper, or otherwise channel the behavior and choices of majorities. What determines if the entire system is democratic is whether it's rule-bound, transparent, and ultimately accountable to the public.

That description fits the Democratic nomination process, and insofar as it doesn't, only minor tweaks are needed. State parties—which control most on-the-ground election procedures—need to devise and follow common standards for registration, party-switching, and caucus participation (in states that use caucuses). If you need to register with the party to participate, it should be easy and straightforward (what happened ahead of the New York primary, for example, is unacceptable). Actual delegate selection—as opposed to allocation—should be as public as possible. And it might be time to restrict superdelegate status to elected officials, so that they can be held directly accountable by their voters.

Jamelle Bouie is the chief political correspondent for *Slate* magazine, and a political analyst for CBS News. He covers campaigns, elections, and national affairs. His work has appeared either online or in print at the *New Yorker*, the *Washington Post*, *The Nation*, and other publications.

William Saletan

The Primaries Aren't Democratic? They're Not Supposed to Be Democratic

Donald Trump says the process of picking Republican presidential delegates is "rigged." His son compares the process to "Communist China." Bernie Sanders says unelected Democratic superdelegates are propping up Hillary Clinton. Sanders and Trump are running as populists, challenging a corrupt nomination system in the name of democracy.

It's true that the system is full of quirks. Why do some states award their delegates proportionally, others by congressional district, and others by winner-take-all? Why do some conduct open primaries, while others restrict participation to caucusgoers? Why does a Republican delegate elected by Trump supporters get to vote for Ted Cruz at the convention? You can quarrel with any of these rules. But let's not pretend that everyone deserves a say in choosing the nominees. Parties are entitled to privilege their members and choose candidates who best represent their ideas. Trump and Sanders don't necessarily fit the bill.

Last weekend, Trump's top aides went on the Sunday shows to complain about the Republican process. "What this election has shown is that when voters participate, Donald Trump wins," said Trump's convention manager, Paul Manafort. That's misleading. What the election has shown is that in a multicandidate field, Trump usually gets a plurality. So far, the only place in which he has won a majority is his home state, New York.

As the race has narrowed, Trump's advantage has shrunk. That's why he got spanked in Wisconsin. And that raises a hard question: Does Trump truly represent Republican voters? Or is his lead in the delegate race a residual artifact of a multicandidate field? Even now, John Kasich's persistence as a third candidate is propping up Trump. Look at two national polls taken this month. A Fox News poll shows that if Kasich were to drop out, 55 percent of his voters would go to Cruz. Only 24 percent would go to Trump. A CBS News poll indicates that if Kasich were to quit, Trump's lead over Cruz would shrink from 13 points to 10 points, leaving Trump still short of a majority.

So when Trump complains about multistage delegate-selection procedures that leave him with fewer delegates than he should have won based on primaries held two months ago, bear this in mind: He's complaining about a result that might have happened anyway if voters had been allowed to register their second choices and reallocate their votes accordingly. A snapshot isn't necessarily better than a deliberate process.

Trump's campaign manager, Corey Lewandowski, has another objection. On *Fox News Sunday*, he complained:

> Let me give you one example. In the state of Florida, Donald Trump dominated and won by 23 points over all of his competitors down there. He was awarded 99 delegates under the party rules. Of those 99 delegates, the chairman of the party of Florida, who is an avid and outward supporter of Marco Rubio, gets to appoint 30 of those delegates.... That's not what the rules should be. The rules should be that Donald Trump won 99 delegates, and...we should have the opportunity to appoint those people.

Lewandowski botched the story: The Florida GOP chairman didn't take sides in the primary and doesn't appoint any delegates. But even if he did, the bigger outrage is that Trump got all 99 delegates for winning 46 percent of the vote. In three winner-take-all states—Florida, Arizona, and South Carolina—Trump won 43 percent of the combined ballots but was awarded all 207 delegates. That accounts for his entire 200-delegate lead in the nomination race. Overall, Trump has collected 48 percent of the delegates in Republican contests while winning only 37 percent of the vote.

Manafort says Trump wants Republicans and independents, "not the party bosses," to choose the nominee. Lewandowski complains that in some states, delegates are chosen based on "whether they run for statewide office and how much volunteering they have done," while other applicants are slighted "because they haven't been involved the last 25 years. That's everything that's wrong with the party system."

Everything that's wrong with the party system? Dude, that *is* the party system. A party is an organization. It has every right to award clout based on how much work you've put in over the years. Why should drive-by independents get more say than party bosses? I should know: I was one of those independents. In 2000, the Maryland Republican Party allowed people like me to vote in its presidential primary. I voted for John McCain over George W. Bush. McCain was a better fit for people like me. But was he a better fit for the party? And isn't that the point of a Republican primary—to choose a candidate who will represent the GOP?

It's particularly rich to hear all this rhetoric about inclusion from a campaign whose core issue is sealing the nation's borders. According to Trump, we mustn't let in any Muslims, since we don't know who they are. "If you don't have borders, you don't have a country," he says. Meanwhile, Trump brags about flooding Republican primaries with independents who pledge allegiance only to him and his defiance of the Republican platform. Why shouldn't the party reassert its right to nominate someone who shares its beliefs? If you don't have ideological boundaries, you don't have a party.

Sanders shares some of Trump's gripes. Prior to New York, the Vermont senator bragged about winning "eight out of nine caucuses and primaries" since March 22. But he's trailing among superdelegates—Democratic officeholders and party officials who get to vote at the convention, just like delegates elected in primaries and caucuses. Sanders thinks that's rotten. "Hillary Clinton is the candidate of the establishment. And she has many, many times more superdelegates than we have," Sanders noted on *Face the Nation*. On Monday, he said he had "serious problems" with this system. He complained about "the establishment folks—these are elected people, these are money people, who are superdelegates." He also criticized laws in New York that tell "hundreds of thousands or more independents who would like to vote tomorrow, for me or anybody else, [that] they can't participate. I think that that's wrong."

Can't participate? Sure they can. Registering as an independent is a choice. In many states, that choice comes with a price: You don't get to vote in primaries. If you want to vote in a primary, join a party. That's what I did two weeks ago: I saw that the Democratic primary for U.S. Senate in Maryland was really close and that my vote might matter. So after 16 years, I changed my registration. On Monday, I got my new registration letter in the mail. It's that simple.

Yes, Sanders has won a bunch of caucuses and primaries. But do those wins really convey a mandate to represent the Democratic Party? Exit polls show that among self-identified Democrats, Sanders has beaten Clinton in only two primaries: his home state of Vermont (easily) and the neighboring state of New Hampshire (barely). In every other primary, Sanders has either lost to Clinton or won by padding his tally with independents. And regardless of party, Clinton has won 56 percent of all ballots cast in Democratic contests. Sanders has won only 42 percent.

As for the caucuses Sanders has won since March 22, check out the rules. You can't vote absentee. You have to show up at a specific time, usually on a Saturday morning. You're advised to reserve a seat or arrive hours early, since "there will probably be lines." If you miss the start time, you can be locked out. You have to endure "instructions and patriotic ceremonies," "speakers on behalf of all the candidates," and "general discussion and debate." The process can take hours. In most states, your ballot isn't secret: You literally "stand with your neighbors in support of your preferred candidate"—or you go to a different corner of the room and stand against them. And if your candidate doesn't get 15 percent of the vote at your caucus, you have to change your vote or throw it away.

That's why few people attend caucuses. Many states don't register voters by party, so it's hard to say how many Democrats there are. So let's use, as a rough proxy, a uniform standard that can be measured everywhere: the state-by-state vote totals for Barack Obama in the 2012 general election. The turnout in caucus states won by Sanders this year (except Utah, which has a more open process) has ranged from 9 percent to 13 percent of the Obama vote. By contrast, the turnout in primary states won by Clinton—even if you exclude the South, which Sanders claims is her base—has ranged from 40 percent to 67 percent of the Obama vote. Sanders tends to win two types of contests: ornate caucuses with very low turnout and wide-open primaries in which independents compensate for his poor showing among Democrats. Neither of these models certifies him as the candidate who best represents the Democratic Party.

Sanders doesn't even identify himself as a committed Democrat. His Senate bio calls him "the longest serving independent member of Congress." It doesn't mention any party affiliation. A year ago, when Sanders announced his presidential candidacy, he said he wouldn't join the Democratic Party. Since then, he has couched his affiliation with the party as a temporary arrangement.

WILLIAM SALETAN writes about politics, science, technology, and other stuff for *Slate*. He is the author of *Bearing Right*.

EXPLORING THE ISSUE

Is the Current Presidential Nomination System Actually Democratic?

Critical Thinking and Reflection

1. How do elections reflect political values of a society?
2. Why should we want the nomination system to be democratic?
3. How can Americans work to ensure nominations are as democratic as possible?
4. What facets of American elections could be made more democratic?
5. Do you believe American elections operate as they should? Why or why not?

Is There Common Ground?

As long as major political parties are permitted to control the nomination system, there will likely be questions regarding the relative democracy within how nominees for the president are selected. Given that the 2016 cycle produced Donald Trump and Hillary Clinton—two strongly unpopular candidates even within certain wings of their own parties—it is possible that reforms could be on the horizon; yet, it is essential to remember that those reforms would still be controlled by the Democratic and Republican parties. Democrats have been questioning the democratic nature of using superdelegates as part of the nomination system, whereas some Republicans have suggested a similar protocol moving forward to try to prevent extreme candidates from being able to take over the nomination.

If individuals are hoping to see a complete overhaul of the presidential nomination system, they are likely to be disappointed. At the end of the day, the presidential nomination system has never been directly concerned with democracy. Instead, it exists to allow political parties to select the candidate that individual party members believe will best represent the entire party in a general election. There will unquestionably be tweaks that occur prior to the 2020 presidential nomination cycle, but these will be relatively minor in nature. Bernie Sanders supporters will likely push for the Democratic Party to assure more inclusiveness in platform setting, while many non-Trump Republicans will be working to revise rules to help bring the party back to the mainstream identifier. Democrats have already moved to alter the superdelegate structure slightly in 2020, but we are still two years from seeing a new process in action.

Additional Resources

Marty Cohen and David Karol, *The Party Decides: Presidential Nominations Before and After Reform* (University of Chicago Press, 2008).

Elaine C. Kamarck, *Primary Politics: Everything You Need to Know about How America Nominates Its Presidential Candidates* (Brookings Institution Press, 2016).

Barbara Norrander, *The Imperfect Primary: Oddities, Biases, and Strengths of U.S. Presidential Nomination Politics* (Routledge, 2015).

Internet References . . .

How the U.S. Presidential Primary System Works

> http://www.cfr.org/elections/us-presidential-nominating-process/p37522

Presidential Election Process

> https://www.usa.gov/election

Understanding the Nomination Process

> https://billofrightsinstitute.org/educate/educator-resources/lessons-plans/current-events/nomination-process/

Selected, Edited, and with Issue Framing Material by:
William J. Miller, *Campus Labs®*

ISSUE

Are Entitlement Programs Creating a Culture of Dependency?

YES: Nicholas Eberstadt, from "The Rise of Entitlements in Modern America, 1960–2010," Templeton Press (2012)

NO: William A. Galston, from "Have We Become 'A Nation of Takers'?" Templeton Press (2012)

Learning Outcomes
After reading this issue, you will be able to:
• Identify current entitlement programs in the United States.   • Describe what is meant by a culture of dependency.   • Assess current spending on entitlement programs on the United States budget today.   • Explain long-term concerns about entitlement spending and dependency.   • Indicate whether government can afford to maintain current entitlement programs.

ISSUE SUMMARY

YES: Social scientist Nicholas Eberstadt argues that the increase in entitlement programs is unprecedented in American history and has created a large dependency class that has lost the will to work.

NO: Political theorist William A. Galston sees the growth of American entitlement programs as an appropriate response to the needs of an aging population and rising costs of higher education and medicine; he sees them not as evidence of dependency but of "interdependence."

In a conference call with fundraisers and donors after the 2012 presidential election, Governor Mitt Romney attributed his defeat to what he called "gifts" bestowed by President Obama to selected constituencies, "especially the African-American community, the Hispanic community and young people." Similar claims were often voiced in the media. Radio talk-show host Rush Limbaugh and Fox News commentator Bill O'Reilly both talked about the election as being influenced by the prospect of "free stuff" from the White House. On the Internet, the Drudge Report posted a YouTube video of a woman in Cleveland bragging about getting a free "Obamaphone."

Central to the complaint about "free stuff" is what are called "entitlements," defined as "benefits provided by government to which recipients have a legally enforceable

right" (Jack Plano and Milton Greenberg, *The American Political Dictionary*). Entitlement spending, in contrast to "discretionary spending," is spending that the government must make to individuals based upon certain criteria. If a certain individual meets those criteria, he or she can demand payments from the government. Major examples of entitlements include Social Security, Medicare, veterans' benefits, government retirement plans, food stamps, and certain welfare programs. In 2010, the Affordable Care Act, a program of national health insurance, was enacted with some entitlement features, such as subsidies for those unable to purchase health insurance.

Entitlement spending has grown steeply over the past half-century. In 1960 it amounted to less than one-third of the total federal government outlays, the same share it occupied in 1940; today it constitutes roughly two-thirds of the total. At the present rate of growth, the risk is that it may soon crowd out other vital federal programs, from defense and internal security to national health and environmental protection. Most observers today agree that the growth of entitlement spending is a serious issue, though they may disagree on the best means of addressing the issue. Some think the best approach is through spending cuts, while others place greater emphasis on increases in revenues.

But the debate on entitlements is not just about fiscal issues. The complaint about "free stuff" touches one of the deepest nerves of American public morality. Since Puritan times, Americans have honored work as a builder of character and maturity. It follows that idleness is contemptible because it weakens character. "Idleness is the Dead Sea that swallows all virtues," wrote Ben Franklin, an appraisal repeated in various languages over the past 250 years. Idleness becomes particularly problematic in the view of most Americans when it is combined with the prospect of "free stuff." Daniel Patrick Moynihan, the 1973 U.S. Senator, addressed this issue in a discussion of "dependency." At the heart of Moynihan's thesis was a distinction between dependency and poverty. "To be poor is an objective condition; to be dependent, a subjective one as well. . . . Being poor is often combined with considerable personal qualities; being dependent rarely so." Moynihan's conclusion was that long-term dependency tends to leave a person in "an incomplete state of life: normal in a child, abnormal in an adult."

But equating entitlements with dependency is not so easy. Moynihan himself was a strong supporter of Social Security, which fits the *American Political Dictionary's* definition of an entitlement as a "legally enforceable right" to a benefit. It is hard to see how Social Security puts its recipients in "an incomplete state of life," especially since they have spent most of their life paying into it. The same is true of veterans' benefits and others considered in some sense to have been earned. Yet still other benefits such as food stamps are unearned. Entitlements, like many other government programs, are an apples-and-oranges mixture that almost defies definition.

One entitlement program that did seem to fit the category of unearned entitlements was Aid to Families with Dependent Children (AFDC) which was abolished by Congress in 1996 and replaced by Temporary Assistance for Needy Families (TANF), which left to the states much of the administration of the program but directed them to require work from recipients in order to receive benefits. Recently, the Obama administration has modified the administra-

tion of the work requirement, leaving still more discretion in the hands of individual states. Returning to Brandeis' central principles, states are again laboratories of democracy. But in the current iteration, there is the potential for states to negatively impact the economic performance of the nation as a whole. Especially since entitlement spending takes the place of discretionary monies.

The Center on Budget and Policy Priorities examined where entitlement funds go in a February 2012 report. Their finds show, "Some conservative critics of federal social programs, including leading presidential candidates, are sounding an alarm that the United States is rapidly becoming an "entitlement society" in which social programs are undermining the work ethic and creating a large class of Americans who prefer to depend on government benefits rather than work. A new CBPP analysis of budget and Census data, however, shows that more than 90 percent of the benefit dollars that entitlement and other mandatory programs spend go to assist people who are elderly, seriously disabled, or members of working households—not to able-bodied, working-age Americans who choose not to work. This figure has changed little in the past few years." These findings directly refute much of the public perceptions—and especially conservative criticisms. Further, it complements other academic research, including a study that concluded: "The U.S. system favors groups with special needs, such as the disabled and the elderly. Groups like these which are perceived as especially deserving receive disproportionate transfers and those transfers have been increasing over time. Second, the system favors workers over non-workers and has increasingly done so over time. The rise of the EITC and the decline of AFDC/TANF is most illustrative of this trend." The study also found that "the demographic group which is most underserved by the system are non-elderly non-disabled families with no continuously-employed members."

Despite these studies, public perception still seems to believe that entitlements do not always assist those in need. While the current budget request of President Trump is not final and could be changed, sources say it would propose about $800 billion in cuts to projected spending in a wide array of means-tested, mandatory spending programs including Medicaid over the next decade. Trump promised during his campaign to not touch Social Security nor Meidcare, but both could ultimately find themselves impacted as well. It's not clear which programs might be cut beyond Medicaid but means-tested mandatory spending programs include food stamps, Temporary Assistance for Needy Families, Supplemental Security Income, child nutrition programs and the Pell Grant program. Proposed cuts to any of these programs would likely spark great controversy among advocates and pushback among Democrats already trying to capitalize on the health care bill.

In the following selections, social scientist Nicholas Eberstadt argues that the increase in entitlement programs is unprecedented in American history and has created a large dependency class that has lost the will to work. Opposing that view is political theorist William A. Galston, who sees the growth of American entitlement programs as an appropriate response to the needs of an aging population and rising costs of higher education and medicine; for him, the growth of these programs is evidence not of dependency but of "interdependence."

YES

Nicholas Eberstadt

The Rise of Entitlements in Modern America, 1960–2010

Introduction

The American republic has endured for more than two and a quarter centuries; the United States is the world's oldest constitutional democracy. But over the past fifty years, the apparatus of American governance has undergone a fundamental and radical transformation. In some basic respects—its scale, its preoccupations, even many of its purposes—the United States government today would be scarcely recognizable to a Franklin D. Roosevelt, much less an Abraham Lincoln or a Thomas Jefferson.

What is monumentally new about the American state today is the vast and colossal empire of entitlement payments that it protects, manages, and finances. Within living memory, the government of the United States of America has become an entitlements machine. As a day-to-day operation, the U.S. government devotes more attention and resources to the public transfers of money, goods, and services to individual citizens than to any other objective; and for the federal government, more to these ends than to all other purposes combined.

Government entitlement payments are benefits to which a person holds an established right under law (i.e., to which a person is entitled). A defining feature of these payments (also sometimes officially referred to as "current transfer receipts of individuals from government," or simply "transfers") is that they "are benefits received for which no current service is performed." Entitlements are a relatively new concept in U.S. politics and policy; according to Merriam-Webster, the first known use of the term was not until 1942. But entitlements have become very familiar, very fast. By the reckoning of the Bureau of Economic Analysis (BEA), the research group within the Commerce Department that prepares the U.S. government's GNP estimates and related national accounts, income from entitlement programs in the year 2010 was transferred to Americans under a panoply of over fifty separate types of programs, and accounted for almost one-fifth (18 percent) of personal income in that year.

In 1960, U.S. government transfers to individuals from all programs totaled about $24 billion. By 2010, the outlay for entitlements was almost 100 times more. Over that interim, the nominal growth in entitlement payments to Americans by their government was rising by an explosive average of 9.5 percent per annum for fifty straight years. The tempo of growth, of course, is exaggerated by concurrent inflation—but after adjusting for inflation, entitlement payments soared more than twelve-fold (1248 percent), with an implied average real annual growth rate of about 5.2 percent per annum. Even after adjusting for inflation and population growth, entitlement transfers to individuals have more than septupled (727 percent) over the past half-century, rising at an overall average of about 4 percent per annum.

These long-term spending trends mask shorter-run tendencies, to be sure. Over the past two decades, for example, the nominal growth in these entitlement outlays has slowed to an average of "only" 7.1 percent a year (or a doubling every decade). Adjusted for inflation by the Consumer Price Index, real entitlement outlays rose by an average of "just" 4.4 percent over those years—and by a "mere" 3.2 percent a year on a per capita basis. But if the pace of entitlement growth has slowed in recent decades, so has the growth in per capita income. From 1960 to 2010 real per capita income in America grew by a measured 2.2 percent on average—but over the past twenty years, it has increased by 1.6 percent per annum. In other words, total entitlement payouts on a real per capita basis have been growing twice as fast as per capita income over the past twenty years; the disparity between entitlement growth on the one hand and overall income growth on the other is greater in recent times than it was in earlier decades.

The magnitude of entitlement outlays today is staggering. In 2010 alone, government at all levels oversaw a transfer of over $2.2 trillion in money, goods, and services to recipient men, women, and children in the United States. At prevailing official exchange rates, that would have been greater than the entire GDP of Italy, roughly the equivalent of Britain's and close to the total for France—advanced economies all with populations of roughly 60 million each. (The U.S. transfer numbers, incidentally, do not include the cost of administering the entitlement programs.) In 2010 the burden of entitlement transfers came to slightly more than $7,200 for every man, woman, and child in America. Scaled against a notional family of four, the average entitlements burden for that year alone would have approached $29,000. And that pay-out required payment from others, through taxes, borrowing, or some combination of the two.

A half-century of unfettered expansion of entitlement outlays has completely inverted the priorities, structure, and functions of federal administration, as these had been understood by all previous generations of American citizens. Until 1960 the accepted purpose of the federal government, in keeping with its constitutional charge, was governing. The federal government's spending patterns reflected that mandate. The overwhelming share of federal expenditures was allocated to defending the republic against enemies foreign and domestic (defense, justice, interest payments on the national debt) and some limited public services and infrastructural investments (the postal authority, agricultural extension, transport infrastructure, and the like). Historically, transfer payments did not figure prominently (or, sometimes, at all) in our federal ledgers. . . .

In 1960, entitlement program transfer payments accounted for well under one-third of the federal government's total outlays—about the same fraction as in 1940, when the Great Depression was still shaping American life, with unemployment running in the range of 15 percent. But then—in just a decade and a half—the share of entitlements in total federal spending suddenly spurted up from 28 percent to 51 percent. It did not surpass the 50 percent mark again until the early 1990s. But over the past two decades it rose almost relentlessly, until by 2010 it accounted for just about two-thirds of all federal spending, with all other responsibilities of the federal government—defense, justice, and all the other charges specified in the Constitution or undertaken in the intervening decades—making up barely one-third. Thus, in a very real sense, American governance has literally turned upside-down by entitlements—and within living memory. . . .

The New American Way of Life: Our National Declaration of Dependence

From the founding of our state up to the present—or rather, until quite recently—the United States and the citizens who peopled it were regarded, at home and abroad, as "exceptional" in a number of deep and important respects. One of these was their fierce and principled independence, which informed not only the design of the political experiment that is the U.S. Constitution but also the approach to everyday affairs. The proud self-reliance that struck Alexis de Tocqueville in his visit to the United States in the early 1830s extended to personal finances. The American "individualism" about which he wrote included social cooperation, and on a grand scale—the young nation was a hotbed of civic associations and voluntary organizations. Rather, it was that American men and women viewed themselves as accountable for their own situation through their own achievements in an environment bursting with opportunity—a novel outlook at that time, markedly different from the prevailing Old World (or at least Continental) attitudes.

The corollaries of this American ethos (which might be described as a sort of optimistic Puritanism) were, on the one hand, an affinity for personal enterprise and industry; and, on the other hand, a horror of dependency and contempt for anything that smacked of a mendicant mentality. Although many Americans in earlier times were poor—before the twentieth century, practically everyone was living on income that would be considered penurious nowadays—even people in fairly desperate circumstances were known to refuse help or handouts as an affront to their dignity and independence. People who subsisted on public resources were known as "paupers," and provision for these paupers was a local undertaking. Neither beneficiaries nor recipients held the condition of pauperism in high regard.

Overcoming America's historic cultural resistance to government entitlements has been a long and formidable endeavor. But as we know today, this resistance did not ultimately prove an insurmountable obstacle to the establishment of a mass public entitlements regime or to the normalization of the entitlement lifestyle in modern America. The United States is at the verge of a symbolic threshold: the point at which more than half of all American households receive, and accept, transfer benefits from the government. From cradle (strictly speaking, from *before* the cradle) to grave, a treasure chest of government-supplied benefits is open for the taking for every American citizen—and exercising one's legal rights to these many blandishments is now part and parcel of the American way of life. . . .

From a Nation of Takers to a Nation of Gamers to a Nation of Chiselers

With the disappearance of the historical stigma against dependence on government largesse, and the normalization of lifestyles relying upon official resource transfers, it is not surprising that ordinary Americans should have turned their noted entrepreneurial spirit not simply to maximizing their take from the existing entitlement system, but to extracting payouts from the transfer state that were never intended under its programs. In this environment, gaming and defrauding the entitlement system have emerged as a mass phenomenon in modern America, a way of life for millions upon millions of men and women who would no doubt unhesitatingly describe themselves as law-abiding and patriotic American citizens.

Abuse of the generosity of our welfare state has, to be sure, aroused the ire of the American public in the past, and continues to arouse it from time to time today. For decades, a special spot in the rhetorical public square has been reserved for pillorying unemployed "underclass" garners who cadge undeserved social benefits. (This is the "welfare Cadillac" trope, and its many coded alternatives.) Public disapproval of this particular variant of entitlement misuse was sufficiently strong that Congress managed in the mid-1990s to overhaul the notorious AFDC program in a reform of welfare that replaced the old structure with Temporary Assistance for Needy Families (TANF). But entitlement fiddling in modern America is by no means the exclusive preserve of a troubled underclass. Quite the contrary: it is today characteristic of working America, and even those who would identify themselves as middle class.

Exhibit A in the documentation of widespread entitlement abuse in mainstream America is the explosion over the past half-century of disability claims and awards under the disability insurance provisions of the U.S. Social Security program. In 1960 an average of 455,000 erstwhile workers were receiving monthly federal payments for disability. By 2010 that total had skyrocketed to 8.2 million (and by 2011 had risen still further, to almost 8.6 million). Thus, the number of Americans collecting government disability payments soared eighteen-fold over the fifty years from 1960 and 2010. In the early 1960s almost twice as many adults were receiving AFDC checks as disability payments; by 2010, disability payees outnumbered the average calendar-year TANF caseload by more than four to one (8.20 million vs. 1.86 million). Moreover, "workers" who were recipients of government disability payments had jumped from the equivalent of 0.65 percent of the economically active eighteen- to sixty-four-year-old population in 1960 to 5.6 percent by 2010. In 1960, there were over 150 men and women in those age groups working or seeking employment for every person on disability; by 2010, the ratio was 18 to 1 and continuing to decrease. The ratios are even starker when it comes to paid work: in 1960, roughly 134 Americans were engaged in gainful employment for every officially disabled worker; by December 2010 there were just over 16. And by some measures, the situation today looks even more unfavorable than this.

Although the Social Security Administration does not publish data on the ethnicity of its disability payees, it does publish information on a state-by-state basis. These suggest that the proclivity to rely upon government disability payments today is at least as much a "white thing" as a tendency for any other American group. As of December 2011 the state with the very highest ratio of working-age disability awardees to the resident population ages eighteen to sixty-four was West Virginia (9.0 percent—meaning that every eleventh adult in this age group was on paid government disability). According to Census Bureau estimates, 93 percent of West Virginia's population was "non-Hispanic white" in 2011. In New England, by the same token, all-but-lily-white Maine (where ethnic minorities accounted for less than 6 percent of the population in 2011) records a 7.4 percent ratio of working-age disability payees to resident working-age population: more than one out of fourteen. . . .

In "playing" the disability system, or cheating it outright, many millions of Americans are making a living by putting their hands into the pockets of their fellow citizen—be they taxpayers now alive or as yet unborn (a steadily growing phenomenon, as we shall see in a moment). And it is not simply the disability gamers themselves who are complicit in this modern scam. The army of doctors and health-care professionals who are involved in, and paid for their services in, certifying dubious workers' compensation cases are direct—indeed indispensable—collaborators in the operation. The U.S. judicial system—which rules on disability cases and sets the standards for disability qualification—is likewise compromised. More fundamentally, American voters and their elected representatives are ultimately responsible for this state of affairs, as its willing and often knowing enablers. This popular tolerance for widespread dishonesty at the demonstrable expense of fellow citizens leads to an impoverishment of the country's civic spirit and an incalculable degradation of the nation's constituting principles. . . .

NICHOLAS EBERSTADT is a political economist who holds the Henry Wendt Chair in Political Economy at the American Enterprise Institute (AEI). He is also a senior adviser to the National Bureau of Asian Research (NBR), a member of the visiting committee at the Harvard School of Public Health, and a member of the Global Leadership Council at the World Economic Forum.

William A. Galston

Have We Become "A Nation of Takers"?

Nicholas Eberstadt assembles a host of empirical trends to prove a moral conclusion: the growth of the entitlement state over the past half-century has undermined the sturdy self-reliance that has long characterized most Americans, replacing it with a culture of dependence that not only distorts our government but also threatens the American experiment. This claim raises two large questions: Do these trends represent a full and fair account of what has taken place since 1960? And do they warrant the conclusion Eberstadt urges on his readers? After some brief reflections on the former question, I devote the bulk of my remarks to the latter.

What Has Happened in the Past Half-Century?

As far as I can tell, Eberstadt's charts and statistics accurately represent the trends on which he focuses. But they are not the whole truth. In the first place, Eberstadt's accounting does not include all of the public policies that constitute entitlements as he defines them. Tax expenditures—special deductions and exemptions from, and credits against, otherwise taxable income—now constitute more than $1.1 trillion annually and they disproportionately benefit upper-income families. . . .

But suppose we consider only the list of entitlement programs on which Eberstadt focuses. Based on his presentation, one might imagine that U.S. households have become far more dependent on public programs in recent decades. This seems not to be the case, however. A Congressional Budget Report (CBO) report released in October 2011 found that government transfers did not grow as a share of household market income between 1979 (a cyclical peak in the economy) and 2007 (another such peak) but rather oscillated between 10 and 12 percent. From the beginning to the end of that period, Social Security was unchanged at 6 percent of market income; health-care programs (primary Medicare, Medicaid, and the Children's Health Insurance Program) rose from under 2 percent to a bit less than 4 percent while all other transfer programs declined.

There was a change in the distribution of these transfers, however: the share going to the poorest households declined significantly. In 1979, households in the lowest income quintile received fully 54 percent of federal transfer payments, but by 2007 that figure had fallen to only 36 percent—a reduction of one-third. Put another way, during that period, households with low-wage or non-working adults got less, while households in the middle and upper middle classes got more. If there is a problem of growing dependence, these figures suggest that it is located more in Middle America than in the ranks of the poor and near-poor. This possibility raises the question (to which I will return in the next section) of whether transfers going to families conducting themselves in accordance with middle-class norms of work and child-rearing represent dependence in any sense that gives rise to moral concern.

At least three other long-cycle trends need to be taken into account as well if we are to understand what is happening in our society and how we might respond. In the first place, we are an aging society. The massive investments in public schools and university expansion at the height of the baby boom have given way increasingly to the funding of hospitals and nursing homes. And while we typically regard the costs of dependence at the beginning of life as primarily the responsibility of families, this is much less true for dependence at the end of life. It is easy to see why. Aging brings expanding needs for complex and costly medical procedures that exceed the resources of average families. And no matter how hard they try, middle-aged adults often find that caring for aging parents in a family setting requires strength and skills they simply do not possess.

A second trend has exacerbated the consequences of aging: the near-disappearance of the pensions and health insurance for retirees that employers provided during the decades after the World War II. America's dominance of the global industrial economy gave employers the market power to set prices high enough to fund generous contracts with unionized employees. As the devastated nations of Europe and Asia recovered and international competition intensified, the postwar bargain in the United States broke down, and government stepped into the breach. For many Americans, Social Security became the primary (not supplemental) source of retirement income, and Medicare made up the difference between having and going without health insurance.

The third trend is macroeconomic. During the generation after World War II, the economy grew briskly, and the fruits of that growth were widely shared. Since then, growth has slowed, and the distribution of gains has become more concentrated at the top. Between 1947 and 1973, incomes of families in the bottom quintile rose by 117 percent; in the middle quintile, by 103 percent; at the top, by 88 percent. From 1973 to 2000, in contrast, the bottom quintile rose by only 12 percent, the middle by 25 percent, and the top by 66 percent. And in the seven years of the twenty-first century before the Great Recession struck, family incomes at the bottom actually fell by 6 percent and stagnated for everyone else (except for those at the very top). Since 1973, meanwhile, costs for big-ticket items such as higher education and health care have risen far faster than family incomes, increasing pressure on the public sector to step into the breach.

So there are reasons—in my view, compelling ones—why the federal government has undertaken major new responsibilities during the past half-century. Even so, we still have a problem: a huge gap between the promises we have made and the resources we have been willing to devote to fulfilling them. One way or another, we must close this gap. But the moral heart of this fiscal challenge is not dependence but rather a dangerous combination of self-interest, myopia, and denial.

What Is "Dependence"?

To understand why I subordinate dependence to these other concerns, we must begin by clarifying the meaning of the term. One thing is clear at the outset: the dependence/independence dyad is too crude to capture the complexity of social relations. At a minimum, we must take account of a third term, "interdependence," and the norm of reciprocity that undergirds it. When I do something for you that you would be hard-pressed to do for yourself and you respond by helping me with something I find difficult, we depend on one another and are the stronger for it.

Well-functioning societies are replete with relations of this sort and use them as models for public policy. But the move from families and small groups to large-scale collective action makes a difference. Reciprocity becomes

extended not only demographically and geographically but also chronologically. Political communities exist not just for the here and now but for future generations as well. Much contemporary public policy rests on temporally extended interdependence—in other terms, on an intergenerational compact. When we consent to deductions from our salary to help fund our parents' retirement, it is with the expectation that our children will do the same for us. This compact is practically sustainable and morally acceptable, but only with the proviso that the burdens we impose on our children are not disproportionate to the burdens we ourselves are willing to bear. The terms of interdependence matter, not just the fact of it. And so—to descend to cases—if we can honor promises to the current generation of working Americans only by imposing heavier sacrifices on the next generation, then something has gone awry. But—to repeat—"dependence" is the wrong characterization of the problem.

So is the concept of "entitlement." To be entitled to something is not necessarily to be dependent on it—at least not in a way that should trouble us. Consider the definition Eberstadt provides: "Government entitlement payments are benefits to which a person holds an established right under law (i.e., to which a person is entitled). A defining feature of these payments (also sometimes officially referred to as government transfers to individuals) is that they are 'benefits received for which no current service is performed.'"

Note that many nongovernmental relations have the same structure. If I use my life savings to purchase a retirement annuity, I have a legally enforceable expectation of receiving over time the stream of income specified in the contract. When I begin receiving these payments, I am performing no "current service" in exchange for them. And I certainly "depend" on these payments to fund my living expenses when I am no longer working. But surely I am not dependent in the way that so concerned Daniel Patrick Moynihan.

I do not see why transferring this case to the public sector makes a moral difference. Suppose someone pays into a government account throughout his working life, in effect purchasing an annuity to fund his retirement. If the income stream is actuarially fair, then he can expect to get back the equivalent of what he contributed. He may do better or worse, of course. If he lives until ninety-five, he will get back more; if he dies at seventy, less. Relying on these payments doesn't make him dependent in any morally troubling sense.

Social Security works this way for millions of Americans. For many others, it is more complicated: some can expect to receive more than the actuarial value of their contributions, others less. Americans in the latter category are helping to fund retirement for those in the former. In effect, some workers are relying on others for a portion of their retirement income. But again, this quantitative premise does not imply a disturbing moral conclusion. When Moynihan worried about dependence, he was not thinking about individuals who have worked hard all their lives in low-wage jobs but whose payroll taxes do not suffice to fund what society regards as a dignified retirement. . . .

Real Problems of Dependence

Eberstadt presents no direct evidence that the growth of the federal government has changed Americans' character or weakened their moral fiber, perhaps because it is very hard to find. Indeed, in-depth examinations of public attitudes suggest the reverse. In 2009, for example, the Pew Social Mobility Project asked a representative sample of Americans what is essential or very important to getting ahead. Ninety-two percent said hard work; 89 percent, ambition; 83 percent, a good education. In contrast, factors such as race (15 percent), gender (16 percent), luck (21 percent), and family wealth (28 percent) ranked at the bottom. Asked about the role of government in fostering economic mobility, 36 percent of respondents thought it did more to help than to hurt, but many more—46 percent—endorsed the opposite view. A follow-up survey two years later revealed that the share of Americans who considered government helpful for mobility had declined to only 27 percent, while those who thought it detrimental had risen to 52 percent.

That is not to say that government has no role. Large majorities thought that public policy could do more to increase jobs in the United States and reduce college and health-care costs. But in their view, mobility-enhancing programs help individuals help themselves. If the growth of government has created a culture of dependence, it is hard to discern the evidence in these surveys, which are representative of a large body of research.

Eberstadt does offer some indirect evidence of cultural change, two instances of which warrant sustained attention. There is little doubt that the Social Security Disability Insurance program (SSDI) is subject to serious abuse. During the past decade, the number of workers receiving monthly benefits has soared from 5.3 million to 8.6 million. And because SSDI recipients qualify for Medicare after receiving benefits for two years, few working-age beneficiaries leave the program once they have entered. By 2010, annual benefits had reached $115 billion plus $75 billion in added Medicare costs. . . .

But this is not necessarily evidence of a deep cultural change. The desire to get something for nothing is a hardy perennial of human nature, not a late-twentieth-century invention. U.S. history is replete with swindles and get-rich-quick schemes. What may have changed is the willingness of taxpayers to fund programs that prefer compassion to tough love. Over the past three decades, efforts to tighten up the program have repeatedly wrecked on the shoals of public resistance. Tales of individual suffering move many voters, and a prosperous society has been willing to fund public compassion—so far. It will be interesting to see what happens when these generous instincts run up against inevitable future efforts to rein in massive budget deficits.

Far more disturbing than the abuses of a single program is the evidence Eberstadt presents of the long-term withdrawal of working-age men from the labor force. Fifty years ago, more than 85 percent of men age twenty and over were in the labor force. Ever before the Great Recession hit, that figure had declined by ten percentage points, and it has dropped more in the ensuing years. During the same period, female labor force participation rose by more than twenty points, stabilizing at around 60 percent in the late 1990s.

Why have so many men checked out? Eberstadt is sure that the "entitlement society" is responsible; without all the programs that enable men to get by without working, the flight from employment "could not have been possible." Perhaps so. Still, although men and women are equally eligible to participate in these programs, they seem to have responded quite differently, at least in the aggregate. For example, nearly as many women (4.1 million) as men (4.5 million) receive disability benefits, but that has not kept the ranks of women in the paid workforce from swelling. . . .

Conclusion

By bringing together and concisely presenting a wealth of data, Eberstadt has performed a real service. He dramatizes the remarkable rise of the entitlement state and issues warnings about its consequences that we must consider seriously. Still, there are good reasons to question the causal link between entitlement programs and dependence—at least the kind of dependence that should concern us. To be sure, Americans want a reasonable level of security in their retirement years, and they think that government programs such as Social Security and Medicare are essential to that security. But they continue to believe that government is no substitute for hard work, ambition, and the perseverance that enables young people to complete their education and put it to work in the job market. They think that government should make reasonable provision for the poor and disabled, but they do not believe that government should enable people who could be independent to depend on the efforts of others. To the extent that current programs turn out to be inconsistent with that view, they will eventually be trimmed or abolished, as was AFDC in 1996.

Left unchecked, the programs we have created in the past half-century will make it difficult to stabilize our finances, to invest in the future, and to defend the nation. These are compelling reasons to rethink the entitlement state. But they have little to do with an alleged culture of dependence, the evidence for which is thin at best. As long as we do our part,there is no harm in benefitting from programs we help sustain. As long as we contribute our share, taking is morally unproblematic. We can be a nation of takers, as long as we are a nation of givers as well. As long as we honor the norm of reciprocity for our compatriots and for posterity, we can steer a steady course.

Note

1. David H. Autor and Mark Duggan, "Supporting Work: A Proposal for Modernizing the U.S. Disability Insurance System," Center for American Progress and The Hamilton Project, December 2010, http://www.hamiltonproject.org/files/downloads_and_links/FINAL_AutorDugganPaper.pdf

WILLIAM A. GALSTON holds the Ezra Zilkha Chair in the Brookings Institution's Governance Studies Program, where he serves as a senior fellow. A former policy adviser to President Clinton and presidential candidates, Galston is an expert on domestic policy, political campaigns, and elections. His current research focuses on designing a new social contract and the implications of political polarization.

EXPLORING THE ISSUE

Are Entitlement Programs Creating a Culture of Dependency?

Critical Thinking and Reflection

1. Why does Nicholas Eberstadt think that the U.S. government today "would be scarcely recognizable" to Franklin Roosevelt, Abraham Lincoln, or Thomas Jefferson?
2. Eberstadt thinks that, over the last 50 years, the government has "inverted" the historic priorities of federal administration. What does he mean by that?
3. Eberstadt contends that "the United States is at the verge of a symbolic threshold." What kind of threshold?
4. William A. Galston: "If there is a problem of growing dependence . . . it is located more in Middle America than in the ranks of the poor and near-poor." Explain.
5. Galston believes that three long-term trends are better explanations than government extravagance for why entitlement spending has risen so steeply in recent years. Pick two and discuss them.
6. Instead of "dependency," Galston contends, we have moved to an era of "interdependence." Explain.

Is There Common Ground?

The common ground between Eberstadt and Galston lies in the fact that entitlement spending is indeed rising steeply. Eberstadt presents alarming statistics on this, which Galston acknowledges to be accurate "as far as I can tell." Galston also acknowledges that, "left unchecked, the programs we have created in the past half century will make it difficult to stabilize our finances, to invest in the future, and to defend the nation." What he denies is that entitlement programs are making Americans lazy and immature. Instead, he believes they serve their role as a safety net. Most Americans would agree that individuals in certain circumstances deserve help from their government in a temporary manner as they get back on their feet.

A pragmatist might argue that perhaps we can put aside the ideological arguments for the moment and bring together people of all ideologies in a nuts-and-bolts campaign to trim the unnecessary costs of these and other government programs. However, such a decision would be difficult to reach. Multiple parties would need to accept such cuts and many may in fact benefit from the programs being trimmed. Perhaps most worrisome is how to handle a program like Social Security, in which citizens have paid into the program but may not be able to draw returns later in life. For these individuals, middle ground is difficult to find.

Additional Resources

Peter Edelman, *So Rich, So Poor: Why It's Hard to End Poverty in America* (New Press, 2012).

Barbara Ehrenreich, *Nickel and Dimed: On (Not) Getting By in America* (Picador Press, 2011).

Daniel P. Moynihan, *The Politics of a Guaranteed Family Income* (Random House, 1973).

James T. Patterson, *America's Struggle Against Poverty in the Twentieth Century* (Harvard University Press, 2000).

Leonard J. Santow and Mark E. Santow, *Social Security and the Middle-Class Squeeze: Fact and Fiction about America's Entitlement Programs* (Praeger, 2005).

Internet References . . .

Administration for Children and Families

www.acf.hhs.gov/help

Medicaid

www.medicaid.gov/

Medicare

www.medicare.gov/

Supplemental Nutrition Assistance Program

www.fns.usda.gov/snap/supplemental-nutrition-assistance-program-snap

The United States Social Security Administration

www.ssa.gov/

Selected, Edited, and with Issue Framing Material by:
William J. Miller, *Campus Labs®*

ISSUE

Should Free Trade Remain the Backbone of American Trade Policy?

YES: Samuel Gregg, from "Trump's Tariffs and Why America Needs a Patriotic Case for Free Trade," *Public Discourse* (2018)

NO: Daniel McCarthy, from "The Case for Trump's Tariffs and 'America First' Economics," *The New York Times* (2018)

Learning Outcomes

After reading this issue, you will be able to:

- Identify characteristics of free-trade economies.
- Assess the strengths and weaknesses of being a free-market economy.
- Describe the history of the United States with free trade.
- Identify alternatives to free trade.
- Determine ways in which America has limited trade in recent decades.

ISSUE SUMMARY

YES: Researcher Samuel Gregg argues that free-trade supporters need to more actively explain to Americans how free trade serves the nation's long-term national interests and represents the ideals of patriotism more than isolationism.

NO: On the counter, conservative news editor Daniel McCarthy describes how economic nationalism can best serve America's political and economic needs in the current era. Only by building up our domestic economy can the country hope to regain strengths it has seen eroded by foreign nations in recent years.

Since Adam Smith first wrote *The Wealth of Nations* in 1776, economists have steadfastly promoted free trade among all nations in the world as a superior trade policy. Yet practical citizens have occasionally raised arguments demonstrating skepticism with academic arguments. The main point of contention centers on how to best protect vital domestic industries from foreign competition. In short, how do we assure domestic products will sell if they are in a global marketplace? How do we control consumer behaviors if trade is truly free?

Ironically, our personal economic behavior differs in important ways from what we typically demand from our national interests. Anyone reading this has exploited the advantages of free trade and comparative advantage at some point in their life. Many of us use laundromats instead of washing and ironing ourselves. Or we buy imported goods as opposed to more expensive domestic products. Common sense tells us to make use of companies that specialize in such work, paying them with money we earn doing something we do better. We understand intuitively that cutting ourselves off from specialists can only lower our standard of living.

Adam Smith applied the same logic to nations: "It is the maxim of every prudent master of a family, never to attempt to make at home what it will cost him more to make than to buy. . . . If a foreign country can supply us with a commodity cheaper than we ourselves can make it, better buy it of them with some part of the produce of our own industry, employed in a way in which we have some advantage."

Numerous countries across the globe manufacture shoes more cheaply than America does. They offer them for sale in our nation. Should we buy them with money we earn doing things we do well—like drafting software and growing corn or wheat? Or should we forbid foreign shoes and their allegedly cheap quality in order to allow more expensive American shoes to flourish? It's hopefully clear—from a purely economic standpoint—that we would suffer from barring these shoes despite the harm it could cause American shoe manufacturers.

While this argument is largely accepted, it is still important to wonder what would happen if another country—let's say China—becomes able to make everything cheaper than we can. Will it cause mass unemployment in the United States? Will we be able to compete? David Ricardo, writing in 1810, says comparative advantage will keep us afloat. But what does this mean? A company CEO could be a better typist than their secretary. This does not, however, mean the CEO's time would be better spent typing. By concentrating energy on being CEO, the company will prosper more than if the secretary were fired and the CEO spent part of their day at a computer. Such specialization not only makes the economy more efficient but also gives both lawyer and secretary productive work to do.

It's the same with nations. Even in the worst-case scenario where China could manufacture everything more cheaply than the United States, there will be industries in which we both have cost advantages. Given these, it will make sense for everyone involved for each nation to focus on producing what it can do most cheaply. Then, we trade. The two countries, taken together, will get both products cheaper than if each produced them at home to meet all of its domestic needs. And, what is also important, workers in both countries will have jobs.

Many people are skeptical about this argument for the following reason. Suppose the average American worker earns 20 dollars per hour, while the average Chinese worker earns just 2 dollars per hour. Won't free trade make it impossible to defend the higher American wage? Won't there instead be a leveling down until, say, both American and Chinese workers earn 11 dollars per hour? The answer, once again, is no. And specialization is part of the reason.

If there were only one industry and occupation in which people could work, then free trade would indeed force American wages close to Chinese levels if Chinese workers were as good as Americans. But modern economies are composed of many industries and occupations. If America concentrates its employment where it does best, there is no reason why American wages cannot remain far above Chinese wages for a long time—even though the two nations trade freely. A country's wage level depends fundamentally on the productivity of its labor force not on its trade policy. As long as American workers remain more skilled and better educated, work with more capital, and use superior technology, they will continue to earn higher wages than their Chinese counterparts. If and when these advantages end, the wage gap will disappear. Trade is a mere detail that helps ensure that American labor is employed where, in Adam Smith's phrase, it has some advantage.

Americans should appreciate the benefits of free trade more than most people for we inhabit the greatest free-trade zone in the world. Michigan manufactures cars; New York provides banking; and Texas pumps oil and gas. The 50 states trade freely with one another, and that helps them all enjoy great prosperity. Indeed, one reason why the United States did so much better economically than Europe for more than two centuries is that America had free movement of goods and services, while the European countries "protected" themselves from their neighbors. To appreciate the magnitudes involved, try to imagine how much your personal standard of living would suffer if you were not allowed to buy any goods or services that originated outside your home state.

Many estimates have been made of the cost of saving jobs through protectionism—or eliminating complete free trade in order to prop up domestic industry. While the estimates differ widely across industries, they are almost always much larger than the wages of the protected workers. For example, one study in the early 1990s estimated that U.S. consumers paid US$1,285,000 annually for each job in the luggage industry that was preserved by barriers to imports, a sum that greatly exceeded the average earnings of a luggage worker.

But the situation is actually worse, for a little deeper thought leads us to question whether any jobs are really saved overall. It is more likely that protectionist policies save some jobs by jeopardizing others. Why? First, protecting one American industry from foreign competition imposes higher costs on others. Second, efforts to protect favored industries from foreign competition may induce reciprocal actions in other countries, thereby limiting American access to foreign markets. Third, there are the little-understood, but terribly important, effects of trade barriers on the value of the dollar. If we successfully restrict imports, Americans will spend less on foreign goods. With fewer dollars offered for sale on the world's currency markets, the value of the dollar will rise relative to that of other currencies.

On balance, the conclusion seems clear and compelling: while protectionism is sold as job saving, it probably really amounts to job swapping. It protects jobs in some industries only by destroying jobs in others. And this is the economic path President Trump seems to be pushing America toward. The president has placed tariffs on billions of dollars' worth of goods from around the world, in particular China in an effort to cut the trade deficit with China—a nation he has accused of unfair trade practices since before he became president. In theory, taxing foreign steel and aluminum will mean American companies will buy local steel instead. The thinking is that will boost the U.S. steel and aluminum industries, as more companies will want to buy their goods. Steel and aluminum prices will go up in America because there will be less of these goods coming in from abroad—so the greater demand for local steel will push up the price, lifting profits for steel makers.

In the following selections, we examine whether America's long-held free-market ideals are truly best for the economy moving forward. Researcher Samuel Gregg argues that free-trade supporters need to more actively explain to Americans how free trade serves the nation's long-term national interests and represents the ideals of patriotism more than isolationism. On the counter, conservative news editor Daniel McCarthy describes how economic nationalism can best serve America's political and economic needs in the current era. Only by building up our domestic economy can the country hope to regain strengths it has seen eroded by foreign nations in recent years.

YES

Samuel Gregg

Trump's Tariffs and Why America Needs a Patriotic Case for Free Trade

When President Donald Trump announced in March his intention to raise tariffs on steel and aluminum imports, much of the *commentariat* expressed shock and dismay. They should have known, however, that this was coming. Trade policy is one area in which President Trump has long expressed skepticism of establishment opinion.

Until relatively recently, a mildly bipartisan consensus favoring trade liberalization existed in much of America. NAFTA, for example, was backed by Democrat and Republican presidents as well as congressional majorities composed of sizable blocks from both parties.

One reason for this support is that the economic logic for free trade has become difficult to deny. The evidence is overwhelming that opening a nation's markets to the world lowers prices for consumer goods, raises its overall living standards, and enables that country and its communities to refine their comparative advantages.

Politically, however, free trade has acquired some very negative baggage since the late 1990s. This is making trade liberalization much harder to sell to Americans, including many who supported Donald Trump in 2016 because of his trade stance.

Many free traders' bad habit of skipping lightly over the effects that opening markets has had on particular communities is one such burden. Not every American "wins" from trade liberalization in the short-to-medium term. That's not a reason to embrace protectionism. Still, free traders should do more to acknowledge these realities and think harder about how to ameliorate the turmoil in non-protectionist ways.

Another encumbrance is free trade's deeply counterproductive association with "Davos Man." This term was coined by the political scientist Samuel P. Huntington to describe those "academics, international civil servants and executives in global companies, as well as successful high-technology entrepreneurs" who regard nation-states as *passé* and believe that global harmony would ensue

if only they were in charge. Their association in many people's minds with free trade is bound to alienate those Americans who, Huntington noted, "remain the world's most patriotic people" and might otherwise be receptive to open markets if they didn't think it implied being ruled by Goldman Sachs, Silicon Valley liberals, United Nations bureaucrats, and Tony Blair.

All of this underscores the need for American free traders to recalibrate their political arguments for trade liberalization. That doesn't just mean disassociating free trade from naive fantasies of a borderless planet or the one-world globalist ideology that animates the European Union's political-bureaucratic class. It also requires free traders to show how protectionism has undermined America's well-being and, by contrast, how free trade can strengthen the United States' position in the world.

How Protectionism Hurt America?

Until 1947, protectionist measures tended to be the rule rather than the exception in America. This has led some to argue that protectionism contributed to America's rise to the status of economic superpower between 1776 and 1890.

Correlation, however, isn't causation. There is considerable evidence indicating that protectionism actually (1) retarded America's economic development and (2) facilitated some unwholesome political trends. In short, America's economic success story largely occurred *despite* protectionist agendas—not because of them.

One major study of the post–Civil War period, for example, found that protectionism undercut the gains made by America through technological innovation because the artificially high price of imported capital goods made it harder and more costly to build America's transportation system and industrial infrastructure. Another analysis of the late nineteenth-century American economy illustrated that economic growth during this period was driven primarily by population increases and capital accumulation rather than productivity improvements. Indeed, productivity growth was faster in those sectors of America's economy "whose performance was not directly related to the tariff."

Putting aside the economic arguments, protectionism in nineteenth-century America also had deleterious political consequences. Most prominently, it contributed to cronyism's growth among American business leaders. In his monumental work *The Tariff History of the United States* (1888), the Harvard economist F.W. Taussig established that the tariff acts of 1864 and 1867 were largely drafted by those whose industries were to be protected. They also resulted in the imposition of import duties that, Taussig noted, had the "chief effect" of putting "money into the pockets of private individuals."

Moving into the twentieth century, the damage caused by the Smoot-Hawley 1930 Tariff Act is hard to ignore. As Douglas A. Irwin points out in *Peddling Protectionism: Smoot-Hawley and the Great Depression* (2011), the raising of tariffs on more than 20,000 imports provoked significant retaliation against the United States. This helped reduce U.S. exports. As a result, Irwin states, "America's share of world trade fell sharply in the 1930s."

Once again, protectionism's negative effects weren't confined to America's economy. The Act itself amounted, according to Irwin, to "a mass of private legislation carried out with little regard for national interest." For once the door was opened to the prospect of tariff increases, many industries clamored for protection. Smoot-Hawley's drafting was thus distinguished, Irwin writes, by "logrolling, special interest politics, and [an] inability of members of Congress to think beyond their own district."

Put another way, the 20,000 tariff increases had little to do with a concern for America's general well-being. They owed far more to that perennial problem identified long ago in Adam Smith's *Wealth of Nations*: rampant collusion between merchants and legislators at other people's expense—in this case, millions of other Americans.

How Free Trade Makes America Great?

So how does free trade bolster America's standing in the world? Here are three particular benefits that free traders might consider emphasizing.

First, free trade helps make America a more economically flexible and disciplined country. Openness to global competition prevents, for example, American businesses

from becoming complacent. Large, medium, and small companies are constantly required to think about how to innovate, increase efficiencies, and redeploy capital so as to maintain a competitive edge.

American workers are likewise discouraged from supposing that there will be permanent jobs in industries that, despite plenty of protection, are becoming globally uncompetitive. Instead, they are encouraged to be more adaptable and plan their lives accordingly. This is undoubtedly easier said than done. The alternative, however, is fewer job opportunities in declining sectors of the economy and the persistence of false expectations about the future.

A second national benefit of free trade is that it forces American governments to consider what's in the United States' long-term interest. Protectionist measures are invariably about reacting to the here and now. By contrast, reducing tariffs and subsidies facilitates prosperity for the many rather than the few over the long term.

This leads us to a third benefit conferred upon America by free trade: it helps to diminish cronyism.

Protectionism is, after all, usually tied to the promotion of particular interests. Invariably, these are industries and unions with good political connections. By contrast, when a country abandons protectionism, everyone becomes subject to the same trade rules. To that extent, free trade increases fairness throughout the American economy.

Of course, as long as people are human, cronyism won't be eradicated. Many American business leaders want to be shielded from foreign competition instead of doing the hard work of innovating and seeking greater productivity. Nor is there any shortage of legislators happy to implement protectionist measures in return for electoral and financial support. A principled commitment to free trade, however, contributes to cronyism's minimization insofar as it limits lawmakers' ability to offer favors. That can only be good for the body politic.

And China?

Protectionists often contend that trade policy in the real world can't be separated from America's geopolitical challenges. Today this especially concerns an authoritarian Chinese regime's pursuit of some decidedly global ambitions. Protectionist policies, the argument goes, must be part of America's strategy to counter these developments.

If American free traders want to refute such claims, they must show how maintaining a free-trade agenda will make America politically stronger and more economically resilient than countries that play protectionist games.

One way of doing this is to show how protectionism will weaken rivals like China.

While China is often touted as having enthusiastically embraced economic globalization, its opening to the world economy has always been selective and cautious. At different times, the regime has lowered tariffs in some areas while raising them in other sectors. China also subsidizes many exports, restricts foreign investment, and routinely violates World Trade Organization rules and protocols. Moreover, protectionist interventions in China don't just emanate from Beijing. Most Chinese provinces and towns have their own regulations that seek to protect local businesses from foreign competition.

These measures might serve some of the Chinese regime's immediate political goals, such as maintaining its control over society and the economy. But over time, such policies will make China's economy less competitive and less attractive to foreign companies and investors. The consequent waning in economic strength will eventually affect China's ability to project power abroad.

But if this is true, *why* would Americans want to replicate protectionist programs in their own country? Or, stated differently, why would Americans want to make America less competitive, less enticing to investors and innovators, and therefore less able to maintain its position as the world's leading economic power?

American protectionists have long wrapped themselves in the flag. It's time for American free traders to challenge that linkage directly. Free trade advocates need to stop waxing lyrical about perpetual-peace-through-commerce and instead focus on how free trade serves America's long-term national interests. For if free trade doesn't become regarded as a position fit for patriots, it's not just trade liberalization and its undeniable poverty-reducing effects that will be jeopardized. So too, in due course, will America's preeminence across the globe.

Samuel Gregg is a director of research at the Acton Institute. He has written and spoken extensively on questions of political economy, economic history, ethics in finance, and natural law theory.

Daniel McCarthy

The Case for Trump's Tariffs and 'America First' Economics

In his campaign, Donald Trump stressed "America First" economic nationalism. But in his first year in office, the theme languished. So when he recently announced that he intended to impose steep tariffs on steel and aluminum, Republicans were as surprised as anyone.

The conservative press and right-leaning think tanks were outraged. The director of the National Economic Council, Gary Cohn, resigned in protest. Conservatives and free-market theorists could forgive Mr. Trump's many sins, but to actually flirt with economic nationalism was inexcusable.

For 25 years, free-trade orthodoxy has been a bipartisan consensus among America's policy elite. Conservatives might editorialize about it more, but liberal presidents arguably advanced free trade the most, from Bill Clinton's signing of the North American Free Trade Agreement to Barack Obama's negotiation of the Trans-Pacific Partnership. (George W. Bush, by contrast, put tariffs on steel, though he did so without the trade-war rhetoric that Mr. Trump has relished.) With his signing on Thursday of a tariff order, Mr. Trump appears once again to be setting himself against the mandarins of both parties.

That has been a politically successful strategy for him in the past. But while his approval ratings may benefit from a brawl over trade, the more important question is whether economic nationalism is any good for the country. In principle, it is.

Economic nationalism differs from free-trade ideology in having three distinct goals rather than one. The first isn't discussed very often in a time of relative global peace: maintaining the industries necessary for prevailing in a large-scale war. The Civil War might have had a different outcome had the North not possessed an overwhelming advantage in industrial capacity over the confederacy.

Likewise, there would not have been a Western Front in World War II if the United States had not had the industrial strength to back Britain's defiance of Nazi Germany.

That the United States could wage war on Germany, and imperial Japan simultaneously was a function of the rapidity with which civilian industry could be adapted for military needs. The United States had the raw resources, the energy capabilities and the factories necessary to conduct a two-front war. Such capacity in the service of national defense will sooner or later be needed again. Strength has to be held in reserve.

The second goal of economic nationalism is no less important than being prepared for the exigency of war. From the time of the constitution's drafting, American statesmen have seen the need to preserve a middle layer in the nation's economic order. As far back as Aristotle, a secure middle class has been thought essential to the well-being of a constitutional republic.

Such a middle class is hard to imagine in a postindustrial nation consisting of a tiny capital-controlling elite and a vast population of Amazon warehouse workers. That a sort of postindustrial middle class might be sustained by universities and hospitals, as it is in places like Pittsburgh, is not a comforting thought to the conservative kind of economic nationalist. Productive industries with a measure of trade protection are still private, profit-seeking firms; in short, they are capitalist institutions, which hospitals, in effect, and universities, in most cases, are not. Economic nationalists are intent upon protecting not only certain industries but also a multilayered free-market political and economic order that is anchored by a healthy middle class.

The third objective of economic nationalism is the most general and the one that most closely matches the aims of free-market ideology: namely, to foster prosperity. Economic nationalists do not accept the claims made by extreme free traders that any degree of industrial protection must inevitably lead to less national wealth. But so what if it does? If the price of national security and a durable, free middle class is a modest reduction in gross domestic product, the economic nationalist is willing to pay it.

Free traders are not indifferent to national security nor blind to the benefits a nation derives from having a middle class. But the priority of goods is different: free traders tend to believe that only by making economic efficiency the supreme goal of public policy can those other ends be achieved. Division of labor produces greater wealth, and so free trade makes everyone better off, with the harm to those whose manufacturing jobs are lost outweighed by the good that comes from, say, cheaper flat-screen televisions. Dollars decide. The figures are the outward and visible signs of the fundamental economic truth.

The middle class, by this reckoning, must take care of itself, finding new ways to make a living if the factories close. With more wealth available in the aggregate, thanks to the efficiencies of trade and specialization, some happy outcome is sure to materialize. If we cannot say what it is, that only means that spontaneous order has a pleasant surprise in store for us.

As for national security, exceptions might have to be made; even *The Wall Street Journal* has recently editorialized against the takeover of the United States communications chip manufacturer Qualcomm by the Singapore-based Broadcom on national-security grounds. But free-trade ideologues say exceptions should be made only case by case, with the benefit of the doubt falling on the side of trade and foreign deals.

To free traders, economic nationalism is simply unnatural, an effort to artificially prolong the lives of aged industries. And since technology eliminates more jobs than trade does, the free traders ask, is the economic nationalist's next step Luddism?

The fact that technology reduces well-paid industrial employment is no reason to reduce it further through open trade policies. And the example of China today, as well as that of the United States in the 19th century, shows that preference for domestic producers does not have to mean fossilization. Nationalist economies have some of the world's most impressive records of growth and technical advancement.

Tariffs are not magic. Sometimes, the unintended consequences at home and retaliation from overseas can be devastating. But trade wars, like shooting wars, shouldn't be avoided with preemptive surrender, which is what the free-trade regime amounts to for America's long-term security and middle-class prosperity. Steel towns throughout the Northeast and Midwest have been losing a trade war for decades because they cannot count on their leaders in Washington to fight for them.

Free trade is a clear and simple rule, and the economic theory of which it is a part is elegant and logical. But it is only a partial truth. The value of the middle class has to be weighed in political terms, not merely economic ones, and national security has a strategic logic all its own that springs from different and darker assumptions about human nature than the hopeful logic of economic efficiency.

To reduce public policy to a single dimension, as free-trade ideologues do, is foolish and dangerous. Yet it is attractive because it provides definite answers to difficult questions, even if those answers are less than complete.

Economic nationalism, on the other hand, requires constant balancing and adjustment if it is to be pursued correctly. Mr. Trump's steel and aluminum tariffs may not work. But they are a first attempt at finding an alternative to a free-trade system that has built up the People's Republic of China while hollowing out the factory towns that once made America great.

DANIEL MCCARTHY is an editor at large of *The American Conservative*. His writing has appeared in the *New York Times*, *USA Today*, *The Spectator*, *The National Interest*, *Reason*, *Modern Age*, and many other publications. Outside of journalism he has worked as an Internet communications coordinator for the Ron Paul 2008 presidential campaign and as a senior editor of ISI Books.

EXPLORING THE ISSUE

Should Free Trade Remain the Backbone of American Trade Policy?

Critical Thinking and Reflection

1. Why do you think America pushed for free-market practices early in its development?
2. How would your life change if America became a more isolated trade nation?
3. What do you see as the strengths of the free market? The concerns?
4. Do you believe American industry has suffered due to free trade? Cite specific examples?
5. Why do you believe politicians may be reticent to consider moving away from free trade? Why do you think Trump might be approaching it differently?

Is There Common Ground?

Tapping into economic discontent, President Trump has argued for protectionism and asserted that decades of free-trade policies were responsible for the collapse of the American manufacturing industry. He has been feeding on the perception among many Americans that globalization has brought more pain than gain, for example, by bringing cheap consumer goods into the country, costing domestic jobs, and depressing wages. Outsourcing of jobs to cheaper markets has also been a concern. Against that backdrop, Trump's stance on trade is perhaps the clearest of his economic policies.

There appear to be elements of common ground already present in the free-trade debate. Outside of academics and pundits, the average American seems to understand that absolute free trade can be detrimental, along with absolute protectionism. Yet such a simple understanding doesn't translate into a complicated economic world. Playing our competitive advantages with other countries while assuring citizens have all their demand met at affordable prices requires trading with many nations on many different terms. And politics can alter any of these relationships,

which America is experiencing firsthand today. It's a matter of assuring the right industries are protected at the right times for the right lengths and without angering the wrong trade partner. It's about more than dollars and cents, but it seems possible that a delicate balance is possible so long as we are willing to contribute to it.

Additional Resources

Thomas L. Friedman, *The Lexus and the Olive Tree: Understanding Globalization* (Random House, 2000).

Joseph E. Stiglitz, *Globalization and its Discontents Revisited: Anti-Globalization in the Era of Trump* (W. W. Norton & Company, 2017).

Ha-Joon Chang, *Bad Samaritans: The Myth of Free Trade and the Secret History of Capitalism* (Bloomsbury Press, 2009).

Russell Roberts, *The Choice: A Fable of Free Trade and Protection* (Pearson, 2006).

Milton Friedman, *Free to Choose* (Harcourt Brace, 1978).

Internet References . . .

Financial Times

https://www.ft.com/freetrade

Foundation for Economic Education

https://fee.org/

International Monetary Fund

https://www.imf.org/en/Data

John Birch Society

https://www.jbs.org/action-projects/stop-the-free-trade-agenda

Trade Policy and Negotiations

https://www.state.gov/e/eb/tpn/

Unit 2

UNIT

The Institutions of Government

*T*he Constitution divides authority between the national government and the states, delegating certain powers to the national government and providing that those not thus delegated "are reserved to the states, respectively, or to the people." The national government's powers are further divided between three branches: Congress, the president, and the federal judiciary, each of which can exercise significant checks on the others.

Americans are familiar with these bodies—some more than others. Almost everyone is aware of who the president is, but they cannot necessarily determine whether he (or she) is doing a good job using appropriate metrics. They know their member of Congress (and overwhelmingly approve of his or her performance, in most cases), yet they rank the trustworthiness of the body, as a whole, to a degree comparable to lawyers and used cars salesmen. And most Americans know there is a Supreme Court that issues important decisions, but they are unaware of the rest of the federal judiciary, let alone the individuals who sit on the bench. As a result, these powerful institutions must regularly remember to show Americans how they are relevant and how they are fulfilling objectives for the betterment of society.

How vigorously and faithfully are these branches performing their respective functions? Do they remain true to the authentic meaning of the Constitution? What legitimate defenses does each branch possess against encroachment by the others? Are some branches more obstructionist than others? Does the Constitution allow for this to happen? These issues have been debated since the earliest years of the Republic, and the debate continues today.

Selected, Edited, and with Issue Framing Material by:
William J. Miller, *Campus Labs®*

ISSUE

Does the President Have Unilateral War Powers?

YES: John C. Yoo, from "The President's Constitutional Authority to Conduct Military Operations Against Terrorists and Nations Supporting Them: Memorandum Opinion for the Deputy Counsel to the President," *Memorandum Opinion for the Deputy Counsel to the President* (2001)

NO: Kurt Couchman, from "The War Powers Resolution Doesn't Let the President Start Wars," *The Hill* (2018)

Learning Outcomes
After reading this issue, you will be able to:
• Explain how war is declared in the United States.
• Describe the legal precedents that allow the president to have unilateral war powers.
• Assess the arguments against the president having unilateral war powers.
• Discuss how Congress and the presidency work together during times of war.
• Identify when it may be prudent for the president to have unilateral war powers.

ISSUE SUMMARY

YES: John C. Yoo, a Law Professor at the University of California, Berkeley, argues that the language of the Constitution, long-accepted precedents, and the practical need for speedy action in emergencies all support broad executive power during war.

NO: Kurt Couchman, on the other hand, delineates how the War Powers Resolution positions Congress to be the definitive decider of when the American military is sent into action.

Dramatic and bitter as they are, the current struggles between the White House and Congress over the president's unilateral authority to conduct military operations and foreign affairs are not without precedent. Episodically, they have been occurring since the administration of George Washington.

The language of the Constitution relating to war powers almost seems to invite struggles between the two branches. Congress is given the power to declare war and "to raise and support armies." The president is authorized to serve as Commander-in-Chief of the armed forces "when called into actual service of the United States." While the

power to "declare" or authorize war rests squarely with the U.S. Congress, the Founders gave some leeway to the president when it came to war making. At the Constitutional Convention, some delegates wanted to give Congress the exclusive power to make war, not simply to declare it. That would have ruled out any presidential war making. But James Madison successfully argued the need for "leaving to the Executive the power to repel sudden attacks."

Down through the years, several presidents have interpreted very broadly these emergency war-making powers. In 1801, President Jefferson ordered his navy to seize the ships of Barbary pirates in the Mediterranean, and 45 years later President Polk sent American troops into territory claimed by Mexico, thus provoking the Mexican American War. A young congressman named Abraham Lincoln vigorously protested Polk's unilateral assertion of power, but when he came to office and faced the secession of the South, he went much further than Polk in the assertion of power, jailing people without trial, enlarging the size of the army and navy, withdrawing money from the Treasury, and blockading Southern ports without authorization from Congress. In more recent times, President Truman committed America to fight in Korea without a congressional declaration, and President Kennedy ordered a naval blockade of Cuba in 1962 without even consulting Congress.

The mid-1960s marked the high-water period of unchallenged presidential war making. Between 1961 and 1963, Kennedy sent 16,000 armed "advisers" to Vietnam, and between 1964 and 1968, President Johnson escalated American involvement to 500,000 troops—all without a formal declaration of war. But that period of congressional indulgence was soon to end. By the early 1970s, Congress was starting on a course that would culminate in the cut-off of funds for Vietnam and legislative efforts to head off any more undeclared wars. In 1973, over President Nixon's veto, Congress passed the War Powers Resolution, which required the president to notify Congress within 48 hours after putting troops in harm's way, withdraw them within 60–90 days absent a congressional authorization, and submit periodic progress reports to Congress during that period. In practice, the War Powers Resolution has been largely ignored by Ronald Reagan when he sent troops into Grenada, by George H. W. Bush when he sent them to Panama, and by Bill Clinton when he sent them into Somalia, Haiti, and Bosnia.

Perhaps ironically, the War Powers Resolution may even have been useful to President George W. Bush in obtaining congressional authorization for the invasion of Iraq. In October 2002, Congress passed a joint resolution giving the president the authority to use the armed forces "as he determines to be necessary and appropriate" to defend national security and enforce all U.N. resolutions against Iraq. The resolution added that this constituted "specific statutory authorization" for war within the meaning of the War Powers Resolution. Such broadly worded language has come back to haunt many members of Congress who voted for it, but now wish they hadn't. The new Democratic Congress elected in 2006 considered various options for challenging President Bush's war-making ability as it related to Iraq, including the repeal or modification of the 2002 authorization for going to war.

For President Barack Obama, the question of unilateral war powers surfaced most significantly when determining whether to attack Bashar al-Assad (Syrian dictator) after strong evidence emerged showing that he had used chemical weapons against his own people. In 2012, Obama had issued an ultimatum to Assad: if he used chemical weapons, the United States would have no choice but to respond. Yet with over half of Americans polled favoring an intervention (and less than 10 percent actually supporting such action), Obama had to decide whether Syria was worth going against the wishes of Americans in a way similar to his predecessor. The key is that Obama was stuck wondering whether he should or should not proceed, not whether he could or could not. Much like with Libya in 2011, there was never a question on whether Obama possessed the ability to launch attacks against a foreign enemy without a formal declaration from Congress.

Ultimately, Obama opted to move forward with diplomacy and not launch attacks despite his earlier warning. After the Bush administration's battles in Iraq and Afghanistan, many Americans began labeling the Republican Party as the one most tied to superseding Congress when deciding whether to attack foreign countries. But Obama's internal deliberations reminded us that all presidents—regardless of partisanship—are forced to weight these options. President Trump has learned this quickly. An attack on a Syrian air base suspected of housing chemical weapons in 2017 and a larger round of attacks on Syrian targets in 2018 were launched to limit Assad's access to chemical weapons for use on his own citizens. In both cases, Trump claimed power, but the War Powers Act requires the president to "terminate any use of United States Armed Forces" after 60 days unless Congress specifically authorizes future action. While Trump was within his power to launch the strikes with merely notifying Congress, the legal (and ultimately political) question focused on there being two separate attacks. If the 2017 strike counts as initial action, Congress would have needed to be included in any determination for the subsequent strike. Trump, in response, has claimed the second strike is for a second conflict, which restarts the 60-day clock. Unsurprisingly, responses to his actions split by political party.

Only a president with no interest in power would blindly hand off the ability to launch unilateral military action, but a wise one would find a way to work in concert with Congress to assure backing and support. Wag the Dog, after all, does not exist in reality. We cannot simply fabricate conflicts to bump polling numbers. In today's America, such actions would likely harm a leader in the polls. Instead, a majority of Americans are still looking for the branches of government to come together in an effort to solve potential problems.

In the selections that follow, John C. Yoo, a Law Professor at the University of California, Berkeley, argues that the language of the Constitution, long-accepted precedents, and the practical need for speedy action in emergencies all support broad executive power during war. Kurt Couchman, on the other hand, delineates how the War Powers Resolution positions Congress to be the definitive decider of when the American military is sent into action.

Yoo, John C., The President's Constitutional Authority to Conduct Military Operations against Terrorists and Nations Supporting Them: Memorandum Opinion for the Deputy Counsel to the President, *Memorandum Opinion for the Deputy Counsel to the President,* 2001.

YES ←

John C. Yoo

The President's Constitutional Authority to Conduct Military Operations Against Terrorists and Nations Supporting Them: Memorandum Opinion for the Deputy Counsel to the President

Our review establishes that all three branches of the Federal Government—Congress, the Executive, and the Judiciary—agree that the President has broad authority to use military force abroad, including the ability to deter future attacks.

I

The President's constitutional power to defend the United States and the lives of its people must be understood in light of the Founders' express intention to create a federal government "cloathed with all the powers requisite to [the] complete execution of its trust." *The Federalist* No. 23 (Alexander Hamilton). Foremost among the objectives committed to that trust by the Constitution is the security of the Nation. As Hamilton explained in arguing for the Constitution's adoption, because "the circumstances which may affect the public safety are [not] reducible within certain determinate limits, . . . it must be admitted, as a necessary consequence that there can be no limitation of that authority which is to provide for the defense and protection of the community in any matter essential to its efficiency."

"It is 'obvious and unarguable' that no governmental interest is more compelling than the security of the Nation" (1981). Within the limits that the Constitution itself imposes, the scope and distribution of the powers to protect national security must be construed to authorize the most efficacious defense of the Nation and its interests in accordance "with the realistic purposes of the entire instrument" (1948). Nor is the authority to protect national security limited to actions necessary for "victories in the field" (1946). The authority over national security "carries with it the inherent power to guard against the immediate renewal of the conflict."

We now turn to the more precise question of the President's inherent constitutional powers to use military force.

Constitutional Text

The text, structure and history of the Constitution establish that the Founders entrusted the President with the primary responsibility, and therefore the power, to use military force in situations of emergency. Article II, Section 2 states that the "President shall be Commander in Chief of the Army and Navy of the United States, and of the Militia of the several States, when called into the actual Service of the United States." He is further vested with all of "the executive Power" and the duty to execute the laws. These powers give the President broad constitutional authority to use military force in response to threats to the national security and foreign policy of the United States. During the period leading up to the Constitution's ratification, the power to initiate hostilities and to control the escalation of conflict had been long understood to rest in the hands of the executive branch.

By their terms, these provisions vest full control of the military forces of the United States in the President. The power of the President is at its zenith under the Constitution when the President is directing military operations of the armed forces, because the power of Commander-in-Chief is assigned solely to the President. It has long been the view of this Office that the Commander-in-Chief Clause is a substantive grant of authority to the President and that the scope of the President's authority to commit the armed forces to combat is very broad. The President's complete discretion in exercising the Commander-in-Chief power

Yoo, John C. The President's Constitutional Authority to Conduct Military Operations Against Terrorists and Nations Supporting Them: Memorandum Opinion for the Deputy Counsel to the President, 2001.

has also been recognized by the courts. In the *Prize Cases,* (1862), for example, the Court explained that, whether the President "in fulfilling his duties as Commander in Chief" had met with a situation justifying treating the southern States as belligerents and instituting a blockade, was a question "to be *decided by him*" and which the Court could not question, but must leave to "the political department of the Government to which this power was entrusted."

Some commentators have read the constitutional text differently. They argue that the vesting of the power to declare war gives Congress the sole authority to decide whether to make war. This view misreads the constitutional text and misunderstands the nature of a declaration of war. Declaring war is not tantamount to making war—indeed, the Constitutional Convention specifically amended the working draft of the Constitution that had given Congress the power to make war. An earlier draft of the Constitution had given to Congress the power to "make" war. When it took up this clause on August 17, 1787, the Convention voted to change the clause from "make" to "declare." A supporter of the change argued that it would "leav[e] to the Executive the power to repel sudden attacks." Further, other elements of the Constitution describe "engaging" in war, which demonstrates that the Framers understood making and engaging in war to be broader than simply "declaring" war. . . . If the Framers had wanted to require congressional consent before the initiation of military hostilities, they knew how to write such provisions.

Finally, the Framing generation well understood that declarations of war were obsolete. Not all forms of hostilities rose to the level of a declared war: during the seventeenth and eighteenth centuries, Great Britain and colonial America waged numerous conflicts against other states without an official declaration of war. . . . Instead of serving as an authorization to begin hostilities, a declaration of war was only necessary to "perfect" a conflict under international law. A declaration served to fully transform the international legal relationship between two states from one of peace to one of war. Given this context, it is clear that Congress's power to declare war does not constrain the President's independent and plenary constitutional authority over the use of military force.

Constitutional Structure

Our reading of the text is reinforced by analysis of the constitutional structure. First, it is clear that the Constitution secures all federal executive power in the President to ensure a unity in purpose and energy in action. "Decision, activity, secrecy, and dispatch will generally characterize

the proceedings of one man in a much more eminent degree than the proceedings of any greater number." *The Federalist* No. 70 (Alexander Hamilton). The centralization of authority in the President alone is particularly crucial in matters of national defense, war, and foreign policy, where a unitary executive can evaluate threats, consider policy choices, and mobilize national resources with a speed and energy that is far superior to any other branch. As Hamilton noted, "Energy in the executive is a leading character in the definition of good government. It is essential to the protection of the community against foreign attacks." This is no less true in war. "Of all the cares or concerns of government, the direction of war most peculiarly demands those qualities which distinguish the exercise of power by a single hand." *The Federalist* No. 74.

Second, the Constitution makes clear that the process used for conducting military hostilities is different from other government decisionmaking. In the area of domestic legislation, the Constitution creates a detailed, finely wrought procedure in which Congress plays the central role. In foreign affairs, however, the Constitution does not establish a mandatory, detailed, Congress-driven procedure for taking action. Rather, the Constitution vests the two branches with different powers—the President as Commander-in-Chief, Congress with control over funding and declaring war—without requiring that they follow a specific process in making war. By establishing this framework, the Framers expected that the process for warmaking would be far more flexible, and capable of quicker, more decisive action, than the legislative process. Thus, the President may use his Commander-in-Chief and executive powers to use military force to protect the Nation, subject to congressional appropriations and control over domestic legislation.

Third, the constitutional structure requires that any ambiguities in the allocation of a power that is executive in nature—such as the power to conduct military hostilities—must be resolved in favor of the executive branch. Article II, section 1 provides that "[t]he executive Power shall be vested in a President of the United States." By contrast, Article I's Vesting Clause gives Congress only the powers "herein granted." This difference in language indicates that Congress's legislative powers are limited to the list enumerated in Article I, section 8, while the President's powers include inherent executive powers that are unenumerated in the Constitution. To be sure, Article II lists specifically enumerated powers in addition to the Vesting Clause, and some have argued that this limits the "executive Power" granted in the Vesting Clause to the powers on that list. But the purpose of the enumeration of executive powers in Article II was not to define and cabin the grant in the Vesting Clause. Rather, the Framers unbundled some plenary powers that had traditionally been regarded as "executive," assigning elements of those powers to Congress in Article I, while expressly reserving other elements as enumerated executive powers in Article II. So, for example, the King's traditional power to declare war was given to Congress under Article I, while the Commander-in-Chief authority was expressly reserved to the President in Article II. Further, the Framers altered other plenary powers of the King, such as treaties and appointments, assigning the Senate a share in them in Article II itself. Thus, the enumeration in Article II marks the points at which several traditional executive powers were diluted or reallocated. Any *other,* unenumerated executive powers, however, were conveyed to the President by the Vesting Clause.

There can be little doubt that the decision to deploy military force is "executive" in nature, and was traditionally so regarded. It calls for action and energy in execution, rather than the deliberate formulation of rules to govern the conduct of private individuals. Moreover, the Framers understood it to be an attribute of the executive. "The direction of war implies the direction of the common strength," wrote Alexander Hamilton, "and the power of directing and employing the common strength forms a usual and essential part in the definition of the executive authority." *The Federalist* No. 74 (Alexander Hamilton). As a result, to the extent that the constitutional text does not explicitly allocate the power to initiate military hostilities to a particular branch, the Vesting Clause provides that it remain among the President's unenumerated powers.

Fourth, depriving the President of the power to decide when to use military force would disrupt the basic constitutional framework of foreign relations. From the very beginnings of the Republic, the vesting of the executive, Commander-in-Chief, and treaty powers in the executive branch has been understood to grant the President plenary control over the conduct of foreign relations. As Secretary of State Thomas Jefferson observed during the first Washington Administration: "the constitution has divided the powers of government into three branches [and] has declared that the executive powers shall be vested in the president, submitting only special articles of it to a negative by the senate." Due to this structure, Jefferson continued, "the transaction of business with foreign nations is executive altogether; it belongs, then, to the head of that department, except as to such portions of it as are specially submitted to the senate. Exceptions are to be construed strictly." In defending President Washington's authority to issue the Neutrality

Proclamation, Alexander Hamilton came to the same interpretation of the President's foreign affairs powers. According to Hamilton, Article II "ought . . . to be considered as intended . . . to specify and regulate the principal articles implied in the definition of Executive Power; leaving the rest to flow from the general grant of that power." As future Chief Justice John Marshall famously declared a few years later, "The President is the sole organ of the nation in its external relations, and its sole representative with foreign nations. . . . The [executive] department . . . is entrusted with the whole foreign intercourse of the nation. . . ." Given the agreement of Jefferson, Hamilton, and Marshall, it has not been difficult for the executive branch consistently to assert the President's plenary authority in foreign affairs ever since. . . .

II

Executive Branch Construction and Practice

The position we take here has long represented the view of the executive branch and of the Department of Justice. Attorney General (later Justice) Robert Jackson formulated the classic statement of the executive branch's understanding of the President's military powers in 1941:

> Article II, section 2, of the Constitution provides that the President "shall be Commander in Chief of the Army and Navy of the United States." By virtue of this constitutional office he has supreme command over the land and naval forces of the country and may order them to perform such military duties as, in his opinion, are necessary or appropriate for the defense of the United States. These powers exist in time of peace as well as in time of war. . . .

"Thus the President's responsibility as Commander in Chief embraces the authority to command and direct the armed forces in their immediate movements and operations designed to protect the security and effectuate the defense of the United States. . . . [T]his authority undoubtedly includes the power to dispose of troops and equipment in such manner and on such duties as best to promote the safety of the country." . . .

Attorney General (later Justice) Frank Murphy, though declining to define precisely the scope of the President's independent authority to act in emergencies or states of war, stated that: "the Executive has powers not enumerated in the statutes—powers derived not from statutory grants but from the Constitution. It is universally recognized that the constitutional duties of the Executive carry with them the constitutional powers necessary for their proper performance. These constitutional powers have never been specifically defined, and in fact cannot be, since their extent and limitations are largely dependent upon conditions and circumstances. . . . The right to take specific action might not exist under one state of facts, while under another it might be the absolute duty of the Executive to take such action." . . .

Judicial Construction

Judicial decisions since the beginning of the Republic confirm the President's constitutional power and duty to repel military action against the United States through the use of force, and to take measures to deter the recurrence of an attack. As Justice Joseph Story said long ago, "[i]t may be fit and proper for the government, in the exercise of the high discretion confided to the executive, for great public purposes, to act on a sudden emergency, or to prevent an irreparable mischief, by summary measures, which are not found in the text of the laws" (1824). The Constitution entrusts the "power [to] the executive branch of the government to preserve order and insure the public safety in times of emergency, when other branches of the government are unable to function, or their functioning would itself threaten the public safety" (1946, Stone, C.J., concurring).

If the President is confronted with an unforeseen attack on the territory and people of the United States, or other immediate, dangerous threat to American interests and security, the courts have affirmed that it is his constitutional responsibility to respond to that threat with whatever means are necessary, including the use of military force abroad. . . .

III

The historical practice of all three branches confirms the lessons of the constitutional text and structure. The normative role of historical practice in constitutional law, and especially with regard to separation of powers, is well settled. . . . Indeed, as the Court has observed, the role of practice in fixing the meaning of the separation of powers is implicit in the Constitution itself: "'the Constitution . . . contemplates that practice will integrate the dispersed powers into a workable government'" (1989). In addition, governmental practice enjoys significant weight in constitutional analysis for practical reasons, on "the basis of a wise and quieting rule that, in determining . . . the existence of a power, weight shall be given to the usage

itself—even when the validity of the practice is the subject of investigation" (1915). . . .

The historical record demonstrates that the power to initiate military hostilities, particularly in response to the threat of an armed attack, rests exclusively with the President. As the Supreme Court has observed, "[t]he United States frequently employs Armed Forces outside this country—over 200 times in our history—for the protection of American citizens or national security" (1990). On at least 125 such occasions, the President acted without prior express authorization from Congress. Such deployments, based on the President's constitutional authority alone, have occurred since the Administration of George Washington. . . . Perhaps the most significant deployment without specific statutory authorization took place at the time of the Korean War, when President Truman, without prior authorization from Congress, deployed United States troops in a war that lasted for over three years and caused over 142,000 American casualties.

Recent deployments ordered solely on the basis of the President's constitutional authority have also been extremely large, representing a substantial commitment of the Nation's military personnel, diplomatic prestige, and financial resources. On at least one occasion, such a unilateral deployment has constituted full-scale war. On March 24, 1999, without any prior statutory authorization and in the absence of an attack on the United States, President Clinton ordered hostilities to be initiated against the Republic of Yugoslavia. The President informed Congress that, in the initial wave of air strikes, "United States and NATO forces have targeted the [Yugoslavian] government's integrated air defense system, military and security police command and control elements, and military and security police facilities and infrastructure. . . . I have taken these actions pursuant to my constitutional authority to conduct U.S. foreign relations and as Commander in Chief and Chief Executive." Bombing attacks against targets in both Kosovo and Serbia ended on June 10, 1999, seventy-nine days after the war began. More than 30,000 United States military personnel participated in the operations; some 800 U.S. aircraft flew more than 20,000 sorties; more than 23,000 bombs and missiles were used. As part of the peace settlement, NATO deployed some 50,000 troops into Kosovo, 7,000 of them American. . . .

Conclusion

In light of the text, plan, and history of the Constitution, its interpretation by both past Administrations and the courts, the longstanding practice of the executive branch, and the express affirmation of the President's constitutional authorities by Congress, we think it beyond question that the President has the plenary constitutional power to take such military actions as he deems necessary and appropriate to respond to the terrorist attacks upon the United States on September 11, 2001. Force can be used both to retaliate for those attacks, and to prevent and deter future assaults on the Nation. Military actions need not be limited to those individuals, groups, or states that participated in the attacks on the World Trade Center and the Pentagon: the Constitution vests the President with the power to strike terrorist groups or organizations that cannot be demonstrably linked to the September 11 incidents, but that, nonetheless, pose a similar threat to the security of the United States and the lives of its people, whether at home or overseas. In both the War Powers Resolution and the Joint Resolution, Congress has recognized the President's authority to use force in circumstances such as those created by the September 11 incidents. Neither statute, however, can place any limits on the President's determinations as to any terrorist threat, the amount of military force to be used in response, or the method, timing, and nature of the response. These decisions, under our Constitution, are for the President alone to make.

JOHN C. YOO, a Professor of Law at Boalt Hall, University of California, Berkeley, served as Deputy Assistant Attorney General in the Office of Legal Counsel in the U.S. Department of Justice from 2001 to 2003. He is the author of *The Powers of War and Peace* (University of Chicago, 2005) and *War by Other Means: An Insider's Account of the War on Terrorism* (Grove/Atlantic, 2006).

Kurt Couchman

The War Powers Resolution Doesn't Let the President Start Wars

Congress is split on the legality of President Trump's strikes on Syria. On Friday, 88 bipartisan members of the House sent him a letter stating that congressional authorization is required. Others say he has authority for one-off strikes, but not prolonged engagements.

Some even claim the president can make war for up to 60 days at his discretion. This argument is at best a misunderstanding of the War Powers Resolution and the Constitution, and at worst, it is a willful and negligent lie.

The War Powers Resolution of 1973, which Congress passed overriding President Nixon's veto, was meant to implement the Constitution's separation of powers between Congress and the president for the initiation and conduct of war. Congress alone has the power to declare war. Authority over the standards to "suppress Insurrections and repel Invasions" belongs to Congress as well.

The president is Commander-in-Chief of U.S. armed forces. He decides how best to conduct military operations once they have been authorized—by Congress—or how to respond to an actual or imminent attack. Managing an active conflict is an executive function that requires the quick response that a single point of decision-making provides.

The Constitution, however, gives Congress the power to "make all Laws which shall be necessary and proper for carrying into Execution" not only Congress' enumerated powers but also "all other Powers vested by this Constitution in the Government of the United States, or in any Department or Officer thereof." In other words, Congress can shape the president's Commander-in-Chief role through statutory law.

Declaring war is properly a legislative function, as the founders recognized. Thomas Jefferson wrote to James Madison in 1789, "We have already given in example one effectual check to The Dog of War by transferring the power of letting him loose from the Executive to the Legislative body, from those who are to spend to those who are to pay."

Turning to the War Powers Resolution, section 2(c) (50 U.S.C. 1541(c)) states:

The constitutional powers of the president as Commander-in-Chief to introduce United States Armed Forces into hostilities, or into situations where imminent involvement in hostilities is clearly indicated by the circumstances, are exercised only pursuant to (1) a declaration of war, (2) specific statutory authorization, or (3) a national emergency created by attack upon the United States, its territories or possessions, or its armed forces.

If Congress doesn't declare war or authorize the use of military force, the president may only introduce American troops into hostilities if we've been attacked to a degree sufficient to create a national emergency. The War Powers Resolution then—and only then—gives the president 60 days to address the attack. That period can be extended by 30 days if needed, or for such period as Congress authorizes.

Note that the attacker, not the president, initiates hostilities.

Isolated references to specific sections are misleading. Section 4 (50 U.S.C. 1543) requires reporting other than when a declaration of war has been made—that is, under an AUMF or when responding to an attack. Section 5 (50 U.S.C. 1544) includes the misunderstood 60-day period noted above.

But context matters. These provisions are secondary to the general rule specified at the beginning of the Act, not independent of it.

James Madison wrote in Federalist 41, "Nothing is more natural nor common than first to use a general phrase, and then to explain and qualify it by a recital of particulars." The War Powers Resolution must be read in full, in which each provision is related to every other, particularly the general rule in section 2(c).

Finally, section 3 states, "The President in every possible instance shall consult with Congress before introducing United States Armed Forces into hostilities . . ." Without context, it appears to dismiss Congress. When understood as subsidiary to the general principle—no initiating hostilities without Congress—it is an obligation, although too vague to be meaningful.

Claiming that the president has unilateral authority absent an attack is a convenient falsehood. The advocates of expansive presidential power obviously prefer letting him have a relatively free hand. That, of course, includes much of the foreign policy establishment, whose prestige and influence is directly correlated to an activist foreign policy that they can shape.

Presidents prefer discretion, and they use it. Presidential candidates tend to campaign for restraint but end up governing as interventionists:

Presidents have incentives to exercise and expand the powers at their disposal. Since foreign policy is an area where presidents face few constraints, they are especially prone to intervene with military force abroad—regardless of their previous campaign rhetoric or party ideology.

If Members of Congress were serious about separation of powers and their institutional prerogatives, they would exercise their authority and prevent that from happening.

As Jefferson hoped, war making would be accountable to the people and the taxpayers through their representatives in Congress.

But each individual member benefits politically from avoiding difficult subjects like war, which is sometimes necessary but always terrible. A president with a free hand benefits legislators because it lets them avoid accountability and responsibility to the people they are charged with representing.

Compelling Congress to stand up for its powers and against executive branch usurpation requires leadership and courage. The convenient untruth that presidents have unilateral but time-limited war-making power must be rejected.

No single person should have the power to unleash America's colossal military might. In our system, no individual legitimately has such power.

Only Congress can authorize war. Otherwise, the president may only respond to attacks on the United States or U.S. Armed Forces. Doing more is unconstitutional, illegal, undemocratic, immoral, and imprudent.

KURT COUCHMAN serves as a vice president for Defense Priorities. He has more than six years' experience in congressional offices.

EXPLORING THE ISSUE

Does the President Have Unilateral War Powers?

Critical Thinking and Reflection

1. What legal precedents does John Yoo cite to bolster his case that the president has unilateral war powers?
2. The Congress has the sole power to "declare" war, but does that leave the president the sole power to "make" war? Or is there a real difference between the two?
3. Do you believe Yoo would back President Obama's utilization of drone strikes against suspected terrorists in Pakistan and Yemen? Why or why not?
4. Should the president or Congress have ultimate war-making powers? Why?
5. Do you believe Trump's strikes on Syria were executed legally? Why or why not?

Is There Common Ground?

The only thing in common between the two sides is their tendency to occupy each other's position with a change of administration. When a Republican president faced a Democratic Congress in 2007–2009, there was much complaining from the latter about the president's unilateral war making. But a few years later, with a Democratic president, many of the same practices—targeting terrorists, holding them indefinitely, wiretapping, rendition—continued, this time with tacit approval from many Democrats in Congress. Now it was time for the Republicans to make a show of indignation. And with President Trump's emergence and actions in Syria, we have seen a political split on a legal question yet again.

The battle over unilateral war making is not a partisan one. Historically, we have seen both of today's major parties exercising this power at different times they deem appropriate. From a citizen's perspective, this makes any efforts at remedying the situation quite difficult. It will never be as simple as removing a president or a party. Instead, the rules of the game will need to change if citizens are that unhappy with a president's decision to act without Congress's consent. If Congress takes it upon itself to prevent a president from acting, it does little but divide the country from the elites to the masses. And as history has shown, a divided house is the most likely to fall.

Additional Resources

Mark Brandon, *The Constitution in Wartime: Beyond Alarmism and Complacency* (Duke University Press, 2005).

Louis Fisher, *Presidential War Power* (University Press of Kansas, 2004).

Richard Neustadt, *Presidential Power and the Modern Presidents: The Politics of Leadership from Roosevelt to Reagan* (Free Press, 1991).

Richard Posner, *Not a Suicide Pact: The Constitution in a Time of National Emergency* (Oxford University Press, 2006).

John C. Yoo, *The Powers of War and Peace: The Constitution and Foreign Affairs After 9/11* (University of Chicago Press, 2006).

Internet References . . .

Congressional Research Service: The War Powers Resolution: After Thirty Years

www.au.af.mil/au/awc/awcgate/crs/rl32267.htm

Department of Justice on War Powers

www.justice.gov/olc/warpowers925.htm

Liberty Classroom

www.libertyclassroom.com/warpowers/

Reclaiming the War Power

http://object.cato.org/sites/cato.org/files/serials/files/cato-handbook-policymakers/2009/9/hb111-10.pdf

War Powers: Law Library of Congress

http://loc.gov/law/help/usconlaw/war-powers.php

Selected, Edited, and with Issue Framing Material by:
William J. Miller, *Campus Labs®*

ISSUE

Is President Trump's Relationship with Vladimir Putin Detrimental for the United States?

YES: Elena Chernenko, from "An Easy Win for Vladimir Putin," *The New York Times* (2018)

NO: Paris Dennard, from "Trump Meeting with Putin Is the Right Thing for America," *The Hill* (2018)

Learning Outcomes

After reading this issue, you will be able to:

- Discuss the historical relationship between the United States and Russia.
- Identify ways that working with Russia benefits the United States.
- Identify ways that working with Russia harms the United States.
- Analyze current political concerns over America's relationship with Russia.
- Describe how the current relationship with Russia differs from that of four years ago.

ISSUE SUMMARY

YES: Elena Chernenko—foreign editor at *Kommersant*—writes that Russia is holding the power in their relationship with the United States today because President Putin has nothing to lose at home, while President Trump has everything at stake. As a result, Trump's perceived ties to Russia seem to be harmful to the United States' larger interests.

NO: Paris Dennard, on the other hand, argues that Trump's bold approach to international diplomacy is reviving America's clout on the global stage. By requesting action, he can get Putin to listen and respond in kind.

At first glance, the man on *Time* magazine's July 30, 2018, cover might seem familiar: it was created by morphing images of two of the world's most recognizable men, United States President Donald Trump and Russian President Vladimir Putin. The composite image, by visual artist Nancy Burson, is meant to represent this particular era in U.S. foreign policy, following the pair's historic meeting in Helsinki, Finland. As Brian Bennett wrote at the time:

> A year and a half into his presidency, Trump's puzzling affinity for Putin has yet to be explained. Trump is bruised by the idea that Russian election meddling taints his victory, those close to

him say, and can't concede the fact that Russia did try to interfere in the election, regardless of whether it impacted the outcome. He views this problem entirely through a political lens, these people say, unable or unwilling to differentiate between the question of whether his campaign colluded with Russia—which he denies—and the question of whether Russia attempted to influence the election.

To represent that conflict, Burson merged the faces of Trump and Putin into a still image and video which morphs between the shifting appearances of the two world leaders. But why is the world so fascinated with these two men? How much weight do they truly hold?

Today, the United States and Russia maintain diplomatic and trade relations. The relationship was generally warm under Russian President Boris Yeltsin (1991–1999) until the NATO bombing of the Federal Republic of Yugoslavia in the spring of 1999 and has since deteriorated significantly. In 2014, relations greatly strained due to the crisis in Ukraine, Russia's annexation of Crimea in 2014, differences regarding Russian military intervention in the Syrian Civil War, and from the end of 2016 over Russia's alleged interference in the 2016 U.S. elections. Mutual sanctions imposed in 2014 remain in place. Yet since Trump gained power, Russia has experienced an invigorated enthusiasm from some within the United States.

The U.S. presidential election campaign of 2016 saw U.S. security officials accuse the Russian government of being behind massive cyber-hackings and leaks that aimed at influencing the election and discrediting the U.S. political system. The allegations were summarily dismissed by Putin who said the idea that Russia was favoring Donald Trump was a myth created by the Hillary Clinton campaign. The background of tense relationship between Putin and Hillary Clinton was highlighted by U.S. press during the election campaign. Trump had been widely seen as a pro-Russia candidate, with the FBI investigating alleged connections between Donald Trump's former campaign manager Paul Manafort as well as Carter Page and pro-Russian interests.

In mid-November 2016, shortly after the election of Trump as president, the Kremlin accused President Barack Obama's administration of trying to damage the United States' relationship with Russia to a degree that would render normalization thereof impossible for the incoming administration of Donald Trump. In an address to the Russian parliament delivered on December 1, 2016, Russian president Putin said this of United States—Russia relations: "We are prepared to cooperate with the new American administration. It's important to normalize and begin to develop bilateral relations on an equal and mutually beneficial basis. Mutual efforts by Russia and the United States in solving global and regional problems are in the interest of the entire world."

In early December 2016, the White House said that President Obama had ordered the intelligence agencies to review evidence of Russian interference in the 2016 presidential campaign; Eric Schultz, the deputy White House press secretary, denied the review to be led by Director of National Intelligence James R. Clapper was meant to be "an effort to challenge the outcome of the election." Simultaneously, the U.S. press published reports, with reference to senior administration officials, that U.S.

intelligence agencies, specifically the CIA, had concluded with "high confidence" that Russia acted covertly in the latter stages of the presidential campaign to harm Hillary Clinton's chances and promote Donald Trump. President-elect Donald Trump rejected the CIA assessment that Russia was behind the hackers' efforts to sway the campaign in his favor as "ridiculous."

In mid-December, President Obama publicly pledged to retaliate for Russian cyberattacks during the U.S. presidential election in order to "send a clear message to Russia" as both a punishment and a deterrent; however, the press reported that his actionable options were limited, with many of those having been rejected as either ineffective or too risky; *The New York Times*, citing a catalog of U.S.-engineered coups in foreign countries, opined, "There is not much new in tampering with elections, except for the technical sophistication of the tools. For all the outrage voiced by Democrats and Republicans in the past week about the Russian action—with the notable exception of Mr. Trump, who has dismissed the intelligence findings as politically motivated—it is worth remembering that trying to manipulate elections is a well-honed American art form."

At the end of 2016, U.S. president-elect Donald Trump praised Russian president Vladimir Putin for not expelling U.S. diplomats in response to Washington's expulsion of 35 Russian diplomats as well as other punitive measures taken by the Obama administration in retaliation for what U.S. officials had characterized as interference in the U.S. presidential election. On January 6, 2017, the Office of the Director of National Intelligence, in an assessment of "Russian Activities and Intentions in Recent US Elections," asserted that Russian leadership favored presidential candidate Trump over Clinton, and that Russian President Vladimir Putin personally ordered an "influence campaign" to harm Clinton's chances and "undermine public faith in the US democratic process."

Yet even with the United States Intelligence Community claiming Russia was responsible, President Trump refused to back down. Trump's public statements during his first formal meeting with Putin in Helsinki on July 16, 2018, drew criticism from the Democratic members of the U.S. Congress and a number of former senior intelligence officials, as well as some ranking members of the Republican Party, for appearing to have sided with Putin rather than accepting the findings of Russian interference in the 2016 presidential election issued by the United States Intelligence Community. Republican Senator John McCain called the press conference "one of the most disgraceful performances by an American president in memory." The press around the world ran publications that tended to assess the news conference following the presidents' two-hour meeting as an event at which Trump had "projected weakness."

Beyond concerns about Russian meddling in his own election, President Trump has routinely gone to bat for Putin, even seeking to help Russia be readmitted to the G7, from which they were expelled in 2014. In the following selections, Elena Chernenko—foreign editor at *Kommersant*—writes that Russia is holding the power in their relationship with the United States today because President Putin has nothing to lose at home, while President Trump has everything at stake. As a result, Trump's perceived ties to Russia seem to be harmful to the United States' larger interests. Paris Dennard, on the other hand, argues that Trump's bold approach to international diplomacy is reviving America's clout on the global stage. By requesting action, he can get Putin to listen and respond in kind.

Elena Chernenko

An Easy Win for Vladimir Putin

Moscow—A few days before the summit in Helsinki, Finland, between President Trump and President Vladimir Putin of Russia, Yuri Ushakov, one of Mr. Putin's advisers, told journalists that this would be "the most important international event of the summer."

The Kremlin had good reason to put an optimistic spin on the meeting: Mr. Putin had almost nothing to lose from the summit, and he had much to gain.

Russia's president is under pressure at home right now. Despite easily winning reelection in March, his popularity has been slipping. He has even faced protests against his government's pension reform plan. But one way that Mr. Putin knows how to appeal to Russians is by appearing tough and in control on the world stage. Mr. Trump made that easy for him.

Until Monday, Russia's president was probably the last head of a powerful state who had not yet had a full-fledged one-on-one meeting with Mr. Trump. The two leaders have met twice on the margins of international events and have talked eight times over the phone, but the absence of an organized meeting between them was making Mr. Putin, ever eager to appear like a powerful global player, look like an outsider, especially after Mr. Trump even met with Kim Jong-un of North Korea.

The date chosen for the meeting was comfortable for Mr. Putin. After the NATO summit in Brussels and an official visit to London, Mr. Trump spent two days playing golf in Scotland before heading to Helsinki. No doubt the president enjoyed the free weekend, but Mr. Putin came away looking more important. While the American president was relaxing, Mr. Putin was finishing up business in Moscow, where he had assembled several heads of states and governments for the World Cup finals.

The venue also seemed to benefit the Russian side. The city discussed as a possible host for the summit was Vienna. It would have been approximately a three-hour flight away from both Scotland and Moscow, while Helsinki was at least an hour closer for Mr. Putin. This may sound like a small point but at symbolic international summits, such details matter.

And this summit was mostly about optics. Expectations for real policy deliverables were low on the Russian side. Although Mr. Trump is more popular in Moscow than in many capitals—especially in Europe—his erratic behavior and disregard for conventional diplomacy worry many people here, too.

The way Mr. Trump castigated American allies on the way to Helsinki and spoke with open admiration of his Russian counterpart also, of course, played into Mr. Putin's hands. But when he tweeted hours before the summit that "Our relationship with Russia has never been worse thanks to many years of U.S. foolishness and stupidity," it was a gift Moscow would not even have hoped for. No wonder the Russian Ministry of Foreign Affairs reposted it with the words "we agree."

Watching the joint news conference held by the two leaders, it was clear that Mr. Putin had the wind at his back. He made a far more confident impression than his American counterpart. In his opening statement, he articulated several concrete proposals—on arms control, terrorism, Syria, and bilateral economic ties. Mr. Trump, on the other hand, devoted much of his initial statement to justifying his decision to meet with Mr. Putin in the first place.

This might have made sense given the debate over Russia in the United States—though I suspect that even Americans found the references to Hillary Clinton's e-mails out of place—but for Russians, it was bizarre. Several Western countries have disputes with the Kremlin, over Ukraine, Syria, espionage, and other issues, but their leaders regularly meet with Mr. Putin.

During the face-to-face meeting, Mr. Trump let Mr. Putin speak first (no arrangement was made concerning the order of speeches in advance), which created the impression that the Russian president was the host of the summit. The joint news also began with a lengthy statement from the Russian side. Add to that the fact that a Russian journalist got to ask the first question and it would be easy to forget that the presidents met on neutral territory.

Almost any outcome would have been easy for Mr. Putin to sell to the Russian public, but this will be especially helpful. And Mr. Putin needs this boost. On June 14, the government announced a controversial pension reform: it wants to raise the retirement age for men (from 60 to 65) and women (from 55 to 63) for the first time since Stalin. Mr. Putin's popularity immediately took a hit. According to a state-run poll, the president's approval rating fell to 62 percent from 77 percent by the end of June. The independent Levada Center had even worse news for Mr. Putin: According to its research, trust in the president had dropped below 50 percent for the first time in five years.

The success of the World Cup will probably help those numbers grow. But so will President Trump. Mr. Putin's popularity at home has long been helped by his ability to present Russia as a superpower that deserves to be taken seriously. The meeting in Helsinki made him look like he was in charge.

ELENA CHERNENKO is a columnist for the international section of the Russian daily *Kommersant*. She has previously worked for Russian Newsweek, the German editorial office of Voice of Russia, the Moskauer Deutsche Zeitung newspaper, and the EURACTIV news agency. She holds a PhD in history from Moscow State University.

Paris Dennard

Trump Meeting with Putin Is the Right Thing for America

The Fake Rage is real. President Trump's critics outraged at the 2018 Helsinki Summit want to see him fail on the global stage but he just keeps winning.

The 2018 Helsinki Summit is yet more evidence that Trump's bold approach to international diplomacy is reviving America's clout on the global stage. When he speaks requesting action, world leaders listen and respond in kind. He is showing himself to be the outspoken political leader of the free world, with a spine of tempered steel, unwavering in his pursuit to always put America First. The anti-Trump politicians and pundits willing to sacrifice better relations with Russia, in search of a temporary dip in the president's poll numbers should be ashamed.

Trump said at his joint press conference in Helsinki, "I would rather take a political risk in pursuit of peace than to risk peace in pursuit of politics." Let me be clear, to get a result that America has never had, you need a leader willing to do something we have never done. The president understands the risk but it is worth it. Peace is worth it, stability is worth it, honest and fair trade is worth it, and getting along with a country that with the United States shares 90 of the world's nuclear arsenal is a risk worth taking.

Instead of shouting from the sidelines, they should find ways to work with him and the administration rather than seek to undermine it to boost book sales and speaking fees.

Having the U.S. president meet privately, bilaterally or at a summit with the Russian president is not new. The hypocritical fake rage about having a meeting is new because the president is Donald J. Trump. President Trump followed in the diplomatic summit footsteps of President Ford in 1975, President Reagan in 1988, President George H.W. Bush in 1990 and 1992, President Clinton in 1997, and even President George W. Bush hosting President Putin as his private Crawford Ranch in 2001.

President Trump knows that in order to make deals, you actually need to sit down and speak directly with adversaries and allies alike. That's why he met with Putin on Monday. He even said, "During today's meeting, I addressed directly with President Putin the issue of Russian interference in our elections. I felt this was a message best delivered in person."

Trump went on to say, "A productive dialogue is not only good for the United States and good for Russia, but it is good for the world."

"Too often, in both recent past and long ago, we have seen the consequences when diplomacy is left on the table," he added.

The president's diplomatic tactics are arguably unorthodox. He operates on the element of surprise, keeping opponents alert, and on their feet at all times. That said, his engagement strategy is effective and has so far resulted in an unprecedented accord with North Korea, something once thought impossible. He has also won a commitment from NATO countries to finally increase their spending on defense. If President Trump can negotiate successfully with North Korea he can—and should continue to negotiate with Russia.

To some critics, however, Trump's sensible desire to meet with one of America's biggest international competitors is proof positive he's somehow a pawn for Putin. Seriously?

New York Magazine recently published a sensational bit of fantasy fiction that claimed, "It would be dangerous not to consider the possibility that the summit is less a negotiation between two heads of state than a meeting between a Russian-intelligence asset and his handler."

President Trump, Russian Ambassador Jon Huntsman, Secretary of Defense James Mattis, Secretary of State Mike Pompeo, or National Security Advisor John Bolton hardly come close to being Russian assets given the laundry list of sanctions and retaliatory actions from this administration toward Russia.

This will obviously come as a shock to *New York Magazine*, but there was once a time in which presidents did try to negotiate with adversarial countries and were applauded for it. President Nixon famously traveled to Red China, a move that began a diplomatic thaw that fundamentally changed the course of the 20th century and beyond.

Reagan met with Soviet leader Mikhail Gorbachev on four separate occasions. Those meetings did not make the Soviets more powerful nor did they result in cries of collusion from the liberal media. They hastened the demise of the Soviet Union and assured Reagan's place in presidential history. Trump rightfully noted that even during the tensions of the Cold War, the United States and Russia maintained a strong and productive dialogue.

Trump directly criticized Democrats and their allies in the mainstream media who are trying to turn his crucial diplomatic efforts into a political circus. "As president, I cannot make decisions on foreign policy in a futile effort to appease partisan critics, or the media, or Democrats who want to do nothing but resist and obstruct," he said.

There is no doubt that Trump's "We will see what happens" is tantamount to "Trust yet verify." We need a modern Russia working with and not against fighting ISIS and the spread of radical Islamic terrorism, denuclearizing the Korean Peninsula, and bringing stability to Syria.

Trump's willingness to meet openly and honestly with Putin should be applauded. The president's direct engagement strategy to ensure peace and prosperity for the American people is the right thing to do and could herald a new age in diplomatic relations between the United States and Russia.

Paris Dennard is a conservative political speaker. He previously worked in several capacities within the Administration of U.S. President George W. Bush, has appeared as a conservative commentator on CNN and NPR, and is the Senior Director of Strategic Communications for the Thurgood Marshall College Fund.

EXPLORING THE ISSUE

Is President Trump's Relationship with Vladimir Putin Detrimental for the United States?

Critical Thinking and Reflection

1. Why do you think Trump has approached Putin differently than Obama did?
2. What do you see as the costs and benefits of a closer relationship with Russia?
3. Do you believe Trump is being played by Putin? Why or why not?
4. Do you believe the current relationship is only motivated by politics? Why or why not?
5. How do you believe the relationship will change post-Trump? Why?

Is There Common Ground?

In reality, seeking middle ground on this issue almost raises more questions than it does provide answers. There is no question that there is middle ground available on how to work with Russia in the global society; we have seen other nations do so and even our own under previous administrations (both Republican and Democratic). But, when it comes to the relationship between Trump and Putin and any election meddling, middle ground is far more difficult to find. And that's not because Russia is a unique case historically per se but more because these issues serve as proxies for larger political attitudes. It would be difficult to find a Democrat that openly accepts Russian election interference or a Republican that sees fault in Trump working with Putin. As a result, American–Russian relations have gone beyond being a matter of foreign relations and instead a domestic hot button issue. And unlike during the Cold War, there is a difference of opinion in whether Russia is a friend or foe today.

With that said, given the current political context, we still need to find a path forward that attempts to satisfy both sides of the political aisle. One option is to seek Congressional involvement more directly in interactions with Russia. By Congress inserting itself more directly, Republicans maintain control of the conversation but hopefully limit the focus being put on Trump and Putin

as sole actors. This, however, would require an invitation to the table—especially given the current political structures within Russia. Another option would be to better leverage Secretary of State Mike Pompeo's continued trust from President Trump. The same could be said for Chief of Staff John Kelly who appears to be held in high regard still by members of Trump's inner-circle. Again, however, this may not be enough to satisfy Democrats and could be prevented by Trump's insistence on remaining personally involved in all Russian diplomacy efforts.

Additional Resources

Craig Unger, *House of Trump, House of Putin* (Dutton, 2018).

Angela Stent, *The Limits of Partnership: U.S.-Russian Relations in the Twenty-First Century* (Princeton University Press, 2015).

Fiona Hill and Clifford Gaddy, *Mr. Putin: Operative in the Kremlin* (Brookings Institution Press, 2015).

Michael McFaul, *From Cold War to Hot Peace: An American Ambassador in Putin's Russia* (Houghton Mifflin Harcourt, 2018).

Michael Isikoff and David Corn, *Russian Roulette: The Inside Story of Putin's War on America and the Election of Donald Trump* (Twelve, 2018).

Internet References . . .

A Guide to the United States' History of Recognition, Diplomatic, and Consular Relations, by Country, since 1776: Russia

https://history.state.gov/countries/russia

From Cooperation to Confrontation: Russia and the United States since 9/11

https://www.ideals.illinois.edu/bitstream/ handle/2142/27701/FromCooperationto ConfrontationRussiaandtheUnitedStates since911.pdf

Report from the Commission on U.S. Policy toward Russia

https://www.belfercenter.org/publication/report- commission-us-policy-toward-russia-right-direction- us-policy-toward-russia

200 Years of United States–Russia Relations

https://www.state.gov/p/eur/ci/rs/200years/

United States–Russian Relations

https://www.csis.org/programs/russia-and-eurasia- program/archives/us-russian-relations

Selected, Edited, and with Issue Framing Material by:
William J. Miller, *Campus Labs®*

ISSUE

Is Congress a Dysfunctional Institution?

YES: Sheryl Gay Stolberg and Nicholas Fandos, from "As Gridlock Deepens in Congress, Only Gloom Is Bipartisan," *The New York Times* (2018)

NO: Thomas Petri, from "Our Government is Messy—but that Doesn't Mean it isn't Working," *Washington Post* (2016)

Learning Outcomes

After reading this issue, you will be able to:

- Identify sources of institutional deadlock.
- Explain how partisan rancor impacts government.
- Describe how members of Congress view their work within the body.
- Assess whether an insider or outsider perspective is more accurate.
- Describe how Congress compares to other branches of government when it comes to power.

ISSUE SUMMARY

YES: Congressional correspondents Sheryl Gay Stolberg and Nicholas Fandos discuss how gridlock in Congress has reached an all-time low and both parties seem to only agree on how poorly performing Congress is to the American people today.

NO: On the other hand, Thomas Petri, a former member of the U.S. House from Wisconsin, argues that Congress is actually operating exactly how the Framers intended despite public perceptions of dysfunction.

Those who teach introductory American government usually look forward to the unit on the American presidency. It sets off lively class participation, especially when students talk about the actions of whoever happens to be in the White House. The same happens when the topic is the Supreme Court; students can argue about controversial decisions like school prayer, flag-burning, and abortion, and the instructor sometimes has to work hard to keep the discussion from getting too hot.

But when Congress, the third branch of the federal government, comes up for discussion, it is hard to get anything going beyond a few cynical shrugs and wisecracks. Seriously intended comments, when they finally emerge, may range from skeptical questions (What do they do for their money?) to harsh pronouncements (Bunch of crooks!).

Students today can hardly be blamed for these reactions. They are inheritors of a rich American tradition of Congress-bashing. At the end of the nineteenth century, the novelist Mark Twain quipped that "there is no distinctly native American criminal class except Congress." In the 1930s, the humorist Will Rogers suggested that "we have the best Congress money can buy." In the 1940s, President Harry Truman coined the term do-nothing Congress, and Fred Allen's radio comedy show had a loud-mouth "Senator Claghorn" who did nothing but bluster. In the 1950s, *The Washington Post*'s "Herblock" and other cartoonists liked to draw senators as potbellied old guys chewing cigars.

Needless to say, the drafters of the U.S. Constitution did not anticipate that kind of portrayal; they wanted Congress to stand tall in power and stature. Significantly, they listed it first among the three branches, and they gave it an extensive list of powers, 18 in all, rounding them off with the power to "make all laws which shall be necessary and proper" for executing its express powers. Given their fear of a tyrannical king, it makes sense that Congress was supposed to have the power. It was closest to the citizens, had one of its bodies directly elected, and would still be checked on all sides.

Throughout the first half of the nineteenth century, Congress played a very visible role in the business of the nation, and some of its most illustrious members, like Daniel Webster, Henry Clay, and John C. Calhoun, were national superstars. Men and women crowded into the visitors' gallery when Webster was about to deliver one of his powerful orations; during these performances they sometimes wept openly.

What, then, happened to Congress over the years to bring about this fall from grace? A number of factors have come into play, two of which can be cited immediately.

First, Congress has become a very complicated institution. In both houses, especially in the House of Representatives, legislation is not hammered out on the floor but in scores of committees and subcommittees, known to some journalists and political scientists but to relatively few others. Major bills can run hundreds of pages and are written in a kind of lawyerspeak inaccessible to ordinary people. Congressional rules are so arcane that even a bill with clear majority support can fall through the cracks and disappear. The public simply doesn't understand all this, and incomprehension can easily sour into distrust and suspicion.

A second reason why Congress doesn't get much respect these days is connected with the increased visibility of its sometime rival, the presidency. Ever since Abraham Lincoln raised the possibility of what presidents can do during prolonged emergencies, charismatic presidents like Woodrow Wilson, Franklin Roosevelt, and Ronald Reagan, serving during such times, have aggrandized the office of the president, pushing Congress into the background. They have thus stolen much of the prestige and glamour that once attached to the legislative branch. The president has become a very visible "one" and Congress has faded into a shadowy "many." Everyone knows who the president is, but how many people can name the leaders of Congress? Can you?

Congress is regularly lambasted in the mainstream media for being unproductive. As *USA Today* explains, "Congress is on track to beat its own low record of productivity, enacting fewer laws this year than at any point in the past 66 years." While there are obvious concerns about using such a simple metric to show productivity, it does demonstrate some of the issues currently at play in Congress. With political parties ideologically polarized like never before, it is hard to find compromises that are meaningful while still being agreeable. This was witnessed during the September/October 2013 government shutdown. Knowing that government would stop working if a compromise was not reached, neither Republicans nor Democrats would come to a middling solution prior to reaching the crisis point. One member of the Senate opted to read *Green Eggs and Ham* rather than attempt to reach a workable solution.

President Trump has not been able to fare better with the Ryan-McConnell Congress. One measure of what Congress is likely to do the rest of the year is to look at bills that have already passed the House but are awaiting action in the Senate. There were 238 of them when examined in 2017. Amazingly, GovTrack gives only 13 a better than 50 percent chance of actually arriving on President Trump's desk in their current form. If that holds up, Trump will have signed just 56 laws by the beginning of the 2018 congressional session. If this tortoise-like pace continues, he will preside over the least productive Congress since Millard Fillmore signed just 74 bills sent to him by the brink-of-war 32nd Congress between 1851 and 1853.

The demands on members of Congress have increased. Citizens hold high expectations that their representative will be able and willing to fill their every need and desire. With these expectations, there is less time to spend focusing on national issues. And with the advent and development of social media, members of Congress need to have more time focused on what is occurring at the national level. Any decision leading to increased taxes, bureaucracy, or size of government will be broadcasted to the world via Twitter and blogs and used against the offending Congressperson in their next election campaign. No matter how well-intentioned or skilled a politician, it seems that Washington, DC, has the ability to change people these days. The founders were careful to make sure that Congress would need consensus to accomplish any meaningful goals, but today, legislative nuances are used to stall progress in the name of politics. It is not that there is something wrong with a policy that leads to it being killed anymore. Instead, it can be just a matter of taste.

In the following selections, Congressional correspondent Sheryl Gay Stolberg and Nicholas Fandos discuss how gridlock in Congress has reached an all-time low and both parties seem to only agree on how poorly performing Congress is to the American people today. On the other hand, Thomas Petri, a former member of the U.S. House from Wisconsin, argues that Congress is actually operating exactly how the Framers intended despite public perceptions of dysfunction.

YES ⬅

Sheryl Gay Stolberg and Nicholas Fandos

As Gridlock Deepens in Congress, Only Gloom Is Bipartisan

As lawmakers recover from a dispiriting government shutdown and prepare for President Trump's State of the Union address on Tuesday, Capitol Hill is absorbed with concern that Mr. Trump's presidency has pushed an already dysfunctional Congress into a near-permanent state of gridlock that threatens to diminish American democracy itself.

The sense of gloom is bipartisan. A group of Republicans in the House and the Senate are warning of a secret plot in the FBI to overthrow the Trump government. Democrats speak of corruption and creeping authoritarianism, unchecked by a Congress that has turned into an adjunct of the executive.

And few lawmakers can muster a word of pride in their institution.

"The Senate has literally forgotten how to function," said Senator Angus King, independent of Maine. "We're like a high school football team that hasn't won a game in five years. We've forgotten how to win."

Senator Ben Sasse, Republican of Nebraska, is no more sanguine. "Congress is weaker than it has been in decades, the Senate isn't tackling our great national problems, and this has little to do with who sits in the Oval Office," he said. "Both parties—Republicans and Democrats—are obsessed with political survival and incumbency."

The dysfunction has played out in ugly and puzzling ways. The three-day shutdown this month over immigration came and went so fast that even many Democrats saw no point in it. Last year's futile efforts to repeal the Affordable Care Act soured many conservatives. Mr. Trump's sweeping budget proposal to reorder government was simply ignored. And issues that both parties say they agree on—from raising military spending to banning "bump stocks," which allow a semiautomatic weapon to fire like a machine gun—remain undone.

To some Democrats, midterm elections this November that were once seen as a test for lunch-pail issues that could woo back white working-class voters are now seen as about nothing short of the future of pluralism and constitutional democracy.

A Democratic victory would "erect a barricade against Trump, against a dangerous, reckless president and what else he might do," said Representative David E. Price, Democrat of North Carolina, who taught political science at Duke University before coming to Congress in 1987. Democracy, he said, depends on checks and balances. "This is an absolutely critical test of whether we can do that."

Representative Jamie Raskin, a constitutional law professor turned House member, echoed the sentiment.

"We have a chaos presidency and a chaos Congress, and to oppose it, we need a politics that restores people's faith in public things, including Congress itself," Mr. Raskin, a Maryland Democrat, said.

Republicans have their own high stakes in November. Losing control of Congress, they say, could mean a highly politicized impeachment of their president. Worse still, a rising tide for Democrats in 2018 and 2020 could put the party in control of the redrawing of House district lines after the next census.

Congress has long been polarized. Republicans complained bitterly of being frozen out of the big legislative pushes of the early Obama administration, not only the Affordable Care Act but also the Dodd–Frank financial services law and other measures. It was Senator Harry Reid, the Democratic leader at the time, who first used the so-called nuclear option to end filibusters for administration nominees and most judicial ones.

But Ross Baker, a political scientist at Rutgers University, sees something new in the level of vitriol and hyperbole.

"It's something that I think has only become more intense, more conspicuous, because of the outsize personality and idiosyncrasies of President Trump," Mr. Baker said. "It has made Democrats feel that they are under a very heavy obligation to defend the norms and the institution. Republicans feel that Congress was elected with a mandate to bring about change, so what had been a kind of preexisting edgy relationship has simply gone viral."

For most of the Obama presidency, Republican leaders were vexed by a dwindling center and an expanding group of hard-right lawmakers who would accept no negotiations with the Democratic president. That impediment to compromise has now been joined by a similar dynamic in the Democratic Party, where a visceral hatred of Mr. Trump on the left has empowered Democratic lawmakers to refuse to deal with the Republican president. The divide has been deepened as a half-dozen Democratic senators consider a White House run in 2020.

If temperatures are to cool, the next few weeks could prove pivotal. Senator Mitch McConnell, the Republican leader, has promised a "fair and open" debate on immigration, while a new bipartisan coalition has emerged in the Senate to try to break a logjam. Senator Jon Tester, Democrat of Montana, saw something hopeful in that development, a new willingness to go around the parties' feuding leaders.

"If anything positive happened out of this past week, it's the fact that people are talking right now," he said.

But if the effort fails, Congress might career toward another fiscal showdown in February—and possibly another shutdown. Even if the Senate can agree to a bipartisan way to bolster border security and protect young undocumented immigrants brought to the country as children, the House would have to follow suit.

Then there is the matter of the investigations into possible collusion between Russia and the Trump campaign. What began as a bipartisan effort to get to the bottom of Russia's brazen meddling in the 2016 presidential election has devolved in recent weeks into partisan warfare, particularly in the House. House Republicans on the Intelligence Committee have assembled a memo said to accuse officials from the FBI and the Justice Department of improperly spying on a Trump campaign adviser. Democrats are crying foul play, and even the Justice Department is warning that a Republican push to declassify the memo could dangerously compromise American intelligence.

One of the year's most crucial questions is shaping up to be whether Republican control of Congress can withstand all this dysfunction, or whether it will lead to a sweeping realignment of power in the midterm elections in November. The outcome will undoubtedly shape the second half of Mr. Trump's term.

"What we find in every state in the country is that people want Congress to hold the Trump administration accountable," said Senator Chris Van Hollen, Democrat of Maryland, who leads the committee charged with electing Democrats to the Senate. He added, "Congress has been totally AWOL."

For Democrats, the dysfunction has made the quest to regain power more urgent. They argue that outside of a few moments of independence—the passage last summer of a Russia sanctions bill opposed by Mr. Trump, for example, and statements by a few Republican senators like Jeff Flake of Arizona and Bob Corker of Tennessee—Republicans have shown themselves unwilling to challenge Mr. Trump and his administration.

"Among the gravest disappointments of this year was not finding out how awful a president Donald Trump has turned out to be, but rather how docile the Congress has been," said Representative Adam Schiff of California, the top Democrat on the Intelligence Committee. "The most important thing people can do right now who are concerned about the direction of the Congress is change the majority in Congress. That's the single most important thing we can do right now for the health of the democracy."

Republicans fiercely contest Democrats' assessment. They take pride in having passed a tax overhaul written by lawmakers—as opposed to the White House—and say they have continued to investigate the election meddling despite Mr. Trump's clear opposition. There is nothing wrong, they argue, with Republicans' advancing an agenda they share with the White House and have long waited to enact.

"If we were really in the tank for Trump, we wouldn't even be doing this investigation," said Representative Tom Rooney, Republican of Florida, who is helping to lead the Intelligence Committee's Russia-related work. "It would have been much easier not to."

For the moment, Congress simply needs to show it can perform its most basic function: controlling the government's purse. The fiscal year began on October 1, but for four months, the government has been functioning on short-term stopgap spending bills that provide no reordering or new direction to government programs.

"There's nothing more basic than the power of the purse, and there's no more systemic failure than what we've had for years: not to exercise that power in an orderly and prescribed way," Mr. Price, the North Carolina Democrat, said.

The latest round of continuing resolutions (CRs), as the stopgap spending laws are known on Capitol Hill, has infuriated Democrats and Republicans alike. The one adopted on Monday—which will fund the government until February 8—was the fourth since September.

"We keep trying to claim victories on both sides and talk about who is going to be blamed," Mr. Rooney said. "In the meantime, we are just living in CR hell. I don't think people out there care that this side or another side was able to jam the other side. This is all just posturing for 2018. In the meantime, we don't govern."

Neither chamber of Congress works as it was intended. Representative Rick Nolan, a Minnesota Democrat who was first elected to Congress in 1974, left for 30 years and then won election again in 2012, noted that bills once went to the floor were open for amendment, then passed after input from both parties. Now, leaders bring fully formed legislation to the floor with little or no opportunity to change it.

"The complaint I am registering is not just voiced by Democrats. Republicans feel the same way," he said. "They did not get elected to Congress for photo ops. They have almost relegated members of Congress to become middle-level telemarketers dialing for dollars."

In the Senate, business is so rushed that Senator Lamar Alexander, Republican of Tennessee, complained that many of the newer senators are unaware of the chamber's most basic rules.

"We don't do enough legislation on the floor to give them experience with how to pass a bill," Mr. Alexander said.

Tom Daschle, a former Democratic Senate majority leader, lamented that the dysfunction might be permanent.

"I worry about whether or not it's reversible, the loss of norms and the loss of institutional process and the lack of institutional memory," he said. "I doubt that there are more than a handful of senators today who have really experienced what regular order feels like."

The shutdown last week produced a nascent effort at pushback: a bipartisan group calling itself the Common Sense Coalition has been meeting in the office of Senator Susan Collins, Republican of Maine and one of the last centrists in the Senate. While passing around a Masai talking stick to discourage talking over one another, the senators provided their leaders a blueprint for reopening the government. Now, they are working to come up with a bipartisan immigration bill.

"That's indicative of how bad it's gotten—that you need rump groups in the Senate to do anything, and often they fail," said Matt Bennett, a senior vice president at Third Way, a centrist Democratic group. "It so happens they succeeded this time, but the bar was kind of low, which was to open the government."

SHERYL GAY STOLBERG is a congressional correspondent. In 21 years at *The New York Times*, she has been a science correspondent, national correspondent, political features reporter, and White House correspondent. Previously, at The *Los Angeles Times*, she shared in two Pulitzer Prizes won by that newspaper's Metro staff.

NICHOLAS FANDOS is a reporter in the Washington bureau covering Congress.

Thomas Petri

 **NO**

Our Government Is Messy—But That Doesn't Mean It Isn't Working

Listening to most commentators, you'd think there is not much hope for the country's political future. Congress is polarized. Extremes are the norm. The branches of government can't work together. Dysfunction abounds. The presidential election is out of control, and there is gridlock when it comes to the next Supreme Court nominee. Doomsday is the only scenario for American politics.

But I beg to differ! The American political system is generally alive and well—and functioning as the architects of our Constitution intended.

George Washington would surely think so. When asked at a reception about the design of Congress, our first president compared it to the cup and saucer he was holding: The House, he said, is like the tea cup into which the popular passions of the moment are poured; the Senate, like the saucer where popular passions cool down.

As any student of history will know, passions, disputes, and conflict are nothing new in politics. The wildly popular musical "Hamilton" surely makes that clear, reminding us that our times look almost pacific when compared to the days of "10 Duel Commandments," when political disagreements resulted not only in insults but actually put politicians' lives at risk.

The fact is that members of the House reflect on and do their best to represent their constituents. They are an able and increasingly well-educated and diverse group of citizens.

So what's holding up the process? It's simple: we're divided because the people are divided, and when there is a lack of consensus, it is reflected in the Congress.

Even when there has been unity in Washington, citizens' disagreement can make it difficult to get things done. In the 1980s, for example, President Reagan, House Speaker Thomas P. "Tip" O'Neill (D-Mass.), Rep. Dan Rostenkowski (D-Ill.), and other members of Congress in both parties were determined to put our senior citizen safety net programs on a more sustainable financial footing. The logic was simple: senior citizens as a group were better off than

younger citizens, so increasing taxes on wealthier senior citizens to strengthen programs to help the less fortunate elderly made sense. The responsible way to do it was to increase taxes before increasing benefits, though both were included in the same legislative package. The legislation passed the House and Senate with large bipartisan majorities and was signed into law by President Reagan.

Members of Congress—myself included—proudly went back to our districts to explain the new law, only to discover that the elderly were rising up in protest. Across the country, elderly citizens objected, many of them quite strongly. The revolt was vividly symbolized by the picture of an old woman in Chicago clinging to the grill of Rostenkowski's car as he attempted to drive away from a senior citizen gathering where he had been explaining the merits of the new act. Similar scenes occurred across the country. Congress returned to Washington and quickly repealed the legislation it had so proudly passed, thanks to long bipartisan deliberations and compromise. It was back to the bargaining table, no compromise allowed. This was when politicians from both parties were in relative agreement. Imagine how much more difficult it is to pass legislation when both politicians and populace are at odds.

Self-government is hard, messy, and often frustrating for everyone. But it is important to remember that the American system is based not on the *support* of the governed (Congress is currently viewed favorably by about 11 percent of voters) but rather on the sometimes grudging *consent* of the governed. There is a difference.

Good leadership can help, and both Speaker Paul Ryan (R-Wis.) and Senate Majority Leader Mitch McConnell (R-Ky.) have moved to reverse the centralization of power in the hands of a few House and Senate leaders back to committee chairmen. This should increase their ability to reach consensus on issues within the jurisdiction of their committees.

[The growth of executive power has turned politics into war]

It's a step in the right direction, but it is no magic bullet. Where the country is divided, on issues such as on immigration, progress will not be as rapid as many would like. And for now, the situation is made worse by a president who, despite being very able in some areas, has not been as effective as many of his recent predecessors in using his bully pulpit to develop common ground. This has increased frustration in the country, but that frustration, as intended by the drafters of our Constitution, is being channeled into this year's presidential and congressional elections.

Winston Churchill once said, "Democracy is the worst form of government, except all those others that have been tried." In the United States, a presidential election is an occasion for us to take a good look at ourselves, at our fellow citizens and at our country. The picture is not always pretty, but it is illuminating. As we take stock of our hopes, fears, frustrations, and aspirations, we can develop a better sense of what we can do through our national governmental institutions and what we cannot, and what we should not do in order to avoid creating more problems than we solve.

THOMAS PETRI (R) represented Wisconsin's sixth congressional district in the U.S. House from 1979 to 2015.

EXPLORING THE ISSUE

Is Congress a Dysfunctional Institution?

Critical Thinking and Reflection

1. Do we really want a speedy system in which laws would be pushed through before a consensus develops?
2. Do we really want a system in which the viewpoint of the minority gets trampled by a rush to action by the majority?
3. How does the public tend to view the work of Congress? Do you agree or disagree? Why?
4. Why is Congress viewed as dysfunctional by some Americans?
5. How could Congress make itself appear less dysfunctional?

Is There Common Ground?

In theory, at least, there is common ground between the assertion that bills should not be hastily run through Congress and the assertion that the passage of laws should not be hamstrung indefinitely by a minority. The problem comes in trying to craft a synthesis of those two assertions in today's polarized Congress. Some hope that a temporary solution—there is never a permanent one—will come when a new election gives one of the parties decisive control of both houses of Congress. Yet that happened in 2008, and, while it did result in the passage of at least three important pieces of legislation, it also set off a powerful backlash against the majority party in the political arena.

In 2013, with a divided Congress, we have seen the smallest amount of legislative output in over a half century. But to much surprise, the 2017 Congress proved to be even less successful in producing legislation despite unified rule. Some will argue that this is a positive fact since it means that unnecessary legislation was not created. Critics, on the other hand, will point to the fact that we elect members of Congress into office to pass legislation. Instead of seeing new laws, recently we have seen little except partisan bickering and utilization of loopholes for political reasons. As a nation, we seem to be missing opportunities to take concentrated efforts to fix the problems ailing our fellow citizens.

Additional Resources

Charles B. Cushman, *An Introduction to the U.S.-Congress* (Shape, 2006).

Lawrence C. Dodd and Bruce Oppenheimer, *Congress Reconsidered* (CQ Press, 2004).

Diana Evans, *Greasing the Wheels: Using Pork Barrel Projects to Build Majority Coalitions in Congress* (Cambridge University Press, 2004).

Richard Fenno, *Home Style: House Members in Their Districts* (Longman, 2002).

Sally Friedman, *Dilemmas of Representation: Local-Politics, National Factors, and the Home Styles of Modern U.S. Congress Members* (State University of New York, 2007).

Internet References . . .

No Labels

www.nolabels.org/gridlock

Reclamation of the U.S. Congress

http://repositories.lib.utexas.edu/bitstream/
handle/2152/20957/FinalReclamationofthe
USCongress_9-27.pdf?sequence=6

Steven Kull on Congressional Gridlock

www.c-spanvideo.org/program/Kul

The Gridlock Illusion

www.wilsonquarterly.com/essays/gridlock-illusion

U.S. Electoral System and Congressional Gridlock

www.c-spanvideo.org/program/316150-4

Selected, Edited, and with Issue Framing Material by:
William J. Miller, *Campus Labs®*

ISSUE

Should Supreme Court Justices Have Term Limits?

YES: Norm Ornstein, from "Why the Supreme Court Needs Term Limits," *The Atlantic* (2014)

NO: Alexander Hamilton, from "Federalist No. 78," *The Federalist Papers* (1788)

Learning Outcomes

After reading this issue, you will be able to:

- Explain the history of judicial term limits.
- Discuss arguments for term limiting Supreme Court justices.
- Discuss arguments against term limiting Supreme Court justices.
- Assess the potential impact term limits would have on judicial decision-making.
- Discuss how term limits would impact checks and balances within the federal government.

ISSUE SUMMARY

YES: Writer Norm Ornstein argues that the most effective way to address the problems created by an increasingly politicized Supreme Court is to limit all justices to 18-year terms.

NO: Founding Father Alexander Hamilton, on the other hand, argues that the judiciary will be the weakest branch of government, and life terms protect judges from political pressures while preventing the invasion of their powers by either the president or Congress.

On the third season of "House of Cards," a fictional Supreme Court justice mulls retirement when he is diagnosed with Alzheimer's. Nobody is speculating that anybody on the real-life Supreme Court is suffering from a degenerative brain disease. But the show's plotline calls attention to the fact that, barring death or an impeachable offence, the justices themselves decide when to hang up their robes. And today's Supremes are not all spring chickens. Ruth Bader Ginsburg, the liberal lion who has resisted calls to retire during Donald Trump's presidency, is 85. Stephen Breyer is 79. Four justices—Clarence Thomas (70), Samuel Alito (68), Sonia Sotomayor (64), and the chief, John Roberts (63)—are sexagenarians. Elena Kagan is 55, and the new kid on the bench, Neil Gorsuch, is a wee 50. Justice Kennedy retired at age 81 in 2018, and Brett Kavanaugh—who stands nominated for his seat

today—is 53. While making nominations to the Supreme Court—and the federal courts at large—President Trump has been clear with his intent to nominate judges who will be able to have a lasting impact on the bench, given the number of years they may be able to serve.

Article III, Section I of the United States Constitution states: "The judicial power of the United States, shall be vested in one Supreme Court, and in such inferior courts as the Congress may from time to time ordain and establish. The judges, both of the supreme and inferior courts, shall hold their offices during good behavior, and shall, at stated times, receive for their services, a compensation, which shall not be diminished during their continuance in office."

The clear implication of this statement has been for Supreme Court justices to serve life terms so long as they have avoided impeachable offenses. The life term has been largely blamed for the increased politicization of the nomination and confirmation process. The idea of term-limiting justices has been brought up repeatedly—most recently after the death of Justice Antonin Scalia, who served 30 years on the Supreme Court. Many, after his death, believed that three decades on the bench was simply too long.

Most Americans would support imposing a term limit on the nine U.S. Supreme Court justices, who now serve for life, a 2018 Morning Consult/POLITICO poll opinion poll has found, including 67 percent of Democrats and 58 percent of Republicans. Limiting terms would be difficult, requiring an amendment to the U.S. Constitution. Congress shows no signs of taking up the idea, though Republican Senator Ted Cruz has suggested the possibility of justices being voted out of office.

Support for the 10-year term limit proposed was also bipartisan, with 66 percent saying they favored such a change, while 17 percent supported life tenure. Sixty-six percent of Democrats, 74 percent of Republicans, and 68 percent of independents said they favored the 10-year term limit idea, according to another recent poll. Respondents were not asked their preference on how long the justices' terms should last. Over the years, legal experts have debated 8-, 10-, 14-, and 18-year limits.

The poll showed broad understanding of the court, with 68 percent saying they knew justices are appointed, not elected, and 60 percent saying they knew the appointments are for life. Under the Constitution, presidents appoint the justices subject to confirmation by the U.S. Senate, a process only 32 percent of respondents backed. Forty-eight percent said justices should be elected. There was little support in the poll for tinkering with the court's role as the final arbiter of U.S. law. Only 29 percent said they would support allowing Congress or the president to overrule court decisions.

While the Constitution was clear about the Founders' intentions, many citizens have taken the opposite stance. Staying too long is not necessarily good behavior—Congress has the ability to define good behavior. But, on the other hand, the tradition in the Supreme Court of the United States that was practiced into the twentieth century was the justices would keep an eye on one another. If somebody got a little bit attenuated and fragile, the others would come to him and say, "Judge, it's time for you to quit." And he would.

But the job has become more politicized, and justices have a large sense of power. Moreover, they have got a lot of help, they've got a huge number, three or four law clerks who can do the heavy lifting. They don't have very many decisions they have to make so it's a relatively easy job in that sense. Part of what was a concern is that increasingly, the Supreme Court has been making decisions that are highly political. They are interpreting the Constitution in ways that bear heavily on a lot of decisions that people want to vote on. And that wasn't going on in the eighteenth century; it wasn't going on until the last few decades.

Justices have always been told to avoid public opinion when making decisions, and it seems like they have largely remained isolated from the views of the masses. But if they are going to be making political decisions, then it's not necessarily too bad of an idea for them to at least be thinking about, in a democratic government, what the people want or believe or would anticipate.

No matter how wise or enlightened they may be, a bench of seven or nine octogenarians will have a circumscribed perspective on the country for which they are adjudicating fundamental questions. Encrusted jurisprudence won't necessarily be bad for the country: as Alexander Hamilton pointed out in *Federalist*, vol. 79, the "danger of a superannuated bench" resulting from aged judges is "imaginary." Indeed, Justice Ginsburg shows in both her written opinions and incisive questions during oral argument that she is as vigorous intellectually as she has ever been. But breathing new life into the nation's highest court more often—even if it does not make the tribunal any less political—would bring more dynamism to the judiciary, jog the justices' decision-making patterns and narrow, even if only slightly, the yawning gap between the enrobed ones and everyday citizens.

In the following selections, writer Norm Ornstein argues that the most effective way to address the problems created by an increasingly politicized Supreme Court is to limit all justices to 18-year terms. Founding Father Alexander Hamilton, on the other hand, argues that the judiciary will be the weakest branch of government, and life terms protect judges from political pressures while preventing the invasion of their powers by either the president or Congress.

YES

Norm Ornstein

Why the Supreme Court Needs Term Limits

This has been quite a time for anniversaries: the 50th of the 1964 Civil Rights Act, the 50th of the Great Society, the 60th of *Brown v. Board of Education*. Each has produced a flurry of celebrations and analyses, including the latest, on *Brown*. Here's one more.

Ten years ago, on the occasion of the 50th anniversary of *Brown*, I attended one of the most interesting and moving panels ever. Yale Law School brought together six luminaries who had been clerks to Supreme Court justices during the deliberations over the *Brown* decision. They talked about the internal discussions and struggles to reach agreement, and the fact that the decision actually took two years. The justices—including Chief Justice Earl Warren and Justices Hugo Black, Felix Frankfurter, Sherman Minton, and others—tried mightily to build a consensus. Whatever their ideological predispositions, they all understood that this decision would alter the fabric of American society. They also knew it would reverberate for a long time, exacerbating some deep-seated societal divisions even as it would heal so many others and right so many wrongs.

The two terms allowed the justices to reach a unanimous conclusion. Afterward, Frankfurter penned a handwritten note to Warren that read: "Dear Chief: This is a day that will live in glory. It is also a great day in the history of the Court, and not in the least for the course of deliberation which brought about the result. I congratulate you."

As I read that letter, I thought about what would have happened if the current Supreme Court were transported back to decide *Brown*. Two years of deliberation? No way. Unanimous or even near-unanimous decision? Forget it. The decision would have been 5-4 the other way, with Chief Justice John Roberts writing for the majority, "The way to stop discrimination on the basis of race is to stop discriminating on the basis of race"—leaving separate but equal as the standard. The idea that finding unanimity or near-unanimity was important for the fabric of the society would never have come up.

Recent analyses have underscored the new reality of today's Supreme Court: It is polarized along partisan lines in a way that parallels other political institutions and the rest of society, in a fashion we have never seen. A couple of years ago, David Paul Kuhn, writing here, noted that the percentage of rulings by one-vote margins is higher under Roberts than any previous chief justice in American history. Of course, many decisions are unanimous—but it is the tough, divisive, and most important ones that end up with the one-vote margins.

The *New York Times's* Adam Liptak weighed in recently with a piece called "The Polarized Court," in which he said, "For the first time, the Supreme Court is closely divided along party lines." Scott Lemieux, in *The Week*, noted further that the polarization on the Court, like the polarization in Congress, is asymmetric; conservative justices have moved very sharply to the right, liberals a bit more modestly to the left. Much of the movement did occur before Roberts was elevated to the Supreme Court, but his leadership has sharpened the divisions much more, on issues ranging from race and voting rights to campaign finance and corporate power.

How did we get here? As politics have become polarized and as two-party competition intensified, control of the courts—which are increasingly making major policy decisions—became more important. With lifetime appointments, a party in power for two or four years could have sway over policy for decades after it left power. But to ensure that sway meant picking judges who were virtual locks to rule the way the party in power wanted. That meant track records in judicial opinions, and that in turn meant choosing sitting judges to move up to the Supreme Court. It also meant choosing younger individuals with more ideology and less seasoning; better to have a justice serving for 30 years or more than for 20 or less.

The Warren Court that decided *Brown* had five members who had been elected to office—three former U.S. senators, one of whom had also been mayor of Cleveland; one state legislator; and one governor. They were mature, they understood the law, but also understood politics and the impact of their decisions on society. As a consequence, they did not always vote in predictable fashion. Only one of the justices, Sherman Minton, had served on a U.S. appellate court—and he had been a senator before that appointment.

Now, zero members of the Supreme Court have served in elective office, and only Stephen Breyer has significant experience serving on a staff in Congress. Eight of the nine justices previously were on U.S. courts of appeal. Few have had real-world experience outside of the legal and judicial realm. And few of their opinions and decisions come as surprises. That is not to say that all the justices are naïve (although Anthony Kennedy's opinion in *Citizens United*, blithely dismissing the idea that there could be any corruption in campaign money spent "independently" in campaigns, was the epitome of naiveté). Roberts is political in the most Machiavellian sense; he understood the zeitgeist enough to repeatedly assure the Senate during his confirmation hearings that he would strive to issue narrow opinions that respected *stare decisis* and achieved 9-0 or 8-1 consensus, even as he lay the groundwork during his tenure for the opposite. His surprising ruling on the Affordable Care Act was clearly done with an eye toward softening the criticism that was sure to come with the series of 5-4 decisions on campaign finance and voting rights that lay ahead.

With a Court that is increasingly active in overturning laws passed by Congress and checking presidential authority when there is a president of the opposite party, that means nominations both to appeals courts and to the Supreme Court have become increasingly divisive and polarized, for both parties. And the policy future of the country depends as much on the actuarial tables and the luck of the draw for presidents as it does on the larger trends in politics and society. We could have one one-term president shaping the Court for decades, and another two-term president having zero appointments. And we could end up with a Supreme Court dramatically out of step for decades with the larger shape of the society, and likely losing much of its prestige and sense of legitimacy as an impartial arbiter, creating in turn a serious crisis of confidence in the rule of law.

For more than a decade, I have strongly advocated moving toward term limits for appellate judges and Supreme Court justices. I would like to have single, 18-year terms, staggered so that each president in a term would have two vacancies to fill. Doing so would open opportunities for men and women in their 60s, given modern life expectancies, and not just those in their 40s. It would to some degree lower the temperature on confirmation battles by making the stakes a bit lower. And it would mean a Court that more accurately reflects the changes and judgments of the society.

If we could combine term limits for justices with a sensitivity by presidents to find some judges who actually understand the real world of politics and life, and not just the cloistered one of the bench, we might get somewhere.

NORM ORNSTEIN is a contributing writer for *The Atlantic*, a contributing editor and columnist for *National Journal*, and a resident scholar at the American Enterprise Institute for Public Policy Research.

Alexander Hamilton

 **NO**

Federalist No. 78

To the People of the State of New York:

WE PROCEED now to an examination of the judiciary department of the proposed government.

In unfolding the defects of the existing Confederation, the utility and necessity of a federal judicature have been clearly pointed out. It is less necessary to recapitulate the considerations there urged, as the propriety of the institution in the abstract is not disputed; the only questions which have been raised being relative to the manner of constituting it, and to its extent. To these points, therefore, our observations shall be confined.

The manner of constituting it seems to embrace these several objects: first, the mode of appointing the judges; second, the tenure by which they are to hold their places; third, the partition of the judiciary authority between different courts and their relations to each other.

First, as to the mode of appointing the judges, this is the same with that of appointing the officers of the Union in general and has been so fully discussed in the two last numbers, that nothing can be said here which would not be useless repetition.

Second, as to the tenure by which the judges are to hold their places, this chiefly concerns their duration in office, the provisions for their support, and the precautions for their responsibility.

According to the plan of the convention, all judges who may be appointed by the United States are to hold their offices DURING GOOD BEHAVIOR, which is conformable to the most approved of the State constitutions and among the rest to that of this State. Its propriety having been drawn into question by the adversaries of that plan is no light symptom of the rage for objection, which disorders their imaginations and judgments. The standard of good behavior for the continuance in office of the judicial magistracy is certainly one of the most valuable of the modern improvements in the practice of government. In a monarchy, it is an excellent barrier to the despotism of the prince; in a republic, it is a no less excellent barrier to the encroachments and oppressions of the representative body. And it is the best expedient which can be devised in any government, to secure a steady, upright, and impartial administration of the laws.

Whoever attentively considers the different departments of power must perceive, that, in a government in which they are separated from each other, the judiciary, from the nature of its functions, will always be the least dangerous to the political rights of the Constitution because it will be least in a capacity to annoy or injure them. The Executive not only dispenses the honors but holds the sword of the community. The legislature not only commands the purse but prescribes the rules by which the duties and rights of every citizen are to be regulated. The judiciary, on the contrary, has no influence over either the sword or the purse, no direction either of the strength or of the wealth of the society, and can take no active resolution whatever. It may truly be said to have neither FORCE nor WILL, but merely judgment, and must ultimately depend upon the aid of the executive arm even for the efficacy of its judgments.

This simple view of the matter suggests several important consequences. It proves incontestably that the judiciary is beyond comparison with the weakest of the three departments of power[1]; that it can never attack with success either of the other two; and that all possible care is requisite to enable it to defend itself against their attacks. It equally proves that though individual oppression may now and then proceed from the courts of justice, the general liberty of the people can never be endangered from that quarter; I mean so long as the judiciary remains truly distinct from both the legislature and the Executive. For I agree that "there is no liberty, if the power of judging be not separated from the legislative and executive powers."[2] And it proves, in the last place, that as liberty can have nothing to fear from the judiciary alone, but would have everything to fear from its union with either of the other departments; that as all the effects of such a union must ensue from a dependence of the former on the latter, notwithstanding a nominal and apparent separation; that as, from the natural feebleness of the judiciary, it is in

Hamilton, Alexander. Federalist No. 78. New York, NY: McLean's, 1788.

continual jeopardy of being overpowered, awed, or influenced by its coordinate branches; and that as nothing can contribute so much to its firmness and independence as permanency in office, this quality may therefore be justly regarded as an indispensable ingredient in its constitution and, in a great measure, as the citadel of the public justice and the public security.

The complete independence of the courts of justice is peculiarly essential in a limited Constitution. By a limited Constitution, I understand one which contains certain specified exceptions to the legislative authority; such, for instance, as that it shall pass no bills of attainder, no ex post facto laws, and the like. Limitations of this kind can be preserved in practice no other way than through the medium of courts of justice, whose duty must be to declare all acts contrary to the manifest tenor of the Constitution void. Without this, all the reservations of particular rights or privileges would amount to nothing.

Some perplexity respecting the rights of the courts to pronounce legislative acts void, because contrary to the Constitution, has arisen from an imagination that the doctrine would imply a superiority of the judiciary to the legislative power. It is urged that the authority which can declare the acts of another void must necessarily be superior to the one whose acts may be declared void. As this doctrine is of great importance in all the American constitutions, a brief discussion of the ground on which it rests cannot be unacceptable.

There is no position which depends on clearer principles than that every act of a delegated authority, contrary to the tenor of the commission under which it is exercised, is void. No legislative act, therefore, contrary to the Constitution, can be valid. To deny this would be to affirm that the deputy is greater than his principal; that the servant is above his master; that the representatives of the people are superior to the people themselves; and that men acting by virtue of powers may do not only what their powers do not authorize but what they forbid.

If it be said that the legislative body are themselves the constitutional judges of their own powers and that the construction they put upon them is conclusive upon the other departments, it may be answered that this cannot be the natural presumption, where it is not to be collected from any particular provisions in the Constitution. It is not otherwise to be supposed that the Constitution could intend to enable the representatives of the people to substitute their WILL to that of their constituents. It is far more rational to suppose that the courts were designed to be an intermediate body between the people and the legislature, in order, among other things, to keep the latter

within the limits assigned to their authority. The interpretation of the laws is the proper and peculiar province of the courts. A constitution is in fact, and must be regarded by the judges as, a fundamental law. It therefore belongs to them to ascertain its meaning as well as the meaning of any particular act proceeding from the legislative body. If there should happen to be an irreconcilable variance between the two, that which has the superior obligation and validity ought, of course, to be preferred; or, in other words, the Constitution ought to be preferred to the statute, the intention of the people to the intention of their agents.

Nor does this conclusion by any means suppose a superiority of the judicial to the legislative power. It only supposes that the power of the people is superior to both; and that where the will of the legislature, declared in its statutes, stands in opposition to that of the people, declared in the Constitution, the judges ought to be governed by the latter rather than the former. They ought to regulate their decisions by the fundamental laws, rather than by those which are not fundamental.

This exercise of judicial discretion, in determining between two contradictory laws, is exemplified in a familiar instance. It not uncommonly happens that there are two statutes existing at one time, clashing in whole or in part with each other and neither of them containing any repealing clause or expression. In such a case, it is the province of the courts to liquidate and fix their meaning and operation. So far as they can, by any fair construction, be reconciled to each other, reason and law conspire to dictate that this should be done; where this is impracticable, it becomes a matter of necessity to give effect to one in exclusion of the other. The rule which has obtained in the courts for determining their relative validity is that the last in order of time shall be preferred to the first. But this is a mere rule of construction, not derived from any positive law but from the nature and reason of the thing. It is a rule not enjoined upon the courts by legislative provision but adopted by themselves, as consonant to truth and propriety, for the direction of their conduct as interpreters of the law. They thought it reasonable that between the interfering acts of an EQUAL authority, that which was the last indication of its will should have the preference.

But in regard to the interfering acts of a superior and subordinate authority, of an original and derivative power, the nature and reason of the thing indicate the converse of that rule as proper to be followed. They teach us that the prior act of a superior ought to be preferred to the subsequent act of an inferior and subordinate authority; and that accordingly, whenever a particular statute contravenes the

Constitution, it will be the duty of the judicial tribunals to adhere to the latter and disregard the former.

It can be of no weight to say that the courts, on the pretense of a repugnancy, may substitute their own pleasure to the constitutional intentions of the legislature. This might as well happen in the case of two contradictory statutes, or it might as well happen in every adjudication upon any single statute. The courts must declare the sense of the law; and if they should be disposed to exercise WILL instead of JUDGMENT, the consequence would equally be the substitution of their pleasure to that of the legislative body. The observation, if it proves anything, would prove that there ought to be no judges distinct from that body.

If the courts of justice are to be considered as the bulwarks of a limited Constitution against legislative encroachments, then this consideration will afford a strong argument for the permanent tenure of judicial offices, since nothing will contribute so much as this to that independent spirit in the judges, which must be essential to the faithful performance of so arduous a duty.

This independence of the judges is equally requisite to guard the Constitution and the rights of individuals from the effects of those ill humors, which the arts of designing men, or the influence of particular conjunctures, sometimes disseminate among the people themselves, and which, though they speedily give place to better information, and more deliberate reflection, have a tendency, in the meantime, to occasion dangerous innovations in the government and serious oppressions of the minor party in the community. Though I trust the friends of the proposed Constitution will never concur with its enemies,[3] in questioning that fundamental principle of republican government, which admits the right of the people to alter or abolish the established Constitution, whenever they find it inconsistent with their happiness, yet it is not to be inferred from this principle, that the representatives of the people, whenever a momentary inclination happens to lay hold of a majority of their constituents, incompatible with the provisions in the existing Constitution would, on that account, be justifiable in a violation of those provisions; or that the courts would be under a greater obligation to connive at infractions in this shape than when they had proceeded wholly from the cabals of the representative body. Until the people have, by some solemn and authoritative act, annulled or changed the established form, it is binding upon themselves collectively, as well as individually; and no presumption, or even knowledge, of their sentiments can warrant their representatives in a departure from it, prior to such an act. But it is easy to see that it would require an uncommon portion of fortitude

in the judges to do their duty as faithful guardians of the Constitution, where legislative invasions of it had been instigated by the major voice of the community.

But it is not with a view to infractions of the Constitution only that the independence of the judges may be an essential safeguard against the effects of occasional ill humors in the society. These sometimes extend no farther than to the injury of the private rights of particular classes of citizens, by unjust and partial laws. Here also the firmness of the judicial magistracy is of vast importance in mitigating the severity and confining the operation of such laws. It not only serves to moderate the immediate mischiefs of those which may have been passed, but it operates as a check upon the legislative body in passing them, who, perceiving that obstacles to the success of iniquitous intention are to be expected from the scruples of the courts, are in a manner compelled, by the very motives of the injustice they meditate, to qualify their attempts. This is a circumstance calculated to have more influence upon the character of our governments than but few may be aware of. The benefits of the integrity and moderation of the judiciary have already been felt in more States than one, and though they may have displeased those whose sinister expectations they may have disappointed, they must have commanded the esteem and applause of all the virtuous and disinterested. Considerate men, of every description, ought to prize whatever will tend to beget or fortify that temper in the courts: as no man can be sure that he may not be tomorrow the victim of a spirit of injustice, by which he may be a gainer today. And every man must now feel that the inevitable tendency of such a spirit is to sap the foundations of public and private confidence and to introduce in its stead universal distrust and distress.

That inflexible and uniform adherence to the rights of the Constitution, and of individuals, which we perceive to be indispensable in the courts of justice, can certainly not be expected from judges who hold their offices by a temporary commission. Periodical appointments, however, regulated, or by whomsoever made, would, in some way or other, be fatal to their necessary independence. If the power of making them was committed either to the Executive or legislature, there would be danger of an improper complaisance to the branch which possessed it; if to both, there would be an unwillingness to hazard the displeasure of either; if to the people, or to persons chosen by them for the special purpose, there would be too great a disposition to consult popularity, to justify a reliance that nothing would be consulted but the Constitution and the laws.

There is yet a further and a weightier reason for the permanency of the judicial offices, which is deducible from the nature of the qualifications they require. It has been frequently remarked, with great propriety, that a voluminous code of laws is one of the inconveniences necessarily connected with the advantages of a free government. To avoid an arbitrary discretion in the courts, it is indispensable that they should be bound down by strict rules and precedents, which serve to define and point out their duty in every particular case that comes before them; and it will readily be conceived from the variety of controversies which grow out of the folly and wickedness of mankind that the records of those precedents must unavoidably swell to a very considerable bulk and must demand long and laborious study to acquire a competent knowledge of them. Hence, it is that there can be but few men in the society who will have sufficient skill in the laws to qualify them for the stations of judges. And making the proper deductions for the ordinary depravity of human nature, the number must be still smaller of those who unite the requisite integrity with the requisite knowledge. These considerations apprise us that the government can have no great option between fit character; and that a temporary duration in office, which would naturally discourage such characters from quitting a lucrative line of practice to accept a seat on the bench, would have a tendency to throw the administration of justice into hands less able, and less well qualified, to conduct it with utility and dignity. In the present circumstances of this country, and in those in which it is likely to be for a long time to come, the disadvantages on this score would be greater than they may at first sight appear, but it must be confessed that they are far inferior to those which present themselves under the other aspects of the subject.

Upon the whole, there can be no room to doubt that the convention acted wisely in copying from the models of those constitutions which have established GOOD BEHAVIOR as the tenure of their judicial offices, in point of duration; and that so far from being blamable on this account, their plan would have been inexcusably defective, if it had wanted this important feature of good government. The experience of Great Britain affords an illustrious comment on the excellence of the institution.

PUBLIUS.

1. The celebrated Montesquieu, speaking of them, says: "Of the three powers above mentioned, the judiciary is next to nothing." "Spirit of Laws." vol. i, page 186.
2. Idem, page 181.
3. Vide "Protest of the Minority of the Convention of Pennsylvania," Martin's Speech, etc.

ALEXANDER HAMILTON was an American statesman and one of the Founding Fathers of the United States. He was an influential interpreter and promoter of the U.S. Constitution, as well as the founder of the nation's financial system, the Federalist Party, the United States Coast Guard, and the *New York Post* newspaper.

EXPLORING THE ISSUE

Should Supreme Court Justices Have Term Limits?

Critical Thinking and Reflection

1. What are the benefits of Supreme Court justices not having term limits?
2. What are the negative aspects of Supreme Court justices not having term limits?
3. How do you believe term limits would change how justices behave? Why?
4. What benefits do term limits present in other offices of government?
5. Do you believe an age limit would fulfill the same purpose as term limits? Why or why not?

Is There Common Ground?

Like most things related to the courts, it's hard to imagine finding common ground on an issue like term limits. Those opposed to term limits are able to quite easily point to the Constitution's clearly defined statement of no term limits, along with the Federalist Paper discussion concerning why it's important for Supreme Court justices to not have to be concerned with leaving office after a term. Likewise, those who wish to see term limits imposed are not likely to be swayed by counterarguments waged by those who disagree. They believe a level of accountability—along with a limit on how long a justice has the capability to determine legal decisions—is essential to making government as democratic as possible.

To reach any common ground would take an agreement that any type of term limit was desired. But what good would a hypothetical 20-year term limit serve? At that point, a judge appointed at 50 would leave the bench at 70 and have two decades to influence policy without fear of the public's sentiments. At the same time, a proposed 5-year term would make it much more difficult for judges to accept appointments since they would be out of work much more quickly. Thus, even if there were to be an agreement reached on a desire for term limits at all, there would still be significant work needed to shape exactly what this new system would look like. Further, a 37-year-old Supreme Court nominee (which one of President Trump's shortlisted nominees is) could serve for five decades on the bench. Most importantly, we need to remember that the individuals who would need to make this decision are members of Congress that also do not have term limits today—and the Supreme Court would be able to determine the constitutionality of this change, barring a Constitutional amendment.

Additional Resources

Roger C. Cramton and Paul D. Carrington, *Reforming the Court: Term Limits for the Supreme Court Justices* (Carolina Academic Press, 2005).

Mark Levin, *The Liberty Amendments: Restoring the American Republic* (Threshold Editions, 2013).

James D. Zirin and Kermit Roosevelt, *Supremely Partisan: How Raw Politics Tips the Scales in the United States Supreme Court* (Rowman & Littlefield, 2016).

Internet References . . .

Running the Numbers on Supreme Court Term Limits

https://www.brennancenter.org/blog/running-numbers-supreme-court-term-limits

Term Limits

http://fixthecourt.com/fix/term-limits/

The Supreme Court and Term Limits

https://www.termlimits.org/the-supreme-court-and-term-limits/

Selected, Edited, and with Issue Framing Material by:
William J. Miller, *Campus Labs*®

ISSUE

Should the Senate Be Able to Delay Hearings on Nominations While Waiting for an Investigation to Conclude?

YES: Paul Schiff Berman, from "A Better Reason to Delay Kennedy's Replacement," *The New York Times* (2018)

NO: Jonathan Turley, from "No One Can Use Mueller Probe to Hold Up Supreme Court Nominee," *The Hill* (2018)

Learning Outcomes

After reading this issue, you will be able to:

- Discuss the process of Supreme Court nominations.
- Explain the factors presidents consider in determining whom to nominate.
- Assess the responsibilities of the Senate with regard to confirming court nominees.
- List potential impacts of the Senate choosing to not act.
- Describe the politics behind nominations and confirmations.

ISSUE SUMMARY

YES: Law Professor Paul Schiff Berman argues that people under the cloud of investigation do not get to pick the judges who may preside over their cases. Consequently, he believes presidents under any type of investigation should not be able to appoint judges who may ultimately be involved in deciding their legal fate.

NO: Jonathan Turley—also a public law academic—instead points to a complete lack of historical precedent or statue for holding such a view. Instead, he argues such arguments are typically politically opportunistic and not rooted in substantive law.

Article II, Section 2 states: "[The President] shall have power, by and with the advice and consent of the Senate, to make treaties, provided two thirds of the Senators present concur; and he shall nominate, and by and with the advice and consent of the Senate, shall appoint ambassadors, other public ministers and consuls, judges of the Supreme Court, and all other officers of the United States, whose appointments are not herein otherwise provided for, and which shall be established by law: but the Congress may by law vest the appointment of such inferior officers,

as they think proper, in the President alone, in the courts of law, or in the heads of departments." Thus, Supreme Court nominations involve two parties: the President, who nominates individuals to the Court, and the Senate, who confirms the nomination.

Merrick Garland officially made Supreme Court history in July 2016—not for something he did, but for something others haven't done. President Barack Obama's choice to replace the late Justice Antonin Scalia has surpassed the record for the high court nominee who has waited the longest to be confirmed for the job.

The milestone couldn't be more symbolic. Garland, who was nominated in March 2016, surpassed Louis Brandeis, one of the greatest justices to ever live, who exactly 100 years ago endured the largest gap between nomination and confirmation of any Supreme Court nominee: 125 days.

Congress took summer recess, and then Republican leadership in the Senate—all but set on the idea to have Donald Trump fill this and other Supreme Court vacancies—showed no intention of even granting Garland a hearing. Senate Majority Leader Mitch McConnell (R-KY) stated at the time: "The American people should have a voice in the selection of their next Supreme Court Justice. Therefore, this vacancy should not be filled until we have a new President."

For more than 40 years, there has been an average of just over two months between a president nominating someone to the Supreme Court and that person receiving a hearing in Congress. What is occurring with Judge Garland appears to be quite different than the typical dysfunction one may expect from Washington, DC. Every Supreme Court nominee since 1875 who hasn't withdrawn from the process has received a hearing or a vote, even when the nominee was controversial and when the Senate and the White House were held by different parties.

But Judge Garland wasn't even necessarily controversial. He had more federal judicial experience than any Supreme Court nominee in our history. He was widely respected by people of both political parties as a man of experience, integrity, and unimpeachable qualifications. The partisan decision of Senate Republicans to deny a hearing to a judge was viewed by many Democrats—including President Obama—as an unprecedented escalation of the stakes. As Obama stated: "Historically, when a president nominates a Supreme Court justice—regardless of when in the presidential term this occurs—the Senate is obligated to act. Senators are free to vote their conscience. But they vote. That's their job."

When Republicans in the Senate refused even to consider a nominee in order to run out the clock until they could elect a president from their own party, so that he could nominate his own justice to the Supreme Court, they effectively nullified the ability of any president from the opposing party to make an appointment to the nation's highest court. They reduced the very functioning of the judicial branch of the government to just another political leverage point. And this is why many are now debating whether hearings should be mandated, or perhaps required to occur within a certain period of time.

But, this also opened the door for Democrats to return the favor, which we are witnessing today. Brett Kavanaugh—although ripe with questions regarding his confirmability—has been caught in the Mueller investigation. But it's Kavanaugh's views of the presidency, especially a Republican presidency, that make his nomination even more alarming to Democrats, given the potential legal perils confronting this president and his family. Put aside whether he thinks a president can be indicted. Kavanaugh suggested that he believes the landmark case, *United States v. Nixon*, that forced the president to turn over his tapes leading to the only presidential resignation in U.S. history, was wrongly decided.

This is damning in the eyes of liberals, given the current president's legal team's constant signaling that it would fight any subpoena to testify before the Mueller probe. Cory Booker—Democratic Senator from New Jersey and likely 2020 presidential hopeful—had the following to say: "President Trump is currently a subject of an ongoing criminal investigation, and any nomination of a Supreme Court justice while that investigation continues is unacceptable because of the clear conflict of interest inherent in the president installing someone who could be the deciding vote on a number of potential issues from that investigation."

The growing politicization of the judiciary is troubling for two reasons. First, a functioning judiciary—at every level—is essential to the business of the nation. For example, in the term in which Justice Scalia died, a deadlocked Supreme Court was unable to reach a decision on several major issues, leaving the law itself in limbo. Across the country, judicial vacancies are leaving some lower courts so overwhelmed they can barely make it through their dockets. Twenty-nine judicial emergencies have been declared by lower courts across the country. This has real implications for jurisprudence, real financial costs to the judicial system, and real consequences in the lives of people awaiting the outcomes of those cases.

Second, treating the Supreme Court like a political football makes the American people more cynical about democracy. When the Supreme Court becomes a proxy for political parties, public confidence in the notion of an impartial, independent judiciary breaks down. And the resulting lack of trust can undermine the rule of law.

So here's an idea that's been proposed in recent administrations—by both major political parties. Democrats and Republicans in the Senate could agree to give every future qualified Supreme Court nominee a hearing and a vote within an established timeframe. This reasonable proposal would prevent the confirmation process from breaking down beyond repair and help restore good faith between the two parties. Democracies depend on the institutions we build, the rules upon which the nation is founded, and the traditions, customs, and habits of heart that guide our behavior and ensure that political differences never override the founding ideals that bind us.

While the arguments for forcing Congress to act are clear, if we return to a reading of the Constitution, there is no mandate for when confirmation hearings would take place on a nominee. While it is quite unlikely that the Founders would approve of a judge waiting well over six months for a hearing for no reason other than politics, nothing they left in writing assures this to be the case. Maybe the confirmation process needs to be political. Maybe the country has reached a point where this type of dysfunction is viewed as more important politically than working together to grow the country as a whole. While this would not bode well for long-term democratic values, it may be the best way to look at the situation we find ourselves in today. Ironically, if Hillary Clinton were to win the White House in November, Senate Republicans may be the ones to try to push through a Garrick appointment given his relatively moderate tendencies and views as compared to a potentially more liberal nominee coming from a new president.

In the following selections, law professor Paul Schiff Berman argues that people under the cloud of investigation do not get to pick the judges who may preside over their cases. Consequently, he believes presidents under any type of investigation should not be able to appoint judges who may ultimately be involved in deciding their legal fate. Jonathan Turley—also a public law academic—instead points to a complete lack of historical precedent or statue for holding such a view. Instead, he argues such arguments are typically politically opportunistic and not rooted in substantive law.

YES ←

Paul Schiff Berman

A Better Reason to Delay Kennedy's Replacement

Almost immediately after Justice Anthony Kennedy announced his retirement on Wednesday, Senate Democrats argued that his replacement should not be confirmed until after the midterm elections this fall—a version of the same argument that Mitch McConnell, the Senate majority leader, used to stymie President Barack Obama's nomination of Merrick Garland to the Supreme Court in 2016.

This is surely a valid argument, not least because Mr. McConnell's blatantly antidemocratic ploy stole a judicial appointment from a popularly elected president and gave it to one who lost the popular vote by millions.

But there is another reason to withhold confirmation that both Republicans and Democrats should be able to agree on: people under the cloud of investigation do not get to pick the judges who may preside over their cases. By this logic, President Trump should not be permitted to appoint a new Supreme Court justice until after the special counsel investigation is over, and we know for sure whether there is evidence of wrongdoing.

True, that point is unlikely to stop Mr. McConnell or his colleagues. But it highlights the real risk involved in letting a deeply compromised president shape a court that may one day stand between him and impeachment.

Much of the conversation since Justice Kennedy announced his retirement has been focused on whether a more conservative replacement might lead to the overthrow of landmark decisions on abortion rights, gay marriage, and other issues. These are undoubtedly important concerns. But not enough attention has been placed on the crucial question of whether the Supreme Court in the Trump era will provide an effective bulwark against autocratic lawless rule.

Indeed, legal experts are already debating several knotty constitutional questions that involve the president and may one day soon have to be decided by the court. Can the president pardon himself or others specifically to extricate himself from criminal investigation? Can the

president be compelled to testify before a grand jury? Can a sitting president be criminally indicted?

Did the appointment of the special counsel somehow violate the Appointments Clause of the Constitution, as some conservatives implausibly insist? Can a president ever obstruct justice? What is the proper legal remedy for Mr. Trump's repeated violations of the Emoluments Clause? It is no exaggeration to say that never before has the selection of a Supreme Court nominee been so thoroughly compromised by the president's profound personal interest in appointing a judge he can count on to protect him.

While we cannot know how Justice Kennedy would have ruled on these questions, we do know that at least at times he was willing to stand up to assertions of power by the executive branch, most notably in *Boumediene v. Bush*, when he wrote a five-to-four decision defying the president and extending the constitutional right of habeas corpus to wartime detainees at Guantánamo Bay.

Mr. Trump's possible crimes are inextricable from his desire for unilateral control of the federal government. It is no secret that the power of the executive branch has grown over the past several decades, under both Republican and Democratic presidents. Our executive now has surveillance capacities never before seen, vast power to conduct drone strikes and conduct lethal military operations abroad, broad authority to set immigration and law enforcement priorities, and the ability to regulate enormous areas of economic and personal life.

Add to this sweeping institutional power a president who refuses to acknowledge *any* checks on his power as legitimate, whether those checks come from the courts, the legislature, the media, the government bureaucracy, or his political opponents. This is the perfect recipe for autocracy. In such a world, the importance of checks and balances has never been greater.

This would be dangerous regardless of Mr. Trump's legal shortcomings. But this president has, by his own admission, already taken steps to thwart an investigation into his own potential criminality. Both Democrats and Republicans in the Senate should therefore resist calls for a quick confirmation process.

Otherwise, there will be a stain on the legitimacy of this nomination, on the performance of whomever is confirmed, and, even, on the Supreme Court itself. The fact that the president has every motive to ensure that happens—to promote his political agenda and to protect him personally—makes the present moment all the more frightening.

Paul Schiff Berman is an American lawyer and the Walter S. Cox Professor of Law at The George Washington University. From 2013 to 2016, he served as the University's Vice Provost for Online Education and Academic Innovation.

Jonathan Turley

 **NO**

No One Can Use Mueller Probe to Hold Up Supreme Court Nominee

In a city where necessity has long been the mother of invention, the retirement of Associate Justice Anthony Kennedy has unleashed a frenzy of creative arguments of why President Trump should not be able to appoint a second member to the Supreme Court. Panic can lead to many things, but principle is not one of them.

According to Democratic politicians and advocates, there is a long-standing principle that any nomination by Trump at this time would be clearly improper. This convenient discovery was explained by Sen. Cory Booker (D-NJ) in a judiciary hearing, where he insisted that, as "a subject of an ongoing criminal investigation," any nomination or confirmation must wait "until the Mueller investigation is concluded."

This suggested barrier for a Trump nomination is both artificial and opportunistic. Initially, Democrats argued that Trump should wait until after the midterm elections, given the earlier blocking of a vote by Republicans on Merrick Garland's nomination at the end of the Obama administration. I was critical of the denial of Garland of a vote, but Republicans have noted that this is not a presidential election year and, more importantly, they have no intention of being "Garlanded."

That has led to this new argument that, somehow, a nomination by Trump would be improper due to special counsel Robert Mueller's ongoing investigation. It shares the same motivation with the Garland rationale, which is to avoid a vote on the merits of a nomination while claiming that principle, not politics, is guiding the decision.

Even if Trump were an actual target of the investigation, this argument would still be dubious. However, Trump repeatedly has been told that he is not a target but a subject of the special counsel investigation. This position has not changed over the course of two years when former FBI Director James Comey told both Congress and Trump that he was not a target. Moreover, Mueller reportedly told

the White House in March that Trump still was not a target but, rather, a subject.

In the U.S. attorney's manual, a "subject" is any "person whose conduct is within the scope of the grand jury's investigation." Nevertheless, the mere fact that conduct is relevant to an investigation is being claimed by Democrats as a barrier to a president carrying out a constitutional duty. So, a president is expected to leave the Supreme Court with just eight members, and likely deadlock votes, until there is no longer even a chance and no matter how remote that he could be elevated to target status and then elevated to being a defendant.

Worse yet, this same logic applies to both state and federal investigations. In either case, the Supreme Court could be the ultimate deciding body on questions related to such investigations. Thus, hostile state attorneys general or district attorneys could effectively block a nomination or confirmation by launching investigations into a president's conduct.

A special or independent counsel investigation can easily go on for years, so merely starting an investigation into a matter touching on a president's conduct would be enough to strip presidents of their Article II authority of appointments to the highest court. After all, the Whitewater investigation went on for 2,978 days. Trump has roughly 930 days left in his presidency. Mueller was appointed roughly 400 days ago, so even if he moved at twice the pace of Whitewater independent counsel Kenneth Starr, it could be another 1,100 days until Trump would be free to make an appointment, under this theory. That period conveniently would end more than two months into the term of the next presidential term.

If Democrats thought the failure of the Senate to vote on Garland was wrong after roughly 300 days, try a denial of the right of a president to nominate a justice for potentially 10 times that period. Putting such practical considerations aside, the constitutional implications are staggering if a president could be effectively blocked by the mere initiation of a criminal investigation on the state or federal levels.

One of my colleagues, Paul Berman, explained in *The New York Times* that "people under the cloud of investigation do not get to pick the judges who may preside over their cases. By this logic, President Trump should not be permitted to appoint a new Supreme Court justice until after the special counsel investigation is over, and we know for sure whether there is evidence of wrongdoing." Of course, by this same logic, presidents "under a cloud" should be denied the appointment of judges on lower courts as well as Supreme Court justices.

Nothing in the Constitution or history supports the claim that any "cloud of investigation" over a president is a barrier to the confirmation of a nominee. Indeed, not a single such objection was voiced when President Clinton appointed Stephen Breyer on April 6, 1994, to replace Associate Justice Harry Blackmun, three months after the appointment of the Whitewater independent counsel. During the summer Breyer was confirmed, Congress subpoenaed 29 Clinton administration officials in its own investigation, and the Clinton legal team ramped up for challenges.

Of course, Trump is not Clinton, and that seems precisely the point. Berman argued that Trump's "possible crimes are inextricable from his desire for unilateral control of the federal government" and that he is "a president who refuses to acknowledge any checks on his power as legitimate, whether those checks come from the courts, the legislature, the media, the government bureaucracy, or his political opponents. This is the perfect recipe for autocracy. In such a world, the importance of checks and balances has never been greater."

The last point appears to be most important for politicians and advocates alike. The primary check on a president's appointment power is to deny confirmation. This argument offers Democratic senators the pretense of principle in refusing to vote to confirm any nominee of Trump. The duty of senators is not to refuse to confirm but to insist that a nominee has the intellectual and ethical independence to fulfill the oath of office.

It often seems that both the U.S. criminal code and the Constitution are endlessly flexible when the subject is Trump. However, if necessity is the very mother of invention, consistency is the very meaning of the rule of law. Whoever Trump's nominee may be, it is the nominee, not the nominating president, who should be the focus of a confirmation vote.

JONATHAN TURLEY is an American lawyer, legal scholar, writer, commentator, and legal analyst in broadcast and print journalism. He is currently a professor of law at the George Washington University Law School.

EXPLORING THE ISSUE

Should the Senate Be Able to Delay Hearings on Nominations While Waiting for an Investigation to Conclude?

Critical Thinking and Reflection

1. Does the Senate have too much power with regard to court nominations?
2. Should the Senate consider politics when deciding whether to confirm a nominee?
3. Do you believe presidents should be able to appoint court members without the Senate's approval? Why or why not?
4. How could the Senate best be enticed to hold hearings, even when they politically may not want to?
5. Why do you believe the Founders created the process that is in place today?

Is There Common Ground?

It is hard to argue that the decision to delay hearings on a nominee during a presidential election year is not something explicitly political in nature. In 2016, Republicans more or less admitted that they did not take action on Merrick Garland's nomination to the Supreme Court because they hoped a Republican would win the presidency and bring forward a more conservative candidate. This ultimately went according to plan on Garland watched as Neil Gorsuch took the seat on the Supreme Court. But now the tides have turned. As Brett Kavanaugh awaits his fate, many Democrats are arguing his nomination should be held until Robert Mueller's investigation into President Trump is complete. Some go as far as to argue that Trump is picking his own potential juror.

The Constitution is unfortunately silent on the question of timing, which means both sides are able to claim legal status. While the Founders were clear that the President would make a nomination to the Supreme Court and the Senate would confirm the appointment if it believed it to be in the best of the interests of the country, it makes no mention of the process of how this should occur.

What makes common ground difficult on this issue is that it has become a political, rather than a procedural, topic. Both the parties believe nominees should face confirmation hearings as soon as possible—when they control the White House. While Democrats may be unhappy with the Republican-controlled Senate today, there is little doubt they would be doing the same thing to a lame duck Republican president if they found themselves in the same situation. Thus, until both the parties are willing to put their own self-interest aside and attempt to determine what would lead to the most effective appointment and confirmation process, we will likely never see common ground reached on this issue. What would common ground look like regardless? A timeline of when the Senate has to act based on how much time a president has left in office?

Additional Resources

Jan C. Greenburg, *Supreme Conflict: The Inside Story of the Struggle for Control of the United States Supreme Court* (Penguin Press, 2007).

Wil Haygood, *Showdown: Thurgood Marshall and the Supreme Court Nomination That Changed America* (Vintage, 2016).

Jeffrey Toobin, *The Nine: Inside the Secret World of the Supreme Court* (Doubleday, 2007).

Internet References . . .

Nomination and Confirmation Process

http://guides.ll.georgetown.edu/c.
php?g=365722&p=2471070

President Trump's Supreme Court Nomination

https://www.whitehouse.gov/scotus

Seven Things to Know about Presidential Appointments to the Supreme Court

http://www.npr.org/2016/02/14/466723547/7-things-
to-know-about-presidential-appointments-to-the-
supreme-court

Unit 3

UNIT

Social Change and Public Policy

*E*conomic and moral issues divide Americans along an ideological spectrum from "left" to "right." The issues are exceedingly diverse; they include economic equality, social welfare, gay rights, abortion, race relations, capital punishment, religious freedom, drug legalization, and whether there should be limits on speech activities. Disagreements break out on the floor of Congress, in state legislatures, in the nation's courtrooms, and sometimes in the streets. These controversial issues generate intense emotions because they force us to defend our most deeply held values and explain how they can be worked out in public policy.

In some cases, debate and deliberation can lead to individuals altering their views or opinions. Yet for other issues, there is no budging, and this is especially true for morally centered issues. While institutions and culture may have an impact on the functioning of American government and its relationship to the citizenry, it is through policy issues where we see citizens becoming most active and involved. Look at recent history to see how the international community has experienced the power of protest. From the Tea Party Movement to Occupy to the Arab Spring to Black Lives Matter to the emerging #MeToo movement, citizens react when policy decisions do not reflect their perceived interests. Hence, the importance of the following debates.

Selected, Edited, and with Issue Framing Material by:
William J. Miller, *Campus Labs*®

ISSUE

Should Access to Abortions Be Restricted?

YES: Berny Belvedere, from "Abortion is Wrong Even if the Fetus is not a Person," *National Review* (2017)

NO: Julie Hirschfield Davis, from "How New Abortion Restrictions Would Affect Women's Health Care," *The New York Times* (2018)

Learning Outcomes
After reading this issue, you will be able to: • Identify arguments in support of abortion.   • Identify arguments in support of banning abortion.   • Assess the impact abortions have on American society.   • Discuss whether it's possible to legislate moral policy.   • Explain why Americans regularly debate the issue of abortion.

ISSUE SUMMARY

YES: Philosopher and writer Berny Belvedere argues that debates between pro-life and pro-choice groups are rooted too much in rhetoric and not enough in reality. Regardless, he examines how moral arguments suggest abortion should not be legalized in any way.

NO: On the other hand, Julie Hirschfield Davis—a reporter and political analyst—examines how increased restrictions regarding abortion access would negatively affect women's health care, which directly counters arguments made by some antiabortion advocates.

Until 1973, the laws governing abortion were set by the states, most of which barred legal abortion except where pregnancy imperiled the life of the pregnant woman. In that year, the U.S. Supreme Court decided the controversial case *Roe v. Wade.* The *Roe* decision acknowledged both a woman's "fundamental right" to terminate a pregnancy before fetal viability and the state's legitimate interest in protecting both the woman's health and the "potential life" of the fetus. It prohibited states from banning abortion to protect the fetus before the third trimester of a pregnancy, and it ruled that even during that final trimester, a woman could obtain an abortion if she could prove that her life or health would be endangered by carrying to term. (In a companion case to *Roe,* decided on

the same day, the Court defined health broadly enough to include "all factors—physical, emotional, psychological, familial, and the woman's age—relevant to the well-being of the patient.") These holdings, together with the requirement that state regulation of abortion had to survive "strict scrutiny" and demonstrate a "compelling state interest," resulted in later decisions striking down mandatory 24-hour waiting periods, requirements that abortions be performed in hospitals, and so-called informed consent laws.

The Supreme Court did uphold state laws requiring parental notification and consent for minors (though it provided that minors could seek permission from a judge if they feared notifying their parents). And federal courts have affirmed the right of Congress not to pay for abortions. Proabortion groups, proclaiming the "right to choose," have charged that this and similar action at the state level discriminate against poor women because it does not inhibit the ability of women who are able to pay for abortions to obtain them. Efforts to adopt a constitutional amendment or federal law barring abortion have failed, but antiabortion forces have influenced legislation in many states.

Can legislatures and courts establish the existence of a scientific fact? Opponents of abortion believe that it is a fact that life begins at conception and that the law must therefore uphold and enforce this concept. They argue that the human fetus is a live human being, and they note all the familiar signs of life displayed by the fetus: a beating heart, brain waves, thumb sucking, and so on. Those who defend abortion maintain that human life does not begin before the development of specifically human characteristics and possibly not until the birth of a child. As Justice Harry A. Blackmun put it in 1973, "There has always been strong support for the view that life does not begin until live birth."

Antiabortion forces sought a court case that might lead to the overturning of *Roe v. Wade*. Pro-choice forces rallied to oppose new state laws limiting or prohibiting abortion. In *Webster v. Reproductive Health Services* (1989), with four new justices, the Supreme Court upheld a Missouri law that banned abortions in public hospitals and abortions that were performed by public employees (except to save a woman's life). The law also required that tests be performed on any fetus more than 20 weeks old to determine its viability. In the later decision of *Planned Parenthood v. Casey* (1992), however, the Court affirmed what it called the "essence" of the constitutional right to abortion while permitting some state restrictions, such as a 24-hour waiting period and parental notification in the case of minors.

In 2000, a five-to-four decision of the Supreme Court in *Stenberg v. Carhart* overturned a Nebraska law that outlawed "partial birth" abortions. The law defined "partial birth abortion" as a procedure in which the doctor "partially delivers vaginally a living child before killing" the child, further defining the process as "intentionally delivering into the vagina a living unborn child, or a substantial portion thereof, for the purpose of performing a procedure that the [abortionist] knows will kill the child." The Court's stated reason for striking down the law was that it lacked a "health" exception. Critics complained that the Court has defined "health" so broadly that it includes not only physical health but also "emotional, psychological," and "familial" health, and that the person the Court has

authorized to make these judgments is the attendant physician, that is, the abortionist himself.

In recent years, the United States has witnessed a rebirth of restrictive abortion measures that have yet to fully play their way through the federal court system. Perhaps the most prominent example has been the Texas abortion debate, which drew national attention; thanks to the filibustering of Texas State Senator Wendy Davis. Texas HB 2 criminalizes abortions after 20 weeks and imposes harsh regulations on abortion providers that will force the vast majority of them to close their doors. HB 2 combines several pieces of antiabortion legislation that were unable to advance during Texas' regular legislative session. Perry called two special sessions specifically to give lawmakers more time to push them through. During the first session, thousands of protesters helped delay the abortion restrictions until the last minute, giving Davis a chance to block the bill with a dramatic filibuster that lasted for more than 11 hours. But those tactics weren't enough to prevent the bill's advancement during a second special session. The Supreme Court voted 5-4 to leave in effect a provision requiring doctors who perform abortions in clinics to have admitting privileges at a nearby hospital. Challenges to the bill still exist in federal appellate court, meaning the Texas law could find itself back in the court sooner rather than later.

Ohio, on the other hand, has spent the past decade enacting more restrictive controls on the availability of abortion without drawing as much negative attention at Texas. The state has become a laboratory of sorts for what antiabortion leaders call the incremental strategy. Under this plan, the state, under the leadership of Republican Governor John Kasich, has passed a series of rules aimed at pushing the limits set by the Supreme Court without directly violating them. The provisions put in place attempt to both discourage women from choosing to have an abortion and hampering clinic operations. There have been two recently passed provisions that will unquestionably make abortions more difficult to receive. First, Ohio has passed a heartbeat bill, which requires women about to have an abortion to both view an ultrasound and watch its beating heart. Through guilt the hope is the woman will have a change of heart. The second provision will perhaps be even more effective. Ohio has required abortion clinics to have formal transfer agreements with nearby hospitals for emergency care for some time despite this being largely unnecessary as hospitals must treat emergency patients. But now public hospitals are barred from signing these agreements, meaning a few clinics will likely have to shut down unless they find a suitable private hospital partner.

In short, it is clear that states are still working to find ways to restrict abortion within their borders, and the Supreme Court sits in waiting to consider appeals.

Even within the past year, we have seen changes to abortion law in a number of states. Mississippi has banned abortions after 15 weeks with no exemptions for rape and incest. Governor Kim Reynolds signed into law Iowa's new "heartbeat" abortion bill, which blocks abortions once a fetal heartbeat is detected. Essentially, the law could ban abortions by the sixth week of pregnancy—though many women don't even know they're pregnant at that time—and it includes some exceptions for rape and incest victims, abnormalities, and medical emergencies. Kentucky passed House Bill 454, which would block a typical abortion procedure after the 11th week of pregnancy. The procedure is known as dilation and evacuation and is normally used during a woman's second trimester. Governor Eric Holcomb of Indiana signed into law a bill that requires medical providers to report information about patients who've experienced complications from abortions. All of these new laws remain open with the federal court system, suggesting that abortion law remains largely unsettled.

In the following selections, philosopher and writer Berny Belvedere argues that debates between pro-life and pro-choice groups are rooted too much in rhetoric and not enough in reality. Regardless, he examines how moral arguments suggest abortion should not be legalized in any way. On the other hand, Julie Hirschfield Davis—a reporter and political analyst—examines how increased restrictions regarding abortion access would negatively affect women's health care, which directly counters arguments made by some antiabortion advocates.

YES ⬅

Berny Belvedere

Abortion Is Wrong Even If the Fetus Is Not a Person

A case for the irrelevance of personhood.

Have you noticed how political debates over abortion often degenerate into egregious and intellectually unserious demagoguery?

This shouldn't surprise—such debates often function as arenas for persuasion at any cost, which has the unfortunate consequence of making truth less important than rhetorical finesse. If maximal effectiveness, in this context, means getting people to buy into a particular viewpoint, then each presentation is in service to the pragmatic ideal of political success.

The political world, not academia, is responsible for the "pro-life" and "pro-choice" designations—labels that are rhetorically effective but intellectually vacuous. They can be useful for shorthand, sure, so long as the antiabortion camp doesn't go so far as to believe that its opponents take life to be bad, and so long as the proabortion advocates don't caricature their opponents as thinking it's wrong to make choices.

Despite academia's recent tendency to intensify (or incubate) the vulgarities of broader culture, and despite the self-satisfaction of its cloistered, professional thinkers, there is great value to exploring what the academic version of the abortion debate has been like.

In what follows, I'll run through two of the most prominent arguments in this debate. The first is Judith Jarvis Thomson's "A Defense of Abortion," and the second is Don Marquis's "Why Abortion Is Immoral." I'll explain why I think Thomson is wrong and Marquis is right.

In the rarefied air of philosophical ethics, arguments can seem a bit strange and unsettling. That is certainly true of Thomson's article, which relies on fanciful thought experiments to advance her thesis that most abortions are permissible.

Consider these scenarios she dreams up:

- To help preserve the life of a comatose violinist, the Society of Music Lovers kidnaps you and connects your body to the violinist, so that he can recover his health in nine months.

- You are trapped in a tiny house with a growing child. Soon, you'll be crushed to death, whereas the child will burst free from the house, damaged but alive.

- You are terminally ill, though a magic cure exists: if Henry Fonda travels from California to where you live and he caresses your face, you will live.

- People-seeds, like pollen, float about in the air. If they enter your house and land on a special carpet, they become full-blown persons. You open the window, because you want a breeze, and you make sure to put up your screen protector, which is 99.9 percent effective in keeping out people-seeds. Yet one manages to get in.

- You are a guest at a palace in the Middle East. The sultan's chandelier intercepts a wolf's howling cry and releases it as a mist that purifies the hearts of everyone in attendance at the ball.

I made the last one up. Here's the point: Could you tell? The more important question is: Just what is Thomson up to?

Thomson has a viewpoint in her sights that she is trying to systematically take down. Her target is the claim that abortion is wrong. So she starts by devising a way to challenge the most extreme form of this claim, the claim that no abortion is ever justified.

Her thought experiment about the violinist is designed to be the strongest possible response to this most stringent form of antiabortionism. The idea being: if you think abortion is always wrong, what about a case such as this, in which someone was violated (kidnapped) and as a result now has a person her body is responsible for keeping alive?

There is a very interesting development here. Notice the last sentence in the preceding paragraph. Did I mistakenly use the word "person"? Doesn't the "pro-choice" camp recoil at designating the fetus as a person? In fact, for many people, doesn't the entire issue hinge on whether we classify the life inside the womb as a person?

In other words, if the life inside is indeed a human person, then the "pro-life" side wins; if the life inside is *not* a person, then the "pro-choice" side wins. Isn't that how it goes?

If there's something philosophy revels in, it's upending the assumptions thought to be rigidly fixed in a debate. Thomson is basically raising the hurdle that a "pro-lifer" needs to clear. Whereas before, all that the antiabortion advocate had to do was to show that the fetus is a person, now, in light of Thomson's argument, even if the "pro-lifer" does this, that is no longer enough to secure a victory in the debate. Thomson argues that abortion is permissible even if the fetus is a person. I don't think she is successful.

How, exactly, does she assume that the fetus is a person—the very thing opponents of abortion work so hard to establish? She does so by building into her thought experiments the personhood of the relevant characters. The violinist, for example, is obviously a person; in other words, no one would deny that an adult human being who skillfully plays an instrument is a person. Even in the examples after this one, as in the people-seeds scenario, the moment a person-seed lands on the carpet (i.e., fertilization), it's a person.

By assuming the truth of the central claim that antiabortion advocates typically make—that the fetus is a person—Thomson is attempting to strengthen the pro-abortion case.

In my judgment, the scenarios she constructs suffer from irreparable problems; in the most important places, they do not work as analogies.

> The level of inconvenience caused by having a fully grown violinist attached to your body far exceeds the inconveniences of pregnancy.

To give one example: the level of inconvenience caused by having a fully grown violinist attached to your body far exceeds the inconveniences of pregnancy. You would have to cart around a hospital bed with an adult lying on it everywhere you went.

Why does this pose a problem for Thomson's argument? Because if you agree with Thomson that it should be permissible for you to disconnect yourself from the violinist and effectively kill him, it's *possible* your reason for saying so is that having a comatose adult connected to your body is too much of an inconvenience to endure for nine months. But that's not applicable to the real-life situation of pregnancy.

Even weaker analogies plague her other scenarios. The people-seeds thought experiment obviously is intended to resemble a pregnancy that results from a consensual sexual encounter in which the partners used contraception. Recall my description:

> People-seeds, like pollen, float about in the air. If they enter your house and land on a special carpet, they become full-blown persons. You open the window, because you want a breeze, and you make sure to put up your screen protector, which is 99.9 percent effective in keeping out people-seeds. Yet one manages to get in.
>
> Are we really supposed to dispassionately weigh the importance of a person when that person is likened to pollen?

Are we really supposed to dispassionately weigh the importance of a person when that person is likened to pollen? Of course, it's going to be easy to say, with Thomson, that it is permissible to eliminate a people-seed: Thomson strips the real-life being, which is the result of a biological process carrying the biological code of her parents, of her connection to the sexual partners who created her. A person becomes a foreign invader; a falling leaf from an outside tree; something alien and utterly unlike us. But that is nothing like a pregnancy.

Thomson believed her readers would agree with her. But I see no reason to.

Don Marquis argues for the contrary conclusion: abortion is immoral.

What's interesting is that Marquis follows Thomson in assuming his opponents' central claim. Just as Thomson tries to strengthen her position by assuming that the fetus is a person, Marquis tries to strengthen the antiabortion position by assuming that the fetus is not a person. In other words, Marquis thinks abortion is seriously immoral even if the being inside the womb lacks personhood.

Here's his argument:

(1) What makes killing someone wrong is that doing so deprives her of a future of value.

(2) When a fetus is killed, it suffers the same kind of loss.

Thus,

(3) Abortion is immoral just as killing an adult or a child is immoral.

As Marquis puts it:

When I am killed . . . I am deprived of all the value of my future. Inflicting this loss on me is ultimately what makes killing me wrong. This being the case, it would seem that what makes killing any adult human being prima facie seriously wrong is the loss of his or her future . . . .

The future of a standard fetus includes a set of experiences, projects, activities, and such that are identical with the futures of adult human beings and are identical with the futures of young children. Since the reason that is sufficient to explain why it is wrong to kill human beings after the time of birth is a reason that also applies to fetuses, it follows that abortion is prima facie seriously morally wrong.

Notice that Marquis's argument doesn't rely on the fetus's being a person. Marquis is essentially shoving the question of personhood aside and looking strictly at what it is that makes killing someone wrong.

If it turned out that what made killing someone wrong crucially relied on personhood, then Marquis wouldn't have an argument against abortion. But what he identifies as the reason that killing is wrong—a future of value—is a feature that adults, children, and fetuses share. If the reason that makes killing someone from the first two groups wrong is that it deprives them of a future of value, then the same reason provides an argument against abortion because the fetus, like the child and the adult, has a future of value.

(Interestingly, Marquis's argument does not provide grounds for seeing euthanasia as wrong, given that in many cases the candidate for euthanasia does not have a future of value.)

It's important to note that the argument is *not* claiming that abortion is wrong because it deprives a fetus of life. The idea here isn't that it's the destruction of *life* that makes abortion wrong. Bacteria are alive, yet they are missing the capacity to have a *future like ours*—that is the crucial feature. We don't prosecute people for mowing the lawn, despite all the plant life that their John Deeres are destroying; we make a distinction between taking a machete to a beanstalk and taking a machete to a human throat. If a being doesn't have a future like ours—an ongoing life in pursuit of hobbies, interests, relationships, thoughts, experiences, and so on—then it is not protected by the principle Marquis is operating with.

Notice, also, that Marquis is not vulnerable to the familiar "pro-choice" lament that he is relying on the notion of a being's *potential*. When an adult is killed, no one comforts the killer by saying, "Don't worry about it— your victim only possessed a future of value in a *potential* sense." No one would accept this reasoning. That's because, as Marquis notes, we see this future of value as something an adult possesses *in the present*. That's precisely why we're so scandalized when someone is killed; they are robbed of something; indeed, they are robbed of the most precious thing they possess: their future of value.

Marquis isn't saying that a fetus *potentially* has a future of value, but that a fetus *presently* has a future of value. Having a potential future of value means I could go on to have a future of value or I could go on to not have a future of value. But that's not what Marquis is saying. Marquis is saying the fetus presently has a future of value. A remarkable psychological fact about us is that we find our way to value—not, necessarily, in an objective sense, as though we always pursue the things we should from God's vantage point; rather, we pursue the things we subjectively find ourselves interested in.

A fetus will go on to fill up his or her life with value. This is what we think adults go on to do.

Marquis is making the utterly uncontroversial psychological claim that a fetus will go on to fill up his or her life with value. This is what we think adults go on to do— whether they collect stamps, or follow the NBA, or spend time with their family, or travel the world, and so on, the point is that they find their way to what they value. It is no different with fetuses.

Marquis writes:

The future of a standard fetus includes a set of experiences, projects, activities, and such, which are identical with the futures of adult human beings and are identical with the futures of young children.

All this to say: a fetus doesn't possess this future of value potentially any more than an adult possesses his or her future of value potentially. Maybe *what* we value goes on to change, but even if there's a change, the valuing remains, just based on different things.

A fetus doesn't merely potentially have a future of value, just like an adult doesn't merely potentially have a future of value. It's a safe assumption that adults who aren't seriously unwell (in terms of health) will go on to derive value in life. The same goes for fetuses.

Marquis has made the case that the same thing that makes killing an adult wrong is what makes killing a fetus wrong. If any of us are killed, we are deprived of a future of value. Killing a fetus is the same, Marquis thinks. From a unified theory about the wrongness of killing comes the result that the same thing that makes killing an adult wrong is what makes killing a fetus wrong.

He's in essence saying: "See that activity that you and I and everyone else thinks is so very wrong? Abortion is like *that*." If he's right, it would mean abortion is seriously immoral.

Berny Belvedere is a professor of philosophy and a writer based in Miami, FL. He is also the editor-in-chief of *ARC*.

Julie Hirschfield Davis

How New Abortion Restrictions Would Affect Women's Health Care

Washington—A Trump administration proposal to bar federally funded family planning facilities from providing or referring patients for abortions is aimed at forcing organizations like Planned Parenthood to make a simple choice: cease offering abortion services or lose some of their government money.

But the proposed rules, which the Department of Health and Human Services submitted Thursday night, have raised complicated questions about the fate of Planned Parenthood and other reproductive health organizations that provide both family planning and abortion services—and the potential health effects on women who depend on such providers for basic care.

At issue are the regulations surrounding Title X, the 1970 law that created the federal family planning program. The statute already bans direct funding of abortion, but many organizations that provide abortions, including Planned Parenthood, use Title X money to subsidize other women's health services, such as dispensing birth control and providing cancer screenings. The proposal—a top priority of social conservatives who are staunch supporters of President Trump—seeks to end that commingling, or at least make it more difficult for reproductive health providers to do both.

To qualify for Title X money under the new policy, an organization would have to have "a bright line of physical as well as financial separation" between family planning programs and facilities where abortion is "performed, supported, or referred for as a method of family planning," according to a summary of the proposal obtained by *The New York Times*.

Sarah Huckabee Sanders, the White House press secretary, said in a statement that the proposal fulfilled Mr. Trump's "promise to continue to improve women's health and ensure that federal funds are not used to fund the abortion industry in violation of the law."

The changes could have real-life effects on the four million women who receive birth control and basic preventive services from federally subsidized providers.

How Planned Parenthood Says the Proposal Would Affect Women

Planned Parenthood and its supporters say the move would essentially bar the organization from receiving Title X funding, costing millions of women throughout the United States access to basic care, including contraceptives and screenings for cancer and sexually transmitted diseases. The organization says it has no intention of ceasing to provide abortions or referrals as part of its reproductive health services.

"This is a far-reaching attack and attempt to take away women's basic rights and reproductive rights, period," said Dawn Laguens, the group's executive vice president and chief executive.

Social conservative activists who pushed hard for the change appeared to agree, saying the organization would lose access to $60 million in federal funding under the new rules.

"Planned Parenthood and other abortion centers will now have to choose between dropping their abortion services from any location that gets Title X dollars and moving those abortion operations off-site," said Tony Perkins, the president of the Family Research Council. "Either way, this will loosen the group's hold on tens of millions of tax dollars."

Because Planned Parenthood has an outsize role in providing federally subsidized family planning services—it serves 41 percent of women who receive them—cutting the organization off from Title X money could have major consequences. An analysis in the journal Health Affairs found that in ⅔ of the 491 counties in which they are located, Planned Parenthood health centers serve at least

½ of all women obtaining contraceptive care from federally subsidized facilities. In ⅕ of the counties in which they are located, Planned Parenthood centers are the only federally funded option for obtaining family planning services.

The analysis of data compiled by the Guttmacher Institute found that, without Planned Parenthood facilities, "in the short term, it is doubtful that other providers could step up in a timely way to absorb the millions of women suddenly left without their preferred source of care."

Still, stripping Title X money from the organization would not decimate it. Three-quarters of the federal money its clinics receive comes through Medicaid, the federal health program for the poor. The largest effect would most likely be felt by women who do not have health insurance, particularly in states that did not expand Medicaid under the 2010 Affordable Care Act.

Abortion Opponents Said They Dropped the "Domestic Gag Rule." It's Not That Simple

The policy is modeled on a Reagan-era rule that required the same physical separation between abortion and family planning services that the Trump administration is seeking to mandate. But there is a difference: while the 1988 regulations specifically barred Title X facilities from even mentioning abortion as an option for pregnant women—a prohibition that came to be known as the "domestic gag rule"—the version proposed this week does not ban such counseling.

Abortion opponents said the Trump administration plan would not silence any family planning organization, and thus could not be regarded as a domestic gag rule.

The proposal is "a recognition that when providers provide women with the real facts about abortion, there's nothing to fear from that information," said Steven H. Aden, the general counsel of Americans United for Life, "and that ordinarily women will choose not to engage in abortion. The old rule was both obsolete and unnecessary."

But Democrats and abortion rights advocates said the practical result of the proposal would be to silence medical caregivers the same way that an explicit gag rule would because they would no longer be allowed to refer women to providers that perform abortions.

"It is a distinction without a difference," said Kashif Syed, a senior analyst at the Planned Parenthood Federation of America. "Blocking doctors from telling patients where they can get specific health services in this country is the very definition of a gag rule."

The policy, according to the summary, would also scrap a requirement imposed by the Clinton administration, which rescinded the Reagan rules in 1994, that Title X providers give patients information about abortion.

One Near Certainty: Legal Challenges

When President Ronald Reagan issued similar guidelines in 1988, they were swiftly blocked in court, prompting a battle that went all the way to the Supreme Court. In its 1991 ruling in *Rust v. Sullivan*, the Supreme Court upheld the Title X restrictions in a 5-4 decision. The court rejected the plaintiffs' contention that the policy violated the free-speech rights of clinic employees and the constitutional rights of patients to choose whether to end a pregnancy.

On Friday, officials at Planned Parenthood said they would have to wait to see the text of the proposed Trump administration rules before determining whether to bring a similar legal challenge. But they did not rule out the possibility.

"We will do everything we can to fight for our patients," said Carrie Flaxman, Planned Parenthood's deputy director of public policy litigation.

Governor Jay Inslee of Washington State, a Democrat, said the state's attorney general was looking into "our legal options."

"If this administration insists on weaponizing the Title X program, I will work with our legislative leaders to make sure that no matter what happens in DC, every woman in Washington State has access to all the family planning and health care services she needs," he said in a statement.

Proponents of the policy said they were confident that their side would prevail in any legal confrontation.

"The constitutionality of this approach has been tried and tested and affirmed by the United States Supreme Court," said Mr. Aden, who added that he anticipated "a big court fight."

JULIE HIRSCHFIELD DAVIS is a White House correspondent at *The New York Times*. She has covered politics from Washington for 19 years, writing on Congress, three presidential campaigns, and three presidents.

EXPLORING THE ISSUE

Should Access to Abortions Be Restricted?

Critical Thinking and Reflection

1. What arguments are made for restricting abortion in the United States?
2. What arguments are made for not restricting abortion in the United States?
3. Do you believe the government should be involved in abortion policy? Why or why not?
4. Is being a "person" different from being a "human being"? Why does this question matter?
5. When does human life begin? Is an eight-month fetus essentially different from a two-minute-old baby? If so, how? If not, what does that mean for policy moving forward?

Is There Common Ground?

There are some areas where common ground can be found. They include help for women who decide not to abort, such as medical assistance during pregnancy and after birth, care for their babies, assistance in housing, and job searches for the mothers. Pro-lifers would also like greater information about child development in the womb, so that women can make a more informed decision about whether to abort. Likewise, we see more legislation aimed at disclosing medical issues faced by women who have had abortions. Pro-choicers would like more information to be given to young people about methods of birth control, to which pro-lifers would rejoin that information about the advantages of "waiting until marriage" would be better. If *Roe v. Wade* is ever overturned, still other areas of common ground might be found in various states, such as banning late-term abortions, favored by large majorities of Americans.

Yet there are other areas where there can simply be no common ground. When it comes to abortions that are not medically necessary, for example, it will be difficult to convince the two sides to come to any meaningful middle point. The main issue is the absence of firm data or agreement on when life begins and at what stage a fetus is viable. If such information could be universally proven, it may be easier to convince the two sides of the argument to find neutral ground. But as the political environment stands today, it is hard to imagine circumstances in which an individual who sees an action as murder and another who views the same action as free choice will be able to agree on much of anything.

Additional Resources

Jack M. Balkin, *What Roe v. Wade Should Have Said* (New York University Press, 2005).

Francis J. Beckwith, *Defending Life: A Moral and Legal Case against Abortion Choice* (Cambridge University Press, 2007).

Barbara H. Craig and David M. O'Brien, *Abortion and American Politics* (Chatham House, 1993).

Peter C. Hoffer, *The Abortion Rights Controversy in America: A Legal Reader* (University of North Carolina Press, 2004).

William Saletan, *Bearing Right: How Conservatives Won the Abortion War* (University of California Press, 2000).

Internet References . . .

Americans United for Life

www.aul.org

Center for Disease Control Abortion Surveillance

www.cdc.gov/mmwr/preview/mmwrhtml/ss6208a1.
htm?s_cid=ss6208a1_w

National Abortion Federation

www.prochoice.org

National Right to Life

www.nrlc.org

Planned Parenthood

www.plannedparenthood.org

Selected, Edited, and with Issue Framing Material by:
William J. Miller, *Campus Labs*®

ISSUE

Is Lethal Injection as a Method of Execution Still Constitutional?

YES: **Samuel Alito**, from *"Glossip v. Gross,"* United States Supreme Court (2015)

NO: **Sonia Sotomayor**, from *"Glossip v. Gross,"* United States Supreme Court (2015)

Learning Outcomes
After reading this issue, you will be able to:
• List reasons advocates have for supporting capital punishment.   • List reasons opponents have for not supporting capital punishment.   • Assess the meaning of cruel and unusual punishment.   • Explain the new processes of lethal injection used in some states.   • Assess the immediate future of capital punishment in the United States.

ISSUE SUMMARY

YES: Supreme Court Justice Samuel Alito argues that lethal injection remains a viable and constitutional method of execution despite some states experimenting with different protocols given the inability to acquire sodium thiopental or pentobarbital.

NO: Writing for the minority, Justice Sonia Sotomayor argued that she believes capital punishment, in any form, likely violates the Eighth Amendment protection against cruel and unusual punishment. As such, too much responsibility is being placed on petitioners to demonstrate certain drugs are not available, leading to a slippery slope of possible execution methods.

The Eighth Amendment to the United States Constitution states: "Excessive bail shall not be required, nor excessive fines imposed, nor cruel and unusual punishments inflicted." Whenever the Supreme Court rules on a question surrounding capital punishment, it typically examines from the lens of cruel and unusual punishment. In the issue at hand, we are focusing on whether a particular manner of executing an individual is constitutional—not whether the death penalty itself is (or should continue to be).

In Wilkerson v. Utah, the Court stated: "Difficulty would attend the effort to define with exactness the extent of the constitutional provision which provides that cruel and unusual punishments shall not be inflicted; but it is safe to affirm that punishments of torture [such as drawing and quartering, embowelling alive, beheading, public dissecting, and burning alive], and all others in the same line of unnecessary cruelty, are forbidden by that amendment to the Constitution." In thus upholding capital punishment inflicted by a firing squad, the Court not only looked to traditional practices, but also examined the history of executions in the territory concerned, the military practice, and current writings on the death penalty. The Court next approved, under the Fourteenth Amendment's due process clause rather than under the Eighth Amendment, electrocution as a permissible method of administering punishment. Many years later, a divided Court, assuming the applicability of the Eighth Amendment to the States, held that a second electrocution following a mechanical failure at the first, which injured but did not kill the condemned man, did not violate the proscription.

Thus, the Supreme Court has a clear history of ruling on individual methods of execution. In some cases, such as lethal gas and the electric chair, states have turned away from methods before the Supreme Court ultimately ruled on their constitutionality. Skeptics will argue this occurred to keep the Court from possibly being able to use potentially cruel mechanisms as a means for ruling all forms of capital punishment unconstitutional. While electrocution, hanging, the gas chamber, and the firing squad are options in some states, more than 30 states authorize lethal injections with over 1250 individuals killed by lethal injection in the United States since 1976. But, today, even the lethal injection is under scrutiny.

Why is it so hard to kill someone via lethal injection? After all, veterinarians manage to euthanize pets rapidly every day, with minimal discomfort. Why aren't those drugs used in executions? Prison officials think the same way. The problem, however, is not that these drugs can't be used on humans, for the most part. It's with supply. Nearly every drug that prison officials turn to for lethal injections has been restricted from that use by manufacturers.

Until 2009, most states used a three-drug combination for lethal injections: an anesthetic (usually sodium thiopental, until pentobarbital was introduced at the end of 2010), pancuronium bromide (a paralytic agent, also called Pavulon), and potassium chloride (stops the heart and causes death). In 2011, however, Hospira Pharmaceuticals, the only U.S. manufacturer of sodium thiopental, stopped making the drug because of its use in executions. That same year, the European Union banned the export of sodium thiopental as well as other barbiturate drugs used in executions, ruling that companies had to ensure any exports would not be used for lethal injections. Pentobarbital, the barbiturate often used in animal euthanasia, was covered under the ban. Due to drug shortages, states have adopted new lethal injection methods including the following:

- Eight states have used a single-drug method for executions--a lethal dose of an anesthetic (Arizona, Georgia, Idaho, Missouri, Ohio, South Dakota, Texas, and Washington). Six other states have at one point or another announced plans to use a one-drug protocol, but have not carried out such an execution (Arkansas, California, Kentucky, Louisiana, North Carolina, and Tennessee).
- Fourteen states have used pentobarbital in executions: Alabama, Arizona, Delaware, Florida,

Georgia, Idaho, Mississippi, Missouri, Ohio, Oklahoma, South Carolina, South Dakota, Texas, and Virginia. Five additional states plan to use pentobarbital: Kentucky, Louisiana, Montana, North Carolina, and Tennessee. Colorado includes pentobarbital as a backup drug in its lethal-injection procedure.
- Seven states have used **midazolam** as the first drug in the three-drug protocol: Florida, Ohio, Oklahoma, Alabama, Virginia, Arkansas, and Tennessee. Oklahoma used midazolam in the botched execution of Clayton Lockett in April 2014, and Lockett died after the procedure was halted. Alabama's use of midazolam in the execution of Ronald Smith in December 2016, resulted in nearly fifteen minutes of Smith heaving and gasping for breath. Arkansas's use of use midazolam in four executions in April 2017 raised concerns and in the execution of Kenneth Williams, witnesses reported coughing, convulsing, lurching and jerking. In January 2017, Florida abandoned its use of midazolam as the first drug in its three-drug protocol and replaced it with etomidate. Two states have used midazolam in a two-drug protocol consisting of midazolam and hydromorphone: Ohio (Dennis McGuire) and Arizona (Joseph Wood). Both of those executions, which were carried out in 2014, were prolonged and accompanied by the prisoners' gasping for breath. After its botched execution of McGuire, Ohio abandoned its use of midazolam in a two-drug protocol, but then in October 2016 decided to keep midazolam in a three-drug protocol. In December 2016, Arizona abandoned its use of midazolam in either a two-drug or a three-drug protocol. Three states have, at some point, proposed using midazolam in a two-drug protocol (Louisiana, Kentucky, and Oklahoma) but none of those states has followed through with that formula. Some states have proposed multiple protocols. Missouri administered midazolam to inmates as a sedative before the official execution protocol began.
- Nebraska first used fentanyl in the August 14, 2018 execution of Carey Dean Moore. Nevada has also announced that they will use fentanyl in combination with other drugs to carry out executions.
- At least ten states have either used or intend to use compounding pharmacies to obtain their drugs for lethal injection. **South Dakota** carried out 2 executions in October 2012, obtaining drugs from compounders. Missouri first used pentobarbital from a compounding pharmacy in the November 20, 2013 execution of Joseph Franklin. Texas first used pentobarbital from a compounding pharmacy in the execution of Michael Yowell

on October 9, 2013. Georgia used drugs from an unnamed compounding pharmacy for an execution on June 17, 2014. Oklahoma has used drugs from compounding pharmacies in executions, including in the botched execution of Lockett. Virginia first used compounded pentobarbital obtained through the Texas Department of Criminal Justice in the execution of Alfredo Prieto on October 1, 2015. Ohio announced plans to obtain drugs from compounding pharmacies in October 2013. In March 2014, Mississippi announced plans to use pentobarbital from a compounding pharmacy. Documents released in January 2014, show that Louisiana had contacted a compounding pharmacy regarding execution drugs, but it is unclear whether the drugs were obtained there. Pennsylvania may have obtained drugs from a compounder, but has not used them. Colorado sent out inquiries to compounding pharmacies for lethal injection drugs, but all executions are on hold.

- In federal executions, the method is lethal injection, which was the method used in all three of the federal executions in the modern era have been by lethal injection carried out in a federal facility in Indiana. Apparently, a three-drug combination was used, though prison officials did not reveal the exact ingredients. The U.S. Military has not carried out any executions since reinstatement. It plans to use lethal injection.

The supply problem highlights a long-standing issue with the medicalization of the death penalty: Doctors are not, generally speaking, on board. The American Medical Association (AMA) opposes physician involvement in capital punishment, as does the American Board of Anesthesiology (ABA). "Patients should never confuse the death chamber with the operating room, lethal doses of execution drugs with anesthetic drugs, or the executioner with the anesthesiologist," J. Jeffrey Andrews, the secretary of the AMA, wrote in a commentary in May 2014. "Physicians should not be expected to act in ways that violate the ethics of medical practice, even if these acts are legal. Anesthesiologists are healers, not executioners."

While prisons can often find physicians to preside over executions, the involvement of the medical profession in executions does not always proceed smoothly. In 2006, executions in California halted when two anesthesiologists resigned from participation in the execution of Michael Morales. They quit after finding out that they would be expected to intervene directly if the execution procedure went wrong. "The Morales case unearthed a nagging paradox. The people most knowledgeable about the process of lethal injection—doctors, particularly anesthesiologists—are often reluctant to impart their insights and skills," wrote Deborah Denno, a professor at the Fordham University School of Law, in a 2007 paper on medicine and the death penalty.

A doctor was presiding over the June 2014 execution of Clayton D. Lockett, who died of heart failure 43 minutes after Oklahoma prison officials began his execution. But a medical technician was doing the actual procedure. Witnesses reported that it took nearly an hour of poking and prodding before the technician gave up on setting a catheter in Lockett's arms, legs, or feet, and instead tried to place a line through the femoral artery. An independent autopsy commissioned by the condemned man's lawyers found that the line was not placed properly, perhaps explaining why Lockett appeared to wake up after the first sedative drug was injected.

Thus, it is perhaps not surprising to know that the Supreme Court has taken a renewed interest in the constitutionality of lethal injection protocols across the country. In the following selections, Supreme Court Justice Samuel Alito argues that lethal injection remains a viable and constitutional method of execution despite some states experimenting with different protocols given the inability to acquire sodium thiopental or pentobarbital. While writing for the minority, Justice Sonia Sotomayor believes capital punishment, in any form, likely violates the Eighth Amendment protection against cruel and unusual punishment. As such, too much responsibility is being placed on petitioners to demonstrate certain drugs are not available, leading to a slippery slope of possible execution methods.

YES ↵

Samuel Alito

Glossip v. Gross

Prisoners sentenced to death in the State of Oklahoma filed an action in federal court under Rev. Stat. §1979, 42 U.S. C. §1983, contending that the method of execution now used by the State violates the Eighth Amendment because it creates an unacceptable risk of severe pain. They argue that midazolam, the first drug employed in the State's current three-drug protocol, fails to render a person insensate to pain. After holding an evidentiary hearing, the District Court denied four prisoners' application for a preliminary injunction, finding that they had failed to prove that midazolam is ineffective. The Court of Appeals for the Tenth Circuit affirmed and accepted the District Court's finding of fact regarding midazolam's efficacy.

For two independent reasons, we also affirm. First, the prisoners failed to identify a known and available alternative method of execution that entails a lesser risk of pain, a requirement of all Eighth Amendment method-of-execution claims. See *Baze v. Rees,* 553 U.S. 35, 61 (2008) (plurality opinion). Second, the District Court did not commit clear error when it found that the prisoners failed to establish that Oklahoma's use of a massive dose of midazolam in its execution protocol entails a substantial risk of severe pain.

I
A

The death penalty was an accepted punishment at the time of the adoption of the Constitution and the Bill of Rights. In that era, death sentences were usually carried out by hanging. The Death Penalty in America: Current Controversies 4 (H. Bedau ed. 1997). Hanging remained the standard method of execution through much of the 19th century, but that began to change in the century's later years. See *Baze, supra,* at 41–42. In the 1880's, the Legislature of the State of New York appointed a commission to find "the most humane and practical method known to modern science of carrying into effect the sentence of death in capital cases." *In re Kemmler*, 136 U.S. 436, 444 (1890). The commission recommended electrocution, and in 1888, the Legislature enacted a law providing for

this method of execution. *Id.,* at 444–445. In subsequent years, other States followed New York's lead in the "'belief that electrocution is less painful and more humane than hanging.'" Baze, 553 U.S., at 42 (quoting *Malloy* v. *South Carolina,* 237 U.S. 180, 185 (1915)).

. . .

After *Gregg* reaffirmed that the death penalty does not violate the Constitution, some States once again sought a more humane way to carry out death sentences. They eventually adopted lethal injection, which today is "by far the most prevalent method of execution in the United States." *Baze, supra,* at 42. Oklahoma adopted lethal injection in 1977, see 1977 Okla. Sess. Laws p. 89, and it eventually settled on a protocol that called for the use of three drugs: (1) sodium thiopental, "a fast-acting barbiturate sedative that induces a deep, comalike unconsciousness when given in the amounts used for lethal injection," (2) a paralytic agent, which "inhibits all muscular-skeletal movements and, by paralyzing the diaphragm, stops respiration," and (3) potassium chloride, which "interferes with the electrical signals that stimulate the contractions of the heart, inducing cardiac arrest." *Baze, supra,* at 44; see also Brief for Respondents 9. By 2008, at least 30 of the 36 States that used lethal injection employed that particular three-drug protocol. 553 U.S., at 44.

While methods of execution have changed over the years, "[t]his Court has never invalidated a State's chosen procedure for carrying out a sentence of death as the infliction of cruel and unusual punishment." *Id.,* at 48. In *Wilkerson* v. *Utah,* 99 U.S. 130, 134–135 (1879), the Court upheld a sentence of death by firing squad. In *In re Kemmler, supra,* at 447–449, the Court rejected a challenge to the use of the electric chair. And the Court did not retreat from that holding even when presented with a case in which a State's initial attempt to execute a prisoner by electrocution was unsuccessful. *Louisiana ex rel. Francis* v. *Resweber,* 329 U.S. 459, 463–464 (1947) (plurality opinion). Most recently, in *Baze, supra,* seven Justices agreed that the three-drug protocol just discussed does not violate the Eighth Amendment.

. . .

Alito, Samuel. "*Glossip v. Gross,*" United States Supreme Court, October 2015.

B

Baze cleared any legal obstacle to use of the most common three-drug protocol that had enabled States to carry out the death penalty in a quick and painless fashion. But a practical obstacle soon emerged, as anti-death-penalty advocates pressured pharmaceutical companies to refuse to supply the drugs used to carry out death sentences. The sole American manufacturer of sodium thiopental, the first drug used in the standard three-drug protocol, was persuaded to cease production of the drug. After suspending domestic production in 2009, the company planned to resume production in Italy. Koppel, Execution Drug Halt Raises Ire of Doctors, Wall Street Journal, Jan. 25, 2011, p. A6. Activists then pressured both the company and the Italian Government to stop the sale of sodium thiopental for use in lethal injections in this country. Bonner, Letter from Europe: Drug Company in Cross Hairs of Death Penalty Opponents, N. Y. Times, Mar. 30, 2011; Koppel, Drug Halt Hinders Executions in the U.S., Wall Street Journal, Jan. 22, 2011, p. A1. That effort proved successful, and in January 2011, the company announced that it would exit the sodium thiopental market entirely. See Hospira, Press Release, Hospira Statement Regarding Pentothal™ (sodium thiopental) Market Exit (Jan. 21, 2011).

After other efforts to procure sodium thiopental proved unsuccessful, States sought an alternative, and they eventually replaced sodium thiopental with pentobarbital, another barbiturate. In December 2010, Oklahoma became the first State to execute an inmate using pentobarbital. See Reuters, Chicago Tribune, New Drug Mix Used in Oklahoma Execution, Dec. 17 2010, p. 41. That execution occurred without incident, and States gradually shifted to pentobarbital as their supplies of sodium thiopental ran out. It is reported that pentobarbital was used in all of the 43 executions carried out in 2012. The Death Penalty Institute, Execution List 2012, online at www.deathpenaltyinfo.org/execution-list-2012 (all Internet materials as visited June 26, 2015, and available in Clerk of Court's case file). Petitioners concede that pentobarbital, like sodium thiopental, can "reliably induce and maintain a comalike state that renders a person insensate to pain" caused by administration of the second and third drugs in the protocol. Brief for Petitioners 2. And courts across the country have held that the use of pentobarbital in executions does not violate the Eighth Amendment. See, *e.g.*, *Jackson* v. *Danberg*, 656 F. 3d 157 (CA3 2011); *Beaty* v. *Brewer*, 649 F. 3d 1071 (CA9 2011); *DeYoung* v. *Owens*, 646 F. 3d 1319 (CA11 2011); *Pavatt* v. *Jones*, 627 F. 3d 1336 (CA10 2010).

Before long, however, pentobarbital also became unavailable. Anti-death-penalty advocates lobbied the Danish manufacturer of the drug to stop selling it for use in executions. See Bonner, *supra*. That manufacturer opposed the death penalty and took steps to block the shipment of pentobarbital for use in executions in the United States. Stein, New Obstacle to Death Penalty in U.S., Washington Post, July 3, 2011, p. A4. Oklahoma eventually became unable to acquire the drug through any means. The District Court below found that both sodium thiopental and pentobarbital are now unavailable to Oklahoma. App. 67–68.

C

Unable to acquire either sodium thiopental or pentobarbital, some States have turned to midazolam, a sedative in the benzodiazepine family of drugs. In October 2013, Florida became the first State to substitute midazolam for pentobarbital as part of a three-drug lethal injection protocol. Fernandez, Executions Stall As States Seek Different Drugs, N. Y. Times, Nov. 9, 2013, p. A1. To date, Florida has conducted 11 executions using that protocol, which calls for midazolam followed by a paralytic agent and potassium chloride. See Brief for State of Florida as *Amicus Curiae* 2–3; *Chavez* v. *Florida SP Warden*, 742 F. 3d 1267, 1269 (CA11 2014). In 2014, Oklahoma also substituted midazolam for pentobarbital as part of its three-drug protocol. Oklahoma has already used this three-drug protocol twice: to execute Clayton Lockett in April 2014 and Charles Warner in January 2015. (Warner was one of the four inmates who moved for a preliminary injunction in this case.)

The Lockett execution caused Oklahoma to implement new safety precautions as part of its lethal injection protocol. When Oklahoma executed Lockett, its protocol called for the administration of 100 milligrams of midazolam, as compared to the 500 milligrams that are currently required. On the morning of his execution, Lockett cut himself twice at "the bend of the elbow." App. 50. That evening, the execution team spent nearly an hour making at least one dozen attempts to establish intravenous (IV) access to Lockett's cardiovascular system, including at his arms and elsewhere on his body. The team eventually believed that it had established intravenous access through Lockett's right femoral vein, and it covered the injection access point with a sheet, in part to preserve Lockett's dignity during the execution. After the team administered the midazolam and a physician determined that Lockett was unconscious, the team next administered the paralytic agent (vecuronium bromide) and most of the potassium chloride. Lockett began to move and speak, at which point the physician lifted the sheet and determined that the IV had "infiltrated," which means that "the IV fluid, rather than entering Lockett's blood stream, had leaked into the tissue surrounding the IV access point." *Warner* v. *Gross*, 776 F. 3d 721, 725 (CA10 2015) (case below). The execution team stopped administering the remaining potassium chloride and terminated the execution about 33 minutes after the midazolam was first injected. About 10 minutes later, Lockett was pronounced dead.

. . .

II
A

In June 2014, after Oklahoma switched from pentobarbital to midazolam and executed Lockett, 21 Oklahoma death row inmates filed an action under 42 U.S. C. §1983 challenging the State's new lethal injection protocol. The complaint alleged that Oklahoma's use of midazolam violates the Eighth Amendment's prohibition of cruel and unusual punishment.

In November 2014, four of those plaintiffs—Richard Glossip, Benjamin Cole, John Grant, and Warner—filed a motion for a preliminary injunction. All four men had been convicted of murder and sentenced to death by Oklahoma juries. Glossip hired Justin Sneed to kill his employer, Barry Van Treese. Sneed entered a room where Van Treese was sleeping and beat him to death with a baseball bat. See *Glossip* v. *State*, 2007 OK CR 12, 157 P. 3d 143, 147–149. Cole murdered his 9-month-old daughter after she would not stop crying. Cole bent her body backwards until he snapped her spine in half. After the child died, Cole played video games. See *Cole* v. *State*, 2007 OK CR 27, 164 P. 3d 1089, 1092–1093. Grant, while serving terms of imprisonment totaling 130 years, killed Gay Carter, a prison food service supervisor, by pulling her into a mop closet and stabbing her numerous times with a shank. See *Grant* v. *State*, 2002 OK CR 36, 58 P. 3d 783, 789. Warner anally raped and murdered an 11-month-old girl. The child's injuries included two skull fractures, internal brain injuries, two fractures to her jaw, a lacerated liver, and a bruised spleen and lungs. See *Warner* v. *State*, 2006 OK CR 40, 144 P. 3d 838, 856–857.

The Oklahoma Court of Criminal Appeals affirmed the murder conviction and death sentence of each offender. Each of the men then unsuccessfully sought both state postconviction and federal habeas corpus relief. Having exhausted the avenues for challenging their convictions and sentences, they moved for a preliminary injunction against Oklahoma's lethal injection protocol.

B

In December 2014, after discovery, the District Court held a 3-day evidentiary hearing on the preliminary injunction motion. The District Court heard testimony from 17 witnesses and reviewed numerous exhibits. Dr. David Lubarsky, an anesthesiologist, and Dr. Larry Sasich, a doctor of pharmacy, provided expert testimony about midazolam for petitioners, and Dr. Roswell Evans, a doctor of pharmacy, provided expert testimony for respondents.

After reviewing the evidence, the District Court issued an oral ruling denying the motion for a preliminary injunction. The District Court first rejected petitioners' challenge under *Daubert* v. *Merrell Dow Pharmaceuticals, Inc.*, 509 U.S. 579 (1993), to the testimony of Dr. Evans. It concluded that Dr. Evans, the Dean of Auburn University's School of Pharmacy, was well qualified to testify about midazolam's properties and that he offered reliable testimony. The District Court then held that petitioners failed to establish a likelihood of success on the merits of their claim that the use of midazolam violates the Eighth Amendment. The court provided two independent reasons for this conclusion. First, the court held that petitioners failed to identify a known and available method of execution that presented a substantially less severe risk of pain than the method that the State proposed to use. Second, the court found that petitioners failed to prove that Oklahoma's protocol "presents a risk that is 'sure or very likely to cause serious illness and needless suffering,' amounting to 'an objectively intolerable risk of harm.'" App. 96 (quoting *Baze*, 553 U.S., at 50). The court emphasized that the Oklahoma protocol featured numerous safeguards, including the establishment of two IV access sites, confirmation of the viability of those sites, and monitoring of the offender's level of consciousness throughout the procedure.

The District Court supported its decision with findings of fact about midazolam. It found that a 500-milligram dose of midazolam "would make it a virtual certainty that any individual will be at a sufficient level of unconsciousness to resist the noxious stimuli which could occur from the application of the second and third drugs." App. 77. Indeed, it found that a 500-milligram dose alone would likely cause death by respiratory arrest within 30 minutes or an hour.

. . .

Oklahoma executed Warner on January 15, 2015, but we subsequently voted to grant review and then stayed the executions of Glossip, Cole, and Grant pending the resolution of this case. 574 U.S.___(2015).

. . .

IV

Our first ground for affirmance is based on petitioners' failure to satisfy their burden of establishing that any risk of harm was substantial when compared to a known and available alternative method of execution. In their amended complaint, petitioners proffered that the State could use sodium thiopental as part of a single-drug protocol. They have since suggested that it might also be constitutional for Oklahoma to use pentobarbital. But the District Court found that both sodium thiopental and pentobarbital are now unavailable to Oklahoma's Department of Corrections. The Court of Appeals affirmed that finding, and it is not clearly erroneous. On the contrary, the record shows that Oklahoma has been unable to procure those drugs despite a good-faith effort to do so.

Petitioners do not seriously contest this factual finding, and they have not identified any available drug or drugs that could be used in place of those that Oklahoma is now unable to obtain. Nor have they shown a risk of pain so great that other acceptable, available methods must be used. Instead, they argue that they need not identify a known and available method of execution that presents less risk. But this argument is inconsistent with the controlling opinion in *Baze*, 553 U.S., at 61, which imposed a requirement that the Court now follows.

Petitioners contend that the requirement to identify an alternative method of execution contravenes our pre-*Baze* decision in *Hill* v. *McDonough,* 547 U.S. 573 (2006), but they misread that decision. The portion of the opinion in *Hill* on which they rely concerned a question of civil procedure, not a substantive Eighth Amendment question. In *Hill*, the issue was whether a challenge to a method of execution must be brought by means of an application for a writ of habeas corpus or a civil action under §1983. *Id.,* at 576. We held that a method-of-execution claim must be brought under §1983 because such a claim does not attack the validity of the prisoner's conviction or death sentence. *Id.,* at 579–580. The United States as *amicus curiae* argued that we should adopt a special pleading requirement to stop inmates from using §1983 actions to attack, not just a particular means of execution, but the death penalty itself. To achieve this end, the United States proposed that an inmate asserting a method-of-execution claim should be required to plead an acceptable alternative method of execution. *Id.,* at 582. We rejected that argument because "[s]pecific pleading requirements are mandated by the Federal Rules of Civil Procedure, and not, as a general rule, through case-by-case determinations of the federal courts." *Ibid. Hill* thus held that §1983 alone does not impose a heightened pleading requirement. *Baze*, on the other hand, addressed the substantive elements of an Eighth Amendment method-of-execution claim, and it made clear that the Eighth Amendment requires a prisoner to plead and prove a known and available alternative. Because petitioners failed to do this, the District Court properly held that they did not establish a likelihood of success on their Eighth Amendment claim.

Readers can judge for themselves how much distance there is between the principal dissent's argument against requiring prisoners to identify an alternative and the view, now announced by JUSTICES BREYER and GINSBURG, that the death penalty is categorically unconstitutional. *Post*, p. __ (BREYER, J., dissenting). The principal dissent goes out of its way to suggest that a State would violate the Eighth Amendment if it used one of the methods of execution employed before the advent of lethal injection *Post*, at 30–31. And the principal dissent makes this suggestion even though the Court held in *Wilkerson* that this method (the firing squad) is constitutional and even though, in the words of the principal dissent, "there is some reason to think that it is relatively quick and painless." *Post*, at 30. Tellingly silent about the methods of execution most commonly used before States switched to lethal injection (the electric chair and gas chamber), the principal dissent implies that it would be unconstitutional to use a method that "could be seen as a devolution to a more primitive era." *Ibid.* If States cannot return to any of the "more primitive" methods used in the past and if no drug that meets with the principal dissent's approval is available for use in carrying out a death sentence, the logical conclusion is clear. But we have time and again reaffirmed that capital punishment is not *per se* unconstitutional. See, *e.g.*, *Baze*, 553 U.S., at 47; *id.*, at 87–88 (SCALIA, J., concurring in judgment); *Gregg*, 428 U.S., at 187 (joint opinion of Stewart, Powell, and Stevens, JJ.); *id.*, at 226 (White, J., concurring in judgment); *Resweber*, 329 U.S., at 464; *In re Kemmler*, 136 U.S., at 447; *Wilkerson*, 99 U.S., at 134–135. We decline to effectively overrule these decisions.

V

We also affirm for a second reason: The District Court did not commit clear error when it found that midazolam is highly likely to render a person unable to feel pain during an execution. We emphasize four points at the outset of our analysis.

First, we review the District Court's factual findings under the deferential "clear error" standard. This standard does not entitle us to overturn a finding "simply because [we are] convinced that [we] would have decided the case differently." *Anderson* v. *Bessemer City*, 470 U.S. 564, 573 (1985).

Second, petitioners bear the burden of persuasion on this issue. *Baze, supra,* at 41. Although petitioners expend great effort attacking peripheral aspects of Dr. Evans' testimony, they make little attempt to prove what is critical, *i.e.,* that the evidence they presented to the District Court establishes that the use of midazolam is sure or very likely to result in needless suffering.

Third, numerous courts have concluded that the use of midazolam as the first drug in a three-drug protocol is likely to render an inmate insensate to pain that might result from administration of the paralytic agent and potassium chloride. See, *e.g.,* 776 F. 3d 721 (case below affirming the District Court); *Chavez* v. *Florida SP Warden,* 742 F. 3d 1267 (affirming the District Court); *Banks* v. *State,* 150 So. 3d 797 (Fla. 2014) (affirming the lower court); *Howell* v. *State,* 133 So. 3d 511 (Fla. 2014) (same); *Muhammad* v. *State,* 132 So. 3d 176 (Fla. 2013) (same). (It is noteworthy that one or both of the two key witnesses in this case —Dr. Lubarsky for petitioners and Dr. Evans for respondents— were witnesses in the *Chavez, Howell,* and *Muhammad* cases.) "Where an intermediate court reviews, and affirms, a trial court's factual findings, this Court will not 'lightly overturn' the concurrent findings of the two lower courts." *Easley* v. *Cromartie,* 532 U.S. 234, 242 (2001). Our review is even more deferential where, as here, multiple trial courts have reached the same finding, and multiple appellate courts have affirmed those findings. Cf. *Exxon Co., U.S.A.* v. *Sofec, Inc.,* 517 U.S. 830, 841 (1996) (explaining that this Court "'cannot undertake to review concurrent findings of fact by two courts below in the absence of a very obvious and exceptional showing of error'" (quoting *Graver Tank & Mfg. Co.* v. *Linde Air Products Co.,* 336 U.S. 271, 275 (1949))).

Fourth, challenges to lethal injection protocols test the boundaries of the authority and competency of federal courts. Although we must invalidate a lethal injection protocol if it violates the Eighth Amendment, federal courts should not "embroil [themselves] in ongoing scientific controversies beyond their expertise." *Baze, supra,* at 51. Accordingly, an inmate challenging a protocol bears the burden to show, based on evidence presented to the court, that there is a substantial risk of severe pain.

. . .

Oklahoma has also adopted important safeguards to ensure that midazolam is properly administered. The District Court emphasized three requirements in particular: The execution team must secure both a primary and backup IV access site, it must confirm the viability of the IV sites, and it must continuously monitor the offender's level of consciousness. The District Court did not commit clear error in concluding that these safeguards help to minimize any risk that might occur in the event that midazolam does not operate as intended. Indeed, we concluded in *Baze* that many of the safeguards that Oklahoma employs— including the establishment of a primary and backup IV and the presence of personnel to monitor an inmate—help in significantly reducing the risk that an execution protocol will violate the Eighth Amendment. *Id.,* at 55–56. And many other safeguards that Oklahoma has adopted mirror those that the dissent in *Baze* complained were absent from Kentucky's protocol in that case. For example, the dissent argued that because a consciousness check before injection of the second drug "can reduce a risk of dreadful pain," Kentucky's failure to include that step in its procedure was unconstitutional. *Id.,* at 119 (opinion of GINSBURG, J.). The dissent also complained that Kentucky did not monitor the effectiveness of the first drug or pause between injection of the first and second drugs. *Id.,* at 120–121. Oklahoma has accommodated each of those concerns.

. . .

Petitioners' remaining arguments about midazolam all lack merit. First, we are not persuaded by petitioners' argument that Dr. Evans' testimony should have been rejected because of some of the sources listed in his report. Petitioners criticize two of the "selected references" that Dr. Evans cited in his expert report: the Web site drugs.com and a material safety data sheet (MSDS) about midazolam. Petitioners' argument is more of a *Daubert* challenge to Dr. Evans' testimony than an argument that the District Court's findings were clearly erroneous. The District Court concluded that Dr. Evans was "well-qualified to give the expert testimony that he gave" and that "his testimony was the product of reliable principles and methods reliably applied to the facts of this case." App. 75–76. To the extent that the reliability of Dr. Evans' testimony is even before us, the District Court's conclusion that his testimony was based on reliable sources is reviewed under the deferential "abuse-of-discretion" standard. *General Elec. Co.* v. *Joiner,* 522 U.S. 136, 142–143 (1997). Dr. Evans relied on multiple sources and his own expertise, and his testimony may not be disqualified simply because one source (drugs.com) warns that it "'is not intended for medical advice'" and another (the MSDS) states that its information is provided "'without any warranty, express or implied, regarding its correctness.'" Brief for Petitioners 36. Medical journals that both parties rely upon typically contain similar disclaimers. See, *e.g.,* Anesthesiology, Terms and Conditions of Use, online at http://anesthesiology.pubs.asahq.org/ss/terms.aspx ("None of the information on this Site shall be used to diagnose or treat any health problem or disease"). Dr. Lubarsky—petitioners' own expert—relied on an MSDS to argue that midazolam has a ceiling effect. And petitioners do not identify any incorrect statements from drugs.com on which Dr. Evans relied. In fact, although Dr. Sasich submitted a declaration to the Court of Appeals criticizing Dr. Evans' reference to drugs.com, that declaration does not identify a single fact from that site's discussion of midazolam that was materially inaccurate.

Second, petitioners argue that Dr. Evans' expert report contained a mathematical error, but we find this argument insignificant. Dr. Evans stated in his expert report that the lowest dose of midazolam resulting in human deaths, according to an MSDS, is 0.071 mg/kg delivered intravenously. App. 294. Dr. Lubarsky agreed with this statement. Specifically, he testified that fatalities have occurred in doses ranging from 0.04 to 0.07 mg/kg, and he stated that Dr. Evans' testimony to that effect was "a true statement" (though he added those fatalities occurred among the elderly). *Id.,* at 217. We do not understand petitioners to dispute the testimony of Dr. Evans and their own expert that 0.071 mg/kg is a potentially fatal dose of midazolam. Instead, they make much of the fact that the MSDS attached to Dr. Evans' report apparently contained a typographical error and reported the lowest toxic dose as 71 mg/kg. That Dr. Evans did not repeat that incorrect figure but instead reported the correct dose supports rather than undermines his testimony. In any event, the alleged error in the MSDS is irrelevant because the District Court expressly stated that it did not rely on the figure in the MSDS. See *id.,* at 75.

Third, petitioners argue that there is no consensus among the States regarding midazolam's efficacy because only four States (Oklahoma, Arizona, Florida, and Ohio) have used midazolam as part of an execution. Petitioners rely on the plurality's statement in *Baze* that "it is difficult to regard a practice as 'objectively intolerable' when it is in fact widely tolerated," and the plurality's emphasis on the fact that 36 States had adopted lethal injection and 30 States used the particular three-drug protocol at issue in that case.

553 U.S., at 53. But while the near-universal use of the particular protocol at issue in *Baze* supported our conclusion that this protocol did not violate the Eighth Amendment, we did not say that the converse was true, *i.e.,* that other protocols or methods of execution are of doubtful constitutionality. That argument, if accepted, would hamper the adoption of new and potentially more humane methods of execution and would prevent States from adapting to changes in the availability of suitable drugs.

Fourth, petitioners argue that difficulties with Oklahoma's execution of Lockett and Arizona's July 2014 execution of Joseph Wood establish that midazolam is sure or very likely to cause serious pain. We are not persuaded. Aside from the Lockett execution, 12 other executions have been conducted using the three-drug protocol at issue here, and those appear to have been conducted without any significant problems. See Brief for Respondents 32; Brief for State of Florida as *Amicus Curiae* 1. Moreover, Lockett was administered only 100 milligrams of midazolam, and Oklahoma's investigation into that execution concluded that the difficulties were due primarily to the execution team's inability to obtain an IV access site. And the Wood execution did not involve the protocol at issue here. Wood did not receive a single dose of 500 milligrams of midazolam; instead, he received fifteen 50-milligram doses over the span of two hours. Brief for Respondents 12, n. 9. And Arizona used a different two-drug protocol that paired midazolam with hydromorphone, a drug that is not at issue in this case. *Ibid.* When all of the circumstances are considered, the Lockett and Wood executions have little probative value for present purposes.

Finally, we find it appropriate to respond to the principal dissent's groundless suggestion that our decision is tantamount to allowing prisoners to be "drawn and quartered, slowly tortured to death, or actually burned at the stake." *Post,* at 28. That is simply not true, and the principal dissent's resort to this outlandish rhetoric reveals the weakness of its legal arguments.

VI

For these reasons, the judgment of the Court of Appeals for the Tenth Circuit is affirmed.

It is so ordered.

Samuel Alito is an associate justice of the United States Supreme Court. He was appointed in 2005 by President George W. Bush.

Sonia Sotomayor

 **NO**

Glossip v. Gross

Petitioners, three inmates on Oklahoma's death row, challenge the constitutionality of the State's lethal injection protocol. The State plans to execute petitioners using three drugs: midazolam, rocuronium bromide, and potassium chloride. The latter two drugs are intended to paralyze the inmate and stop his heart. But they do so in a torturous manner, causing burning, searing pain. It is thus critical that the first drug, midazolam, do what it is supposed to do, which is to render and keep the inmate unconscious. Petitioners claim that midazolam cannot be expected to perform that function, and they have presented ample evidence showing that the State's planned use of this drug poses substantial, constitutionally intolerable risks.

Nevertheless, the Court today turns aside petitioners' plea that they at least be allowed a stay of execution while they seek to prove midazolam's inadequacy. The Court achieves this result in two ways: first, by deferring to the District Court's decision to credit the scientifically unsupported and implausible testimony of a single expert witness; and second, by faulting petitioners for failing to satisfy the wholly novel requirement of proving the avail ability of an alternative means for their own executions.

On both counts the Court errs. As a result, it leaves petitioners exposed to what may well be the chemical equivalent of being burned at the stake.

I

A

The Eighth Amendment succinctly prohibits the infliction of "cruel and unusual punishments." Seven years ago, in *Baze* v. *Rees*, 553 U.S. 35 (2008), the Court addressed the application of this mandate to Kentucky's lethal injection protocol. At that time, Kentucky, like at least 29 of the 35 other States with the death penalty, utilized a series of three drugs to perform executions: (1) sodium thiopental, a "fast-acting barbiturate sedative that induces a deep, comalike unconsciousness when given in the amounts

used for lethal injection"; (2) pancuronium bromide, "a paralytic agent that inhibits all muscular-skeletal movements and . . . stops respiration"; and (3) potassium chloride, which "interferes with the electrical signals that stimulate the contractions of the heart, inducing cardiac arrest." *Id.*, at 44 (plurality opinion of ROBERTS, C. J.).

In *Baze*, it was undisputed that absent a "proper dose of sodium thiopental," there would be a "substantial, constitutionally unacceptable risk of suffocation from the administration of pancuronium bromide and pain from the injection of potassium chloride." *Id.*, at 53. That is because, if given to a conscious inmate, pancuronium bromide would leave him or her asphyxiated and unable to demonstrate "any outward sign of distress," while potassium chloride would cause "excruciating pain." *Id.*, at 71 (Stevens, J., concurring in judgment). But the Baze petitioners conceded that if administered as intended, Kentucky's method of execution would nevertheless "result in a humane death," *id.*, at 41 (plurality opinion), as the "proper administration" of sodium thiopental "eliminates any meaningful risk that a prisoner would experience pain from the subsequent injections of pancuronium and potassium chloride," *id.*, at 49. Based on that premise, the Court ultimately rejected the challenge to Kentucky's protocol, with the plurality opinion concluding that the State's procedures for administering these three drugs ensured there was no "objectively intolerable risk" of severe pain. *Id.*, at 61–62 (internal quotation marks omitted).

. . .

D

The District Court denied petitioners' motion for a preliminary injunction. It began by making a series of factual findings regarding the characteristics of midazolam and its use in Oklahoma's execution protocol. Most relevant here, the District Court found that "[t]he proper administration of 500 milligrams of midazolam . . . would make it a virtual certainty that an individual will be at a sufficient level of unconsciousness to resist the noxious stimuli which could occur from the application of the second and third drugs." *Id.*, at 77. Respecting petitioners' contention that there is a "ceiling effect which prevents an increase in dosage from having a corresponding incremental effect on anesthetic depth," the District Court concluded:

> "Dr. Evans testified persuasively . . . that whatever the ceiling effect of midazolam may be with respect to anesthesia, which takes effect at the spinal cord level, there is no ceiling effect with respect to the ability of a 500 milligram dose of midazolam to effectively paralyze the brain, a phenomenon which is not anesthesia but does have the effect of shutting down respiration and eliminating the individual's awareness of pain." *Id.*, at 78.

Having made these findings, the District Court held that petitioners had shown no likelihood of success on the merits of their Eighth Amendment claim for two independent reasons. First, it determined that petitioners had "failed to establish that proceeding with [their] execution[s] . . . on the basis of the revised protocol presents . . . 'an objectively intolerable risk of harm.'" *Id.*, at 96. Second, the District Court held that petitioners were unlikely to prevail because they had not identified any "'known and available alternative'" means by which they could be executed—a requirement it understood *Baze* to impose. *Id.*, at 97. The District Court concluded that the State "ha[d] affirmatively shown that sodium thiopental and pentobarbital, the only alternatives to which the [petitioners] have even alluded, are not available to the [State]." *Id.*, at 98.

. . .

A

To begin, Dr. Evans identified no scientific literature to support his opinion regarding midazolam's properties at higher-than-normal doses. Apart from a Material Safety Data Sheet that was relevant only insofar as it suggests that a low dose of midazolam may occasionally be toxic, see *ante*, at 27—an issue I discuss further below—Dr. Evans' testimony seems to have been based on the Web site www.drugs.com. The Court may be right that "petitioners do not identify any incorrect statements from drugs.com on which Dr. Evans relied." *Ante*, at 27. But that is because there were *no* statements from drugs.com that supported the critically disputed aspects of Dr. Evans' opinion. If anything, the Web site supported petitioners' contentions, as it expressly cautioned that midazolam

"[s]hould not be used alone for maintenance of anesthesia," App. H to Pet. for Cert. 6159, and contained no warning that an excessive dose of midazolam could "paralyze the brain," see *id.*, at 6528–6529.

Most importantly, nothing from drugs.com—or, for that matter, any other source in the record—corroborated Dr. Evans' key testimony that midazolam's ceiling effect is limited to the spinal cord and does not pertain to the brain. Indeed, the State appears to have disavowed Dr. Evans' spinal-cord theory, refraining from even mentioning it in its brief despite the fact that the District Court expressly relied on this testimony as the basis for finding that larger doses of midazolam will have greater anesthetic effects. App. 78. The Court likewise assiduously avoids defending this theory.

. . .

In sum, then, Dr. Evans' conclusions were entirely unsupported by any study or third-party source, contradicted by the extrinsic evidence proffered by petitioners, inconsistent with the scientific understanding of midazolam's properties, and apparently premised on basic logical errors. Given these glaring flaws, the District Court's acceptance of Dr. Evans' claim that 500 milligrams of midazolam would "paralyz[e] the brain" cannot be credited. This is not a case "[w]here there are two permissible views of the evidence," and the District Court chose one; rather, it is one where the trial judge credited "one of two or more witnesses" even though that witness failed to tell "a coherent and facially plausible story that is not contradicted by extrinsic evidence." *Anderson* v. *Bessemer City*, 470 U.S. 564, 574–575 (1985). In other words, this is a case in which the District Court clearly erred. See *ibid.*

B

Setting aside the District Court's erroneous factual finding that 500 milligrams of midazolam will necessarily "paralyze the brain," the question is whether the Court is nevertheless correct to hold that petitioners failed to demonstrate that the use of midazolam poses an "objectively intolerable *risk*" of severe pain. See *Baze*, 553 U.S., at 50 (plurality opinion) (internal quotation marks omitted). I would hold that they made this showing. That is because, in stark contrast to Dr. Evans, petitioners' experts were able to point to objective evidence indicating that midazolam cannot serve as an effective anesthetic that "render[s] a person insensate to pain caused by the second and third [lethal injection] drugs." *Ante*, at 23.

As observed above, these experts cited multiple sources supporting the existence of midazolam's ceiling effect. That evidence alone provides ample reason to doubt midazolam's efficacy. Again, to prevail on their claim, petitioners need only establish an intolerable *risk* of pain, not a certainty. See *Baze*, 553 U.S., at 50. Here, the State is attempting to use midazolam to produce an effect the drug has never previously been demonstrated to produce, and despite studies indicating that at some point increasing the dose will not actually increase the drug's effect. The State is thus proceeding in the face of a very real risk that the drug will not work in the manner it claims.

Moreover, and perhaps more importantly, the record provides good reason to think this risk is substantial. The Court insists that petitioners failed to provide "probative evidence" as to whether "midazolam's ceiling effect occurs below the level of a 500-milligram dose and at a point at which the drug does not have the effect of rendering a person insensate to pain." *Ante*, at 23. It emphasizes that Dr. Lubarsky was unable to say "at what dose the ceiling effect occurs," and could only estimate that it was "'[p]robably after about . . . 40 to 50 milligrams.'" *Ante*, at 23 (quoting App. 225).

But the precise dose at which midazolam reaches its ceiling effect is irrelevant if there is no dose at which the drug can, in the Court's words, render a person "insensate to pain." *Ante*, at 23. On this critical point, Dr. Lubarsky was quite clear. He explained that the drug "does not work to produce" a "lack of consciousness as noxious stimuli are applied," and is "not sufficient to produce a surgical plane of anesthesia in human beings." App. 204. He also noted that "[t]he drug would never be used and has never been used as a sole anesthetic to give anesthesia during a surgery," *id.*, at 223, and asserted that "the drug was not approved by the FDA as a sole anesthetic because after the use of fairly large doses that were sufficient to reach the ceiling effect and produce induction of unconscious ness, the patients responded to the surgery," *id.*, at 219. Thus, Dr. Lubarsky may not have been able to identify whether this effect would be reached at 40, 50, or 60 milligrams or some higher threshold, but he could specify that at no level would midazolam reliably keep an inmate unconscious once the second and third drugs were delivered.

. . .

This evidence was alone sufficient, but if one wanted further support for these conclusions it was provided by the Lockett and Wood executions. The procedural flaws that marred the Lockett execution created the conditions for an unintended (and grotesque) experiment on midazolam's efficacy. Due to problems with the IV line, Lockett was not fully paralyzed after the second and third drugs were administered. He had, however, been administered more than enough midazolam to "render an average person unconscious," as the District Court found. App. 57. When Lockett awoke and began to write and speak, he demonstrated the critical difference between midazolam's ability to render an inmate unconscious and its ability to maintain the inmate in that state. The Court insists that Lockett's execution involved "only 100 milligrams of midazolam," *ante*, at 28, but as explained previously, more is not necessarily better given midazolam's ceiling effect.

The Wood execution is perhaps even more probative. Despite being given over 750 milligrams of midazolam, Wood gasped and snorted for nearly two hours. These reactions were, according to Dr. Lubarsky, inconsistent with Wood being fully anesthetized, App. 177–178, and belie the claim that a lesser dose of 500 milligrams would somehow suffice. The Court attempts to distinguish the Wood execution on the ground that the timing of Arizona's administration of midazolam was different. *Ante*, at 28. But as Dr. Lubarsky testified, it did not "matter" whether in Wood's execution the "midazolam was introduced all at once or over . . . multiple doses," because "[t]he drug has a sufficient half life that the effect is cumulative." App. 220; see also Saari 253 (midazolam's "elimination half-life ranges from 1.7 to 3.5 h[ours]"). Nor does the fact that Wood's dose of midazolam was paired with hydromorphone rather than a paralytic and potassium chromide, see *ante*, at 29, appear to have any relevance—other than that the use of this analgesic drug may have meant that Wood did not experience the same degree of searing pain that an inmate executed under Oklahoma's protocol may face.

. . .

C

The Court not only disregards this record evidence of midazolam's inadequacy, but also fails to fully appreciate the procedural posture in which this case arises. Petitioners have not been accorded a full hearing on the merits of their claim. They were granted only an abbreviated evidentiary proceeding that began less than three months after the State issued its amended execution protocol; they did not even have the opportunity to present rebuttal evidence after Dr. Evans testified. They sought a preliminary injunction, and thus were not required to prove their claim, but only to show that they were likely to succeed on the merits. See *Winter* v. *Natural Resources Defense Council, Inc.*, 555 U.S. 7, 20 (2008); *Hill* v. *McDonough,* 547 U.S. 573, 584 (2006).

. . .

III

The Court's determination that the use of midazolam poses no objectively intolerable risk of severe pain is factually wrong. The Court's conclusion that petitioners' challenge also fails because they identified no available alternative means by which the State may kill them is legally indefensible.

A

This Court has long recognized that certain methods of execution are categorically off-limits. The Court first confronted an Eighth Amendment challenge to a method of execution in *Wilkerson* v. *Utah,* 99 U.S. 130 (1879). Although *Wilkerson* approved the particular method at issue—the firing squad—it made clear that "public dissection," "burning alive," and other "punishments of torture . . . in the same line of unnecessary cruelty, are forbidden by [the Eighth A]mendment to the Constitution." *Id.,* at 135–136. Eleven years later, in rejecting a challenge to the first proposed use of the electric chair, the Court again reiterated that "if the punishment prescribed for an offense against the laws of the State were manifestly cruel and unusual, as burning at the stake, crucifixion, breaking on the wheel, or the like, it would be the duty of the courts to adjudge such penalties to be within the constitutional prohibition." *In re Kemmler,* 136 U.S. 436, 446 (1890).

In the more than a century since, the Members of this Court have often had cause to debate the full scope of the Eighth Amendment's prohibition of cruel and unusual punishment. See, *e.g., Furman* v. *Georgia,* 408 U.S. 238 (1972). But there has been little dispute that it at the very least precludes the imposition of "barbarous physical punishments." *Rhodes* v. *Chapman,* 452 U.S. 337, 345 (1981); see, *e.g., Solem* v. *Helm,* 463 U.S. 277, 284 (1983); *id.,* at 312–313 (Burger, C. J., dissenting); *Baze,* 553 U.S., at 97–99 (THOMAS, J., concurring in judgment); *Harmelin* v. *Michigan,* 501 U.S. 957, 976 (1991) (opinion of SCALIA, J.). Nor has there been any question that the Amendment prohibits such "inherently barbaric punishments *under all circumstances.*" *Graham* v. *Florida,* 560 U.S. 48, 59 (2010)

(emphasis added). Simply stated, the "Eighth Amendment *categorically* prohibits the infliction of cruel and unusual punishments." *Penry* v. *Lynaugh,* 492 U.S. 302, 330 (1989) (emphasis added).

B

The Court today, however, would convert this categorical prohibition into a conditional one. A method of execution that is intolerably painful—even to the point of being the chemical equivalent of burning alive—will, the Court holds, be unconstitutional *if,* and only if, there is a "known and available alternative" method of execution. *Ante,* at 15. It deems *Baze* to foreclose any argument to the contrary. *Ante,* at 14.

Baze held no such thing. In the first place, the Court cites only the plurality opinion in *Baze* as support for its known-and-available-alternative requirement. See *ibid.* Even assuming that the *Baze* plurality set forth such a requirement—which it did not—none of the Members of the Court whose concurrences were necessary to sustain the *Baze* Court's judgment articulated a similar view. See 553 U.S., at 71–77, 87 (Stevens, J., concurring in judgment); *id.,* at 94, 99–107 (THOMAS, J., concurring in judgment); *id.,* at 107–108, 113 (BREYER, J., concurring in judgment). In general, "the holding of the Court may be viewed as that position taken by those Members who concurred in the judgments on the narrowest grounds." *Marks* v. *United States,* 430 U.S. 188, 193 (1977) (internal quotation marks omitted). And as the Court observes, *ante,* at 14, n. 2, the opinion of JUSTICE THOMAS, joined by JUSTICE SCALIA, took the broadest position with respect to the degree of intent that state officials must have in order to have violated the Eighth Amendment, concluding that only a method of execution deliberately designed to inflict pain, and not one simply designed with deliberate indifference to the risk of severe pain, would be unconstitutional. 553 U.S., at 94 (THOMAS, J., concurring in judgment). But this understanding of the Eighth Amendment's intent requirement is unrelated to, and thus not any broader or narrower than, the requirement the Court now divines from *Baze.* Because the position that a plaintiff challenging a method of execution under the Eighth Amendment must prove the availability of an alternative means of execution did not "represent the views of a majority of the Court," it was not the holding of the *Baze* Court. *CTS Corp.* v. *Dynamics Corp. of America,* 481 U.S. 69, 81 (1987).

In any event, even the *Baze* plurality opinion provides no support for the Court's proposition. To be sure, that opinion contains the following sentence: "[The condemned] must show that the risk is substantial when compared to the known and available alternatives." 553 U.S., at 61. But the meaning of that key sentence and the limits of the requirement it imposed are made clear by the sentence directly preceding it: "A stay of execution may not be granted *on grounds such as those asserted here* unless the condemned prisoner establishes that the State's lethal injection protocol creates a demonstrated risk of severe pain." *Ibid.* (emphasis added). In *Baze*, the very premise of the petitioners' Eighth Amendment claim was that they had "identified a significant risk of harm [in Kentucky's protocol] that [could] be eliminated by adopting alternative procedures." *Id.*, at 51. Their basic theory was that even if the risk of pain was only, say, 25%, that risk would be objectively intolerable if there was an obvious alternative that would reduce the risk to 5%. See Brief for Petitioners in *Baze* v. *Rees*, O. T. 2007, No. 07–5439, p. 29 ("In view of the severity of the pain risked and the ease with which it could be avoided, Petitioners should not have been required to show a high likelihood that they would suffer such pain . . ."). Thus, the "grounds . . . asserted" for relief in *Baze* were that the State's protocol was intolerably risky given the alternative procedures the State could have employed.

Addressing this claim, the *Baze* plurality clarified that "a condemned prisoner cannot successfully challenge a State's method of execution merely by showing a slightly or marginally safer alternative," 553 U.S., at 51; instead, to succeed in a challenge of this type, the comparative risk must be "substantial," *id.*, at 61. Nowhere did the plurality suggest that *all* challenges to a State's method of execution would require this sort of comparative-risk analysis. Recognizing the relevance of available alternatives is not at all the same as concluding that their absence precludes a claimant from showing that a chosen method carries objectively intolerable risks. If, for example, prison officials chose a method of execution that has a 99% chance of causing lingering and excruciating pain, certainly that risk would be objectively intolerable whether or not the officials ignored other methods in making this choice. Irrespective of the existence of alternatives, there are some risks "so grave that it violates contemporary standards of decency to expose *anyone* unwillingly to" them. *Helling* v. *McKinney*, 509 U.S. 25, 36 (1993) (emphasis in original).

That the *Baze* plurality's statement regarding a condemned inmate's ability to point to an available alternative means of execution pertained only to challenges premised on the existence of such alternatives is further evidenced by the opinion's failure to distinguish or even mention the Court's unanimous decision in

Hill v. *McDonough,* 547 U.S. 573. *Hill* held that a §1983 plaintiff challenging a State's method of execution need not "identif[y] an alternative, authorized method of execution." *Id.*, at 582. True, as the Court notes, *ante*, at 14–15, *Hill* did so in the context of addressing §1983's pleading standard, rejecting the proposed alternative-means requirement because the Court saw no basis for the "[i]mposition of heightened pleading requirements." 547 U.S., at 582. But that only confirms that the Court in *Hill* did not view the availability of an alternative means of execution as an element of an Eighth Amendment claim: If it had, then requiring the plaintiff to plead this element would not have meant imposing a heightened standard at all, but rather would have been entirely consistent with "traditional pleading requirements." *Ibid.*; see *Ashcroft* v. *Iqbal*, 556 U.S. 662, 678 (2009). The *Baze* plurality opinion should not be understood to have so carelessly tossed aside *Hill*'s underlying premise less than two years later.

. . .

D

In concocting this additional requirement, the Court is motivated by a desire to preserve States' ability to conduct executions in the face of changing circumstances. See *ante*, at 4–6, 27–28. It is true, as the Court details, that States have faced "practical obstacle[s]" to obtaining lethal injection drugs since *Baze* was decided. *Ante*, at 4. One study concluded that recent years have seen States change their protocols "with a frequency that is unprecedented among execution methods in this country's history." Denno, Lethal Injection Chaos Post-*Baze*, 102 Geo. L. J. 1331, 1335 (2014).

But why such developments compel the Court's imposition of further burdens on those facing execution is a mystery. Petitioners here had no part in creating the shortage of execution drugs; it is odd to punish them for the actions of pharmaceutical companies and others who seek to disassociate themselves from the death penalty—actions which are, of course, wholly lawful. Nor, certainly, should these rapidly changing circumstances give us any greater confidence that the execution methods ultimately selected will be sufficiently humane to satisfy the Eighth Amendment. Quite the contrary. The execution protocols States hurriedly devise as they scramble to locate new and untested drugs, see *supra*, at 3, are all the more likely to be cruel and unusual—presumably, these drugs would have been the States' first choice were they in fact more effective. But see Denno, The Lethal Injection

Quandry: How Medicine Has Dismantled the Death Penalty, 76 Ford. L. Rev. 49, 65–79 (2007) (describing the hurried and unreasoned process by which States first adopted the original three-drug protocol). Courts' review of execution methods should be more, not less, searching when States are engaged in what is in effect human experimentation.

It is also worth noting that some condemned inmates may read the Court's surreal requirement that they identify the means of their death as an invitation to propose methods of executions less consistent with modern sensibilities. Petitioners here failed to meet the Court's new test because of their assumption that the alternative drugs to which they pointed, pentobarbital and sodium thiopental, were available to the State. See *ante*, at 13–14. This was perhaps a reasonable assumption, especially given that neighboring Texas and Missouri still to this day continue to use pentobarbital in executions. See The Death Penalty Institute, Execution List 2015, online at www.deathpenaltyinfo.org/execution-list-2015 (as visited June 26, 2015, and available in the Clerk of the Court's case file).

In the future, however, condemned inmates might well decline to accept States' current reliance on lethal injection. In particular, some inmates may suggest the firing squad as an alternative. Since the 1920's, only Utah has utilized this method of execution. See S. Banner, The Death Penalty 203 (2002); Johnson, Double Murderer Executed by Firing Squad in Utah, N. Y. Times, June 19, 2010, p. A12. But there is evidence to suggest that the firing squad is significantly more reliable than other methods, including lethal injection using the various combinations of drugs thus far developed. See A. Sarat, Gruesome Spectacles: Botched Executions and America's Death Penalty, App. A, p. 177 (2014) (calculating that while 7.12% of the 1,054 executions by lethal injection between 1900 and 2010 were "botched," none of the 34 executions by firing squad had been). Just as important, there is some reason to think that it is relatively quick and painless. See Banner, *supra*, at 203.

Certainly, use of the firing squad could be seen as a devolution to a more primitive era. See *Wood* v. *Ryan*, 759 F. 3d 1076, 1103 (CA9 2014) (Kozinski, C. J.,

dissenting from denial of rehearing en banc). That is not to say, of course, that it would therefore be unconstitutional. But lethal injection represents just the latest iteration of the States' centuries-long search for "neat and non-disfiguring homicidal methods." C. Brandon, The Electric Chair: An Unnatural American History 39 (1999) (quoting Editorial, New York Herald, Aug. 10, 1884); see generally Banner, *supra*, at 169–207. A return to the firing squad—and the blood and physical violence that comes with it—is a step in the opposite direction. And some might argue that the visible brutality of such a death could conceivably give rise to its own Eighth Amendment concerns. See *Campbell* v. *Wood*, 511 U.S. 1119, 1121–1123 (1994) (Blackmun, J., dissenting from denial of stay of execution and certiorari); *Glass* v. *Louisiana*, 471 U.S. 1080, 1085 (1985) (Brennan, J., dissenting from denial of certiorari). At least from a condemned inmate's perspective, however, such visible yet relatively painless violence may be vastly preferable to an excruciatingly painful death hidden behind a veneer of medication. The States may well be reluctant to pull back the curtain for fear of how the rest of us might react to what we see. But we deserve to know the price of our collective comfort before we blindly allow a State to make condemned inmates pay it in our names.

* * *

"By protecting even those convicted of heinous crimes, the Eighth Amendment reaffirms the duty of the government to respect the dignity of all persons." *Roper* v. *Simmons*, 543 U.S. 551, 560 (2005). Today, however, the Court absolves the State of Oklahoma of this duty. It does so by misconstruing and ignoring the record evidence regarding the constitutional insufficiency of midazolam as a sedative in a three-drug lethal injection cocktail, and by imposing a wholly unprecedented obligation on the condemned inmate to identify an available means for his or her own execution. The contortions necessary to save this particular lethal injection protocol are not worth the price. I dissent.

SONIA SOTOMAYOR is an associate justice of the United States Supreme Court. She was appointed in 2009 by President Barack Obama.

EXPLORING THE ISSUE

Is Lethal Injection as a Method of Execution Still Constitutional?

Critical Thinking and Reflection

1. Do you believe in capital punishment? Why or why not?
2. What purpose do you believe capital punishment serves?
3. Why do you believe some states have abandoned capital punishment?
4. What do you believe would happen if capital punishment was found to be unconstitutional?
5. Do you believe lethal injection is an improvement on previous methods of capital punishment? Why or why not?

Is There Common Ground?

When it comes to an issue like capital punishment, there is little room for common ground. Societally, we either accept the right of the state to take the life of an individual who has been convicted and sentenced by a jury of peers, or we do not. Capital punishment plays out like most moral-based issues with strong advocates on both sides and fewer individuals waffling between the two sides. One either believes the state possesses a right to end the life of another as punishment for the most severe crimes, or it does not. While we have seen middle ground reached on issues pertaining to what crimes should be capital punishment eligible, the use of capital punishment against juveniles and the mentally handicapped, and the appeal rights of inmates condemned to die, we have not been able to reach it on the issue at large.

Most importantly for the question at hand is the reality that today the method of execution is not as debated as the presence of capital punishment at all. In the past, America has witnessed debates over the "cruel and unusual" aspects of the electric chair, the gas chamber, hanging, firing squads, and hangings, but today even the most staunchly opposed to the death penalty is likely to agree that lethal injection is the most humane option—if we choose to execute at all. Drug companies continue to impact the debate, as well. If lethal injection is not possible, does it introduce questions as to whether capital punishment is appropriate at all?

Additional Resources

David M. Oshinsky, Capital Punishment on Trial: Furman v. Georgia and the Death Penalty in Modern America (University Press of Kansas, 2010).

Jon Sorensen and Rocky L-A. Pilgrim, *Lethal Injection: Capital Punishment in Texas during the Modern Era* (University of Texas, 2013).

Carol S. Steiker and Jordan M. Steiker, *Courting Death: The Supreme Court and Capital Punishment* (Belknap, 2016).

Internet References . . .

Capital Punishment

http://www.bjs.gov/index.cfm?ty=tp&tid=18

Lethal Injection

http://www.deathpenaltyinfo.org/lethal-injection

Lethal Injection

http://www.amnestyusa.org/our-work/issues/death-penalty/lethal-injection

Selected, Edited, and with Issue Framing Material by:
William J. Miller, *Campus Labs®*

ISSUE

Should Colleges and Universities Consider an Applicant's Race When Deciding Whether to Accept a Student?

YES: Maureen Downey, from "Trump Doesn't Think College Admissions Should Consider Race. Do You?" *The Atlanta Journal-Constitution* (2018)

NO: Shane Croucher, from "Campus Diversity: Will Trump End Affirmative Action in College Admissions?" *Newsweek* (2018)

Learning Outcomes

After reading this issue, you will be able to:

- Explain the typical college admissions process.
- Describe why race may be considered in making college admissions decisions.
- Assess the costs and benefits of including race in college admissions decisions.
- Explain support and opposition for using race as a factor in college admissions decisions.
- Assess how colleges and universities will likely respond to recent court decisions.

ISSUE SUMMARY

YES: Reporter Maureen Downey argues that not considering affirmative action as part of college admissions will have negative—and potentially unanticipated—consequences on the composition of campuses across the country.

NO: Shane Croucher, on the other hand, describes the changes being administered by the Trump administration and why they believe they assure federal guidelines better align with the prevailing sentiment of recent Supreme Court decisions.

In a number of recent incidents across the country—perhaps most prominently during protests at the University of Missouri—black students have expressed how they continue to experience hostility because of their skin color. These students have spoken of their feelings of isolation and disempowerment. These are the two values higher education does not intend to promote. Instead, all colleges and universities urgently need policies to address these challenges. One such existing policy includes the Supreme Court–endorsed limited consideration of race in admission decisions. This policy allows institutions to build a racially and ethnically diverse student body, which helps assure the development of well-rounded individual graduates

In its 2015–2016 term, the Supreme Court considered the *Fisher v. University of Texas* case. This will be the second time the court rules on the constitutionality of a race-sensitive postsecondary admissions policy at The University of Texas. In 2008, Abigail Fisher, a white female, applied to The University of Texas at Austin (UT-Austin) and was denied admission. She then sued the university on the grounds that the university's race-conscious admissions policy violated the equal protection clause of the Fourteenth Amendment. The case is now back before the Supreme Court.

In its earlier 2013 decision, the Supreme Court had sent the case back to the lower court to conduct a more rigorous assessment of whether UT-Austin needed to consider race in admissions to advance its interest in the educational benefits of diversity. The Supreme Court was concerned that the lower court's decision had relied primarily on the university's judgment, without conducting an independent review. After reconsidering the case, the Fifth Circuit ruled that the university's policy was necessary. Court rules, however, allow the parties to appeal the decision back to the Supreme Court, which Fisher did. In June 2015, the Court agreed to hear the case for a second time, despite her having now graduated and earned a degree from another institution.

Individuals who favor admissions that assure increased diversity in higher education believe any efforts to limit the use of race in admissions can have harmful consequences for the diversity of the student body. Research focusing on the impacts of bans on race-sensitive admissions in the field of medicine found that following these bans, underrepresented students of color at public medical schools dropped from 18.5 percent to about 15.3 percent in examined states. While the drop may seem minor, before bans on affirmative action, for every 100 students matriculated in medical schools in states with bans, there were 18 students of color, whereas after the ban, for every 100 students matriculated, about 15 were students of color. In an era where diversity grew in the general population, medical schools were becoming more homogenous—and more white.

These declines in racial student body diversity can isolate and stigmatize students of color who are admitted and make it more difficult for institutions to create a welcoming campus environment for students of color. In addition to leading to less diversity in the student body, barring the consideration of race in admissions can prevent institutions from addressing the ways in which race shapes the educational experiences of all students. We might not think that admission policies can have an influence on the work of administrators charged with supporting students of color once they are on campus, but findings from a more recent study suggest that the influence of these laws extend beyond the composition of the student body. Bans on affirmative action can have a detrimental influence on work that is critical to the success of students of color on campus.

Race influences thoughts and behavior of individuals of all races in subconscious ways—through implicit biases, such as attitudes toward particular social groups—and other psychological phenomena such as stereotype threat, classically manifested in high-stakes test performance, involving the threatening experience of conforming to negative race-based stereotypes present in the larger society. Because race often shapes attitudes and behaviors subconsciously, not paying attention to race in admissions can further harm race relations. At the same time, permitting its consideration can lead to social cohesion. Justice Anthony Kennedy, a decisive vote in the original Fisher case, has acknowledged in past decisions how much race continues to matter. This understanding, however, needs to reflect the ways in which race matters and also take into account the impact of the court's decisions in a post-Ferguson, post-University of Missouri society. Colleges and universities need all tools they can have at their disposal to improve race relations on their campuses.

While cultivating diversity can be seen as an important virtue in higher education, there remains the question of why lesser qualified students might be admitted over more qualified students due to the color of their skin or their ethnic background. Some ask: but without affirmative action, wouldn't our universities become all white, thus shutting off upward mobility for blacks and other minority groups? That's the sky will fall argument, but it may not stand up. The use of racial admission quotas does not lead to an increase in the total number of minority students; it only leads to their redistribution. The most academically challenging schools, such as the University of Michigan, wind up with more minority students than they would if academic preparation were all that mattered, but if Michigan just admitted students based on merit, those who didn't make it into the flagship university in Ann Arbor would instead go to some other school, where they might be a better academic fit.

If one wants to look at strong arguments against race-based admissions, they can turn to *Brown v. Board of Education*, when Thurgood Marshall, then executive director of the Legal Defense Fund of the National Association for the Advancement of Colored People, wrote "Distinctions by race are so evil, so arbitrary and invidious that a state, bound to defend the equal protection of the laws must not invoke them in any public sphere." The argument applies to our public universities with special force because here the habits of democracy are molded. But many universities now give very marked preference by race and seek to justify what they do by the quest for diversity.

A diverse student body is an appropriate goal for a university—but that goal, as Justice Lewis F. Powell said explicitly in his opinion in *University of California v. Bakke*, is intellectual diversity, diversity of judgment, and viewpoint. When our universities announce that they are striving for diversity, we know that what they are really seeking to achieve is racial proportionality; they profess an intellectual objective, but their real goal is racial balance. This passion for racial balance "misconceives"—that is Justice Powell's word—the diversity that might serve educative ends. And however meritorious those educative ends, it is worth noting that they cannot possibly serve as the "compelling" objective that is required for the constitutional use of racial classifications by the state.

The Trump administration in July rescinded guidance issued by the Obama administration on how colleges can legally consider race and ethnicity in admissions decisions. The move is the latest sign that the Trump administration is skeptical of the way some colleges consider race in admissions. But the immediate impact may be minimal. Court rulings already are more powerful than guidance from any administration. The move may indicate how the administration would respond to complaints it receives, but those complaints could well end up in courts and not be decided by federal agency officials. In all, the Justice Department and Education Department withdrew seven separate documents—issued by the agencies between 2011 and 2016—on the use of race in decisions by schools and by colleges. The guidance in those documents generally said that colleges had ways to consider race in admissions, consistent with various Supreme Court decisions.

In the following selections, reporter Maureen Dowd argues that not considering affirmative action as part of college admissions will have negative—and potentially unanticipated—consequences on the composition of campuses across the country. Shane Croucher, on the other hand, describes the changes being administered by the Trump administration and why they believe they assure federal guidelines better align with the prevailing sentiment of recent Supreme Court decisions.

YES ←

Maureen Downey

Trump Doesn't Think College Admissions Should Consider Race. Do You?

*T*he *Wall Street Journal* and *The New York Times* report today the Trump White House plans to rescind Obama administration policies designed to foster greater racial diversity on America's college campuses.

The news was not a surprise as newly confirmed Assistant Secretary for Civil Rights Ken Marcus is not a proponent of race-conscious college admissions.

The reversal of federal admissions guidelines reflects a general retreat by the administration from policies that pressure schools to scrutinize their practices through a lens of racial bias. For example, the U.S. Department of Education said last week it would push back the imposition of an Obama-era rule mandating states review how districts identify and serve minority students with disabilities for two years.

The "Equity in IDEA" rule was due to go into effect this fall and came in response to findings that minority students in special education were disproportionately disciplined and placed in more.

> We found that, under Secretary of Education Betsy DeVos, the department has scuttled more than 1,200 civil rights investigations that were begun under the Obama administration and lasted at least six months. These cases, which investigated complaints of civil rights violations ranging from discriminatory discipline to sexual violence in school districts and colleges around the country, were closed without any findings of wrongdoing or corrective action, often due to insufficient evidence.

Today, *The New York Times* reports:

> The Trump administration will encourage the nation's school superintendents and college presidents to adopt race-blind admissions standards, abandoning an Obama administration policy that called on universities to consider race as a factor in diversifying their campuses, Trump administration officials said . . . As part of that process, the Justice Department rescinded seven policy guidances from the Education Department's civil rights division on Tuesday.

The Supreme Court has steadily narrowed the ways that schools can consider race when trying to diversify their student bodies. But it has not banned the practice. Now, affirmative action is at a crossroads. The Trump administration is moving against any use of race as a measurement of diversity in education. And the retirement of Justice Anthony M. Kennedy at the end of this month will leave the court without its swing vote on affirmative action and allow President Trump to nominate a justice opposed to a policy that for decades has tried to integrate elite educational institutions.

Reaction was swift.

"While I am not surprised, I continue to be disappointed that the President of this great country demonstrably cares so little for its nonwhite residents and their interests," said Louisiana Congressman Cedric L. Richmond, chairman of the Congressional Black Caucus.

"The reported actions come as the Department of Justice appears ready to tee up a challenge to lawful race-conscious admissions or affirmative action programs. Diverse campuses play an integral part in how our students collaborate and thrive. Although today's action does not change any laws, it sends a clear signal that Attorney General Sessions and Secretary DeVos are advancing a vision of America that is particularly hostile to students of color, but that will impact all students," said Vanita Gupta, president and CEO of the Leadership Conference on Civil and Human Rights.

Many readers of this blog endorse the elimination of race as one of the factors that colleges weigh. Yet, they don't seem to object to athletic ability as a factor in admissions, especially for their favorite college team.

As the AJC reported, the 2014 freshman class at Georgia Tech had an average SAT score of 1,445. However, for incoming football players, the average SAT was 420 points below the class as a whole. Gaps were also found among athletes at the University of Georgia, Georgia State, and Georgia Southern. The AJC reported that in some years, as many as 100 percent of football players have SAT scores in the bottom quarter of their freshman class at Tech. At the University of Georgia, the AJC found about 8 of 10 football players were in the bottom quarter.

But no one in the Georgia Legislature, the U.S. Congress, or the White House is speaking out against affirmative action for football players. Nor are any elected officials or millionaire congress members arguing against the admissions edge sometimes accorded legacies or the children of influential lawmakers and big donors.

Those insisting college acceptances be blind to any factors outside student performance would likely not welcome the result—campuses that are overwhelmingly women. Girls are outperforming boys across the country, which is why 58 percent of students on college campuses are women.

Admissions directors bypass more qualified females to admit enough males to keep the campus somewhat balanced as neither young women nor young men want to attend a school that is nearly all women. As Richard Whitmire, author of "Why Boys Fail," wrote in a column seven months ago:

When it comes to college, middle-class and upper-middle-class parents with underperforming sons get a break that helps disguise these gaps. Many colleges, desperate to recruit more men, are more than willing to admit less-qualified males. The takeaway for parents: if you've got the tuition money, you'll find a spot for your son somewhere.

Colleges seek out running backs, math scholars, tuba players, ballet dancers, and nice kids willing to organize dorm Halloween parties. They search out students with an array of backgrounds and talents. The admissions process is designed to produce a well-rounded class of students whose interests and backgrounds are not identical. And that's a worthwhile goal for campuses and students.

I recently talked to a Walton High School grad who turned down a prestigious University of Georgia scholarship to go to an urban campus in the northeast. She told me, "I thought UGA would just be Walton on a bigger scale. I wanted to meet people who were different than the ones I went to school with since first grade."

Maureen Downey, winner of the 1999 Pulitzer Prize for distinguished commentary and author of three *The New York Times* best sellers, became an Op-Ed columnist in 1995. In August 2014, she also became a writer for *The Times Magazine*.

Shane Croucher

 **NO**

Campus Diversity: Will Trump End Affirmative Action in College Admissions?

As the Trump administration dumps Obama-era affirmative action guidelines encouraging schools to increase campus diversity by using race as a factor in admissions policies, many wonder what impact it will have on nonwhite students trying to get into their college of choice.

While ditching the guidance does not change the law, and schools and colleges that want to improve diversity can still use affirmative action despite a lack of federal support, the Supreme Court precedent underpinning such policies could be under threat.

Justice Anthony Kennedy, who has supported affirmative action in college admissions as constitutional, retired on July 31. President Donald Trump's pick to replace Kennedy could tilt the fine balance of votes on this issue.

Attorney General Jeff Sessions announced that the guidelines would be scrapped, signaling the administration's direction on affirmative action, of which it has been highly critical. Sessions said the Obama-era guidelines go beyond what the Supreme Court permits.

In place of race-aware guidance for education providers will be the instruction to adopt race-neutral admission policies, The Wall Street Journal reported.

The Supreme Court first ruled that race-conscious admissions policies were compatible with the Constitution in the 1978 case *Regents of the University of California v. Bakke*. Race was ruled permissible as one of the number of considerations in school admissions.

This decision was affirmed in the 2003 Supreme Court case *Grutter v. Bollinger*, on which Kennedy dissented, when it was ruled that race-aware admissions in the pursuit of campus diversity were not a breach of the Constitution.

The ruling sanctions the "narrowly tailored use of race in admissions decisions to further a compelling interest in obtaining the educational benefits that flow from a diverse student body."

Twice again, in 2013 and 2016, race-aware admissions policies were affirmed by the Supreme Court as within the bounds of the Constitution. However, it has also been consistently affirmed that race-based quota systems for admissions are unconstitutional.

The Obama administration developed guidelines for schools and colleges wanting to use race in admissions and remain within the scope of the law. They were jointly issued by the education and justice departments.

"Ensuring that our nation's students are provided with learning environments comprised of students of diverse backgrounds is not just a lofty ideal," the guidelines say.

"As the Supreme Court has recognized, the benefits of participating in diverse learning environments flow to an individual, his or her classmates, and the community as a whole. These benefits greatly contribute to the educational, economic, and civic life of this nation."

Now President Trump has scrapped those guidelines in what is likely a broader move against affirmative action in general, despite research that suggests the most effective way of increasing campus diversity and leveling the playing field for nonwhite students is an affirmative action.

A 2015 paper from the education nonprofit Educational Testing Service modeled what the impact would be of substituting socioeconomic status for race in affirmative action admissions policies.

"Our analysis here suggests that affirmative action policies based on socioeconomic status are unlikely to achieve meaningful increases in racial diversity," the researchers concluded.

"That is not to say that socioeconomic affirmative action would not be valuable in its own right—it would increase socioeconomic diversity on university campuses and would benefit low-income college applicants—but only that it is not an effective or efficient means to achieving racial diversity."

"Race-conscious affirmative action does, however, increase racial diversity effectively at the schools that use it. Although imperfect, it may be the best strategy we currently have."

Lily Eskelsen García, president of the National Education Association, a professional group, said in a statement that "affirmative action has proven to be one of the most effective ways to create diverse and inclusive classrooms."

"But by telling schools and universities that they should not use affirmative action to achieve inclusive classrooms, the Education Department has again failed our students," she said.

"President Trump has indicated he intends to appoint a nominee to the Supreme Court who will declare that affirmative action is unconstitutional in our schools."

"The Education Department's action forecasts how much is at stake in the upcoming Supreme Court nomination process. Our nation must join together and fight to ensure all our students have what they need to succeed."

One case that may give the Supreme Court—which will likely include—Trump's next nominee—an opportunity to overturn the precedent involves a group of Asian-American students suing Harvard University for its admissions policy.

They allege Harvard rejected them despite high test scores because of their race in favor of other, lower performing students from different minority groups.

This amounts to an unconstitutional race-based quota system for admissions, they claim. Harvard says it does not discriminate against applicants.

In a sign of what may be yet to come, the Trump administration has backed those Asian-American students in their attempt to make public internal documents and information about Harvard's admissions policies.

SHANE CROUCHER is a senior reporter for *Newsweek*.

EXPLORING THE ISSUE

Should Colleges and Universities Consider an Applicant's Race When Deciding Whether to Accept a Student?

Critical Thinking and Reflection

1. How do you believe colleges should select students they want to attend?
2. Should race play a role in determining whether someone is accepted to a college?
3. In what cases do you believe it is most appropriate to consider race when making a college admissions decision?
4. Should colleges always admit the most qualified students based on test scores and high-school performance? Why or why not?
5. Do you believe the college admissions process is fair? Why or why not?

Is There Common Ground?

Of all the issues discussed in this volume, perhaps there is the greatest opportunity for common ground to be reached on the question of including race as a factor in college admissions. The Supreme Court, after all, has already created a template by which schools can legally do this, without causing harm to nonminority students, through the *Gratz v. Grutter* decisions. Yet we can expect to continue to hear discussions about the role of race in college admissions as long as higher education is as emphasized in American society as it is today.

From a college or university's perspective, diversity is a key component of the student experience. Beyond textbook learning, college is a time for young adults to be exposed to new and different situations, people, and ways of thinking. This cannot be easily accomplished in a homogenous setting. Yet, standardized tests have been shown by repeated studies to be easier for white students than for minority groups—especially African Americans and Hispanics. As a result, if colleges and universities want to assure diverse student populations—and the greatest potential for well-rounded educations for all students—it may mean admitting students of color with lower academic profiles than white applicants. Through the court's recent rulings, we have witnessed the creation of common ground that has been largely accepted by those impacted. Future rulings, including an upcoming case surrounding Harvard's treatment of Asian-American applicants, will dictate future policy.

Additional Resources

Elizabeth Armstrong, *Paying for the Party: How College Maintains Inequality* (Harvard University Press, 2013).

Annette Lareau, *Unequal Childhoods: Class, Race, and Family Life* (University of California Press, 2011).

Lois Weis, Kristin Cipollone, and Heather Jenkins, *Class Warfare: Class, Race, and College Admissions in Top-Tier Secondary Schools* (University of Chicago Press, 2014).

Internet References . . .

Diverse Issues in Higher Education

http://diverseeducation.com/

Diversity in Admission

http://www.nacacnet.org/issues-action/Legislative
News/Pages/Diversity-in-Admission.aspx

Why Diversity Matters in Higher Education

http://www.collegexpress.com/counselors-and-
parents/parents/articles/college-journey/why-
diversity-matters-college-admissions/

Selected, Edited, and with Issue Framing Material by:
William J. Miller, *Campus Labs*®

ISSUE

Does the NRA Hold Too Much Power in the Gun Control Debate?

YES: Bill Scher, from "Why the NRA Will Always Win," *Politico* (2018)

NO: Mel Robbins, from "The Real Gun Problem Is Mental Health, Not the NRA," CNN (2014)

Learning Outcomes

After reading this issue, you will be able to:

- Discuss current gun ownership restrictions in the United States.
- Assess the threats gun pose to society.
- Identify key political players in the battle over gun control.
- Assess the role the NRA plays in the fun control debate.
- Determine if the NRA's influence is appropriate in the gun control debate.

ISSUE SUMMARY

YES: Author and editor Bill Scher argues that the National Rifle Association's power as a lobbying group is not rooted in the money it has been able to raise but instead in the permeation of a culture that believe gun ownership is a way of life, central to one's freedom, and deserving of defense on a daily basis. Either way, the influence of the organization is vast.

NO: Mel Robbins—a legal analyst—argues that the NRA is not the main problem with gun violence in the United States. Instead, she points to concrete examples that demonstrate how and increased focus on mental health could better alleviate current issues.

Should Americans have the right to self-defense? Does the Second Amendment not give all Americans a fundamental right to bear arms in order to protect themselves and their property in the pursuit of life and liberty? Without guns, rebellion against a tyrannical government would not have been possible and the American Revolution would not mark the beginning of America's independence from England. In fact, search and seizure of firearms and ammunition were a major catalyst for events leading to the American Revolution. While the Second Amendment laid the foundation for gun rights in America, it was not until recently that courts began to clarify exactly whom the Second Amendment impacts. Without such clarification,

state and local governments have been slowly stripping away access to firearms, and therefore, a citizen's right to self-defense with false claims of more guns equals more violence.

The Second Amendment, ratified in 1791, states, "A well-regulated militia, being necessary to the security of a free State, the right of the people to keep and bear Arms, shall not be infringed." Proponents of gun control believe the word "militia" was specifically used to guarantee the right of states to have an armed militia, like our current National Guard. Of course, opponents of gun control believe it to be an individual right to bear arms and a denial of access to guns is unconstitutional. Prior to *District of Columbia v. Heller* in 2008, the Supreme Court had not reviewed a Second Amendment case since *United States v. Miller* in 1939, which did not answer if the Second Amendment was an individual right or one specifically held by the state militia. Without a Supreme Court standing on the issue, states and local governments spent nearly 70 years with a little authoritative guidance and have been able to push gun restrictions to the edge, including all-out handgun bans in places like the District of Columbia and the city of Chicago.

In 2008, *District of Columbia v. Heller* finally answered the question as to individual rights granted by the Second Amendment. In 1976, the District of Columbia banned all handguns within the district, and all long guns had to be disassembled and a trigger lock used at all times, ultimately defeating the usefulness of a firearm for self-defense in one's home. In siding with *Heller*, the Supreme Court showed that such stringent controls are unconstitutional and obstruct a person's right of self-defense. The *Heller* case was a monumental movement to solidifying the individual right to bear arms, at least at the federal level, but did not express whether the case was enforceable against the states. In 2010, the Supreme Court heard the case of *McDonald v. Chicago*, in which the Supreme Court ruled that the Second Amendment was enforceable against the state under the Privileges and Immunities Clause of the Fourteenth Amendment. *District of Columbia v. Heller* and *McDonald v. Chicago* have been two of the most influential cases in decades to address the right to bear arms, but as is often the result with major court decisions, the rulings have raised many new questions.

The problem with imposing excessive gun bans like those in Chicago and the District of Columbia is that they may not do much to actually reduce crime. Instead, they hinder the law-abiding citizen's right to self-defense, and at best create unreasonable barriers to access firearms. According to a Harvard study by Don Kates and Gary Mauser, Russia's gun controls are so stringent that very few civilians have access to firearms, yet as of 2002, Russia had the highest murder rate of any developed country. Russia is not alone, ownership of any gun in Luxembourg is minimal, and handguns are banned, yet they have a murder rate nine times that of countries with high gun ownership such as Germany, Norway, Switzerland, and Austria. In 1996, Australia banned most guns and made the defensive use of a firearm illegal, which resulted in armed robberies rising 51 percent, unarmed robberies by 37 percent, assaults by 24 percent, and kidnappings by 43 percent in the four years following the ban. England has fared no better; during the late 1990s, handguns were banned resulting in a 40 percent increase in firearm-related crimes, yet hundreds of thousands of guns were confiscated from law-abiding

citizens. Countries like Australia and England are proving when stringent gun restrictions are imposed, and the right to self-defense is taken away, there are only two people with access to guns: the government and criminals.

The idiom "guns don't kill people, people kill people" is being tested in public opinion in the United States every time a mass shooting occurs within the nation's borders. In recent months, we have experienced two such incidents that helped assure gun control remains active on the federal agenda. First, on February 14, 2018, a former student unleashed a hail of gunfire at Marjory Stoneman Douglas High School in Parkland, FL, killing at least 17 adults and children. Nikolas Cruz, 19, has been charged with 17 counts of premeditated murder. Less than three months later, Dimitrios Pagourtzis, 17, allegedly walks into an art class and begins firing, killing eight students and two teachers at Santa Fe High School in Santa Fe, TX. Pagourtzis is arrested and charged with capital murder and aggravated assault of a public servant. In both the cases, there were concerns raised about gun control: How did these men gain access to weapons despite displaying signs of mental illness? Why do we have semiautomatic weapons available? Is there any way to prevent possible criminals from getting access to guns without preventing Americans from protecting themselves?

Speaking after a mass shooting in the Navy Yard, President Obama explained: "By now . . . it should be clear that the change we need will not come from Washington. . . . Change will come the only way it ever has come, and that's from the American people. . . . Part of what wears on . . . is the sense that this has happened before," the president said. "What wears on us, what troubles us so deeply, as we gather here today is this senseless violence that took place in the Navy Yard echoes other recent tragedies. . . . I do not accept that we cannot find a commonsense way to preserve our traditions, including our basic Second Amendment freedoms and the rights of law-abiding gun owners while at the same time reducing the gun violence that unleashed so much mayhem on a regular basis." Yet the National Rifle Association (NRA) remains a significant obstacle to any gun control in the United States. With strong membership numbers, funds, and a knack for lobbying, even after a string of massacres, the NRA has successfully prevented any new restrictions to gun ownership.

The NRA was founded over 144 years. The NRA's mission is to promote public safety, train members of law enforcement agencies, adopt and encourage the shooting sports, and promote hunter safety. The research results showed that the NRA operates at over $250 million a year, and most of the money is spent on ads, lobbying, and Political Action Committees. The research concluded that the primary source of power for the NRA is its 5 million dedicated members. The NRA's members are engaged in the political arena and feel passionate about their gun rights. The NRA has also a strong access to policy makers; they have hired former legislators and government officials, since they can use their friendships and personal connections to gain access to policy makers.

The NRA has lobbied heavily against all forms of gun control and argued aggressively that more guns make the country safer. It relies on, and staunchly defends, a disputed interpretation of the Second Amendment to the U.S. Constitution, which it argues gives U.S. citizens the rights to bear arms. The association faced criticism from both sides of the political spectrum in the wake of the Sandy Hook shooting, when Wayne La Pierre said that the lack of an armed guard at the school was to blame for the tragedy. It staunchly opposes most local, state, and federal legislation that would restrict gun ownership. For example, the NRA recently has lobbied for guns confiscated by the police to be resold, arguing that destroying the weapons is, in effect, a waste of perfectly good guns. Likewise, it strongly supports legislation that expand gun rights such as "open-carry" laws, which allow gun owners to carry their weapons, unconcealed, in most public places.

In the following selections, we hear from author and editor Bill Scher who argues that the NRA's power as a lobbying group is not rooted in the money it has been able to raise but instead in the permeation of a culture that believe gun ownership is a way of life, central to one's freedom, and deserving of defense on a daily basis. Either way, the influence of the organization is vast. Mel Robbins—a legal analyst—argues that the NRA is not the main problem with gun violence in the United States. Instead, she points to concrete examples that demonstrate how and increased focused on mental health could better alleviate current issues.

YES

Bill Scher

Why the NRA Will Always Wins

It's not the money. It's the culture.

Your burning outrage about the Parkland school massacre is already starting to flicker. The special counsel's indictments of the Russian hacker operation and President Donald Trump's dizzying response to them is competing for your attention ("This is code red" says *The New York Times* columnist Thomas Friedman). And what's that shiny object over there? A case for impeaching Justice Clarence Thomas? ("Drop everything and read this" urged HuffPost's Editor-in-Chief Lydia Polgreen.)

Meanwhile, the National Rifle Association (NRA) and its allies are maintaining their maniacal focus. Rush Limbaugh went on Fox News, right after an interview with several Parkland survivors critical of the gun lobby, to scold those who "bash the NRA" and insist the only solution to school shootings is "concealed carry in the schools." The NRA's 24/7 streaming network NRATV echoed the sentiment with the familiar refrain, "we need more good guys with guns." Hosts complained that the school had only one armed guard, while advertising the NRA's "School Shield" security initiative to freshly terrified school administrations.

Why does the NRA always win, despite the repeated national traumas, and despite poll after poll showing a majority in favor of stronger gun control measures? It's not the money. It's because the NRA has built a movement that has convinced its followers that gun ownership is a way of life, central to one's freedom and safety, that must be defended on a daily basis.

The gun control majority gets worked up only in the days after public mass shootings, even though such events accounted for only 71 of the 38,658 annual gun fatalities in 2016. Then the news coverage shifts, political prospects for action diminish, and the majority gravitates to other political matters while guns continue to take lives in suicides, domestic violence incidents, other crimes, and accidents every day.

Since the progressive political prism views campaign cash as the scourge of democracy, gun control proponents are quick to blame NRA donations for why Congress seems immune to public opinion. In a powerful speech last week in Florida, Marjory Stoneman Douglas High School senior Emma Gonzalez excoriated "politicians who sit in their gilded House and Senate seats funded by the NRA telling us nothing could have been done to prevent this" and added, "To every politician who is taking donations from the NRA, shame on you."

But it's a mistake to attribute the NRA's success entirely to its campaign spending. The dollar amount was considerable in 2016: $54.4 million. But that money was not spent on the entire Congress. Thirty million went to Donald Trump and the rest mainly to six Republican Senate candidates in competitive races, five of whom won. For most members of Congress, the amount of money they get from the NRA is a tiny percentage of their overall hauls. If money were the only reason for their gun rights stances, Michael Bloomberg could offer to double whatever the NRA gives them and flip their votes.

To beat the NRA at its own game, the gun control movement needs to better understand how the NRA has built an army of single-issue voters.

NRATV is a new piece of the puzzle, having been launched only in the late 2016. But it's a window into the culture that the NRA has nurtured for decades. Every minute, the network pumps out a message that can be delivered regardless of external events: liberal elites want to take away your guns and freedom. Terrorists and criminals lurk everywhere and you need to know how to defend yourself. And by the way, look how cool guns are and how powerful they make you feel!

Some shows are standard conservative political talk show fare, with hosts who wear T-shirts emblazoned with "Socialist Tears" and mock mainstream media figures for alleged bias (the network is particularly obsessed with CNN's Don Lemon).

Other shows are more like reality TV, such as "Love at First Shot," which follows women novices as they get firearms training for "hunting, personal protection, and competition" and learn the "lifestyle and cultural elements of being a gun owner." The show "Noir" recently offered a slow-motion tutorial on how to be that "good guy with a gun" if you're in a movie theater when a mass shooter enters. "They don't always talk about gun issues," gun policy expert Dr. Robert Spitzer said of the network to *Time* magazine, "It's about beliefs and how people view the world."

Who knows how many watch NRATV—the point is that it's a distilled version of the message the gun lobby has been pushing into the culture for decades. That worldview keeps the NRA on message when events don't cooperate. But for frustrated and desperate gun control advocates, mass shootings goad them into chasing marginal proposals that have a real, or perceived, link to the immediate crime.

The Columbine school shooting prompted activists to prioritize the "gun show loophole" since the killers bought guns at a gun show where a background check wasn't required. The Charleston church massacre led to calls to close the "Charleston loophole," which allows someone to get a gun if a background check isn't completed after three days. After the Las Vegas massacre, many demanded a ban on "bump stocks" that allow for more rapid firing.

Not only did activists fail to enact these policy ideas, the ideas, however laudable, don't have much relevance to the vast majority of gun deaths. They can't help motivate people after memories of the last massacre fade.

Gun control proponents don't necessarily have to emulate the NRA and, say, launch a TV network. But they might consider marshaling the financial resources of Bloomberg, and other multimillionaires, and emulating one of the most successful public service advertising campaigns in history: the anti-tobacco "truth" campaign.

Hundreds of millions have been spent since 2000 by what is now called the "Truth Initiative" on edgy ads that turned teenage perception of what smoking represents from cool rebellion to corporate dishonesty. The ad campaign is not the sole reason, but it is widely credited for helping drive smoking levels among teens down from 23 percent to 6 percent.

Like the tobacco industry, the NRA has been cultivating an image of guns as a source of freedom and cool, with the extra value of protection from grievous harm. A large-scale countercampaign could help reverse that image, highlighting the damage guns do every day: the depressed never getting another chance for mental health services, the children dying from home accidents, and the domestic abuse victims who never could escape. Other spots could depict life where guns are controlled around the world, to show what is possible. A partnership with Hollywood could bring gun issues into more TV shows and movies, similar to how Hollywood was successfully pressured to stop making cigarettes look cool.

Such a campaign would have two main objectives: in the short run, keep the gun control majority engaged on a daily basis, and in the long run, reduce the demand for guns in areas where the NRA exerts political influence.

As heartwarming as it is to see high school students organize anti-gun marches, they are no more likely to be successful in busting the NRA narrative, or separating politicians from NRA money, than the parents of Columbine and Sandy Hook. The gun rights community is steeled against succumbing to sympathetic victims, as they have convinced themselves that they are above the politics of knee-jerk emotion.

Social conservatives are fond of the insight, "Politics is downstream from culture." There is a big gun-rights culture that has a grip on our politics. Until there is a gun-free culture that can rival what the NRA has cultivated over decades, no national trauma, no matter how searing, is going to move the political needle.

BILL SCHER is a liberal pundit and political analyst. He is a contributing editor to POLITICO Magazine and a contributor to RealClearPolitics. He also cohosts "The DMZ," an online TV show with conservative pundit Matt Lewis on Bloggingheads.tv.

Mel Robbins    **NO**

The Real Gun Problem Is Mental Health, Not the NRA

Next time there's a mass shooting, don't jump to blame the National Rifle Association (NRA) and lax gun laws. Look first at the shooter and the mental health services he did or didn't get, and the commitment laws in the state where the shooting took place.

Strengthening gun control won't stop the next mass shooter, but changing our attitudes, the treatment options we offer, and the laws for holding the mentally unstable and mentally ill for treatment just might.

Take the case of the recent mass shooting incident in Isla Vista, CA. Police say Elliot Rodger went on a killing spree near the University of California campus in Santa Barbara, shooting and stabbing victims, killing six, and wounding 13 before he killed himself.

He had legally purchased three guns, passed a federal background check, and met several other requirements in one of the most liberal states with the toughest gun control laws in the country. California was one of eight states that passed major gun reforms in the wake of 2012's Sandy Hook Elementary School shooting, in which a lone gunman killed 20 children and 6 adults.

In fact, California's gun control laws received an "A-" grade from both The Brady Campaign to Prevent Gun Violence and the Law Center to Prevent Gun Violence, the Los Angeles Times reported.

Analyzed the state of mental commitment laws state by state, looking at both the "quality of involuntary treatment (civil commitment) laws, which facilitate emergency hospitalization during a psychiatric emergency, and the availability of court orders mandating continued treatment as a condition of living in a community."

On virtually all counts, California received an "F" (it got a "C" on emergency evaluation). In Rodger's case, a friend concerned about alarming videos he'd posted on YouTube had alerted a county mental health staff member, and police had conferred with his mother, but this was not enough to get him committed.

Under California's Welfare and Institutions Code Section 5150, a person must be a danger to himself or others before he can be held for 72 hours for evaluation, and the standard is even higher to mandate treatment. Police visiting Rodger found him to be "polite and courteous" and not an apparent danger, so they had no authority to detain him or search his home for weapons to seize. The reason had nothing to do with gun laws. It had to do with the commitment laws in California.

We need to adopt a nationwide standard for involuntary civil commitment, and that standard should be "need for treatment." If a family member, law enforcement officer, or mental health professional is concerned about the well-being of an individual, they should be able to have that individual held for a mental health evaluation.

Indeed, the Treatment Advocacy Center's report describes the exact situation police found themselves in when they conducted that "well-being" check on Rodger:

"But what if the person is neither threatening violence against anyone nor at any apparent imminent risk of injuring himself? What if the concern spurring the family member to seek help is simply that the person is suffering, tormented by terrifying delusions, yet somehow unaware that he is ill? Do we as a society have reason to intervene? To answer 'yes,' we must believe there is a compelling societal imperative beyond preventing imminent injury or death—an imperative to liberate a person from a hellish existence he would never—in his 'right mind'—choose."

The truth is that commitment laws shouldn't be a stopgap to prevent imminent harm, but rather seen as an essential tool to help a loved one needing treatment before things reach the imminent harm stage.

Next, we've got to connect the dots between mental health records and National Instant Background Check. In 2014, Mayors Against Illegal Guns released a report calling for states to close this gap. It found that 11 states and the District of Columbia have no reporting laws, and another 12 states have submitted fewer than 100 mental health records to the national background check system.

But connecting the dots won't help unless every gun sale is subject to an instant background check imposed on all licensed gun retailers.

And finally, the police need tools as well. They need training and the discretion to ask about and remove guns from any household where there is a domestic dispute, a call for a "well-being check," or a person who exhibits violent or unstable behavior. They also need a mental health professional on call for such checks.

Connecticut, Indiana, and, yes, even Texas have firearms seizure statutes aimed at dangerous persons. Laws like these enable the police to temporarily remove guns from someone who is exhibiting dangerous behavior until

a judge can make a final determination on fitness for gun ownership based on evidence presented at a hearing.

mental illness are nonviolent." You're right about that, too. Indeed, mentally ill people only account for a small fraction of the gun deaths in America every year and the vast majority of those are suicide, not homicide. Violence by the mentally ill is usually a symptom of the untreated mental illness—that's why access to treatment, not gun control, is the answer.

Overhauling mental health laws would give family members and professionals more responsibility and authority in care decisions. And in some cases, medications and therapies should not be optional.

We've got a major problem on our hands. And since guns aren't going anywhere, the discussion about solutions needs to place the focus somewhere else.

Even the NRA agrees that the seriously mentally ill should never own a gun. So let's finally do something about it.

Mel Robbins is an American on-air CNN commentator, television host, author, and motivational speaker. Robbins is widely known for covering the George Zimmerman trial; her TED X talk, How to Stop Screwing Yourself Over, with over 15 million views; and her book, *The 5 Second Rule.*

EXPLORING THE ISSUE

Does the NRA Hold Too Much Power in the Gun Control Debate?

Critical Thinking and Reflection

1. What are the arguments for placing greater restrictions on gun ownership in the United States? Which argument do you believe is most persuasive, why?
2. What are the arguments for loosening present restrictions on gun ownership in the United States? Which argument do you believe is most persuasive, why?
3. Cities like Chicago, which have some of the strictest gun control laws in the country, have the highest rates of gun violence in the United States. How does this happen? How can it be prevented?
4. Do you believe the Second Amendment is properly applied and understood in the United States? Why or why not?
5. Does the NRA yield too much power? Why or why not? How could its influence be curbed moving forward, if necessary?

Is There Common Ground?

While it may seem that lines are clearly drawn in the sand when it comes to gun control in the United States, in reality there is great potential for middle ground to be discovered. Throughout the history of guns in America, compromises have been reached. There are certain restrictions and purchasing protocols in place currently trying to assure that malintentioned individuals struggle to gain access to a firearm. In another vein, across the country, concealed carry laws are becoming prominent, permitting skilled individuals to keep their piece on their person at all times. What these examples show is that both sides of the argument have made certain sacrifices already.

But there are concerns that are perhaps more difficult to bridge the gap on. Those opposed to gun control, for example, routinely point to the fact that criminals are not likely to obey any form of law passed related to access to weapons. In this scenario, law-abiding citizens could find themselves vulnerable as only lawbreakers maintain firearms. At the same time, those in favor of curbing access will seemingly always have a fresh mass shooting to use when driving home key arguments. Few Americans are on the fence with regard to gun control, and consequently, the sharpness of opinions leads one to believe that

middle ground may be more difficult to realize than we originally expected.

Perhaps most importantly, groups like the NRA continue to carry great influence on the gun control debate. Their interests run counter to practices that many believe could curb gun violence across the nation. But there has been little success in circumventing their organized efforts and financial power. Much like the gun control debate, it's rare to find anyone who doesn't hold strong feelings toward the NRA one way or the other.

Additional Resources

Gregg L. Carter, *Gun Control in the United States: A Reference Handbook* (ABC-CLIO, 2006).

Saul Cornell, *A Well-Regulated Militia: The Founding Fathers and the Origins of Gun Control in America* (Oxford University Press, 2008).

John R. Lott Jr., *More Guns, Less Crime: Understanding Crime and Gun Control Laws* (University of Chicago Press, 2010).

Robert Spitzer, *The Politics of Gun Control* (Paradigm, 2011).

Craig Whitney, *Living with Guns: A Liberal's Case for the Second Amendment* (PublicAffairs, 2012).

Internet References . . .

Brady Campaign to Prevent Gun Violence

www.handguncontrol.org

Coalition to Stop Gun Violence

www.gunfree.org

National Criminal Justice Reference Service

www.ncjrs.gov/App/Topics/Topic.aspx?topicid=87

National Rifle Association

www.nra.org

Revolution PAC

www.revolutionpac.com

Selected, Edited, and with Issue Framing Material by:
William J. Miller, *Campus Labs*®

ISSUE

Should "Recreational" Drugs Be Legalized?

YES: **Alex Suskind**, from "Cory Booker Explains Why He's Making Legal Weed His Signature Issue," *Vice* (2017)

NO: **David Brooks**, from "Weed: Been There. Done That," *The New York Times* (2014)

Learning Outcomes
After reading this issue, you will be able to:
• Identify different interpretations of what should be classified as recreational drugs. • Explain how individual choices can impact public well-being. • Discuss the potential long-term health effects of drug usage. • Explain why some argue that using certain drugs is not risky behavior. • Identify the possible impacts to law enforcement of legalizing or not legalizing recreational drugs.

ISSUE SUMMARY

YES: Writer and interviewer Alex Suskind interviews New Jersey Democratic Senator Cory Booker about his proposed legislation to legalize marijuana at the federal level. Through the interview, Booker explains why he wants to see marijuana legalized and how he sees government being able to repair the egregious harm the War on Drugs has caused to targeted communities.

NO: David Brooks—*The New York Times* columnist—argues that making marijuana more accessible raises important moral and ethical questions that must be considered as part of the larger policy argument.

Prohibition is a word Americans associate with the prohibition of liquor, which was adopted as a national policy with the ratification of the Eighteenth Amendment to the U.S. Constitution in 1920 and repealed with the adoption of the Twenty-first Amendment in 1933. Many states had earlier banned whiskey and other intoxicating beverages, and some states have had various restrictions since repeal.

Similarly, certain categories of illicit drugs were banned in some states prior to the passage of the Controlled Substance Act in 1970, which made the prohibition a national policy. Unlike the Prohibition Amendment, this was achieved by an Act of Congress. Many claimed then, and many still do today, that to do this in the absence of a constitutional amendment exceeds the power of the national government. Nevertheless, it has been upheld by

the federal courts and has continued to function for more than four decades.

The principal substances that are banned include opium, heroin, cocaine, and marijuana. Marijuana is also known as cannabis (the plant from which it is obtained) and by a variety of informal names, most familiarly "pot." Its use dates back several thousand years, sometimes for religious or medical purposes. However, it is a so-called recreational drug that a United Nations committee characterized as "the most widely used illicit substance in the world." Because opium, heroin, and cocaine are more powerful, more addictive, and less prevalent, advocates of legalization often restrict their appeal to removing the ban on marijuana.

In the 50 years following an international convention in 1912 that urged the restriction of dangerous drugs, the use in the United States of illicit drugs other than marijuana was consistently below ½ of 1 percent of the population, with cocaine rising somewhat in the counter culture climate that began in the late 1950s. Illicit drug use was widely promoted as mind-expanding and relatively harmless. It is estimated that its use peaked in the 1970s. Present estimates for drugs other than marijuana suggest that between 5 percent and 10 percent of the population at least occasionally engages in the use of some illicit drugs.

In 2006, there were approximately 1.9 million drug arrests in the United States. Of these, 829,625 (44 percent of the total) were marijuana arrests. During the past two decades, the price of marijuana has gone down, its potency has increased, and it has become more readily available. Further, it has begun being mixed with other substances, increasing the potential for unintended side effects.

Studies, principally conducted in Sweden, Holland, and other nations with more tolerant drug policies, conclude that social factors influence drug use. Apart from peer pressure, particularly in the use of marijuana, hard drugs generally become more common in times of higher unemployment and lower income. Apart from cannabis, which is easily grown, the illicit character of hard drugs makes them expensive, but the profit motive induces growers, distributors, and "pushers" to risk arrest and punishment. It has been estimated that as many as $\frac{1}{6}$ of all persons in federal prisons have been convicted of selling, possessing, or using marijuana.

The movement to legalize these drugs, often with a focus on marijuana, has existed as long as their prohibition, but in recent years has won recruits from both liberal and conservative ranks. As with the prohibition of alcohol, experience with the unintended consequences of prohibition of drugs led some to wonder whether this has not only failed to eliminate their use but increased public health problems. Under the Prohibition Amendment, people drank unlicensed alcohol, often adulterated by the addition of poisonous substances. Illicit drug prohibition has led to the sale of toxic ingredients added to the drugs resulting in more impure and more dangerous products. Drug users injecting the drugs employ dirty reused needles that spread HIV and hepatitis B and C. While illicit drug use has never rivaled the widespread public acceptance of alcohol, their use has been extensive enough to spawn new networks of organized crime, violence related to the drug market, and the corruption of law enforcement and governments. We have recently witnessed this in the drug gang wars in Mexico that have slipped over into the American southwest.

Milton Friedman, who was America's most influential conservative economist, reached the interesting conclusion that drug prohibition has led to the rise of drug cartels. His reasoning was that only major retailers can handle massive shipments, own aircraft fleets, have armed troops, and employ lawyers and methods of eluding and bribing the police. Consequently, law enforcement as well as competition drives out smaller, less ruthless, and less efficient drug dealers.

The economic cost of legislating and attempting to enforce drug prohibition is very high. When the national policy went to effect, the federal cost was $350 million in 1971. Thirty-five years later in 2006, the cost was $30 billion. To this should be added the revenue that could be obtained if marijuana were subject to taxation. If it were taxed at the same rate as alcohol or tobacco, it has been estimated that it would yield as much as $7.7 billion. It may be, as advocates of legalization suggest, that the financial costs exceed the damages that the drugs themselves cause.

Against these arguments for repeal, those who support the war on drugs claim that prohibitive drug laws suppress drug use. Compare the large majority of Americans who consume legal alcohol with the very much smaller proportion who use illicit drugs. The Drug Enforcement Administration (DEA) has demonstrated that people under the influence of drugs are more than six times more likely to commit homicides than people looking for money to buy drugs. Drug use changes behavior and causes criminal activity. Cocaine-related paranoia frequently results in assaults, drugged driving, and domestic violence. These crimes are likely to increase when drugs are more readily available.

The point that liberalization advocates miss is that the illicit drugs are inherently harmful. In the short term, illicit drugs cause memory loss, distorted perception, a decline of motor skills, and an increased heart rate and anxiety. Particularly, for young people, drug use produces a decline in mental development and motivation, as well as a reduced ability to concentrate in school.

The United States Centers for Disease Control and Prevention has concluded that although there are more than seven times more Americans who use alcohol than drugs, during a single year alone (2000), there were almost as many drug-induced deaths (158,520) as alcohol-induced (18,539). The DEA concludes that drugs are "far more deadly than alcohol." This is true even for marijuana, which is deemed more potent than it was a generation ago. It contains more than 400 chemicals (the toxicity of some is clear and of many others is unknown), and one marijuana cigarette deposits four times more tar than a filtered tobacco cigarette.

The widespread support for medicinal marijuana seems to be changing public attitudes toward potential legalization. Colorado and Washington voters have sent a message that their respective states will exercise their rights under the Constitution legalizing the recreational use of marijuana. This process began with the legalization of medical marijuana in over a dozen states, opening the doors of debate with regard to the benefits of marijuana and dispelling some misconceptions. Party support has increased across the board. Republican support increased from 33 percent to 35 percent between November 2012 and October 2013, with Democratic changes increasing from 61 percent to 65 percent and Independents from 50 percent to 62 percent within the same time period, respectively. While marijuana is still illegal at the federal level, the Obama administration has made it clear that they will not go after users in states that choose to legalize. A memo sent from former Attorney General Eric Holder to all U.S. attorneys informs them that the federal government will not intervene with state laws as long as the states follow certain protocols and guidelines in regulating products. Perhaps, the tides are actually changing.

A new administration has meant new interpretations, however. The spread of marijuana legalization has led to a reimagining of the US drug policy and how, exactly, it should change as people seek alternatives to punitive criminal justice policies that have led to more incarceration and a black market that supports violent criminal enterprises. But marijuana remains illegal under federal law. And although the Obama administration said it would allow state-level rules to stand without much federal interference, the Trump administration has taken a tougher line. Supporters, such as the Marijuana Policy Project and the Drug Policy Alliance, say that legalization is the only way to cut off a major source of revenue from criminal organizations and totally end the arrests of nonviolent marijuana users and sellers. But there's

disagreement among some supporters, such as New York University drug policy expert Mark Kleiman, about *how* to legalize pot, and whether for-profit companies should be allowed to sell and aggressively market the drug.

Opponents, such as Smart Approaches to Marijuana, worry about the consequences of legalization—whether legally allowing pot could make it more accessible and therefore easier to misuse, especially if for-profit enterprises are able to advertise the drug similar to how alcohol companies promote their products during major public events like the Super Bowl. Some critics of full legalization instead favor smaller steps toward reform, like allowing pot only for medical uses or decriminalization, which would remove criminal penalties for possession but keep distribution and sales illegal. The legalization debate, then, isn't about whether reform should happen at all, but if a certain kind of change goes too far. This is typical of drug policy: it's not about which option is perfect, but about which option is the least bad. In the case of marijuana, both sides are weighing whether the costs of prohibition—more arrests and drug-related violence—outweigh the risks of increased access to marijuana, given its potential harms to society and personal health.

In the following selections, writer and interviewer Alex Suskind interviews New Jersey Democratic Senator Cory Booker about his proposed legislation to legalize marijuana at the federal level. Through the interview, Booker explains why he wants to see marijuana legalized and how he sees government being able to repair the egregious harm the War on Drugs has caused to targeted communities. David Brooks—*The New York Times* columnist—argues that making marijuana more accessible raises important moral and ethical questions that must be considered as part of the larger policy argument.

YES ←

Alex Suskind

Cory Booker Explains Why He's Making Legal Weed His Signature Issue

The New Jersey Senator and Potential 2020 Candidate Talks about His Far-Reaching Legalization Bill and Whether He's Ever Inhaled.

We're at a pot precipice in America. Twenty-nine states (and Washington, DC) have given residents access to some form of medical marijuana, eight have legalized recreational use, and a contingent of politicians, policy experts, and advocacy groups continue to fight for further decriminalization. This push has helped many people like me—I have Crohn's disease and frequently use medical weed as a deterrent for flare-ups. But even though some Republicans have embraced the cause of legalizing weed, the current White House seems devoted to keeping the war on drugs alive.

Yet despite the current climate, and even though the conversation over marijuana legalization has been less prominent in the age of Trump, politicians like Senator Cory Booker believe full legalization is all but inevitable. "We are on the right side of history," the New Jersey Democratic senator told me over the phone from Washington, DC, two months after introducing his Marijuana Justice Act, a bill that calls for a full federal legalization as well as the establishment of a fund to repair communities hit hardest by the drug war.

It's an ambitious plan that, given the Republican domination of Congress and the White House, almost certainly won't become law. But it marked Booker as perhaps the Senate's leading antidrug war advocate, which is important, given that many observers are already assuming he is one of the top contenders for the 2020 Democratic presidential nomination. (When he was asked this summer about 2020, Booker said, "I don't know what the future's going to bring.")

Booker recently talked about the future of weed in America, how his bill fits in, and why he's pushing for legalization while Trump is the president.

VICE: When Did You First Begin to Consider a Full Federal Legalization of Pot, and How Did It Manifest into the Marijuana Justice Act?

Cory Booker: I was talking about what the art of the possible was, and why one of the first things I led with was (the CARERS Act), a bipartisan bill on medical marijuana. I thought that that would be a great move and something that could get a lot more momentum. And it did—it is a bill that the Judiciary Committee is willing to hold a hearing on. . . . It's been this experience of seeing the hypocrisy within marijuana prohibition, and how it destroyed so many lives and communities who get caught up in the war on drugs, while other communities are more easily able to have their breaking of the law exonerated or overlooked. There is a massive injustice being done in a nation that believes in equal justice under the law; marijuana enforcement makes a mockery of that ideal.

I came to the conclusion that I am not going to wait until pragmatic politics shows me a pathway. I want to start to change the conversation and *make* the pathway, no matter how many obstacles there may be.

Do You Think That That Conversation Can Even Be Had in the Current Political Climate? Every Day Brings a Dozen News Items from the Administration, and a Lot of Important Topics End Up Buried

I was very moved at how in the day after introducing this bill a few Republican senators, who I wouldn't have expected, came up to share with me how they felt. One senator talked to me about college students that he knew who were having their lives ruined because they were caught with a little bit of marijuana. And it led to good conversations, and my desire for my colleagues to understand that it doesn't matter if they are a college student or a teenager in an inner city who is unemployed and still searching for an opportunity.

Nationally, I am questioned about it all the time. I am trying to use my platform not to follow consensus but to shape consensus, and to reveal to people what our current laws are doing in terms of how they're destroying our nation.

Though You've Had GOP Members Like Orrin Hatch Come Out in Support of Medical Marijuana, Republicans are Typically Seen as Being against Legalization. Why Put Forth Something the Trump Administration Will Toss Aside? Is This More about Broadening Discussion than Passing Your Bill as Is?

Well, I don't know when that time is going to be. But I know this: we've got to start that journey. I have been making the analogy to marriage equality. It was not that long ago that I was so frustrated that everybody from President Obama to Secretary of State Clinton were not in favor of marriage equality. But before you knew it, people were talking about it and pushing for the change. I don't want to wait to start calling for what's right when the political climate might seem advantageous. There is no time like the present to fight for what's right, to advocate for justice. There is no doubt in my mind that the federal government should not be in the marijuana prohibition business. It's making us less safe, it's costing taxpayers too

much money, and it's violating our values. From every perspective—a libertarian perspective, fiscal conservative's perspective, Christian evangelical perspective, and progressive perspective—marijuana prohibition is just wrong. So I am not going to read the political tea leaves anymore, and I am not going to be silent on this issue, especially when I can see—as the only senator that lives in a low-income inner-city community—the damage that has been done over decades of a failed war on drugs.

It's important to note that this is not just ending prohibition on the federal level. My legislation is really about beginning to repair the egregious harm that has been done to the communities that have been targeted. . . . Nobody is setting up FBI sting operations or stopping and frisking people as they come home from a fraternity party. This war on drugs is a war on people, and not all people: it's a war on poor people, on mentally ill people, on addicted people, and on people of color. My bill is focused on understanding that it's not just about ending prohibition. It has to be about retroactively expunging records. It has to be about community repair and addressing the generational damage that's been done by stripping communities of their economic strength.

In Your Initial Announcement of the Bill, You Spoke about Hearing Members in Congress Openly Admit to Drug Use. Do You Remember the First Time You Heard That? How Did You React?

I was graduating from college by the time Bill Clinton admitting to smoking marijuana—without inhaling. And that seemed like a radical revelation at the time—and risky. That's 1992, so about 15 years later—or I'm sorry, 21 years later (God, I am getting old) when I became a U.S. senator—it was a commonplace to having elected leaders admitting to having smoked marijuana, not to mention staffers. There is a privilege of people that get to positions of Senate and congressional staff—you're coming through privileged portals where you see no consequences for having done these things. Which is *dramatically* different than the community that I call home, where you don't have that privilege to be able to experiment with drugs without consequences. Remember, two of the last three presidents admitted to doing drugs far more serious than alcohol and marijuana. They copped to felony drug use, and they became the president of the United States.

Yet there are kids in my community and in communities around this country who have had their lives destroyed, and lifetime sentences for using drugs. The consequences for that "youthful indiscretion," as some might call it, will follow them for the rest of their lives.

Have You Ever Smoked Weed?

I have never smoked marijuana, I have never smoked a cigarette, I have never eaten marijuana, I have never tried another drug, and I have never drank alcohol*[laughs].* I think the most alcohol I have had may be a sip of beer to get my friends off my back, or maybe the church wine. This to me is not an issue I come at through my own experimentations. I come at this as an issue of justice, as an issue of safety for our communities, and as an issue of utter fairness. But I will tell you what, I might have my first drink of alcohol if my bill can become a law.

So What Are the Next Steps? Do You See a Clear Path for This Bill Passing?

I hate to be dramatic about it, but I don't see the pathway to passage right now. And—this is what I mean by being dramatic—I know that the first abolitionists that got together and started fighting for abolition didn't see the likelihood of passage in Congress at that point, I know that the first activists who started pressing for voting rights legislation and civil rights legislation didn't see a pathway . . . This is the beginning of a journey, and I think it's going to be a far shorter journey than many people think. Millennials in this country, Republican and Democrat, *overwhelmingly* believe in legalization. So we are getting there, and as experiments in a dozen plus states continue to forge forward on medical marijuana, and as decriminalization and legalization begin to show more instructive ways for dealing with marijuana, I think the momentum for our movement is going to continue. I am just proud to be a part of a group of people down here in Washington that believes we shouldn't follow. It's about time that we lead.

David Brooks  **NO**

Weed: Been There. Done That

For a little while in my teenage years, my friends and I smoked marijuana. It was fun. I have some fond memories of us all being silly together. I think those moments of uninhibited frolic deepened our friendships.

But then we all sort of moved away from it. I don't remember any big group decision that we should give up weed. It just sort of petered out, and, before long, we were scarcely using it.

We didn't give it up for the obvious health reasons: that it is addictive in about one in six teenagers; that smoking and driving is a good way to get yourself killed; that young people who smoke go on to suffer I.Q. loss and perform worse on other cognitive tests.

I think we gave it up, first, because we each had had a few embarrassing incidents. Stoned people do stupid things (that's basically the point). I smoked one day during lunch and then had to give a presentation in English class. I stumbled through it, incapable of putting together simple phrases, feeling like a total loser. It is still one of those embarrassing memories that pop up unbidden at 4 in the morning.

We gave it up, second, I think, because one member of our clique became a full-on stoner. He may have been the smartest of us, but something sad happened to him as he sunk deeper into pothead life.

Third, most of us developed higher pleasures. Smoking was fun, for a bit, but it was kind of repetitive. Most of us figured out early on that smoking weed doesn't really make you funnier or more creative (academic studies more or less confirm this). We graduated to more satisfying pleasures. The deeper sources of happiness usually involve a state of going somewhere, becoming better at something, learning more about something, overcoming difficulty, and experiencing a sense of satisfaction and accomplishment.

One close friend devoted himself to track. Others fell deeply in love and got thrills from the enlargements of the heart. A few developed passions for science or literature.

Finally, I think we had a vague sense that smoking weed was not exactly something you were proud of yourself for. It's not something people admire. We were in the stage, which I guess all of us are still in, of trying to become more integrated, coherent, and responsible people. This process usually involves using the powers of reason, temperance, and self-control—not qualities one associates with being high.

I think we had a sense, which all people have, or should have, that the actions you take change you inside, making you a little more or a little less coherent. Not smoking, or only smoking sporadically, gave you a better shot at becoming a little more integrated and interesting. Smoking all the time seemed likely to cumulatively fragment a person's deep center, or at least not do much to enhance it.

So, like the vast majority of people who try drugs, we aged out. We left marijuana behind. I don't have any problem with somebody who gets high from time to time, but I guess, on the whole, I think being stoned is not a particularly uplifting form of pleasure and should be discouraged more than encouraged.

We now have a couple states—Colorado and Washington—that have gone into the business of effectively encouraging drug use. By making weed legal, they are creating a situation in which the price will drop substantially. One RAND study suggests that prices could plummet by up to 90 percent, before taxes and such. As prices drop and legal fears go away, usage is bound to increase. This is simple economics, and it is confirmed by much research. Colorado and Washington, in other words, are producing more users.

The people who debate these policy changes usually cite the health risks users would face or the tax revenues the state might realize. Many people these days shy away from talk about the moral status of drug use because that would imply that one sort of life you might choose is better than another sort of life.

But, of course, these are the core questions: laws profoundly mold culture, so what sort of community do we want our laws to nurture? What sort of individuals and behaviors do our governments want to encourage? I'd say that in healthy societies, government wants to subtly tip the scale to favor temperate, prudent, self-governing citizenship. In those societies, government subtly encourages the highest pleasures, like enjoying the arts or being in nature, and discourages lesser pleasures, like being stoned.

In legalizing weed, citizens of Colorado are, indeed, enhancing individual freedom. But they are also nurturing a moral ecology in which it is a bit harder to be the sort of person most of us want to be.

DAVID BROOKS became an Op-Ed columnist for *The New York Times* in September 2003.

EXPLORING THE ISSUE

Should "Recreational" Drugs Be Legalized?

Critical Thinking and Reflection

1. How harmful are illegal drugs? Are they more dangerous than alcohol? Can we distinguish among them?
2. Is the history of prohibition of alcohol relevant in revealing the consequences of prohibition? Are the indicted substances sufficiently different so that comparisons are not useful?
3. In view of crowded prisons, should we consider alternative means of punishment for some categories of drug offenders? Does prohibition inspire its violation?
4. Why shouldn't we have a civil right to do what may be harmful to ourselves?
5. Do you believe there would be a larger societal impact if recreational drugs were to be legalized? If so, what could it be? If not, why not?

Is There Common Ground?

Advocates of legalization mostly believe that it must be accompanied by restraints on drug usage. Just as alcohol is subject to restrictions regarding its manufacturing and sale, and states vary in their requirements regarding the sale of alcohol, so legal drugs may be subject to strict controls. Absolute libertarians will dissent, arguing that there should be no regulation, but a vast majority of Americans would disagree. It would be likely that legalization would involve laws on purity of contents and other requirements that apply to alcohol and other legal drugs.

It is possible that supporters of prohibition may distinguish among the illicit drugs based on present awareness of their different effects. Defenders of drug prohibition might consent to the sale of medical marijuana, due to the claim that its use can reduce the pain of certain diseases. However, the experience in California and elsewhere is that licensing medical marijuana is likely to lead to the easy medical dispensing of medical marijuana to persons who are not legally entitled to it.

Perhaps, the true common ground has already begun to emerge. States are able to legalize within their boundaries and not fear federal crackdowns so long as they regulate the drug within federal guidelines. While such a measure works well for the time being, questions will continue to arise surrounding the Trump Administration's stance on enforcing federal law. After all, the current setup keeps recreational drugs illegal at the federal level and relies on policy memos from a political appointee. For the states to feel safe in their status, it will be necessary for a clearer relationship to develop between federal and state authorities on these issues, so enforcement does not ultimately become a political whim of the sitting president.

Additional Resources

Jonathan P. Caulkins, Angela Hawken, Beau Kilmer, and Mark A.R. Kleiman, *Marijuana Legalization: What Everyone Needs to Know* (Oxford University Press, 2012).

Larry Gaines, *Drug, Crimes, & Justice* (Waveland Press, 2002).

James A. Inciardi, *The Drug Legalization Debate* (Greenhaven Press, 2013).

Robert J. MacCoun and Peter Reuter, *Drug War -Heresies* (Cambridge University Press, 2001).

U.S. Department of Justice and Drug Enforcement Administration, *Speaking Out Against Drug Legalization* (CreateSpace, 2012).

Internet References . . .

Citizens against Legalizing Marijuana

www.calmca.org/about/

Marijuana Policy Project

www.mpp.org/

National Organization for the Reform of Marijuana Laws

http://norml.org/

Public Broadcasting Service

www.pbs.org/wnet/need-to-know/ask-the-experts/ ask-the-experts-legalizing-marijuana/15474/

Selected, Edited, and with Issue Framing Material by:
William J. Miller, *Campus Labs®*

ISSUE

Should Business Owners Be Able to Refuse Clients Based on Religious Beliefs?

YES: Anthony Kennedy, from *"Masterpiece Cakeshop, Ltd., et al., v. Colorado Civil Rights Commission, et al.,"* United States Supreme Court (2018)

NO: Ruth Bader Ginsburg, from *"Masterpiece Cakeshop, Ltd., et al., v. Colorado Civil Rights Commission, et al.,"* United States Supreme Court (2018)

Learning Outcomes
After reading this issue, you will be able to:
• Explain the Supreme Court's role in determining religious freedom.
• Discuss religious freedom in the American context.
• Assess the impact of recent Supreme Court rulings on religion.
• Explain the freedoms of corporations in the United States.
• Assess the relationship between law and religion.

ISSUE SUMMARY

YES: Supreme Court Justice Anthony Kennedy, writing for the Court, identifies the fundamental conflict between freedom of religion and civil rights. In the matter of a businessman's decision on whether to serve a gay couple, Kennedy acknowledges how imperative it is to balance religious sincerity with the rights of a group to be served. In this case, however, he sides with the business.

NO: Justice Ruth Bader Ginsburg agrees with much of Kennedy's argument but believes at a fundamental level it is not right that a business provides services to one group that it wouldn't provide to another.

Within the United States, a volume of legal scholarship exists deeming that a corporation (an entity consisting of a group of people) may be recognized as having many of the same legal rights—and responsibilities—as an individual. Corporations, for example, can enter contracts or seek legal remedies much the same as individual American citizens can. While corporations are given many rights, they are not viewed by the courts as people. Likewise, they are not provided with all of the same rights as human beings.

This legal phenomenon is not particularly new— despite numerous public claims that corporations have never had such rights in the country's past. In 1819, the Supreme Court—in *Trustees of Dartmouth college v. Woodward*—recognized that corporations possess the same rights as natural persons to enforce contracts. Six decades later, in *Santa Clara v. Southern Pacific Railroad*, Justice Morrison White stated at the beginning of oral arguments that "The court does not wish to hear argument on the question whether the provision in the Fourteenth Amendment to the Constitution, which forbids a State to deny to any person within its jurisdiction the equal protection of the laws, applies to these corporations. We are all of the opinion that it does." Since White's statement was not part of the official opinion, it did not immediately become legal precedent. Shortly thereafter, however, White's proclamation became part of the official record in *Pembina Consolidated Silver Mining Co. v. Pennsylvania*. Within the ruling, the Court held that "Under the designation of 'person' there is no doubt that a private corporation is included (in the Fourteenth Amendment). Such corporations are merely associations of individuals united for a special purpose and permitted to do business under a particular name and have a succession of members without dissolution." In the next century, this finding would be reaffirmed regularly.

If we look at why corporations are viewed as persons, we can turn to the Fourteenth Amendment, which clearly mentions the powers of people. If one is to interpret a group of people (a corporation) as a person, it becomes possible to understand the assumption of some individual rights being granted to the aggregate. After all, if corporations are just organizations of people, how could the courts justify the deprivation of individual constitutional rights simply because of collective action? By treating corporations as people, it becomes easier to legally consider them. They can be sued, taxed, regulated, and observed far more easily. Perhaps even more importantly, corporations are simplified and allow individuals to reap the benefits of working together without being forced to sacrifice their right of association. Not all Americans are accepting of these rules, however. Instead, opponents believe the Constitution should only apply to natural born persons and that only state laws should be permitted to provide corporations with rights and responsibilities.

It is important to remember that not all individual rights are automatically given to corporations; the Supreme Court utilizes cases and selective incorporation to make rulings on an independent basis. As a rough estimate, if groups of people do not possess the protection, odds are corporations do not either. Corporations, for example, cannot claim a Fifth Amendment protection against self-incrimination. Corporations have tried to argue for such protections, but they have yet to succeed (most recently failing in *United States v. Sourapas and Crest Beverage*).

Suffice it to say, corporate personhood was not a particularly controversial concept prior to the Supreme Court's ruling in *Citizens United v. Federal Election Commission* in 2010. In the *Citizens United* case, the Court upheld the rights of corporations to make political expenditures under the First Amendment. Despite making no references to either corporate personhood or the Fourteenth Amendment, public outcry has begun to demand the revocation of individual rights from corporate organizations. Yet, as stated above, the debate was not new when it arose in 2010—with questions of campaign finance

and corporate impact on democratic governance leading the considerations. In 1990, the Court ruled in *Austin v. Michigan Chamber of Commerce* that corporations could be prohibited from using money from their aggregate treasury to directly support or oppose federal candidates due to the potential for unfair influence. Ultimately, in the *Citizens United* case, the Court opted to overrule *Austin*. And the influence has not stopped in 2010 as the newly created precedent has already been applied—most notably in *Western Tradition Partnership Inc v. Attorney General of Montana* in 2012. In this case, the Court reversed a Montana Supreme Court ruling that *Citizens United* did not preclude a Montana state law regarding the illegality of corporate spending in election.

At the end of the day, in the past half-decade, the Supreme Court has decided that corporations are entitled to the same free speech protections that individuals received from the *Buckley v. Valeo* ruling in 1976—at least when it comes to campaign donations. Opponents of these recent decisions have argued that if all corporate rights under the Constitution were abolished, it would clear the way for greater regulation of campaign spending and contributions. It should be noted, however, that neither decision relied on the concept of corporate personhood, and the Buckley decision in particular deals with the rights of individuals and political committees, not corporations. But—taken on the whole—the cases show corporations are gaining significantly more rights. Enter the discussion on religion.

The U.S. Supreme Court heard arguments last year in the latest challenge to the Affordable Care Act with Hobby Lobby, a chain of arts and crafts stores owned by Christians who object to certain methods of birth control—IUDs and morning after pills—because they can interfere with the creation of life once an egg is fertilized, resulting in abortion, serving as the lead plaintiff. The issue in the case was clear: can for-profit corporations, citing religious objections, refuse some or potentially all contraceptive services in health plans offered to employees? It's a hot-button issue that had Americans watching carefully for the Court's decision as siding with Hobby Lobby would provide additional freedoms to corporations. Ultimately, the Court ruled with Hobby Lobby for a number of reasons. They discussed how corporations, while having independent legal existences, are formed through individuals. Further, they noted concerns with restricting the First Amendment and removing the private aspect of private enterprise.

At the end of the day, granting individual freedoms to a corporation looks ridiculous on its face. Mitt Romney was mocked from making such claims when campaigning for president in 2012. Yet the U.S. Code defines corporations as people in its opening line. Even if corporations have individual rights—especially those espoused in the First Amendment—there are still questions about exactly how far Americans want the courts to go in expanding freedoms to these created groups. When asked their opinion, Americans consistently agree that religious liberty is important for both individual employees and owners. Yet, in contrast, they were significantly and consistently less willing to grant the same scope of protection to all the for-profit companies we presented them.

In the following readings, Supreme Court Justice Anthony Kennedy, writing for the Court, identifies the fundamental conflict between freedom of religion and civil rights. In the matter of a businessman's decision on whether to serve a gay couple, Kennedy acknowledges how imperative it is to balance religious sincerity with the rights of a group to be served. In this case, however, he sides with the business. Justice Ruth Bader Ginsburg agrees with much of Kennedy's argument but believes at a fundamental level it is not right that a business provides services to one group that it wouldn't provide to another.

Anthony Kennedy

Masterpiece Cakeshop, Ltd., et al., v. Colorado Civil Rights Commission, et al.

Justice Kennedy delivered the opinion of the Court.

In 2012, a same-sex couple visited Masterpiece Cakeshop, a bakery in Colorado, to make inquiries about ordering a cake for their wedding reception. The shop's owner told the couple that he would not create a cake for their wedding because of his religious opposition to same-sex marriages—marriages the State of Colorado itself did not recognize at that time. The couple filed a charge with the Colorado Civil Rights Commission alleging discrimination on the basis of sexual orientation in violation of the Colorado Anti-Discrimination Act.

The Commission determined that the shop's actions violated the Act and ruled in the couple's favor. The Colorado state courts affirmed the ruling and its enforcement order, and this Court now must decide whether the Commission's order violated the Constitution.

The case presents difficult questions as to the proper reconciliation of at least two principles. The first is the authority of a State and its governmental entities to protect the rights and dignity of gay persons who are, or wish to be, married but who face discrimination when they seek goods or services. The second is the right of all persons to exercise fundamental freedoms under the First Amendment, as applied to the States through the Fourteenth Amendment.

The freedoms asserted here are both the freedom of speech and the free exercise of religion. The free speech aspect of this case is difficult, for few persons who have seen a beautiful wedding cake might have thought of its creation as an exercise of protected speech. This is an instructive example, however, of the proposition that the application of constitutional freedoms in new contexts can deepen our understanding of their meaning.

One of the difficulties in this case is that the parties disagree as to the extent of the baker's refusal to provide service. If a baker refused to design a special cake with words or images celebrating the marriage—for instance, a cake showing words with religious meaning—that might be different from a refusal to sell any cake at all. In defining whether a baker's creation can be protected, these details might make a difference.

The same difficulties arise in determining whether a baker has a valid free exercise claim. A baker's refusal to attend the wedding to ensure that the cake is cut the right way, or a refusal to put certain religious words or decorations on the cake, or even a refusal to sell a cake that has been baked for the public generally but includes certain religious words or symbols on it are just three examples of possibilities that seem all but endless.

Whatever the confluence of speech and free exercise principles might be in some cases, the Colorado Civil Rights Commission's consideration of this case was inconsistent with the State's obligation of religious neutrality. The reason and motive for the baker's refusal were based on his sincere religious beliefs and convictions. The Court's precedents make clear that the baker, in his capacity as the owner of a business serving the public, might have his right to the free exercise of religion limited by generally applicable laws. Still, the delicate question of when the free exercise of his religion must yield to an otherwise valid exercise of state power needed to be determined in an adjudication in which religious hostility on the part of the State itself would not be a factor in the balance the State sought to reach. That requirement, however, was not met here. When the Colorado Civil Rights Commission considered this case, it did not do so with the religious neutrality that the Constitution requires.

Given all these considerations, it is proper to hold that whatever the outcome of some future controversy involving facts similar to these, the Commission's actions here violated the Free Exercise Clause, and its order must be set aside.

I

A

Masterpiece Cakeshop, Ltd., is a bakery in Lakewood, CO, a suburb of Denver. The shop offers a variety of baked goods, ranging from everyday cookies and brownies to elaborate custom-designed cakes for birthday parties, weddings, and other events.

Jack Phillips is an expert baker who has owned and operated the shop for 24 years. Phillips is a devout Christian. He has explained that his "main goal in life is to be obedient to" Jesus Christ and Christ's "teachings in all aspects of his life." App. 148. And he seeks to "honor God through his work at Masterpiece Cakeshop." *Ibid.* One of Phillips' religious beliefs is that "God's intention for marriage from the beginning of history is that it is and should be the union of one man and one woman." *Id.,* at 149. To Phillips, creating a wedding cake for a same-sex wedding would be equivalent to participating in a celebration that is contrary to his own most deeply held beliefs.

Phillips met Charlie Craig and Dave Mullins when they entered his shop in the summer of 2012. Craig and Mullins were planning to marry. At that time, Colorado did not recognize same-sex marriages, so the couple planned to wed legally in Massachusetts and afterward to host a reception for their family and friends in Denver. To prepare for their celebration, Craig and Mullins visited the shop and told Phillips that they were interested in ordering a cake for "our wedding." *Id.,* at 152 (emphasis deleted). They did not mention the design of the cake they envisioned.

Phillips informed the couple that he does not "create" wedding cakes for same-sex weddings. *Ibid.* He explained, "I'll make your birthday cakes, shower cakes, sell you cookies and brownies, I just don't make cakes for same-sex weddings." *Ibid.* The couple left the shop without further discussion.

The following day, Craig's mother, who had accompanied the couple to the cakeshop and been present for their interaction with Phillips, telephoned to ask Phillips why he had declined to serve her son. Phillips explained that he does not create wedding cakes for same-sex weddings because of his religious opposition to same-sex marriage and also because Colorado (at that time) did not recognize same-sex marriages. *Id.,* at 153. He later explained his belief that "to create a wedding cake for an event that celebrates something that directly goes against the teachings of the Bible, would have been a personal endorsement and participation in the ceremony and relationship that they were entering into." *Ibid.* (emphasis deleted).

C

Craig and Mullins filed a discrimination complaint against Masterpiece Cakeshop and Phillips in August 2012, shortly after the couple's visit to the shop. App. 31. The complaint alleged that Craig and Mullins had been denied "full and equal service" at the bakery because of their sexual orientation, *id.,* at 35, 48, and that it was Phillips' "standard business practice" not to provide cakes for same-sex weddings, *id.,* at 43.

The Civil Rights Division opened an investigation. The investigator found that "on multiple occasions," Phillips "turned away potential customers on the basis of their sexual orientation, stating that he could not create a cake for a same-sex wedding ceremony or reception" because his religious beliefs prohibited it and because the potential customers "were doing something illegal" at that time. *Id.,* at 76. The investigation found that Phillips had declined to sell custom wedding cakes to about six other same-sex couples on this basis. *Id.,* at 72. The investigator also recounted that, according to affidavits submitted by Craig and Mullins, Phillips' shop had refused to sell cupcakes to a lesbian couple for their commitment celebration because the shop "had a policy of not selling baked goods to same-sex couples for this type of event." *Id.,* at 73. Based on these findings, the Division found probable cause that Phillips violated Colorado Antidiscrimination Act and referred the case to the Civil Rights Commission. *Id.,* at 69.

II

A

Our society has come to the recognition that gay persons and gay couples cannot be treated as social outcasts or as inferior in dignity and worth. For that reason the laws and the Constitution can, and in some instances must, protect them in the exercise of their civil rights. The exercise of their freedom on terms equal to others must be given great weight and respect by the courts. At the same time, the religious and philosophical objections to gay marriage are protected views and in some instances protected forms of expression. As this Court observed in *Obergefell v. Hodges,* 576 U.S. _____ (2015), "[t]he First Amendment ensures that religious organizations and persons are given proper protection as they seek to teach the principles that are so fulfilling and so central to their lives and faiths." *Id.,* at _____ (slip op., at 27). Nevertheless, while those religious and philosophical objections are protected, it is a general rule that such objections do not allow business owners and other actors in the economy and in society to deny protected persons equal access to goods and services under a neutral and generally applicable public accommodations law. See *Newman v. Piggy Park Enterprises, Inc.*, 390 U.S. 400, 402, n. 5 (1968) (*per curiam*); see also *Hurley v. Irish-American Gay, Lesbian and Bisexual Group of Boston, Inc.*, 515 U.S. 557, 572 (1995) (Provisions like these are well within the State's usual power to enact when a legislature has reason to believe that a given group is the target of discrimination, and they do not, as a general matter, violate the First or Fourteenth Amendments).

When it comes to weddings, it can be assumed that a member of the clergy who objects to gay marriage on moral and religious grounds could not be compelled to perform the ceremony without denial of his or her right to the free exercise of religion. This refusal would be well understood in our constitutional order as an exercise of religion, an exercise that gay persons could recognize and accept without serious diminishment to their own dignity and worth. Yet if that exception were not confined, then a long list of persons who provide goods and services for marriages and weddings might refuse to do so for gay persons, thus resulting in a community-wide stigma inconsistent with the history and dynamics of civil rights laws that ensure equal access to goods, services, and public accommodations.

It is unexceptional that Colorado law can protect gay persons, just as it can protect other classes of individuals, in acquiring whatever products and services they choose on the same terms and conditions as are offered to other members of the public. And there are no doubt innumerable goods and services that no one could argue implicate the First Amendment. Petitioners conceded, moreover, that if a baker refused to sell any goods or any cakes for gay weddings, that would be a different matter and the State would have a strong case under this Court's precedents that this would be a denial of goods and services that went beyond any protected rights of a baker who offers goods and services to the general public and is subject to a neutrally applied and generally applicable public accommodations law. See Tr. of Oral Arg. 4–7, 10.

Phillips claims, however, that a narrower issue is presented. He argues that he had to use his artistic skills to make an expressive statement, a wedding endorsement in his own voice and of his own creation. As Phillips would see the case, this contention has a significant First Amendment speech component and implicates his deep and sincere religious beliefs. In this context, the baker likely found it difficult to find a line where the customers' rights to goods and services became a demand for him to exercise the right of his own personal expression for their message, a message he could not express in a way consistent with his religious beliefs.

B

The neutral and respectful consideration to which Phillips was entitled was compromised here, however. The Civil Rights Commission's treatment of his case has some elements of a clear and impermissible hostility toward the sincere religious beliefs that motivated his objection.

That hostility surfaced at the Commission's formal, public hearings, as shown by the record. On May 30, 2014, the seven-member Commission convened publicly to consider Phillips' case. At several points during its meeting, commissioners endorsed the view that religious beliefs cannot legitimately be carried into the public sphere or commercial domain, implying that religious beliefs and persons are less than fully welcome in Colorado's business community. One commissioner suggested that Phillips can believe "what he wants to believe," but cannot act on his religious beliefs "if he decides to do business in the state." Tr. 23. A few moments later, the commissioner restated the same position: "[I]f a businessman wants to do business in the state and he's got an issue with the—the law's impacting his personal belief system, he needs to look at being able to compromise." *Id.*, at 30. Standing alone, these statements are susceptible of different interpretations. On the one hand, they might mean simply that a business cannot refuse to provide services based on sexual orientation, regardless of the proprietor's personal views. On the other hand, they might be seen as inappropriate and dismissive comments showing lack of due consideration for Phillips' free exercise rights and the dilemma he faced. In view of the comments that followed, the latter seems the more likely.

On July 25, 2014, the Commission met again. This meeting, too, was conducted in public and on the record. On this occasion, another commissioner made specific reference to the previous meeting's discussion but said far more to disparage Phillips' beliefs. The commissioner stated:

> "I would also like to reiterate what we said in the hearing or the last meeting. Freedom of religion and religion has been used to justify all kinds of discrimination throughout history, whether it be slavery, whether it be the holocaust, whether it be—I mean, we—we can list hundreds of situations where freedom of religion has been used to justify discrimination. And to me it is one of the most despicable pieces of rhetoric that people can use to—to use their religion to hurt others." Tr. 11–12.

To describe a man's faith as "one of the most despicable pieces of rhetoric that people can use" is to disparage his religion in at least two distinct ways: by describing it as despicable and also by characterizing it as merely rhetorical—something insubstantial and even insincere. The commissioner even went so far as to compare Phillips' invocation of his sincerely held religious beliefs to defenses of slavery and the Holocaust. This sentiment is inappropriate for a Commission charged with the solemn responsibility of fair and neutral enforcement of Colorado's antidiscrimination law—a law that protects discrimination on the basis of religion as well as sexual orientation.

For the reasons just described, the Commission's treatment of Phillips' case violated the State's duty under the First Amendment not to base laws or regulations on hostility to a religion or religious viewpoint.

In *Church of Lukumi Babalu Aye, supra*, the Court made clear that the government, if it is to respect the Constitution's guarantee of free exercise, cannot impose regulations that are hostile to the religious beliefs of affected citizens and cannot act in a manner that passes judgment upon or presupposes the illegitimacy of religious beliefs and practices. The Free Exercise Clause bars even "subtle departures from neutrality" on matters of religion. *Id.*, at 534. Here, that means the Commission was obliged under the Free Exercise Clause to proceed in a manner neutral toward and tolerant of Phillips' religious beliefs. The Constitution "commits government itself to religious tolerance, and upon even slight suspicion that proposals for state intervention stem from animosity to religion or distrust of its practices, all officials must pause to remember their own high duty to the Constitution and to the rights it secures." *Id.*, at 547.

Factors relevant to the assessment of governmental neutrality include "the historical background of the decision under challenge, the specific series of events leading to the enactment or official policy in question, and the legislative or administrative history, including contemporaneous statements made by members of the decision-making body." *Id.*, at 540. In view of these factors, the record here demonstrates that the Commission's consideration of Phillips' case was neither tolerant nor respectful of Phillips' religious beliefs. The Commission gave "every appearance," *id.*, at 545, of adjudicating Phillips' religious objection based on a negative normative "evaluation of the particular justification" for his objection and the religious grounds for it. *Id.*, at 537. It hardly requires restating that government has no role in deciding or even suggesting whether the religious ground for Phillips' conscience-based objection is legitimate or illegitimate. On these facts, the Court must draw the inference that Phillips' religious objection was not considered with the neutrality that the Free Exercise Clause requires.

While the issues here are difficult to resolve, it must be concluded that the State's interest could have been weighed against Phillips' sincere religious objections in a way consistent with the requisite religious neutrality that must be strictly observed. The official expressions of hostility to religion in some of the commissioners' comments—comments that were not disavowed at the Commission or by the State at any point in the proceedings that led to affirmance of the order—were inconsistent with what the Free Exercise Clause requires. The Commission's disparate consideration of Phillips' case compared to the cases of the other bakers suggests the same. For these reasons, the order must be set aside.

III

The Commission's hostility was inconsistent with the First Amendment's guarantee that our laws be applied in a manner that is neutral toward religion. Phillips was entitled to a neutral decision maker who would give full and fair consideration to his religious objection as he sought to assert it in all of the circumstances in which this case was presented, considered, and decided. In this case, the adjudication concerned a context that may well be different going forward in the respects noted above. However, later cases raising these or similar concerns are resolved in the future, for these reasons the rulings of the Commission and of the state court that enforced the Commission's order must be invalidated.

The outcome of cases like this in other circumstances must await further elaboration in the courts, all in the context of recognizing that these disputes must be resolved with tolerance, without undue disrespect to sincere religious beliefs, and without subjecting gay persons to indignities when they seek goods and services in an open market.

The judgment of the Colorado Court of Appeals is reversed.

It is so ordered.

ANTHONY KENNEDY is an American lawyer and jurist who served as an associate justice of the Supreme Court of the United States from 1988 until his retirement in 2018. He was nominated to the court in 1987 by President Ronald Reagan and sworn in on February 18, 1988.

Ruth Bader Ginsburg

 **NO**

Masterpiece Cakeshop, Ltd., et al., v. Colorado Civil Rights Commission, et al.

Justice Ginsburg, with whom Justice Sotomayor joins, dissenting.

There is much in the Court's opinion with which I agree. "[I]t is a general rule that [religious and philosophical] objections do not allow business owners and other actors in the economy and in society to deny protected persons equal access to goods and services under a neutral and generally applicable public accommodations law." *Ante*, at 9. "Colorado law can protect gay persons, just as it can protect other classes of individuals, in acquiring whatever products and services they choose on the same terms and conditions as are offered to other members of the public." *Ante*, at 10. "[P]urveyors of goods and services who object to gay marriages for moral and religious reasons [may not] put up signs saying 'no goods or services will be sold if they will be used for gay marriages'." *Ante*, at 12. Gay persons may be spared from "indignities when they seek goods and services in an open market." *Ante*, at 18. I strongly disagree, however, with the Court's conclusion that Craig and Mullins should lose this case. All of the above-quoted statements point in the opposite direction.

The Court concludes that "Phillips' religious objection was not considered with the neutrality that the Free Exercise Clause requires." *Ante*, at 17. This conclusion rests on evidence said to show the Colorado Civil Rights Commission's (Commission) hostility to religion. Hostility is discernible, the Court maintains, from the asserted "disparate consideration of Phillips' case compared to the cases of" three other bakers who refused to make cakes requested by William Jack, an amicus here. *Ante*, at 18. The Court also finds hostility in statements made at two public hearings on Phillips' appeal to the Commission. *Ante*, at 12–14. The different outcomes the Court features do not evidence hostility to religion of the kind we have previously held to signal a free exercise violation nor do the comments by one or two members of one of the four

decision-making entities considering this case justify reversing the judgment below.

I

On March 13, 2014—approximately three months after the ALJ ruled in favor of the same-sex couple, Craig and Mullins, and two months before the Commission heard Phillips' appeal from that decision—William Jack visited three Colorado bakeries. His visits followed a similar pattern. He requested two cakes

> "made to resemble an open Bible. He also requested that each cake be decorated with Biblical verses. [He] requested that one of the cakes include an image of two groomsmen, holding hands, with a red 'X' over the image. On one cake, he requested [on] one side[,] . . . 'God hates sin. Psalm 45:7' and on the opposite side of the cake 'Homosexuality is a detestable sin. Leviticus 18:2.' On the second cake, [the one] with the image of the two groomsmen covered by a red 'X' [Jack] requested [these words]: 'God loves sinners' and on the other side 'While we were yet sinners Christ died for us. Romans 5:8.'" App. to Pet. for Cert. 319a; see *id.*, at 300a, 310a.

In contrast to Jack, Craig and Mullins simply requested a wedding cake: they mentioned no message or anything else distinguishing the cake they wanted to buy from any other wedding cake Phillips would have sold.

One bakery told Jack it would make cakes in the shape of Bibles but would not decorate them with the requested messages; the owner told Jack her bakery "does not discriminate" and "accept[s] all humans." *Id.*, at 301a (internal quotation marks omitted). The second bakery owner told Jack he "had done open Bibles and books many times and that they look amazing" but declined to make the specific cakes Jack

Ginsburg, Ruth Bader. *Masterpiece Cakeshop, Ltd., et al., v. Colorado Civil Rights Commission, et al.*

described because the baker regarded the messages as "hateful." *Id.*, at 310a (internal quotation marks omitted). The third bakery, according to Jack, said it would bake the cakes, but would not include the requested message. *Id.*, at 319a.

Jack filed charges against each bakery with the Colorado Civil Rights Division (Division). The Division found no probable cause to support Jack's claims of unequal treatment and denial of goods or services based on his Christian religious beliefs. *Id.*, at 297a, 307a, 316a. In this regard, the Division observed that the bakeries regularly produced cakes and other baked goods with Christian symbols and had denied other customer requests for designs demeaning people whose dignity the Colorado Antidiscrimination Act (CADA) protects. See *id.*, at 305a, 314a, 324a. The Commission summarily affirmed the Division's no-probable-cause finding. See *id.*, at 326a–331a.

The Court concludes that "the Commission's consideration of Phillips' religious objection did not accord with its treatment of [the other bakers'] objections." *Ante*, at 15. See also *ante*, at 5–7 (Gorsuch, J., concurring). But the cases the Court aligns are hardly comparable. The bakers would have refused to make a cake with Jack's requested message for any customer, regardless of his or her religion. And the bakers visited by Jack would have sold him any baked goods they would have sold anyone else. The bakeries' refusal to make Jack cakes of a kind they would not make for any customer scarcely resembles Phillips' refusal to serve Craig and Mullins: Phillips would *not* sell to Craig and Mullins, for no reason other than their sexual orientation, a cake of the kind he regularly sold to others. When a couple contacts a bakery for a wedding cake, the product they are seeking is a cake celebrating *their* wedding—not a cake celebrating heterosexual weddings or same-sex weddings—and that is the service Craig and Mullins were denied. Cf. *ante*, at 3–4, 9–10 (Gorsuch, J., concurring). Colorado, the Court does not gainsay, prohibits precisely the discrimination Craig and Mullins encountered. See *supra*, at 1. Jack, on the other hand, suffered no service refusal on the basis of his religion or any other protected characteristic. He was treated as any other customer would have been treated—no better, no worse.

The fact that Phillips might sell other cakes and cookies to gay and lesbian customers was irrelevant to the issue Craig and Mullins' case presented. What matters is that Phillips would not provide a good or service to a same-sex couple that he would provide to a heterosexual couple. In contrast, the other bakeries' sale of other goods to Christian customers was relevant: It shows that there were no goods the bakeries would sell to a non-Christian customer that they would refuse to sell to a Christian customer. Cf. *ante*, at 15.

Nor was the Colorado Court of Appeals' "difference in treatment of these two instances . . . based on the government's own assessment of offensiveness." *Ante*, at 16. Phillips declined to make a cake he found offensive where the offensiveness of the product was determined solely by the identity of the customer requesting it. The three other bakeries declined to make cakes where their objection to the product was due to the demeaning message the requested product would literally display. As the Court recognizes, a refusal "to design a special cake with words or images . . . might be different from a refusal to sell any cake at all." *Ante*, at 2. The Colorado Court of Appeals did not distinguish Phillips and the other three bakeries based simply on its or the Division's finding that messages in the cakes Jack requested were offensive while any message in a cake for Craig and Mullins was not. The Colorado court distinguished the cases on the ground that Craig and Mullins were denied service based on an aspect of their identity that the State chose to grant vigorous protection from discrimination. See App. to Pet. for Cert. 20a, n. 8 (The Division found that the bakeries did not refuse [Jack's] request because of his creed, but rather because of the offensive nature of the requested message. . . . [T]here was no evidence that the bakeries based their decisions on [Jack's] religion . . . [whereas Phillips] discriminat[ed] on the basis of sexual orientation.). I do not read the Court to suggest that the Colorado Legislature's decision to include certain protected characteristics in CADA is an impermissible government prescription of what is and is not offensive. Cf. *ante*, at 9–10. To repeat, the Court affirms that "Colorado law can protect gay persons, just as it can protect other classes of individuals, in acquiring whatever products and services they choose on the same terms and conditions as are offered to other members of the public." *Ante*, at 10.

II

Statements made at the Commission's public hearings on Phillips' case provide no firmer support for the Court's holding today. Whatever one may think of the statements in historical context, I see no reason why the comments of one or two Commissioners should be taken to overcome Phillips' refusal to sell a wedding cake to Craig and Mullins. The proceedings involved several layers of independent decision-making, of which the Commission was but one. See App. to Pet. for Cert. 5a–6a. First, the Division had to find probable cause that Phillips violated CADA. Second, the ALJ entertained the parties' cross-motions for summary judgment. Third, the Commission heard Phillips' appeal. Fourth, after the Commission's ruling, the Colorado Court of Appeals considered the case de novo.

What prejudice infected the determinations of the adjudicators in the case before and after the Commission? The Court does not say. Phillips' case is thus far removed from the only precedent upon which the Court relies, *Church of Lukumi Babalu Aye, Inc. v. Hialeah*, 508 U.S. 520 (1993), where the government action that violated a principle of religious neutrality implicated a sole decision-making body, the city council, see *id.*, at 526–528.

For the reasons stated, sensible application of CADA to a refusal to sell any wedding cake to a gay couple should occasion affirmance of the Colorado Court of Appeals' judgment. I would so rule.

RUTH BADER GINSBURG is an associate justice of the Supreme Court of the United States. Ginsburg was appointed by President Bill Clinton and took the oath of office on August 10, 1993. She is the second female justice of four to be confirmed to the court.

EXPLORING THE ISSUE

Should Business Owners Be Able to Refuse Clients Based on Religious Beliefs?

Critical Thinking and Reflection

1. How did this case differ from previous business-based religious freedom cases?
2. Do you agree or disagree with the decision? Why?
3. On what other issues do we see politics and religion intersecting in the United States today?
4. How does the Court typically view corporations? In which ways do they have individual rights? In which ways do they not?
5. Is it possible to have a wall between church and state in America today? Why or why not?

Is There Common Ground?

At the end of the day, corporations are either people or they are not. While the Courts continue to discuss what rights and freedoms these legally constructed groups of citizens should possess, at the end of the day, there is little room for common ground in this debate. After all, citizens will either agree that corporations should have First Amendment freedoms or not—and that decision will largely be based on perceptions of the entities themselves. And, most importantly, this opinion is unlikely to be swayed. What citizens believe about corporations and corporate personhood is typically a steadfast attitude, unable to be swayed or penetrated by new ideas or opinions.

When it comes to matters of religion, the issue becomes even more debatable. We are now taking sensitive issues that hit at the inner core of many Americans and suggesting that legal constructions be provided with similar freedoms. Abortion—for example—is a deeply personal issue for many and one that many seek spiritual guidance for understanding and interpreting. Now, the Courts are suggesting that soulless, heartless, and bodiless organizations are potentially capable of making the same interpretations. If citizens do not believe politics should interfere with religion, the odds are they will not appreciate the ability for corporations to do the same—at least if their side is not winning. Unfortunately, when it comes to religion and politics, issues—in reality—are never black and white, despite citizens doing everything in their power to view them that way. Common ground on this issue will be particularly difficult to find as a result.

Additional Resources

Andrew Koppleman, *Defending American Religious Neutrality* (Harvard University Press, 2013).

Brian Leiter, *Why Tolerate Religion?* (Princeton University Press, 2012).

Ira Luple and Robert Tuttle, *Secular Government, Religious People* (Wm. B. Eerdmans Publishing Co., 2014).

Martha Nussbaum, *Liberty of Conscience: In Defense of America's Tradition of Religious Equality* (Basic Books, 2010).

Steven D. Smith, *The Rise and Decline of American Religious Freedom* (Harvard University Press, 2014).

Internet References . . .

Alliance for Defending Freedom

http://www.alliancedefendingfreedom.org/issues/
religious-liberty

Bill of Rights Institute

http://billofrightsinstitute.org/resources/educator-
resources/headlines/freedom-of-religion/

Center for Religious Freedom

http://www.hudson.org/policycenters/7-center-for-
religious-freedom

International Association for Religious Freedom

https://iarf.net/

International Religious Freedom Report for 2017

https://www.state.gov/j/drl/rls/irf/religiousfreedom/
index.htm

Unit 4

UNIT

America and the World

*A*t one time, the United States could isolate itself from much of the world, and it did. But today's America affects and is affected—for good or ill—by what happens anywhere on the planet. Whether the topic is ecology, finance, war, or terrorism, America is integrally tied to the rest of the world. With a globalized economy and instant communication, no nation lives in a bubble, regardless of its intent or desire to. What happens in one country will impact societies across the globe regardless of one's intent.

    The United States, then, simply has no choice but to act and react in relation to a constantly shifting series of events; the arguments turn on over whether it acts morally or immorally, wisely or foolishly, what methods are morally justified in protecting the American homeland from attack? Do they include limiting immigrants from countries known to harbor threats? To build a wall to protect domestic interests along our Southern border, Should we expect enemies to demilitarize under pressure from the United States and her allies? And how should we best utilize our allies in areas prone to conflict without becoming too involved with their domestic needs and wants?

Selected, Edited, and with Issue Framing Material by:
William J. Miller, *Campus Labs®*

ISSUE

Should the President Have the Power to Limit Immigrants and Refugees from Specific Countries?

YES: John Roberts, from *"Majority Opinion: Trump v. Hawaii,"* United States Supreme Court (2018)

NO: Sonia Sotomayor, from *"Dissenting Opinion: Trump v. Hawaii,"* United States Supreme Court (2018)

Learning Outcomes

After reading this issue, you will be able to:

- Discuss immigration trends from Middle Eastern countries.
- Identify concerns about immigration from these countries.
- Describe historical Supreme Court rulings related to immigration.
- Explain political pressures present on both sides of this debate.
- Assess impact of banning immigrants from specific countries.

ISSUE SUMMARY

YES: Writing for the Court, Chief Justice John Roberts argues that the Trump Administration based its immigration policy on a sufficient national security justification to survive a rational basis review. Regardless of politicized statements made, the president's broad power over immigration matters Trump's potential concerns that are not in direct violation of any Constitutional provisions.

NO: Writing for the minority, Justice Sonia Sotomayor points to both Trump's statements about Muslims and the Establishment Clause to argue that the president should not have the power to ban immigrants from specific countries—especially when there is a strong religious correlation.

In passing what became commonly referred to as a Muslim Ban, President Trump stated:

"In Executive Order 13780 of March 6, 2017 (Protecting the Nation from Foreign Terrorist Entry into the United States), on the recommendations of the Secretary of Homeland Security and the Attorney General, I ordered a worldwide review of whether, and if so what, additional information would be needed from each foreign country to assess adequately whether their nationals seeking to enter the United States pose a security or safety

threat. This was the first such review of its kind in United States history. As part of the review, the Secretary of Homeland Security established global requirements for information sharing in support of immigration screening and vetting. The Secretary of Homeland Security developed a comprehensive set of criteria and applied it to the information-sharing practices, policies, and capabilities of foreign governments. The Secretary of State thereafter engaged with the countries reviewed in an effort to address deficiencies and achieve improvements. In many instances, those efforts produced positive results. By obtaining additional information and formal commitments from foreign governments, the United States Government has improved its capacity and ability to assess whether foreign nationals attempting to enter the United States pose a security or safety threat. Our Nation is safer as a result of this work.

Despite those efforts, the Secretary of Homeland Security, in consultation with the Secretary of State and the Attorney General, has determined that a small number of countries—out of nearly 200 evaluated—remain deficient at this time with respect to their identity-management and information-sharing capabilities, protocols, and practices. In some cases, these countries also have a significant terrorist presence within their territory.

"As President, I must act to protect the security and interests of the United States and its people. I am committed to our ongoing efforts to engage those countries willing to cooperate, improve information-sharing and identity-management protocols and procedures, and address both terrorism-related and public-safety risks. Some of the countries with remaining inadequacies face significant challenges. Others have made strides to improve their protocols and procedures, and I commend them for these efforts. But until they satisfactorily address the identified inadequacies, I have determined, on the basis of recommendations from the Secretary of Homeland Security and other members of my Cabinet, to impose certain conditional restrictions and limitations, as set forth more fully below, on entry into the United States of nationals of the countries identified in section 2 of this proclamation."

There were some key revisions to this ban that made it more expansive than its predecessors.

The restrictions targeted more countries than before with the latest ban aimed at travelers from six Muslim-majority countries and all refugees. The new ban targets the issuing of visas for citizens of eight countries, five of which—Syria, Iran, Somalia, Yemen, and Libya—were included in Trump's first two bans, and three of which—North Korea, Chad, and Venezuela—were added in the latest ban. The order will also place Iraqi travelers under additional scrutiny but does not ban entire visa classes as it does with the other eight nations.

Trump's first and second bans sought to freeze the issuing of visas from the targeted countries for 90 days to allow the Department of Homeland Security (DHS) to assess worldwide screening and visa vetting procedures. By contrast, the new restrictions are essentially indefinite, although the administration has said it will review them if the targeted countries improve cooperation with the U.S. government. Sudan had been included in the previous two bans but was dropped this time by the administration without any specific explanation. The president's proclamation says that the DHS vetting review led to some improvements and positive results in certain countries but again provides no specific detail.

Advocates have suggested that the DHS decision to end temporary protected status for Sudan last week, which gave immigration status to Sudanese citizens in the United States due to ongoing conflict in the region, may have had something to do with the decision. According to Becca Heller, the director of the International Refugee Assistance Project, it suggests the government of Sudan was pressured into agreeing to accept massive numbers of deported Sudanese nationals from the United States in exchange for being dropped from the travel ban. The central African nation of Chad, which is 52 percent Muslim, has been added to the ban ostensibly because of a failure to adequately share public-safety and terrorism-related information. But a number of observers have found the Trump administration's move perplexing because of Chad's close counterterrorism partnership with the United States. The additions of North Korea and Venezuela add a further twist. Although the administration argues that both countries fail to share adequate information with the United States, it is probably more accurate to interpret the restrictions on these countries as official sanctions rather than a travel ban.

The curbs placed on Venezuela only affect a small group of government officials and their families. And while the ban on North Korean travel is all-encompassing, with the exception of diplomatic entries, relations with the country have been frozen for some time already. The United States issued only nine immigrant visas to North Koreans last year, one in 2014 and seven in 2015.

The inclusion of these countries, however, could help with part of the administration's legal battle over the bans. In one early challenge, a U.S. district judge in Virginia ruled the first order was unconstitutional because it had religious bias at its heart—an appeals court in the same state ruled along the same lines on the second ban too. Ruling on the second version, the Hawaii court also dismissed the government's argument that the ban is not anti-Muslim because it targets all individuals from the six countries, regardless of religion, and the countries themselves represent only a small fraction of the world's Muslim population. "The illogic of the government's contentions is palpable. The notion that one can demonstrate animus toward any group of people only by targeting all of them at once is fundamentally flawed," the court ruling said, pointing out that the countries' populations were between 90 percent and 99 percent Muslim.

Yet, the final ban put forward by President Trump was ultimately blessed by the United States Supreme Court. In the following selections, writing for the Court, Chief Justice John Roberts argues that the Trump Administration based its immigration policy on a sufficient national security justification to survive a rational basis review. Regardless of politicized statements made, the president's broad power over immigration matters Trump's potential concerns that are not in direct violation of any Constitutional provisions. Writing for the minority, Justice Sonia Sotomayor points to both Trump's statements about Muslims and the Establishment Clause to argue that the president should not have the power to ban immigrants from specific countries—especially when there is a strong religious correlation.

YES ↵

John Roberts

Majority Opinion: Trump v. Hawaii

Chief Justice Roberts delivered the opinion of the Court.

Under the Immigration and Nationality Act (INA), foreign nationals seeking entry into the United States undergo a vetting process to ensure that they satisfy the numerous requirements for admission. The Act also vests the President with authority to restrict the entry of aliens whenever he finds that their entry "would be detrimental to the interests of the United States." 8 U.S.C. §1182(f). Relying on that delegation, the President concluded that it was necessary to impose entry restrictions on nationals of countries that do not share adequate information for an informed entry determination, or that otherwise present national security risks. Presidential Proclamation No. 9645, 82 Fed. Reg. 45161 (2017) (Proclamation). The plaintiffs in this litigation, respondents here, challenged the application of those entry restrictions to certain aliens abroad. We now decide whether the President had authority under the Act to issue the Proclamation, and whether the entry policy violates the Establishment Clause of the First Amendment.

I

A

Shortly after taking office, President Trump signed Executive Order No. 13769, Protecting the Nation From Foreign Terrorist Entry Into the United States. 82 Fed. Reg. 8977 (2017) (EO–1). EO–1 directed the Secretary of Homeland Security to conduct a review to examine the adequacy of information provided by foreign governments about their nationals seeking to enter the United States. §3(a). Pending that review, the order suspended for 90 days the entry of foreign nationals from seven countries—Iran, Iraq, Libya, Somalia, Sudan, Syria, and Yemen—that had been previously identified by Congress or prior administrations as posing heightened terrorism risks. §3(c). The District Court for the Western District of Washington entered a temporary restraining order blocking the entry restrictions, and the Court of Appeals for the Ninth Circuit denied the Government's request to stay that order. *Washington v. Trump*, 847 F. 3d 1151 (2017) (*per curiam*).

In response, the President revoked EO–1, replacing it with Executive Order No. 13780, which again directed a worldwide review. 82 Fed. Reg. 13209 (2017) (EO–2). Citing investigative burdens on agencies and the need to diminish the risk that dangerous individuals would enter without adequate vetting, EO–2 also temporarily restricted the entry (with case-by-case waivers) of foreign nationals from six of the countries covered by EO–1: Iran, Libya, Somalia, Sudan, Syria, and Yemen. §§2(c), 3(a). The order explained that those countries had been selected because each "is a state sponsor of terrorism, has been significantly compromised by terrorist organizations, or contains active conflict zones." §1(d). The entry restriction was to stay in effect for 90 days, pending completion of the worldwide review.

These interim measures were immediately challenged in court. The District Courts for the Districts of Maryland and Hawaii entered nationwide preliminary injunctions barring enforcement of the entry suspension, and the respective Courts of Appeals upheld those injunctions, albeit on different grounds. *International Refugee Assistance Project (IRAP) v. Trump*, 857 F. 3d 554 (CA4 2017); *Hawaii v. Trump*, 859 F. 3d 741 (CA9 2017) (*per curiam*). This Court granted certiorari and stayed the injunctions—allowing the entry suspension to go into effect—with respect to foreign nationals who lacked a "credible claim of a bona fide relationship" with a person or entity in the United States. *Trump v. IRAP*, 582 U.S. _____, _____ (2017) (*per curiam*) (slip op., at 12). The temporary restrictions in EO–2 expired before this Court took any action, and we vacated the lower court decisions as moot. *Trump* v. *IRAP*, 583 U.S. _____ (2017); *Trump* v. *Hawaii*, 583 U.S. _____ (2017).

On September 24, 2017, after completion of the worldwide review, the President issued the Proclamation before us—Proclamation No. 9645, Enhancing Vetting Capabilities and Processes for Detecting Attempted Entry

Roberts, John. *Majority Opinion: Trump v. Hawaii.*

Into the United States by Terrorists or Other Public-Safety Threats. 82 Fed. Reg. 45161. The Proclamation (as its title indicates) sought to improve vetting procedures by identifying ongoing deficiencies in the information needed to assess whether nationals of particular countries present "public safety threats." §1(a). To further that purpose, the Proclamation placed entry restrictions on the nationals of eight foreign states whose systems for managing and sharing information about their nationals the President deemed inadequate.

The Proclamation described how foreign states were selected for inclusion based on the review undertaken pursuant to EO–2. As part of that review, the Department of Homeland Security (DHS), in consultation with the State Department and several intelligence agencies, developed a "baseline" for the information required from foreign governments to confirm the identity of individuals seeking entry into the United States, and to determine whether those individuals pose a security threat. §1(c). The baseline included three components. The first, "identity-management information," focused on whether a foreign government ensures the integrity of travel documents by issuing electronic passports, reporting lost or stolen passports, and making available additional identity-related information. Second, the agencies considered the extent to which the country discloses information on criminal history and suspected terrorist links, provides travel document exemplars, and facilitates the U.S. Government's receipt of information about airline passengers and crews traveling to the United States. Finally, the agencies weighed various indicators of national security risk, including whether the foreign state is a known or potential terrorist safe haven and whether it regularly declines to receive returning nationals following final orders of removal from the United States. *Ibid.*

DHS collected and evaluated data regarding all foreign governments. §1(d). It identified 16 countries as having deficient information-sharing practices and presenting national security concerns, and another 31 countries as "at risk" of similarly failing to meet the baseline. §1(e). The State Department then undertook diplomatic efforts over a 50-day period to encourage all foreign governments to improve their practices. §1(f). As a result of that effort, numerous countries provided DHS with travel document exemplars and agreed to share information on known or suspected terrorists. *Ibid.*

Following the 50-day period, the Acting Secretary of Homeland Security concluded that eight countries—Chad, Iran, Iraq, Libya, North Korea, Syria, Venezuela, and Yemen—remained deficient in terms of their risk profile and willingness to provide requested information. The Acting Secretary recommended that the President impose entry restrictions on certain nationals from all of those countries except Iraq. §§1(g), (h). She also concluded that although Somalia generally satisfied the information-sharing component of the baseline standards, its "identity-management deficiencies" and "significant terrorist presence" presented special circumstances justifying additional limitations. She therefore recommended entry limitations for certain nationals of that country. §1(i). As for Iraq, the Acting Secretary found that entry limitations on its nationals were not warranted, given the close cooperative relationship between the U.S. and Iraqi Governments and Iraq's commitment to combating ISIS. §1(g).

After consulting with multiple Cabinet members and other officials, the President adopted the Acting Secretary's recommendations and issued the Proclamation. Invoking his authority under 8 U.S.C. §§1182(f) and 1185(a), the President determined that certain entry restrictions were necessary to "prevent the entry of those foreign nationals about whom the United States Government lacks sufficient information"; "elicit improved identity-management and information-sharing protocols and practices from foreign governments"; and otherwise "advance [the] foreign policy, national security, and counterterrorism objectives" of the United States. Proclamation §1(h). The President explained that these restrictions would be the "most likely to encourage cooperation" while "protect[ing] the United States until such time as improvements occur." *Ibid.*

The Proclamation imposed a range of restrictions that vary based on the "distinct circumstances" in each of the eight countries. *Ibid.* For countries that do not cooperate with the United States in identifying security risks (Iran, North Korea, and Syria), the Proclamation suspends entry of all nationals, except for Iranians seeking nonimmigrant student and exchange-visitor visas. §§2(b)(ii), (d)(ii), (e)(ii). For countries that have information-sharing deficiencies but are nonetheless "valuable counterterrorism partner[s]" (Chad, Libya, and Yemen), it restricts entry of nationals seeking immigrant visas and nonimmigrant business or tourist visas. §§2(a)(i), (c)(i), (g)(i). Because Somalia generally satisfies the baseline standards but was found to present special risk factors, the Proclamation suspends entry of nationals seeking immigrant visas and requires additional scrutiny of nationals seeking nonimmigrant visas. §2(h)(ii). And for Venezuela, which refuses to cooperate in information sharing but for which alternative means are available to identify its nationals, the Proclamation limits entry only of certain government officials and their family members on nonimmigrant business or tourist visas. §2(f)(ii).

The Proclamation exempts lawful permanent residents and foreign nationals who have been granted asylum. §3(b). It also provides for case-by-case waivers when a foreign national demonstrates undue hardship, and that his entry is in the national interest and would not pose a threat to public safety. §3(c)(i); see also §3(c)(iv) (listing examples of when a waiver might be appropriate, such as if the foreign national seeks to reside with a close family member, obtain urgent medical care, or pursue significant business obligations). The Proclamation further directs DHS to assess on a continuing basis whether entry restrictions should be modified or continued, and to report to the President every 180 days. §4. Upon completion of the first such review period, the President, on the recommendation of the Secretary of Homeland Security, determined that Chad had sufficiently improved its practices, and he accordingly lifted restrictions on its nationals. Presidential Proclamation No. 9723, 83 Fed. Reg. 15937 (2018).

By its plain language, §1182(f) grants the President broad discretion to suspend the entry of aliens into the United States. The President lawfully exercised that discretion based on his findings—following a worldwide, multiagency review—that entry of the covered aliens would be detrimental to the national interest. And plaintiffs' attempts to identify a conflict with other provisions in the INA, and their appeal to the statute's purposes and legislative history, fail to overcome the clear statutory language.

A

The text of §1182(f) states:

> Whenever the President finds that the entry of any aliens or of any class of aliens into the United States would be detrimental to the interests of the United States, he may by proclamation, and for such period as he shall deem necessary, suspend the entry of all aliens or any class of aliens as immigrants or nonimmigrants, or impose on the entry of aliens any restrictions he may deem to be appropriate.

By its terms, §1182(f) exudes deference to the President in every clause. It entrusts to the President the decisions whether and when to suspend entry ("[w]henever [he] finds that the entry" of aliens "would be detrimental" to the national interest); whose entry to suspend ("all aliens or any class of aliens"); for how long ("for such period as he shall deem necessary"); and on what conditions ("any restrictions he may deem to be appropriate"). It is therefore unsurprising that we have previously observed that §1182(f) vests the President with "ample power" to impose entry restrictions in addition to those elsewhere enumerated in the INA. *Sale*, 509 U.S., at 187 (finding it "perfectly clear" that the President could "establish a naval blockade" to prevent illegal migrants from entering the United States); see also *Abourezk v. Reagan*, 785 F. 2d 1043, 1049, n. 2 (CADC 1986) (describing the "sweeping proclamation power" in §1182(f) as enabling the President to supplement the other grounds of inadmissibility in the INA).

The Proclamation falls well within this comprehensive delegation. The sole prerequisite set forth in §1182(f) is that the President "find[]" that the entry of the covered aliens "would be detrimental to the interests of the United States." The President has undoubtedly fulfilled that requirement here. He first ordered DHS and other agencies to conduct a comprehensive evaluation of every single country's compliance with the information and risk assessment baseline. The President then issued a Proclamation setting forth extensive findings describing how deficiencies in the practices of selecting foreign governments—several of which are state sponsors of terrorism—deprive the Government of "sufficient information to assess the risks [those countries' nationals] pose to the United States." Proclamation §1(h)(i). Based on that review, the President found that it was in the national interest to restrict entry of aliens who could not be vetted with adequate information—both to protect national security and public safety, and to induce improvement by their home countries. The Proclamation therefore "craft[ed] . . . country-specific restrictions that would be most likely to encourage cooperation given each country's distinct circumstances," while securing the Nation "until such time as improvements occur." *Ibid.*

Plaintiffs believe that these findings are insufficient. They argue, as an initial matter, that the Proclamation fails to provide a persuasive rationale for why nationality alone renders the covered foreign nationals a security risk. And they further discount the President's stated concern about deficient vetting because the Proclamation allows many aliens from the designated countries to enter on nonimmigrant visas.

Such arguments are grounded on the premise that §1182(f) not only requires the President to *make* a finding that entry "would be detrimental to the interests of the United States" but also to explain that finding with sufficient detail to enable judicial review. That premise is questionable. See *Webster v. Doe*, 486 U.S. 592, 600 (1988) (concluding that a statute authorizing the CIA Director to terminate an employee when the Director "shall deem such termination necessary or advisable in the interests of the United States" forecloses "any meaningful judicial standard of review"). But even assuming that some form of review is appropriate, plaintiffs' attacks on the sufficiency of the President's findings cannot be sustained. The 12-page Proclamation—which thoroughly describes the process, agency evaluations, and recommendations underlying the President's chosen restrictions—is more detailed than any prior order a President has issued under §1182(f). Contrast Presidential Proclamation No. 6958, 3 CFR 133 (1996) (President Clinton) (explaining in one sentence why suspending entry of members of the Sudanese government and armed forces "is in the foreign policy interests of the United States"); Presidential Proclamation No. 4865, 3 CFR 50–51 (1981) (President Reagan) (explaining in five sentences why measures to curtail "the continuing illegal migration by sea of large numbers of undocumented aliens into the southeastern United States" are "necessary").

Moreover, plaintiffs' request for a searching inquiry into the persuasiveness of the President's justifications is inconsistent with the broad statutory text and the deference traditionally accorded the President in this sphere. "Whether the President's chosen method" of addressing perceived risks is justified from a policy perspective is "irrelevant to the scope of his [§1182(f)] authority." *Sale*, 509 U.S., at 187–188. And when the President adopts "a preventive measure . . . in the context of international affairs and national security," he is "not required to conclusively link all of the pieces in the puzzle before [courts] grant weight to [his] empirical conclusions." *Holder v. Humanitarian Law Project*, 561 U.S. 1, 35 (2010).

The Proclamation also comports with the remaining textual limits in §1182(f). We agree with plaintiffs that the word "suspend" often connotes a "defer[ral] till later," Webster's Third New International Dictionary 2303 (1966). But that does not mean that the President is required to prescribe in advance a fixed end date for the entry restrictions. Section 1182(f) authorizes the President to suspend entry "for such period as he shall deem necessary." It follows that when a President suspends entry in response to a diplomatic dispute or policy concern, he may link the duration of those restrictions, implicitly or explicitly, to the resolution of the triggering condition. See, e.g., Presidential Proclamation No. 5829, 3 CFR 88 (1988) (President Reagan) (suspending the entry of certain Panamanian nationals "until such time as . . . democracy has been restored in Panama"); Presidential Proclamation No. 8693, 3 CFR 86–87 (2011) (President Obama) (suspending the entry of individuals subject to a travel restriction under United Nations Security Council resolutions "until such time as the Secretary of State determines that [the suspension] is no longer necessary"). In fact, not one of the 43 suspension orders issued prior to this litigation has specified a precise end date.

Like its predecessors, the Proclamation makes clear that its "conditional restrictions" will remain in force only so long as necessary to "address" the identified "inadequacies and risks" within the covered nations. Proclamation Preamble, and §1(h); see *ibid.* (explaining that the aim is to "relax[] or remove[]" the entry restrictions "as soon as possible"). To that end, the Proclamation establishes an ongoing process to engage covered nations and assess every 180 days whether the entry restrictions should be modified or terminated. §§4(a), (b). Indeed, after the initial review period, the President determined that Chad had made sufficient improvements to its identity-management protocols, and he accordingly lifted the entry suspension on its nationals. See Proclamation No. 9723, 83 Fed. Reg. 15937.

Finally, the Proclamation properly identifies a "class of aliens"—nationals of select countries—whose entry is suspended. Plaintiffs argue that "class" must refer to a well-defined group of individuals who share a common "characteristic" apart from nationality. Brief for Respondents 42. But the text of §1182(f), of course, does not say that, and the word "class" comfortably encompasses a group of people linked by nationality. Plaintiffs also contend that the class cannot be "overbroad." Brief for Respondents 42. But that simply amounts to an unspoken tailoring requirement found nowhere in Congress's grant of authority to suspend entry of not only "any class of aliens" but "all aliens."

In short, the language of §1182(f) is clear, and the Proclamation does not exceed any textual limit on the President's authority.

Three additional features of the entry policy support the Government's claim of a legitimate national security interest. First, since the President introduced entry restrictions in January 2017, three Muslim-majority countries—Iraq, Sudan, and Chad—have been removed from the list of covered countries. The Proclamation emphasizes that its "conditional restrictions" will remain in force only so long as necessary to "address" the identified "inadequacies and risks," Proclamation Preamble, and §1(h), and establishes an ongoing process to engage covered nations and assess every 180 days whether the entry restrictions should be terminated, §§4(a), (b). In fact, in announcing the termination of restrictions on nationals of Chad, the President also described Libya's ongoing engagement with the State Department and the steps Libya is taking "to improve its practices." Proclamation No. 9723, 83 Fed. Reg. 15939.

Second, for those countries that remain subject to entry restrictions, the Proclamation includes significant exceptions for various categories of foreign nationals. The policy permits nationals from nearly every covered country to travel to the United States on a variety of nonimmigrant visas. See, e.g., §§2(b)–(c), (g), (h) (permitting student and exchange visitors from Iran, while restricting only business and tourist nonimmigrant entry for nationals of Libya and Yemen, and imposing no restrictions on nonimmigrant entry for Somali nationals). These carveouts for nonimmigrant visas are substantial: over the last three fiscal years—before the Proclamation was in effect—the majority of visas issued to nationals from the covered countries were nonimmigrant visas. Brief for Petitioners 57. The Proclamation also exempts permanent residents and individuals who have been granted asylum. §§3(b)(i), (vi).

Third, the Proclamation creates a waiver program open to all covered foreign nationals seeking entry as immigrants or nonimmigrants. According to the Proclamation, consular officers are to consider in each admissibility determination whether the alien demonstrates that (1) denying entry would cause undue hardship, (2) entry would not pose a threat to public safety, and (3) entry would be in the interest of the United States. §3(c)(i); see also §3(c)(iv) (listing examples of when a waiver might be appropriate, such as if the foreign national seeks to reside with a close family member, obtain urgent medical care, or pursue significant business obligations). On its face, this program is similar to the humanitarian exceptions set forth in President Carter's order during the Iran hostage crisis. See Exec. Order No. 12206, 3 CFR 249; Public Papers of the Presidents, Jimmy Carter, Sanctions Against Iran, at 611–612 (1980) (outlining exceptions). The Proclamation also directs DHS and the State Department to issue guidance elaborating upon the circumstances that would justify a waiver.

Under these circumstances, the Government has set forth a sufficient national security justification to survive rational basis review. We express no view on the soundness of the policy. We simply hold today that plaintiffs have not demonstrated a likelihood of success on the merits of their constitutional claim.

V

Because plaintiffs have not shown that they are likely to succeed on the merits of their claims, we reverse the grant of the preliminary injunction as an abuse of discretion. *Winter v. Natural Resources Defense Council*, Inc., 555 U.S. 7, 32 (2008). The case now returns to the lower courts for such further proceedings as may be appropriate. Our disposition of the case makes it unnecessary to consider the propriety of the nationwide scope of the injunction issued by the District Court.

The judgment of the Court of Appeals is reversed, and the case is remanded for further proceedings consistent with this opinion.

It is so ordered.

John Glover Roberts Jr. is an American lawyer serving as the 17th and current chief justice of the United States since 2005. He was nominated by President George W. Bush after the death of Chief Justice William Rehnquist and has been described as having a conservative judicial philosophy in his jurisprudence.

Sonia Sotomayor

Dissenting Opinion: Trump v. Hawaii

Justice Sotomayor, with whom Justice Ginsburg joins, dissenting.

The United States of America is a Nation built upon the promise of religious liberty. Our Founders honored that core promise by embedding the principle of religious neutrality in the First Amendment. The Court's decision today fails to safeguard that fundamental principle. It leaves undisturbed a policy first advertised openly and unequivocally as a "total and complete shutdown of Muslims entering the United States" because the policy now masquerades behind a façade of national-security concerns. But this repackaging does little to cleanse Presidential Proclamation No. 9645 of the appearance of discrimination that the President's words have created. Based on the evidence in the record, a reasonable observer would conclude that the Proclamation was motivated by anti-Muslim animus. That alone suffices to show that plaintiffs are likely to succeed on the merits of their Establishment Clause claim. The majority holds otherwise by ignoring the facts, misconstruing our legal precedent, and turning a blind eye to the pain and suffering the Proclamation inflicts upon countless families and individuals, many of whom are United States citizens. Because that troubling result runs contrary to the Constitution and our precedent, I dissent.

I

Plaintiffs challenge the Proclamation on various grounds, both statutory and constitutional. Ordinarily, when a case can be decided on purely statutory grounds, we strive to follow a "prudential rule of avoiding constitutional questions." *Zobrest v. Catalina Foothills School District*, 509 U.S. 1, 8 (1993). But that rule of thumb is far from categorical, and it has limited application where, as here, the constitutional question proves far simpler than the statutory one. Whatever the merits of plaintiffs' complex statutory claims, the Proclamation must be enjoined for a more fundamental reason: it runs afoul of the Establishment Clause's guarantee of religious neutrality.

A

The Establishment Clause forbids government policies "respecting an establishment of religion." U.S. Const., Amdt. 1. The "clearest command" of the Establishment Clause is that the Government cannot favor or disfavor one religion over another. *Larson v. Valente*, 456 U.S. 228, 244 (1982); *Church of Lukumi Babalu Aye, Inc. v. Hialeah*, 508 U.S. 520, 532 (1993) ("[T]he First Amendment forbids an official purpose to disapprove of a particular religion"); *Edwards v. Aguillard*, 482 U.S. 578, 593 (1987) ("The Establishment Clause . . . forbids *alike* the preference of a religious doctrine *or* the prohibition of theory which is deemed antagonistic to a particular dogma" (internal quotation marks omitted)); *Lynch v. Donnelly*, 465 U.S. 668, 673 (1984) (noting that the Establishment Clause "forbids hostility toward any [religion]," because "such hostility would bring us into 'war with our national tradition as embodied in the First Amendmen[t]'"); *Epperson v. Arkansas*, 393 U.S. 97, 106 (1968) ("[T]he State may not adopt programs or practices . . . which aid or oppose any religion. This prohibition is absolute" (citation and internal quotation marks omitted)). Consistent with that clear command, this Court has long acknowledged that governmental actions that favor one religion "inevitabl[y]" foster "the hatred, disrespect, and even contempt of those who [hold] contrary beliefs." *Engel v. Vitale*, 370 U.S. 421, 431 (1962). That is so, this Court has held, because such acts send messages to members of minority faiths "'that they are outsiders, not full members of the political community.'" *Santa Fe Independent School District v. Doe*, 530 U.S. 290, 309 (2000). To guard against this serious harm, the Framers mandated a strict "principle of denominational neutrality." *Larson*, 456 U.S., at 246; *Board of Education of Kiryas Joel Village School District v. Grumet*, 512 U.S. 687, 703 (1994) (recognizing the role of courts in "safeguarding a principle at the heart of the Establishment Clause, that government should not prefer one religion to another, or religion to irreligion").

"When the government acts with the ostensible and predominant purpose" of disfavoring a particular religion, "it violates that central Establishment Clause value of official religious neutrality, there being no neutrality when the government's ostensible object is to take sides." *McCreary County v. American Civil Liberties Union of Ky.*, 545 U.S. 844, 860 (2005). To determine whether plaintiffs have proved an Establishment Clause violation, the Court asks whether a reasonable observer would view the government action as enacted for the purpose of disfavoring a religion. See id., at 862, 866; accord, *Town of Greece v. Galloway*, 572 U.S. _____, _____ (2014) (plurality opinion) (slip op., at 19).

In answering that question, this Court has generally considered the text of the government policy, its operation, and any available evidence regarding "the historical background of the decision under challenge, the specific series of events leading to the enactment or official policy in question, and the legislative or administrative history, including contemporaneous statements made by" the decision maker. *Lukumi*, 508 U.S., at 540 (opinion of Kennedy, J.); *McCreary*, 545 U.S., at 862 (courts must evaluate "text, legislative history, and implementation . . . , or comparable official act" (internal quotation marks omitted)). At the same time, however, courts must take care not to engage in "any judicial psychoanalysis of a drafter's heart of hearts." *Id.*, at 862.

B

1

Although the majority briefly recounts a few of the statements and background events that form the basis of plaintiffs' constitutional challenge, *ante*, at 27–28, that highly abridged account does not tell even half of the story. See Brief for The Roderick and Solange MacArthur Justice Center as *Amicus Curiae* 5–31 (outlining President Trump's public statements expressing animus toward Islam). The full record paints a far more harrowing picture, from which a reasonable observer would readily conclude that the Proclamation was motivated by hostility and animus toward the Muslim faith.

During his Presidential campaign, then-candidate Donald Trump pledged that, if elected, he would ban Muslims from entering the United States. Specifically, on December 7, 2015, he issued a formal statement "calling for a total and complete shutdown of Muslims entering the United States." App. 119. That statement, which remained on his campaign website until May 2017 (several months into his Presidency), read in full:

> "Donald J. Trump is calling for a total and complete shutdown of Muslims entering the United States until our country's representatives can

figure out what is going on." According to Pew Research, among others, there is great hatred towards Americans by large segments of the Muslim population. Most recently, a poll from the Center for Security Policy released data showing '25% of those polled agreed that violence against Americans here in the United States is justified as a part of the global jihad' and 51% of those polled 'agreed that Muslims in America should have the choice of being governed according to Shariah.' Shariah authorizes such atrocities as murder against nonbelievers who won't convert, beheadings and more unthinkable acts that pose great harm to Americans, especially women.

> "Mr. Trum[p] stated, 'Without looking at the various polling data, it is obvious to anybody the hatred is beyond comprehension. Where this hatred comes from and why we will have to determine. Until we are able to determine and understand this problem and the dangerous threat it poses, our country cannot be the victims of the horrendous attacks by people that believe only in Jihad, and have no sense of reason or respect of human life. If I win the election for President, we are going to Make America Great Again.'—Donald J. Trump." *Id.*, at 158; see also *id.*, at 130–131.

On December 8, 2015, Trump justified his proposal during a television interview by noting that President Franklin D. Roosevelt "did the same thing" with respect to the internment of Japanese Americans during World War II. *Id.*, at 120. In January 2016, during a Republican primary debate, Trump was asked whether he wanted to "rethink [his] position" on "banning Muslims from entering the country." *Ibid.* He answered, "No." *Ibid.* A month later, at a rally in South Carolina, Trump told an apocryphal story about United States General John J. Pershing killing a large group of Muslim insurgents in the Philippines with bullets dipped in pigs' blood in the early 1900s. *Id.*, at 163–164. In March 2016, he expressed his belief that "Islam hates us. . . . [W]e can't allow people coming into this country who have this hatred of the United States . . . [a]nd of people that are not Muslim." *Id.*, at 120–121. That same month, Trump asserted that "[w]e're having problems with the Muslims, and we're having problems with Muslims coming into the country." *Id.*, at 121. He therefore called for surveillance of mosques in the United States, blaming terrorist attacks on Muslims' lack of "assimilation" and their commitment to "sharia law." *Ibid.*; *id.*, at 164. A day later, he opined that Muslims "do not respect us at all" and "don't respect a lot of the things that are happening throughout not only our country, but they don't respect other things." *Ibid.*

As Trump's presidential campaign progressed, he began to describe his policy proposal in slightly different terms. In June 2016, for instance, he characterized the policy proposal as a suspension of immigration from countries "where there's a proven history of terrorism." *Id.*, at 121. He also described the proposal as rooted in the need to stop "importing radical Islamic terrorism to the West through a failed immigration system." *Id.*, at 121–122. Asked in July 2016 whether he was "pull[ing] back from" his pledged Muslim ban, Trump responded, "I actually don't think it's a rollback. In fact, you could say it's an expansion." *Id.*, at 122–123. He then explained that he used different terminology because "[p]eople were so upset when [he] used the word Muslim." *Id.*, at 123.

A month before the 2016 election, Trump reiterated that his proposed "Muslim ban" had "morphed into a[n] extreme vetting from certain areas of the world." *Ibid.* Then, on December 21, 2016, President-elect Trump was asked whether he would "rethink" his previous "plans to create a Muslim registry or ban Muslim immigration." *Ibid.* He replied: "You know my plans. All along, I've proven to be right." *Ibid.*

On January 27, 2017, one week after taking office, President Trump signed Executive Order No. 13769, 82 Fed. Reg. 8977 (2017) (EO–1), entitled "Protecting the Nation From Foreign Terrorist Entry Into the United States." As he signed it, President Trump read the title, looked up, and said "We all know what that means." App. 124. That same day, President Trump explained to the media that, under EO–1, Christians would be given priority for entry as refugees into the United States. In particular, he bemoaned the fact that in the past, "[i]f you were a Muslim [refugee from Syria] you could come in, but if you were a Christian, it was almost impossible." *Id.*, at 125. Considering that past policy "very unfair," President Trump explained that EO–1 was designed "to help" the Christians in Syria. *Ibid.* The following day, one of President Trump's key advisers candidly drew the connection between EO–1 and the "Muslim ban" that the President had pledged to implement if elected. *Ibid.* According to that adviser, "[W]hen [Donald Trump] first announced it, he said, 'Muslim ban.' He called me up. He said, 'Put a commission together. Show me the right way to do it legally.'" *Ibid.*

On February 3, 2017, the United States District Court for the Western District of Washington enjoined the enforcement of EO–1. See *Washington v. Trump*, 2017 WL 462040, *3. The Ninth Circuit denied the Government's request to stay that injunction. *Washington v. Trump*, 847 F. 3d 1151, 1169 (2017) (*per curiam*). Rather than appeal the Ninth Circuit's decision, the Government declined to continue defending EO–1 in court and instead announced

that the President intended to issue a new executive order to replace EO–1.

On March 6, 2017, President Trump issued that new executive order, which, like its predecessor, imposed temporary entry and refugee bans.

And in June 2017, the President stated on Twitter that the Justice Department had submitted a "watered down, politically correct version" of the "original Travel Ban" "to S[upreme] C[ourt]." *Id.*, at 132. The President went on to tweet: "People, the lawyers, and the courts can call it whatever they want, but I am calling it what we need and what it is, a TRAVEL BAN!" *Id.*, at 132–133. He added: "That's right, we need a TRAVEL BAN for certain DANGEROUS countries, not some politically correct term that won't help us protect our people!" *Id.*, at 133. Then, on August 17, 2017, President Trump issued yet another tweet about Islam, once more referencing the story about General Pershing's massacre of Muslims in the Philippines: "Study what General Pershing . . . did to terrorists when caught. There was no more Radical Islamic Terror for 35 years!" *IRAP v. Trump*, 883 F. 3d 233, 267 (CA4 2018) (*IRAP II*) (en banc) (alterations in original).

In September 2017, President Trump tweeted that "[t]he travel ban into the United States should be far larger, tougher and more specific—but stupidly, that would not be politically correct!" App. 133. Later that month, on September 24, 2017, President Trump issued Presidential Proclamation No. 9645, 82 Fed. Reg. 45161 (2017) (Proclamation), which restricts entry of certain nationals from six Muslim-majority countries. On November 29, 2017, President Trump "retweeted" three anti-Muslim videos, entitled "Muslim Destroys a Statue of Virgin Mary!," "Islamist mob pushes teenage boy off roof and beats him to death!", and "Muslim migrant beats up Dutch boy on crutches!" *IRAP II*, 883 F. 3d, at 267. Those videos were initially tweeted by a British political party whose mission is to oppose "all alien and destructive politic[al] or religious doctrines, including . . . Islam." *Ibid.* When asked about these videos, the White House Deputy Press Secretary connected them to the Proclamation, responding that the "President has been talking about these security issues for years now, from the campaign trail to the White House" and "has addressed these issues with the travel order that he issued earlier this year and the companion proclamation." *Ibid.*

Government's asserted national-security justifications. Even before being sworn into office, then-candidate Trump stated that "Islam hates us," App. 399, warned that "[w]e're having problems with the Muslims, and we're having problems with Muslims coming into the country," *id.*, at 121, promised to enact a "total and complete shutdown of Muslims entering the United States," *id.*, at 119, and instructed one of his advisers to find a "lega[l]" way to enact a Muslim ban, *id.*, at 125. The President continued to make similar statements well after his inauguration, as detailed above, see *supra*, at 6–10.

Moreover, despite several opportunities to do so, President Trump has never disavowed any of his prior statements about Islam. Instead, he has continued to make remarks that a reasonable observer would view as an unrelenting attack on the Muslim religion and its followers. Given President Trump's failure to correct the reasonable perception of his apparent hostility toward the Islamic faith, it is unsurprising that the President's lawyers have, at every step in the lower courts, failed in their attempts to launder the Proclamation of its discriminatory taint. See *United States v. Fordice*, 505 U.S. 717, 746–747 (1992) ("[G]iven an initially tainted policy, it is eminently reasonable to make the [Government] bear the risk of nonpersuasion with respect to intent at some future time, both because the [Government] has created the dispute through its own prior unlawful conduct, and because discriminatory intent does tend to persist through time" (citation omitted)). Notably, the Court recently found less pervasive official expressions of hostility and the failure to disavow them to be constitutionally significant. Cf. *Masterpiece Cakeshop, Ltd. v. Colorado Civil Rights Commission*, 584 U.S. _____, _____ (2018) (slip op., at 18) ("The official expressions of hostility to religion in some of the commissioners' comments—comments that were not disavowed at the Commission or by the State at any point in the proceedings that led to the affirmance of the order—were inconsistent with what the Free Exercise Clause requires"). It should find the same here.

Ultimately, what began as a policy explicitly "calling for a total and complete shutdown of Muslims entering the United States" has since morphed into a "Proclamation" putatively based on national-security concerns. But this new window dressing cannot conceal an unassailable fact: the words of the President and his advisers create the strong perception that the Proclamation is contaminated by impermissible discriminatory animus against Islam and its followers.

Moreover, the Proclamation purports to mitigate national-security risks by excluding nationals of countries that provide insufficient information to vet their nationals. 82 Fed. Reg. 45164. Yet, as plaintiffs explain, the Proclamation broadly denies immigrant visas to all nationals of those countries, including those whose admission would likely not implicate these information deficiencies (e.g., infants, or nationals of countries included in the Proclamation who are long-term residents of and traveling from a country not covered by the Proclamation). See Brief for

Respondents 72. In addition, the Proclamation permits certain nationals from the countries named in the Proclamation to obtain nonimmigrant visas, which undermines the Government's assertion that it does not already have the capacity and sufficient information to vet these individuals adequately. See 82 Fed. Reg. 45165–45169.

Equally unavailing is the majority's reliance on the Proclamation's waiver program. *Ante*, at 37, and n. 7. As several *amici* thoroughly explain, there is reason to suspect that the Proclamation's waiver program is nothing more than a sham. See Brief for Pars Equality Center et al. as *Amici Curiae* 11, 13–28 (explaining that "waivers under the Proclamation are vanishingly rare" and reporting numerous stories of deserving applicants denied waivers). The remote possibility of obtaining a waiver pursuant to an ad hoc, discretionary, and seemingly arbitrary process scarcely demonstrates that the Proclamation is rooted in a genuine concern for national security. See *ante*, at 3–8 (Breyer, J., dissenting) (outlining evidence suggesting "that the Government is not applying the Proclamation as written," that "waivers are not being processed in an ordinary way," and that consular and other officials "do not, in fact, have discretion to grant waivers").

In sum, none of the features of the Proclamation highlighted by the majority supports the Government's claim that the Proclamation is genuinely and primarily rooted in a legitimate national-security interest. What the unrebutted evidence actually shows is that a reasonable observer would conclude, quite easily, that the primary purpose and function of the Proclamation is to disfavor Islam by banning Muslims from entering our country.

III

As the foregoing analysis makes clear, plaintiffs are likely to succeed on the merits of their Establishment Clause claim. To obtain a preliminary injunction, however, plaintiffs must also show that they are "likely to suffer irreparable harm in the absence of preliminary relief," that "the balance of equities tips in [their] favor," and that "an injunction is in the public interest." *Winter v. Natural Resources Defense Council, Inc.*, 555 U.S. 7, 20 (2008). Plaintiffs readily clear those remaining hurdles.

First, plaintiffs have shown a likelihood of irreparable harm in the absence of an injunction. As the District Court found, plaintiffs have adduced substantial evidence showing that the Proclamation will result in "a multitude of harms that are not compensable with monetary damages and that are irreparable—among them, prolonged separation from family members, constraints to recruiting and retaining students and faculty members to foster diversity and quality within the University community, and the diminished membership of the [Muslim] Association." 265 F. Supp. 3d 1140, 1159 (Haw. 2017).

Second, plaintiffs have demonstrated that the balance of the equities tips in their favor. Against plaintiffs' concrete allegations of serious harm, the Government advances only nebulous national-security concerns. Although national security is unquestionably an issue of paramount public importance, it is not "a talisman" that the Government can use "to ward off inconvenient claims—a 'label' used to 'cover a multitude of sins.'" *Ziglar v. Abbasi*, 582 U.S. _____, _____ (2017) (slip op., at 20). That is especially true here, because, as noted, the Government's other statutory tools, including the existing rigorous individualized vetting process, already address the Proclamation's purported national-security concerns. See *supra*, at 19–22.

Finally, plaintiffs and their amici have convincingly established that "an injunction is in the public interest."

Winter, 555 U.S., at 20. As explained by the scores of amici who have filed briefs in support of plaintiffs, the Proclamation has deleterious effects on our higher education system, national security, health care, artistic culture, and the Nation's technology industry and overall economy. Accordingly, the Court of Appeals correctly affirmed, in part, the District Court's preliminary injunction.

Our Constitution demands, and our country deserves, a Judiciary willing to hold the coordinate branches to account when they defy our most sacred legal commitments. Because the Court's decision today has failed in that respect, with profound regret, I dissent.

Sonia Maria Sotomayor is an Associate Justice of the Supreme Court of the United States, appointed by President Barack Obama in May 2009 and confirmed in August 2009. She has the distinction of being its first Justice of Hispanic descent and the first Latina.

EXPLORING THE ISSUE

Should the President Have the Power to Limit Immigrants and Refugees from Specific Countries?

Critical Thinking and Reflection

1. Why do you believe Trump opted to limit immigrants from particular countries?
2. Do you believe this policy will reduce threats to the United States? Why or why not?
3. How should the United States handle immigration policy today?
4. How do you think these targeted countries will respond? Why?
5. Do you believe this will continue to be a politically polarizing issue? Why or why not?

Is There Common Ground?

It is difficult to imagine meaningful common ground existing between those who favor an executive's right to limit (or ban) immigrants from one country and those who oppose this power. The reasons are plenty: first, some citizens will oppose limiting immigration in any way; second, even those who support the idea may not support the president doing so as opposed to Congress; and third, the Supreme Court has ruled and settled the legal question included within this debate. Given how immigration policy has become even more politicized during President Trump's administration, complete with images of children being ripped from their parents' arms at the border, middle ground is even more difficult to imagine. Determining who to let into your country, and in what number, is not an easy process, especially when attempting to eliminate potential threats. But one would hope that such decisions would be made on policy grounds—not political ones.

With that in mind, it is important to think through ways that we can move toward an acceptable policy that does not discriminate while securing borders. At the basis of a country's immigration policy is the recognition that a country has the right to pursue its interests first and whenever it wishes to be altruistic and humane, this is instantiated without ever risking the danger of its citizens or its cultural values. A country does not need to cede an inch of its sense of security. It does not need to place a single of its citizens at risk. As such, it is unclear how to strike the right balance between suicidal empathy and ill-informed xenophobic rigidity. But somewhere between these two end points of the continuum lies the optimal policy. Those who wish to find that balance are valuable members of this great debate. But it requires meaningful conversations with all involved, which is difficult to experience if one person holds the ability to make policy.

Additional Resources

Sandra Bucerius, *Unwanted: Muslim Immigrants, Dignity, and Drug Dealing* (Oxford University Press, 2014).

Matthew Soerens and Jenny Yang, *Welcoming the Stranger: Justice, Compassion & Truth in the Immigration Debate* (IVP Books, 2018).

Philip Kretsedemas and David C. Brotherton, *Immigration Policy in the Age of Punishment: Detention, Deportation, and Border Control* (Columbia University Press, 2018).

Doug Saunders, *The Myth of the Muslim Tide: Do Immigrants Threaten the West?* (Vintage, 2012).

Sara Cleave, *Banthology: Stories from Banned Nations* (Deep Vellum, 2018).

Internet References . . .

Immigration Data & Statistics

https://www.dhs.gov/immigration-statistics

Migration Policy Institute

https://www.migrationpolicy.org/

Muslim Ban

https://www.americanimmigrationcouncil.org/tags/
muslim-ban

Muslim Immigration Ban Hotline

https://muslimimmigrationhotline.squarespace.com/

Timeline of the Muslim Ban

https://www.aclu-wa.org/pages/timeline-muslim-ban

Selected, Edited, and with Issue Framing Material by:
William J. Miller, *Campus Labs®*

ISSUE

Should the United States Build a Border Wall with Mexico?

YES: Reece Jones, from "Why Build a Border Wall?" *North American Congress on Latin America* (2012)

NO: Vanda Felbab-Brown, from "The Wall: The Real Costs of a Barrier between the United States and Mexico," *Brookings Institute* (2017)

Learning Outcomes

After reading this issue, you will be able to:

- Identify benefits to building a border wall with Mexico.
- Identify the costs to building a border wall with Mexico.
- Describe the political realities of a border wall with Mexico.
- Assess the political ramifications of building a border wall with Mexico.
- Explain the potential economic impact of building a border wall with Mexico.

ISSUE SUMMARY

YES: Geographer Reece Jones writes that a possible border wall would serve a greater purpose than responding to immigration and drug problems. Instead, it can help establish sovereignty, protect the wealth of impacted states, and limit the possible dilution of cultural practices by immigrants.

NO: On the other side, Vanda Felbab-Brown—a senior fellow at the Brookings Institute—demonstrates the true costs of building a wall between the United States and Mexico. Her argument focuses on real costs and potential negative externalities of such a decision.

Throughout his 2016 presidential campaign, Donald Trump called for the construction of larger and fortified wall along the Mexican border, and claimed Mexico will pay for its construction, estimated at $8 to $12 billion. Others estimate there are enough uncertainties to drive up the cost between $15 and $25 billion. In January 2017, Mexican President Enrique Peña Nieto said the country would not pay for any part of the wall. The Trump administration, in the same month, signed the Border Security and Immigration Enforcement Improvements Executive Order 13767 to commence extending the border wall. Trump had planned to meet Nieto at the White House to discuss topics including border security and announced the United States would impose a 20 percent tariff on Mexican goods to effectively pay for the wall. Peña Nieto gave a national televised address confirming they would not pay, adding "Mexico doesn't believe in walls," and canceled the meeting.

In March 2017, the Trump administration submitted a budget amendment for fiscal year 2017 that included a $3 billion continuing budget for border security and immigration enforcement. Trump's FY 2018 Budget Blueprint increases discretionary funds for the Department of Homeland Security (DHS) by $2.8 billion (to $44.1 billion). Then DHS Secretary John F. Kelly told the Senate

Homeland Security and Governmental Affairs Committee during a hearing the Budget Blueprint included $2.6 billion for high-priority border security technology and tactical infrastructure, including funding to plan, design, and construct the border wall.

A survey conducted by the National Border Patrol Council found that 89 percent of border patrol agents said a "wall system in strategic locations is necessary to securing the border." Only 7 percent of agents disagreed. However, the U.S. Senator Claire McCaskill (D-MO) said during a hearing that while Americans want a secure border, she had not met anyone that says the most effective way is to build a wall across the entirety of our southern border. The only one who keeps talking about that in McCaskill's opinion is President Trump.

USA Today asked all 534 members of the House and Senate whether they supported the president's initial $1.6 billion budget request to begin construction and found fewer than 25 percent of Republicans willing to stand up for the plan. When asked by the network whether they support the funding, only 69 of the 292 Republicans on Capitol Hill said "yes." Three Republicans said they oppose the money, several evaded a direct answer, and the rest simply refused to respond.

To date, there is no cost–benefit analysis for what a border wall should accomplish or what cost is acceptable, reporters found. Government analyses show that officials have never established a measure to determine whether current fences are effective, either. No one knows how many miles of wall will be built, or in what locations, or what type of construction will be used.

Trump proposed in a White House meeting that the wall should be covered with solar panels, claiming that this would generate revenue and improve its appearance. On June 21, 2017, Trump told a rally in Iowa that he was working on ways Mexico will have to pay much less money, saying that the wall would be a solar wall that could create energy and pay for itself. Trump also touted a report he had seen on Fox News that cited a study by the Center for Immigration Studies, in which it claimed that a wall along the Mexican border could save taxpayers $64 billion by reducing crime and welfare costs for undocumented immigrants over the next 10 years. Some dispute this, claiming the wall and maintenance would cost more than predicted and that illegal immigrants would just find another way into the nation. In August 2017, while speaking at a rally in Arizona, Trump stated he will close down the U.S. government if necessary to force Congress to pay for the wall. As of the end of 2017, Mexico had not entered into any agreement to pay for any amount of the wall aid and repair fence along the border.

In September 2017, the United States DHS issued a notice that Acting Secretary of Homeland Security Elaine Duke would be waiving certain laws, regulations, and other legal requirements to begin construction of the new wall near Calexico, CA. The waiver allows the DHS to bypass the National Environmental Policy Act, the Endangered Species Act, the Clean Water Act, the Clean Air Act, the National Historic Preservation Act, the Migratory Bird Treaty Act, the Migratory Bird Conservation Act, the Archaeological Resources Protection Act, the Safe Drinking Water Act, the Noise Control Act, the Solid Waste Disposal Act, the Antiquities Act, the Federal Land Policy and Management Act, the Administrative Procedure Act, the Native American Graves Protection and Repatriation Act, and the American Indian Religious Freedom Act. Following the waivers, the federal government announced the start of construction of eight prototype barriers made from concrete and other materials.

Trump's description of the border wall has shifted over time. During his campaign, he indicated the entire border would be walled, but later said only 1,000 miles required a wall. In July 2017, he told reporters the border might need only 700 miles of wall. The nature of the wall was fluid as well. Initially, he seemed to say the wall would be new construction and usually referred to it as concrete, unlike current steel fences. In a February news conference, Trump said, "We are going to have a wall that works, not going to have a wall like they have now which is either nonexistent or a joke." But then later, Trump's statements indicate he may consider existing fences to be part of his wall plan. His July remarks included this: "We're fixing large portions of wall right now."

In the following selections, we seek to examine whether this wall would in fact accomplish its discussed goals—especially since based on Border Patrol apprehension data, illegal traffic on the border is at its lowest point in four decades. It has been falling consistently since 2000, and in some areas is at a 10th of its peak levels. Geographer Reece Jones writes that a possible border wall would serve a greater purpose than responding to immigration and drug problems. Instead, it can help establish sovereignty, protect the wealth of impacted states, and limit the possible dilution of cultural practices by immigrants. On the other side, Vanda Felbab-Brown—a senior fellow at the Brookings Institute—demonstrates the true costs of building a wall between the United States and Mexico. Her argument focuses on real costs and potential negative externalities of such a decision.

YES ←   **Reece Jones**

Why Build a Border Wall?

We live a world of borders and walls. In addition to the massive and expensive barrier on long stretches of the U.S.–Mexico border, in the 23 years since the fall of the Berlin Wall, 26 other new walls and fences have gone up on political borders around the world. These walls are built by both totalitarian regimes and democracies, including India, Thailand, Israel, South Africa, and the European Union. Invariably, the barriers are justified in the language of security—the country must be protected from the terrorists, drug cartels, insurgents, or suicide bombers lurking on the other side.

Despite the external focus of these justifications, in most instances, these walls and fences are actually the result of the internal politics of the state that builds them. There are three specific reasons for constructing a border wall: establishing sovereignty over ungoverned or unruly lands, protecting the wealth of the state and population, and protecting cultural practices within the state from the possible influence of other value systems possessed by immigrants. The decision to build the 664-mile barrier along the U.S.–Mexico border, although often presented as primarily in response to drug-related violence and terrorism, is largely due to these internal factors.

The desire to establish clear sovereign authority over the state's territory is the first factor that underlies the construction of a border barrier. Although we often imagine the territorial outline of countries as sharply drawn lines where the control of one state ends and another begins, most borders on the ground belie this simplicity. The idea that borders (or rivers or coastlines) are lines is a convenience of cartography that is established on the ground many years after a map is drawn, if at all. The oldest political borders in Europe, for example, are only a few hundred years old, and most were established more recently than that. Before the 1600s, most states did not recognize each other's sovereign authority over a territory, and the technological advances in cartography that allowed fixed borders and territories to be represented had not been achieved. Consequently, even the simple idea that states

have clearly defined territories that are marked by a linear border is a very recent development.

The contemporary U.S.–Mexico border was established on maps at the end of the U.S.–Mexican War by the Treaty of Guadalupe Hidalgo. The war settled which territories the expansion-minded United States could claim and transferred almost half of Mexico's territory to the United States. The last sections of the border were finalized with the Gadsden Purchase in 1854, which secured mining rights and a better route for a railroad connection to California. At the time, the territory was part of the United States in name only and, despite the enormous land area, was populated by about 100,000 Mexicans and 200,000 Native Americans. Over the intervening years, sovereign authority over these lands was established by moving Anglo populations onto the land and by violently suppressing any resistance. Land surveying, creating property maps, and the deployment of police forces resignified the landscape. Yet the line existed on the map and in the population's geographic imagination only inchoately, as the practices and performances of sovereignty slowly inscribed the different territories onto the landscape.

This process accelerated in the 1990s as funding for border security increased substantially and the idea of marking the imagined line with a physical barrier took hold. When the Border Patrol was established in 1924, it was tiny and remained underfunded for decades. In 1992, there were 3,555 agents at the U.S.–Mexico border, but by 2010, there were over 20,100. These changes have both practical and symbolic effects on the hardening of the border. The additional agents play a practical enforcement role, while the fence project, which passed Congress in 2006, is much more symbolically significant. Walls and fences are the most efficient way to mark territorial differences on the ground because they take the abstract idea of a territory and materialize it. The construction of the barrier is another step in the process of reimaging these formerly Native American and Mexican lands as firmly part of the territory of the United States. By physically inscribing the line in the landscape, the wall brings the border into being and visually demonstrates where U.S. territory ends and Mexican territory begins.

The second internal factor that results in the construction of a wall or fence on a border is the presence of a poorer country on the other side. In previous eras, political borders served primarily as either military defensive lines where one army prevented the movement of another or as markers of different government regimes where one set of laws and taxes or one cultural system stopped and another began. Over the 20th century, the practice of absolute sovereignty over a bounded territory produced substantial wealth inequalities globally, which increased the desire of many people to move either to avoid deteriorating conditions in their home state or to seek better economic opportunities elsewhere. These movements, along with the possibility of hostile people or items passing into the state, resulted in a much more substantial focus on borders as a location to prevent the unauthorized movement of people.

Just as we often imagine most borders as the sharp lines depicted on maps, we also imagine that historically most borders were fenced and fortified, but this is not the case. The older purposes of borders as defensive military lines or administrative divisions do not necessitate a wall or fence. Fences do not deter tanks and airplanes, and administrative divisions between peaceful neighbors do not require an expensive barrier. The changing purpose for borders is evident in the sheer number of new barriers built in the past 20 years. Twenty-seven have been built since 1998, compared with 11 during the entire Cold War period from 1945 until 1990. Furthermore, several of those Cold War barriers were quite short including the U.S. fence with Cuba at the Guantánamo Bay and the fence between Gibraltar and Spain.

Not only are the new barriers longer than in the past, but many are built along peaceful borders. The significant characteristic that most of these borders share is that they mark a sharp wealth discontinuity. For example, the average annual per capita GDP (in 2010 U.S. dollars) of the countries that have built barriers since the fall of the Berlin Wall is $14,067; the average for the countries on the other side of these barriers is $2,801. The U.S. barrier on the Mexican border fits this pattern. Although the Canadian border is longer and certainly more porous (the Border Patrol estimated in 2009 that it had effective control over less than 1 percent of the Canadian border vs. 35 percent of the Mexican border), the debates about fencing the border focused only on Mexico. The United States' per capita GDP in 2010 was $47,000, Canada's was $39,000, and Mexico's was $14,000.

The final internal factor that plays a role in the decision to build a fence or wall on a political border is the fear that population movements will irreversibly change the way of life inside the state. In the United States, concerns about the threat that immigrant values pose are as old as the country itself. At different points in history, the Irish, the Chinese, and the Italians were all described as posing a grave threat to a particular version of what it meant to be an "American." Today, these debates revolve around both Muslims and Latino immigrants who, anti-immigrant activists argue, bring alternative social codes and do not assimilate into the mainstream of U.S. society. The fence on the border symbolizes the hardened and fixed borderline that marks a clear distinction between the territories where particular people belong.

The construction of a barrier on the border simultaneously legitimates and intensifies the internal exclusionary practices of the sovereign state. It legitimates exclusion by providing a material manifestation of the abstract idea of sovereignty, which brings the claim of territorial difference into being. The barrier also intensifies these exclusionary practices, because once the boundary is marked and "the container" of the state takes form, the perception of the difference between the two places becomes stronger. This process is evident in new restrictive immigration laws at the state level in Alabama and Arizona as well as in the protests and vandalism directed toward proposed Islamic cultural centers in New York and Tennessee. By demonstrating sovereign control, the state simultaneously reifies authority over that territory and defines the limits of the people that belong there. These perceived differences then fuel more passionate feelings of belonging to the in-group and distinction from the other on the outside.

The U.S. fence on the Mexican border should be understood both in terms of the enhanced enforcement capabilities of the government and in the assertion of where the state has authority and who should be allowed in the state's territory. The United States builds the barrier on the U.S.–Mexico border to define its sovereign authority over its territory, to protect the economic privileges of its population, and to protect a particular way of life from other people who are perceived to have different value systems. Rather than a barrier against terrorism and cartel violence, it is a performance of the United States' territory and boundaries.

REECE JONES is an American political geographer. Jones was educated at The University of North Carolina at Chapel Hill and the University of Wisconsin at Madison.

Vanda Felbab-Brown

The Wall

The Real Costs of a Barrier between the United States and Mexico

Many have been separated from their family members for years. Some were deported to Mexico after having lived in the United States for decades without authorization, leaving behind children, spouses, siblings, and parents. Others never left Mexico, but have made their way to the fence to see relatives in the United States. With its prison-like ambience and Orwellian name—Friendship Park—this site is one of the very few places where families separated by immigration rules can have even fleeting contact with their loved ones, from 10 a.m. to 2 p.m. on Saturdays and Sundays. Elsewhere, the tall metal barrier is heavily patrolled.

So is to be the wall that President Donald Trump promises to build along the border. But no matter how tall and thick a wall will be, illicit flows will cross.

Undocumented workers and drugs will still find their way across any barrier the administration ends up building. And such a wall will be irrelevant to those people who become undocumented immigrants by overstaying their visas—who for many years have outnumbered those who become undocumented immigrants by crossing the U.S.–Mexico border.

Nor will the physical wall enhance U.S. security.

The border, and more broadly how the United States defines its relations with Mexico, directly affects the 12 million people who live within 100 miles of the border. In multiple and very significant ways that have not been acknowledged or understood, it will also affect communities all across the United States as well as Mexico.

What the Wall's Price Tag Would Be

The wall comes with many costs, some obvious though hard to estimate, some unforeseen. The most obvious is the large financial outlay required to build it, in whatever form it eventually takes. Although during the election campaign candidate Trump claimed that the wall would cost only $12 billion, a Department of Homeland Security (DHS) internal report in February put the cost at $21.6 billion, but that may be a major underestimate.

The estimates vary so widely because of the lack of clarity about what the wall will actually consist of beyond the first meager Homeland Security specifications that it be either a solid concrete wall or a see-through structure, "physically imposing in height," ideally 30-feet high but no less than 18 feet, sunk at least 6 feet into the ground to prevent tunneling under it; that it should not be scalable with even sophisticated climbing aids; and that it should withstand prolonged attacks with impact tools, cutting tools, and torches. But that description doesn't begin to cover questions about the details of its physical structure. Then, there are the legal fees required to seize land on which to build the wall. The Trump administration can use eminent domain to acquire the land but will still have to negotiate compensation and often face lawsuits. More than 90 such lawsuits in southern Texas alone are still open from the 2008 effort to build a fence there.

The Trump administration cannot simply seize remittances to Mexico to pay for the wall; doing so may increase flows of undocumented workers to the United States. Remittances provide many Mexicans with amenities they could never afford otherwise. But for Mexicans living in poverty—some 46.2 percent in 2015 according to the Mexican social research agency CONEVAL—the remittances are a veritable lifeline, which can represent as much as 80 percent of their income. These families count on that money for the basics of life—food, clothing, health care, and education for their children.

I met the matron of one of those families in a lush but desperately poor mountain village in Guerrero. Rosa, a forceful woman who was initially suspicious, decided to confide in me. Her son had crossed into the United States eight years ago, she said. The remittances he sent allowed Rosa's grandchildren to get medical treatment at the nearest clinic, some 30 miles away. Like Rosa, many people in the village had male relatives working illegally in the United States in order to help their families make ends meet. Sierra de Atoyac may be paradise for a bird-watcher (which I am), but Guerrero is one of Mexico's poorest, most neglected, and crime- and violence-ridden states. "Here you have few chances," Rosa explained to me. "If you're smart, like my son, you make it across the border to the U.S. If you're not so smart, you join the *narcos*. If you're stupid, but lucky, you join the [municipal] police. Otherwise, you're stuck here farming or logging and starving."

Any attempt to seize the remittances from such families would be devastating. Fluctuating between $20 billion and $25 billion annually during the past decade, remittances from the United States have amounted to about 3 percent of Mexico's GDP, representing the third largest source of foreign revenue after oil and tourism. The remittances enable human and economic development throughout the country, and this in turn reduces the incentives for further migration to the United States—precisely what Trump is aiming to do.

A tunnel between Tijuana and a warehouse in California featured an elevator. Getty Images

Why the Wall Wouldn't Stop Smuggling

Why the DHS believes that a 30–foot tall wall cannot be scaled and a tunnel cannot be built deeper than 6 feet below ground is not clear.

Drug smugglers have been using tunnels to get drugs into the United States ever since Mexico's most famous drug trafficker, Joaquín "El Chapo" Guzmán of the Sinaloa Cartel, pioneered the method in 1989. And the sophistication of these tunnels has only grown over time. In April 2016, U.S. law enforcement officials discovered a drug tunnel that ran more than half a mile from Tijuana to San Diego and was equipped with ventilation vents, rails, and electricity. It is the longest such tunnel to be found so far, but one of 13 of great length and technological expertise discovered since 2006. Altogether, between 1990 and 2016, 224 tunnels have been unearthed at the U.S.–Mexico border.

Other smuggling methods increasingly include the use of drones and catapults as well as joint drainage systems between border towns that have wide tunnels or tubes through which people can crawl and drugs can be pulled. But even if the land border were to become much more secure, that would only intensify the trend toward smuggling goods as well as people via boats that sail far to the north, where they land on the California coast.

Another thing to consider is that a barrier in the form of a wall is increasingly irrelevant to the drug trade as it is now practiced because most of the drugs smuggled into the United States from Mexico no longer arrive on the backs of those who cross illegally. Instead, according to the U.S. Drug Enforcement Administration, most of the smuggled marijuana, as well as cocaine, heroin, and methamphetamines, comes through the 52 legal ports of entry on the border. These ports have to process literally millions of people, cars, trucks, and trains every week. Traffickers hide their illicit cargo in secret, state-of-the-art compartments designed for cars, or under legal goods in trailer trucks. And they have learned many techniques for fooling the border patrol. Mike, a grizzled U.S. border official whom I interviewed in El Paso in 2013, shrugged: "The *narcos* sometimes tip us off, letting us find a car full of drugs while they send six other cars elsewhere. Such write-offs are part of their business expense. Other times the tip-offs are false. We search cars and cars, snarl up the traffic for hours on, and find nothing."

Beyond the Sinaloa Cartel, 44 other significant criminal groups operate today in Mexico. The infighting within and among them has made Mexico one of the world's most violent countries. In 2016 alone, this violence claimed between 21,000 and 23,000 lives. Between 2007 and 2017, a staggering 177,000 people were murdered in Mexico, a number that could actually be much higher, as many bodies are buried in mass graves that are hidden and never found. Those Mexican border cities that are principal entry points of drugs into the Unites States have been particularly badly affected by the violence.

Take Ciudad Juárez, for example. Directly across the border from peaceful El Paso. Ciudad Juárez was likely the world's most violent city when I was there in 2011 and it epitomizes what can happen during these drug wars. In 2011, the Sinaloa Cartel was battling the local Juárez Cartel, trying to take over the city's smuggling routes to the United States, and causing a veritable bloodbath. Walking around the contested *colonías* at the time was like touring a cemetery: residents would point out places where people were killed the day before, three days before, and five weeks ago.

Juan, a skinny 19-year old whom I met there that year told me that he was trying to get out of a local gang (the name of which he wouldn't reveal). He had started working for the gang as a *halcone* (a lookout) when he was 15, he said. But now as the drug war raged in the city and the local gangs were pulled into the infighting between the big cartels, his friends in the gang were being asked to do much more than he wanted to do—to kill. Without any training, they were given assault weapons. Having no shooting skills, they just sprayed bullets in the vicinity of their assigned targets, hoping that at least some of the people they killed would be the ones they were supposed to kill, because if they didn't succeed, they themselves might be murdered by those who had contracted them to do the job.

I met Juan through Valeria, whose NGO was trying to help gang members like Juan get on the straight and narrow. But it was tough going for her and her staff to make the case. As Juan had explained to me, a member who refused to do the bidding of the gangs could be killed for his failure to cooperate.

"And America does nothing to stop the weapons coming here!" Valeria exclaimed to me.

While President Trump accuses Mexico of exporting violent crime and drugs to the United States, many Mexican officials as well as people like Valeria, who are on the ground in the fight against the drug wars, complain of a tide of violence and corruption that flows in the opposite direction. Some 70 percent of the firearms seized in Mexico between 2009 and 2014 originated in the United States. Although amounting to over 73,000 guns, these seizures still likely represented only a fraction of the weapons smuggled from the United States. Moreover, billions of dollars per year are made in the illegal retail drug market in the United States and smuggled back to Mexico, where the cartels depend on this money for their basic operations. Sometimes, sophisticated money-laundering schemes, such as trade-based deals, are used; but large parts of the proceeds are smuggled as bulk cash hidden in secret compartments and among goods in the cars and trains daily crossing the border south to Mexico.

And, of course, it is the U.S. demand for drugs that fuels Mexican drug smuggling in the first place. Take, for example, the current heroin epidemic in the United States. It originated in the overprescription of medical opiates to treat pain. The subsequent efforts to reduce the overprescription of painkillers led those Americans who became dependent on them to resort to illegal heroin. That in turn stimulated a vast expansion of poppy cultivation in Mexico, particularly in Guerrero. In 2015, Mexico's opium poppy cultivation reached perhaps 28,000 hectares, enough to distill about 70 tons of heroin (which is even more than the 24–50 tons estimated to be necessary to meet the U.S. demand).

Mexico's large drug cartels, including El Chapo's Sinaloa Cartel, which is estimated to supply between 40 percent and 60 percent of the cocaine and heroin sold on the streets in the United States, are the dominant wholesale suppliers of illegal drugs in the United States. For the retail trade, however, they usually recruit business partners among U.S. crime gangs. And thanks to the deterrence capacity of U.S. law enforcement, insofar as Mexican drug-trafficking groups do have in-country operations in the United States, such as in wholesale supply, they have behaved strikingly peacefully and have not resorted to the vicious aggression and infighting that characterizes their business in Mexico. So the United States has been spared the drug-traffic-related explosions of violence that have ravaged so many of the drug-producing or smuggling areas of Mexico.

Both the George W. Bush administration and the Obama administration recognized the joint responsibility for drug trafficking between the United States and Mexico, an attitude that allowed for unprecedented collaborative efforts to fight crime and secure borders. This collaboration allowed U.S. law enforcement and intelligence agents to operate in Mexico and help their Mexican counterparts in intelligence development, training, vetting, establishment of police procedures and protocols, and interdiction operations. The collaboration also led to Mexico being far more willing than it ever had been before to patrol both its northern border with the United States and its southern border with Central America, as part of the effort to help apprehend undocumented workers trying to cross into the United States.

The Trump administration's hostility to Mexico could jeopardize this progress. In retaliation for building the wall, for any efforts, the United States might make to force Mexico to pay for the wall, or for the collapse of NAFTA, the Mexican government could, for example, give up on its efforts to secure its southern border or stop sharing counterterrorism intelligence with the United States. Yet Mexico's cooperation is far more important for U.S. security than any wall.

Rather than a line of separation, the border should be conceived of as a membrane, connecting the tissues of communities on both sides, enabling mutually beneficial trade, manufacturing, ecosystem improvements, and security, while enhancing intercultural exchanges.

In 1971, when First Lady Pat Nixon attended the inauguration of Friendship Park—that tragic place that allows separated families only the most limited amount of contact—she said, "I hope there won't be a fence here too long." She supported two-way positive exchanges between the United States and Mexico, not barriers. In fact, for her visit, she had the fence in Friendship Park torn down. Unfortunately, it's still there, bigger, taller, and harder than when she visited, and with the wall about to get much worse yet.

VANDA FELBAB-BROWN is an American expert on internal and international organized crime. She is a senior fellow with the Center for 21st Century Security and Intelligence in the Foreign Policy program at the Brookings Institution, a Washington-based think tank.

EXPLORING THE ISSUE

Should the United States Build a Border Wall with Mexico?

Critical Thinking and Reflection

1. Why do you believe Trump and some Republicans want a border wall built?
2. Do you believe a border wall will curb immigration concerns? Why or why not?
3. Do you believe a border wall is a real possibility? Why or why not?
4. How do you believe any potential border wall should be funded?
5. If a wall was erected, how do you believe it would impact the United States politically and economically? Mexico?

Is There Common Ground?

Efforts to build a physical wall suggest common ground has come and gone in quite the physical way. Yet, the reasons for wanting a wall to be built suggest there could still be meaningful alternatives available for consideration. Those who support limiting immigration from Mexico—especially by making it difficult to enter illegally—appear swayed by the idea of a physical structure separating the United States from its southern neighbor. If policies were in place that created an environment where it was as seemingly difficult to enter the United States without permission as if a physical barrier were present, their needs would be met. And if these policies did not adequately satisfy supporters, we would know something besides fear was driving the urge for border security.

Creating effective immigration policies is easier said than done, however. One could argue that a border wall wouldn't even be a political fantasy if we had done a better job of creating and enforcing policies previously. Further, if cases of abuse of the immigration system weren't turned into fodder for extreme political conversation, it might be easier to have more policy-based conversations on the topic. So, how can we find middle ground when it comes to thinking about a wall being built between the United States and Mexico? We can limit the hyperbole surrounding the discussion, make concentrated efforts to improve the flow of individuals through the U.S. southern border, and attempt to correct wrongs when they emerge. All this though depends on a willingness to explore the issue.

Additional Resources

Marty Gitlin, *The Border Wall with Mexico* (Greenhaven, 2017).

John Moore, *Undocumented: Immigration and the Militarization of the United States-Mexico Border* (powerHouse Books, 2018).

Tony Payan, *The Three U.S.-Mexico Border Wars: Drugs, Immigration, and Homeland Security* (Praeger, 2016).

Peter Reich, *The Law of the United States-Mexico Border: A Casebook* (Carolina Academic Press, 2017).

Peter Andres, *Border Games: Policing the U.S.-Mexico Divide* (Cornell University Press, 2009).

Internet References . . .

How Mexican Immigration to the U.S. Has Evolved

> http://time.com/3742067/history-mexican-immigration/

Immigration from Mexico

> https://cis.org/Report/Immigration-Mexico

The Wall

> https://www.usatoday.com/border-wall/us-mexico-interactive-border-map/

U.S.–Mexico Border Woes

> https://www.cfr.org/backgrounder/us-mexico-border-woes

Selected, Edited, and with Issue Framing Material by:
William J. Miller, *Campus Labs®*

ISSUE

Should the United States Expect North Korea to Denuclearize?

YES: Eleanor Albert, from "What Would Denuclearization Look Like in North Korea?" *Council on Foreign Relations* (2018)

NO: Aaron David Miller and Richard Sokolsky, from "Trump Should Learn to Live with a Nuclear North Korea," *Washington Post* (2018)

Learning Outcomes

After reading this issue, you will be able to:

- Describe the historical relationship between the United States and North Korea.
- Identify signs that North Korea may be willing to denuclearize.
- Assess the benefits to the United States of North Korea denuclearizing.
- Describe reasons why North Korea has attempted to nuclearize.
- Explain why this issue matters to the international community.

ISSUE SUMMARY

YES: Eleanor Albert—a writer for the Council on Foreign Relations—interviews Melissa Hanham (a Senior Research Associate in the East Asia Nonproliferation Program) about how denuclearization could happen in North Korea. Through the interview, she emphasizes ways the United States could help encourage and assure a denuclearized North Korea in the future.

NO: On the other hand, Aaron David Miller (a vice president at the Woodrow Wilson Center) and Richard Sokolsky (a fellow at the Carnegie Endowment for International Peace) argue denuclearization is an unreachable dream and instead the United States should identify more achievable outcomes from continuing talks with the once rogue nation.

North Korea (formally, the Democratic People's Republic of Korea (DPRK)), has active and increasingly sophisticated nuclear weapons and ballistic missile programs, and is believed to possess chemical and biological weapons capabilities. Recent interactions with the United States and its neighbor South Korea—including the 2018 meeting with American President Donald Trump—suggest the hermit nation may be interested in mainstreaming relations with the world. But it could come at a cost—their nuclear program.

North Korea unilaterally withdrew from the Treaty on the Non-Proliferation of Nuclear Weapons (NPT) in January 2003, is not a party to the Comprehensive Nuclear-Test-Ban Treaty, and has conducted six increasingly sophisticated nuclear tests since 2006. The DPRK is not a party to the Chemical Weapons Convention and is believed to possess a large chemical weapons program. Despite being a state party to the Biological and Toxin Weapons Convention and Geneva Protocol, evidence suggests North Korea may maintain an offensive biological weapons program. In defiance of the international community, which has imposed heavy sanctions on North Korea for its illicit behavior, the country has continued to escalate its WMD activities. In July 2017, North Korea successfully tested its first intercontinental ballistic missile (ICBM), and in September 2017, it conducted a test of what it claimed was a thermonuclear weapon.

North Korea's nuclear ambitions date to the Korean War in the 1950s, but came to the attention of the international community in 1992, when the International Atomic Energy Agency (IAEA) discovered that its nuclear activities were more extensive than declared. The revelations led North Korea to withdraw from the IAEA in 1994. In an effort to prevent North Korean withdrawal from the NPT, the United States and North Korea negotiated the Agreed Framework, in which Pyongyang agreed to freeze its nuclear activities and give access to IAEA inspectors in exchange for U.S.-supplied light water reactors and energy assistance. The Agreed Framework broke down in 2002, however.

North Korea unilaterally withdrew from the NPT in January 2003, prompting China, Japan, Russia, South Korea, and the United States to engage North Korea in the Six-Party Talks in a further attempt at a diplomatic solution to the country's nuclear program. The talks fell apart in 2009, and no serious diplomatic initiatives to denuclearize North Korea occurred until 2018. At the June 2018 U.S.–North Korean summit, Kim Jong-un "reaffirmed his firm and unwavering commitment to complete denuclearization of the Korean Peninsula," although North Korea's definition of "denuclearization" is ambiguous. No agreement on a method or timetable for dismantling North Korea's nuclear weapons has been reached.

North Korea produces both weapons-usable plutonium and enriched uranium, with one U.S. government estimate in 2017 suggesting the country may be producing enough nuclear material each year for 12 additional nuclear weapons. It possesses a large and increasingly sophisticated ballistic missile program and conducts frequent missile test launches, heightening East Asian tensions. In 2017, North Korea successfully tested the Hwasong-14 and Hwasong-15, its first ICBMs, which some experts believe gives North Korea the capability to deliver a nuclear payload anywhere in the United States. North Korea initiated its ballistic missile program in the late 1970s and early 1980s, when it acquired Soviet Scud–type missiles from Egypt and reverse engineered them. In the early 1990s, with assistance from Iran and several other countries, North Korea began producing Nodong medium-range ballistic missiles. North Korea has developed and tested a number of new missiles since Kim Jong-un's ascension to

leadership in 2011, such as the intermediate-range Hwasong-12 and the extended-range Scud. In addition to its land-based ballistic missiles, North Korea has successfully tested a submarine-launched ballistic missile, the Pukguk-song-1. North Korea also has a Space Launch Vehicle, the Unha, which uses technologies closely related to its ballistic missiles. North Korea is not a member of the Missile Technology Control Regime.

After years of heightened regional tensions and frequent North Korean nuclear and ballistic missile tests, there was a diplomatic thaw in early 2018. On March 9, 2018, South Korean officials announced that North Korean leader Kim Jong-un was committed to denuclearization, would refrain from any further nuclear and missile tests, and wished to meet U.S. President Donald Trump. Trump and Kim met on June 12, 2018, in Singapore—the first face-to-face meeting between leaders of North Korea and the United States in history. At the summit, the DPRK pledged "to work toward complete denuclearization of the Korean Peninsula."

So what has happened since the summit? Is North Korea following through on its commitment? The newest intelligence shows Kim's regime has escalated efforts to conceal its nuclear activity, according to three senior U.S. officials. During the three months since the historic Singapore summit and Trump's proclamation that North Korea intends to denuclearize, North Korea has built structures to obscure the entrance to at least one warhead storage facility, according to the officials. The United States has also observed North Korean workers moving warheads out of the facility, the officials said, though they would not speculate on where the warheads went. U.S. intelligence assesses North Korea could produce five to eight new nuclear weapons in 2018, according to three current and former senior U.S. officials. That pace is virtually identical to their assessment of the regime's production of about six per year prior to the Trump–Kim summit.

Public rhetoric, meanwhile, has a different tone. After his June meeting with Kim in Singapore, Trump said, "There is no longer a Nuclear Threat from North Korea." Trump tweeted a "thank you" to Kim in September for proclaiming his unwavering faith after a South Korean official reported Kim wanted to denuclearize before the end of Trump's first term. The South Korean official said Kim emphasized that he has never said anything negative about President Trump. Also in September, North Korea held its annual Foundation Day military parade to commemorate the 70th anniversary of the founding of the nation. This year, however, North Korea did not display any ICBMs.

In the following sections, we discuss whether denuclearization is actually on the table in North Korea or if it is a bargaining chip being used by a fearless leader to bring his nation back to the international table without any intent of follow through. Eleanor Albert—a writer for the Council on Foreign Relations—interviews Melissa Hanham (a Senior Research Associate in the East Asia Non-Proliferation Program) about how denuclearization could happen in North Korea. Through the interview, she emphasizes ways the United States could help encourage and assure a denuclearized North Korea in the future. On the other hand, Aaron David Miller (a vice president at the Woodrow Wilson Center) and Richard Sokolsky (a fellow at the Carnegie Endowment for International Peace) argue denuclearization is an unreachable dream and instead the United States should identify more achievable outcomes from continuing talks with the once rogue nation.

YES

Eleanor Albert

What Would Denuclearization Look Like in North Korea?

U.S. and North Korean officials are pressing ahead with efforts for a possible summit between U.S. President Donald J. Trump and North Korean leader Kim Jong-un, though both sides appear far apart on goals for the meeting. In particular, the flurry of diplomacy has exposed large gaps between how Washington and Pyongyang view denuclearization, says Melissa Hanham, a senior research associate at the James Martin Center for Nonproliferation Studies at the Middlebury Institute in Monterey, CA. On top of the legal and technical complexities in developing a rigorous inspections regime, Hanham says, past nuclear verification regimes in North Korea have been bedeviled by mistrust.

It depends on what kind of denuclearization we're talking about. North Korea's ideas of denuclearization are different from those of the United States. North Korea believes in the larger idea of denuclearization that is not just North Korea unilaterally giving up nuclear weapons, but instead the whole peninsula. To the regime, this means removing the threat of nuclear weapons against the country. Even though the United States withdrew tactical nuclear weapons from South Korea under the George H. W. Bush administration, North Korea still feels threatened and that is not 100 percent inaccurate. It's not paranoia, because in addition to former threats to use nuclear weapons to attack North Korea, and the more recent talk of "decapitation" of North Korean leadership, the United States still flies bombers and regularly conducts war games in the region. North Korea feels the exercises are a pretext for an eventual war. Meeting North Korea's desired outcome would be a long-term process.

Meanwhile, the United States focuses on complete, verifiable, and irreversible dismantlement (CVID) and is asking for this to be unilateral. The most similar model for an agreement like this is the Iran deal. However, Iran did not actually achieve nuclear weapons. So, in addition to all the measures incorporated in the Iran deal, any agreement between Washington and Pyongyang would additionally have to include securing existing nuclear warheads. The deal would need to acknowledge the existence of the warheads and have a component that would provide for their dismantlement, turnover to another party, or placement where they would not be deemed threatening.

States feel like they have the right to have [warheads], and they don't want to give away military secrets.

On top of that challenge, North Korea has a very advanced missile program. They would also need to negotiate a freeze of rocket production and tests. It is worth noting that a 2012 agreement negotiated by the Obama administration, known as the Leap Day deal, collapsed because of conflicting perceptions. Washington expected the deal to stop all rocket launches, but Pyongyang insisted it covered only missile launches. When North Korea launched a space launch vehicle a few months later, Washington believed Pyongyang had abrogated the deal.

Is There a Timetable for the Denuclearization Process for a Country Like North Korea That Has Arguably Reached Nuclear Weapons Capability?

In the Panmunjom agreement, North Korea and South Korea expressed the common goal of realizing a nuclear-free Korean Peninsula and described denuclearization as a long-term, sort of staged process. They were looking at an undetermined but long time frame. That is very reasonable because logistically it is complicated to implement a system like this. The U.S. side would like something to happen quite quickly. They are cognizant of Trump's time in office and want to enter a negotiation process where it would be able to carry out some deal on denuclearization within his administration.

Who Are the Actors That Would Be Involved?

During the now suspended negotiating process known as the Six-Party Talks, China, Japan, North Korea, Russia, South Korea, and the United States worked together and at many points came close to an agreement, but there were domestic pressures at play beneath the surface.

If an agreement ever materializes, Japan will want something related to the return of Japanese abductees held in North Korea. [Japanese Prime Minister Shinzō] Abe also has an election to think about and his larger aspirations for defending Japan and the country's position in Northeast Asia.

In South Korea, Moon [Jae-in] is extremely popular, but there are still hawks in South Korean politics who could pull a stunt to disrupt the flow of diplomacy. There are also families [on both sides of the Korean peninsula] who want to be reunited. There are different feelings about North Korea across generations. There are young people who want to know why they are estranged from their "brothers" across the border, but there is also an older generation that remembers the horrors of the Korean War.

Beijing didn't want a nuclear North Korea, but now it has one. What it wants is to make sure that nothing becomes so destabilized that the North Korean state collapses and millions of refugees flow into the country. It would also then lose that famous buffer zone between China

Another challenge is if North Korea has a nuclear accident or does an atmospheric test. This seems to be an issue that is followed closely in parts of China bordering North Korea, as there is fear—rightly or wrongly—about radiation.

What Would a Successful Monitoring Program Look Like?

With any kind of denuclearization agreement, there is a legal part and a technical part. Assuming that the United States and North Korea agree to the most invasive verification methods, you would have an international group on the ground. The International Atomic Energy Agency (IAEA) would probably be asked to do this because it was involved in the Iran deal and ensures safeguards around the world. IAEA inspectors were based in North Korea before Pyongyang kicked them out in 2002 and returned in 2007 to monitor the shutdown of the five-megawatt reactor at Yongbyon, although they too were forced to

leave, in April 2009. The best thing is to have humans with sensors on the ground.

North Korea would also need to declare all of its facilities. We know about a lot of them through open-source reporting and satellite imagery, but it's possible that there are a few that we don't know about that might be declared. And we would have to trust them to not leave out any facilities. This is a challenge because uranium enrichment facilities, reprocessing facilities in particular, are hard to identify with satellite imagery because they don't have a big visible signature.

Questions over the veracity of North Korea's declarations would likely extend to warheads as well. Warheads are not that big and they don't have a big footprint. Estimates of how many nuclear warheads the country has require making sense of what fissile material we think North Korea can make and guessing how efficient it is at using that fissile material across different warheads.

An agreement should include cameras, all the different seals and tags that are used in IAEA safeguards, and 24-hour monitoring, making use of satellites and other remote sensing technologies to monitor high-risk facilities. This monitoring would be to make sure that, if facilities are operating to generate nuclear power, none of the nuclear material is being diverted. North Korea doesn't currently use its reactors to generate power, but it has negotiated for energy needs in the past.

Some of the trickiest agreements are about warheads because states feel they have the right to have them, and they don't want to give away military secrets like where, what type, or how powerful they are. To verify a warhead, inspectors need to use what we call an information barrier. This barrier is needed to give the inspecting party the confidence that they have the correct warhead, not a fake or smaller warhead. The host party needs to feel assured that they are not giving away military secrets.

What Kind of Challenges Might an Inspections Regime Face in North Korea?

North Korea is still fairly closed, though it is more open than it has ever been. Still, we don't know much about North Korea's intentions and intentions can change. This process will most likely look like a freeze rather than dismantlement, so it will be imperative to maintain trust. Unfortunately, none of the parties trust each other very much, and North Korea has a history of kicking out inspectors and reversing course.

To make denuclearization truly irreversible, you would want to look at how the facilities are taken apart and how warheads are dismantled. So far, North Korea has been pretty cagey on those sorts of things. It reportedly collapsed the tunnels at the Punggye-ri nuclear test site, but North Korea probably doesn't need to test anymore anyway. Instead, attention should be focused on dismantlement and preventing the production of additional warheads, missiles, and launchers.

Last and most importantly, the parties must agree. We can design an extremely invasive CVID process, but North Korea will just walk away unless it believes it is in its best interest.

Eleanor Albert is a senior online writer/editor at the Council on Foreign Relations.

Aaron David Miller and Richard Sokolsky  **NO**

Trump Should Learn to Live with a Nuclear North Korea

The Rolling Stones' classic, "You Can't Always Get What You Want," with its sobering refrain, "but if you try sometimes, well, you might find, you get what you need," was a staple at then-candidate Donald Trump's 2016 campaign rallies. Today, when it comes to dealing with the North Korean nuclear challenge, President Trump, Secretary of State Mike Pompeo—who left Pyongyang empty-handed Saturday—and other administration officials would be wise to heed those words: they have almost no chance of getting what they want, North Korea's complete, verifiable, and irreversible denuclearization (CVID).

The administration might, however, get what it needs—peace and security on the Korean Peninsula—if Trump is willing to adjust to the reality that America will have to live with a nuclear North Korea and to find the safest, most secure, and least humiliating way to do so. He can accept this outcome while still protecting the security of the United States and its allies.

Trump's haste to declare victory in his negotiations with North Korean leader Kim Jong-un risks locking the United States into a potentially self-defeating game: having tweeted, after returning from his summit last month with Kim, that "There is no longer a Nuclear Threat from North Korea," the president is boxed in on one side by high expectations and on the other by an unnamed official in the North Korean Foreign Ministry describing Pompeo's negotiating position as "gangster-like" and "cancerous." On this latest trip, the secretary of state didn't have face-to-face meeting with Kim and didn't hand-deliver the Elton John CD that Trump said he planned to give Kim as a gift, and there are reports from unnamed individuals saying the North Koreans were merely toying with Pompeo.

In that kind of negotiating climate, it's magical thinking to aim for getting Kim to surrender his nuclear weapons capability and destroying North Korea's nuclear infrastructure. It certainly won't happen in accordance with America's timelines or preferences, and little progress will be made toward this goal as long as Trump thinks he can talk Kim into unilaterally giving him what he wants—CVID—up front without giving Kim what he wants: an end to what North Korea calls America's "hostile policy," security assurances, a halt to joint U.S.–South Korea military exercises, withdrawal of U.S. forces from South Korea, normalization of diplomatic relations, sanctions relief, and economic assistance. That's not going to happen, either. Kim, too, should heed the Rolling Stones.

[*Peace with North Korea seems unlikely. But peace often does ahead of time.*]

But diplomacy can work if the administration is ready to give up on its maximalist goals and engages in the give and take of compromise with North Korea—and if Trump and Pompeo accept that negotiations will be drawn out and difficult, not a quick, easy win. As CNN's senior diplomatic correspondent, Michelle Kosinski, tweeted Wednesday of denuclearization, cue Sir Elton singing, "And I think it's gonna be a long, long time."

Step 1 is for the United States to accept the reality, however unpleasant, that North Korea is now a nuclear-armed state. Next is coming to terms with having to tolerate a North Korea with a nuclear arsenal if the United States, South Korea, and North Korea are successful in eventually establishing terms for reconciliation and a comprehensive security regime for the Korean Peninsula.

As much as separating Kim from his nukes might appear to be the only solution to the threat he poses, and would be received as a diplomatic coup for Trump, the central focus on these weapons does not address North Korea's chemical, biological, and conventional weapons, all of which pose an immediate threat to South Korea and Japan and the roughly 28,000 U.S. troops in South Korea. A preoccupation with denuclearization diminishes the real, and realistic, strategic endgame: reducing the risk of war between North and South Korea, and the United States and North Korea, and creating a more stable Korean Peninsula and northeast Asia.

Given North Korea's extant capabilities, denuclearization should be one means to an end, not an end itself. Indeed, the administration's—official Washington's, really—*idée fixe* with CVID has the effect of crowding out other avenues for reducing the risks of war and holds progress hostage to the most intractable and politically loaded issue. There will come a point in these negotiations, as in all negotiations, where both parties will face each other's nonnegotiable bottom lines. For Kim, that will almost certainly be maintaining some sort of nuclear insurance policy. But apart from that, Trump and Pompeo probably don't know yet what his best offer is, and it would therefore be unwise to contemplate short-circuiting the negotiating process.

Preoccupation with CVID counterproductively plays into Trump's penchant for the grand gesture and ignores a few realities: First, American troops on the peninsula, our naval presence in the region, and our nuclear umbrella are already an effective deterrent, one that's worked for years and will continue to work in the future—we don't want war, but neither does Kim. Second, depending on concessions, and an agreement on effective verification measures (much like the now-scrapped Iran deal), North Korea's nuclear and missile capabilities and programs can be capped and reduced. Third, improved North–South political and economic relations and a more normal U.S.–North Korea relationship will give Kim a greater sense of security and at some future point might encourage him to believe he doesn't need a nuclear shield to safeguard North Korean security, and himself.

The administration is now paying a price for its initial demands, its rush to stage last month's summit, and the president's initially inflammatory rhetoric. Having hyped the threat of war last year in his heated exchanges with Kim—"locked and loaded" "fire and fury" "Rocket Man"—and later having exaggerated the peace dividend post-Singapore, Trump is left with reduced leverage; strained ties with North Korea's main patron, China, over trade; South Korea led by a left-leaning president who believes deeply in the "sunshine" policy of reconciliation and wants a North–South peace deal, and an overall approach to North Korea based on an unrealistic goal. Trump has also created the impression that he's vulnerable

to being played by Kim and that he has already given away too much—in particular, the photo op Kim craved—for almost nothing in return. Give Trump his due for what he acknowledged in Singapore: transforming the U.S.–North Korean political relationship and replacing fear with trust and confidence are the keys to achieving meaningful progress toward North Korea's denuclearization. He secured the release of three Americans held by the North Koreans and worked to bring the remains of U.S. troops killed in the Korean War home. But he must further understand this: Kim sees nuclear weapons as the only effective guarantee of his regime's survival. He will cling to these weapons until he reaches the conclusion that the preservation of the North Korean state, in its current form, no longer depends on this nuclear hedge.

With that acknowledgment, the administration needs to decide exactly what price it is willing to pay to achieve the more realistic goal of capping and building down North Korea's nuclear weapons and ballistic missile capabilities and production infrastructure—and that inevitably means asking how far it is prepared to go in providing reliable security guarantees and assisting North Korea with its economic development goals and with sanctions relief.

If the United States and South Korea are successful in negotiating peace treaties and normalization of relations with North Korea, meeting most of their denuclearization goals, reducing other aspects of the North Korean military threat, and gradually integrating North Korea into the regional and global economy, it's worth Washington, and the world, reconciling with the idea of a nuclear North Korea.

Aaron David Miller is an American Middle East analyst, author, and negotiator. He is the vice president for New Initiatives at the Woodrow Wilson International Center for Scholars and has been an advisor to both Republican and Democratic secretaries of state.

Richard Sokolsky is a nonresident senior fellow in Carnegie's Russia and Eurasia Program. His work focuses on U.S. policy toward Russia in the wake of the Ukraine crisis.

EXPLORING THE ISSUE

Should the United States Expect North Korea to Denuclearize?

Critical Thinking and Reflection

1. Why has North Korea worked to nuclearize throughout their existence?
2. How would you characterize the historical relationship between the United States and North Korea? What factors have shaped this relationship?
3. Do you believe North Korea intends to denuclearize today? Why or why not?
4. How does the increasingly positive relationship between North and South Korea impact this discussion?
5. Should the United States press North Korea more directly to denuclearize? Why or why not? Do you think these efforts would be successful?

Is There Common Ground?

Nuclear arsenals are not an area where one might expect to find middle ground. But, when it comes to a country like North Korea looking to build an arsenal, it may in fact be possible. From an outsider's perspective, there is something hypocritical about the United States—a nation with the largest nuclear arsenal in the world—asking North Korea to not join its ranks. Many—especially from smaller, nonnuclear nations—wonder about questions of fairness and equity. And while there are many countries that share American concerns about a rogue leader like Kim Jong-un controlling nuclear weapons, recent actions to better integrate into global society suggest that change may be coming.

All this to say that if North Korea is willing to allow outside observers to meaningfully monitor their progress and development, it is hard to claim they shouldn't be permitted to. The question of middle ground is what type of observation would assure North Korea didn't go rogue with its arsenal and how quickly (and how much) they would develop. After all, if we are looking for North Korea to normalize relations with larger global society, inviting them to a conversation and to allow other countries in to monitor activities would be an important step.

If we assume that Kim is coming to the table genuinely intent on radically altering his country's place among the family of nations, then both he and President Trump will need to enter negotiations with the understanding that any bargaining positions either may have had that are seen as "extreme" by the other, and which were crafted to either posture ahead of negotiations, or were designed for the benefit of public consumption are unlikely to result in a solution. Both of them will need to embrace the art of

the deal. Kim really will need to consider shelving or dismantling his nuclear weapons, but that is merely a starting point. No doubt, the American negotiators will want to see Kim stop engaging in cyberattacks and the plethora of illegal activities the North Korean regime has become so adept at over the decades. Trump must realize that he cannot get to the finish line with Kim without agreeing to a similar list of demands. He will need to be flexible on how and when Kim either freezes or dismantles his nuclear arsenal. Kim will undoubtedly want the United States to agree to remove its troops from South Korea and to cease its annual war games with Seoul. This would imply a radical transformation of the security posture the United States and South Korea have known since the 1950s. Kim will probably also demand assurances about being allowed to remain in power and never to be invaded as long as he and his successors abide by the terms of the agreement.

Additional Resources

Michael Seth, *North Korea: A History* (Red Globe Press, 2018).

Sung Chull Kim and Michael D. Cohen, *North Korea and Nuclear Weapons: Entering the New Era of Deterrence* (Georgetown University Press, 2017).

Jonathan Pollack, *No Exit: North Korea, Nuclear Weapons, and International Security* (Routledge, 2011).

Andrei Lankov, *The Real North Korea: Life and Politics in the Failed Stalinist Utopia* (Oxford University Press, 2014).

Han Park, *North Korea: The Politics of Unconventional Wisdom* (Lynne Rienner, 2005).

Internet References . . .

Chronology of U.S.-North Korean Nuclear and Missile Diplomacy

https://www.armscontrol.org/factsheets/dprkchron

International Atomic Energy Agency

https://www.iaea.org/

North Korea's Military Capabilities

https://www.cfr.org/backgrounder/north-koreas-military-capabilities

Preparatory Commission for the Comprehensive Nuclear-Test-Ban Treaty Organization

https://www.ctbto.org/

Testing North Korea's Nuclear Offer

http://www.atlanticcouncil.org/blogs/new-atlanticist/testing-north-korea-s-nuclear-offer

Selected, Edited, and with Issue Framing Material by:
William J. Miller, *Campus Labs®*

ISSUE

Is the United States Too Tied to Israel When Deciding Policy in the Middle East?

YES: **Ramzy Baroud,** from "The Uneven Alliance: How America Became Pro-Israel," *Al-Jazeera* (2017)

NO: **Tamara Cofman Wittes and Daniel B. Shapiro,** from "How Not to Measure Americans' Support for Israel," *Brookings Institute* (2018)

Learning Outcomes
After reading this issue, you will be able to:
• Identify why the United States works so closely with Israel.
• Describe the historical relationship between the United States and Israel.
• Assess the costs and benefits of the United States' relationship with Israel.
• Explain concerns identified by other nations about this relationship.
• Examine possible future trajectories of this relationship.

ISSUE SUMMARY

YES: Ramzy Baroud—an author and media consultant—examines how and why Israel's influence on the United States has grown over time. He believes this has had a direct impact on American policy choices within the Middle East and negatively impacted many Arab nations.

NO: Tamara Cofman Wittes, a senior fellow at Brookings, and Daniel B. Shapiro, a former ambassador to Israel, argue that Americans continue to support their country's relationship with Israel even as attitudes regarding the Israeli–Palestinian conflict continue to demonstrate increased polarization.

Benjamin Netanyahu, Israel's prime minister, was one of the first foreign leaders to visit President Donald Trump after his election in November 2017 and his inauguration in January 2018 for a simple reason—the United States and Israel have one of the strongest military to military alliances in the world. But why?

The United States supports Israel in diplomatic and military matters not simply because of the strength of pro-Israel lobbies like the American Israeli Public Affairs Committee (AIPAC), or out of sympathy stemming from the events of World War II, but for practical reasons: intelligence sharing and ideological unity. Israel's intelligence and insights into Middle Eastern affairs is unparalleled throughout the world and benefits the United States in more ways than we can imagine. For decades, intelligence analysts have regarded Israel's Unit 8200 as one of the most elite in the world. The unit functions similarly to our domestic National Security Agency, and the two work closely together. In 2010, for example, the United States and Israel collaborated on one of the most sophisticated malware systems ever created, Stuxnet, to infiltrate Iran's cyber infrastructure and slow progress toward nuclear weapons without firing a shot. In missile defense as well, we have worked together to field some of the most effective systems around.

Unlike other U.S. allies in NATO and the Pacific, we have no forward-based troops in Israel, which could serve as a port of last resorts, should the United States ever need friendly territory to stage troops or equipment. But besides having perhaps the world's greatest intelligence sharing partnership, the United States and Israel see eye to eye on something fundamental to both states: democracy. Israel is the only liberal democracy in the Middle East, and there are many shared societal values between the two nations. Like the United States, Israel has regular and open elections with peaceful transitions of power. In a region with failed and failing states, Israel is really an important ideological ally.

Like ourselves, or virtually any country on earth, Israel is not without its enemies. The United Nations has pushed back on Israel's treatment of Palestinians and their support for Jewish settlements outside of Israel's borders. Specifically, Israel in the past two years pushed through legislation that retroactively legalizes about 4,000 settler homes built on privately owned Palestinian land in a move that a United Nations spokesperson called a contravention of international law. As a result, if you're a supporter of the Palestinian cause, it's reasonable to ask why the United States is supporting Israel. Even within our own country, many take exception to funding given to Israel considering the treatment of Palestinians. Furthermore, American military aid and weapons have been used by the Israelis against Palestinians in their territory.

Others worry about the balance of the United States' aide to Israel. In 2015, more than half of our foreign military aid went to Israel. That's about $3.1 billion dollars. Much of this money Israel spends on U.S. defense projects in return. And it's all noticed. Israel's treatment of the Palestinians, for example, has not gone unnoticed by its neighbors in the Middle East. Historically, support for Israel causes tension with allies in the region for obvious reasons. Many question whether our support for Israel is worth the issues it raises with other, more powerful, allies. But our allies have learned to deal with Israel.

Saudi Arabia and other Gulf nations no longer protest the U.S.–Israeli relationship as they did in the 1970s with the oil embargo, as we now have many sources of oil and the price of crude oil has plummeted. Iran, however, is not an American ally by any means and remains a sworn enemy of Israel. Iran openly supports Hezbollah and Hamas, militant groups in the West Bank, Gaza, and Lebanon, which wage war against Israel. Iran tests ballistic missiles with Israel must be wiped off the face of the planet and launches naval vessels with slogans like death to America.

Today, the United States and Israel find themselves at odds over issues such as the Jewish settlements in the West Bank or whether Israel should pursue a one- or two-state solution to their borders. But, in the past, confrontations have been much more substantial, and sometimes violent. In 1967, Israel's air force attacked the USS Liberty, an American Navy vessel in international waters in the Mediterranean. The attack killed 34 virtually defenseless U.S. sailors as Israeli planes and torpedo boats made multiple attacks. Israel apologized for the attack, claimed it was a mistake, and provided compensation, but survivors of the attack maintain that it was deliberate.

In the 1980s, Jonathan Pollard, an American naval intelligence analyst passed classified information to the Israelis that the United States had withheld despite a memorandum of understanding between the two nations that such intelligence should be shared. Pollard eventually pleaded guilty to one count of conspiracy to commit espionage and served 30 years in prison. So, while the American alliance with Israel puts U.S. diplomats in some tricky situations with the UN over human rights concerns and Iran, the alliance has survived sometimes extreme difficulties to massively benefit both parties while supporting a strong, liberal democracy in the Middle East.

The reality of U.S. policy for years has reflected a broader understanding. President Barack Obama, like his predecessors, pushed hard for progress toward a two-state solution—an effort in which one of us was directly involved as the U.S. ambassador to Israel. Obama's push sometimes created tension or disagreements with Israel's leadership (although he hardly spared the Palestinians the same). At the same time, like other presidents of both parties, he celebrated the shared values at the heart of the U.S.–Israel partnership; encouraged U.S.–Israeli trade, investment, and scientific cooperation; and upheld U.S. commitments to Israel's security. He won praise from Israeli leaders for increased military assistance, investment in lifesaving missile-defense technologies, and expanded intelligence cooperation to deal with regional threats. And he did all this with strong support from the American public.

Americans are far more divided on the Israeli–Palestinian conflict than they are on Israel or the U.S.–Israel relationship—and so when Israel advocates and Israelis themselves use this poll question as a proxy for American support for Israel, they are not doing themselves any favors. The organizations that have traditionally led on advocacy for Israel, like AIPAC, have always prized bipartisanship, recognizing that the pendulum of American politics swings both ways and that Israel never benefits from being used as a partisan political football.

In the following selections, we examine whether this is worth the cost for America today. Ramzy Baroud—an author and media consultant—examines how and why Israel's influence on the United States has grown over time. He believes this has had a direct impact on American policy choices within the Middle East and negatively impacted many Arab nations. Tamara Cofman Wittes, a senior fellow at Brookings, and Daniel Shapiro, a former ambassador to Israel, argue that Americans continue to support their country's relationship with Israel even as attitudes regarding the Israeli–Palestinian conflict continue to demonstrate increased polarization.

YES

Ramzy Baroud

The Uneven Alliance: How America Became Pro-Israel

Mere days after Donald Trump won the US presidential election, American Zionists moved quickly to ensure that Israeli interests were fully guarded by the new administration.

The Zionist Organization of America (ZOA) wasted no time, hobnobbing with notorious racists, also known for their anti-Jewish agendas. ZOA's annual gala on November 20 hosted none other than Steve Bannon, a leader in the so-called alt-right, otherwise known as white supremacy in the United States.

Under his leadership, Breitbart, seen as a major platform for the alt-right, fueled anti-Semitism (needless to say, racisms of all shades) argued Alex Amend and Jonathan Morgan in AlterNet.

Watching top Israeli officials and leaders of the Jewish community in the United States hosting—ever so enthusiastically—Bannon at ZOA's annual gala appeared perplexing to some. Others casually explained it as the nature of politics, as Israel needs its US alliance even if it meant accommodating anti-Semites.

But it is hardly that simple.

Bannon's ties with Zionists go back well before the rather surprising Trump election victory. In fact, Israel has never had a problem with true anti-Semites. Instead, it merely rebranded any criticism of the Israeli occupation of Palestinian land as anti-Semitism.

By conflating the term, the Zionists managed to largely silence all debate on Israel in the United States, and despite stubborn attempts to break Israel's stronghold on Zionist control over the Palestine and Middle East narrative in US media, government, and society as a whole, Israel continues to maintain the upper hand, as it has for decades.

Speaking in the White House's East Room on February 15, in a joint press conference with President Trump, Israeli Prime Minister Benjamin Netanyahu cordially thanked Trump for his hospitality, and then uttered these words: "Israel has no better ally than the United States. And I want to assure you, the United States has no better ally than Israel."

But it was only half true. The United States has indeed been a stalwart supporter of Israel, offering it over $3.1bn in financial assistance each year for the last a few decades, an amount that dramatically increased under President Barack Obama to $3.8 bn. In addition to hundreds of millions more in all kinds of financial, military assistance, and "loans" that went mostly unaccounted for.

However, Netanyahu lied. His country has not been an equally strong ally to the United States; in fact, Israel has been a liability. Let alone the various serious episodes of Israeli spying on Washington and bartering US secrets and technologies with Russia and China, Israel has been the cause of instability in the Middle East region.

Since World War II, the United States has vied to achieve two main foreign policy objectives in the Middle East: control the region and its resources and prop-up its allies (often dictators), while maintaining a degree of "stability" so that the United States is able to conduct its business unhindered.

In March 2010, General David Petraeus, then head of the US Central Command told the Senate Armed Services Committee during a testimony that Israel had become a liability for the United States and that has become a challenge to "security and stability," which his country aimed to achieve.

He said: "Israeli–Palestinian tensions often flare into violence and large-scale armed confrontations. The conflict foments anti-American sentiment, due to a perception of US favoritism for Israel. Arab anger over the Palestinian question limits the strength and depth of US partnerships with governments and peoples in the AOR (Area of Operations) and weakens the legitimacy of moderate regimes in the Arab World. Meanwhile, al-Qaeda and other militant groups exploit that anger to mobilize support."

Although speaking strictly from a US military interest, the Israeli lobby attacked Petraeus almost immediately. Abe Foxman, Director of the Anti-Defamation League, which often mischaracterizes its role as that of combating racism in the United States, lashed out at the top American commander calling his conclusions "dangerous and counterproductive."

In the United States, no one is immune to Israeli criticism, including the president himself, who is expected to accommodate Israeli whims, without expecting any Israeli reciprocation.

A particularly telling episode revealed the degree of Israeli influence in the United States, when then-House Speaker John Boehner plotted with then-Israel's ambassador to Washington, Ron Dermer to arrange a visit and a speech before Congress for Netanyahu, in defiance of President Obama.

Netanyahu then raged and raved before a united Congress (with a few exceptions) that repeatedly endowed the Israeli prime minister with many standing ovations as he belittled their president and strongly criticized US foreign policy on Iran.

But how did Israel achieve such commanding influence over US foreign policy?

In an article entitled: "Steve Bannon's web of Weirdness: Meet the Bizarre Billionaires behind the President-elect's Chief Strategist," Heather Digby Patron named a few of these "bizarre billionaires." They included, Sheldon Adelson, a right-wing billionaire with a gambling empire, who is "singularly focused on the state of Israel." Adelson's relations with Bannon (and Trump) has well preceded Trump's victory and seemed to take little notice of the fact that Bannon and his ilk were viewed by many American Jews as frightening, racist anti-Semites with a menacing agenda.

Adelson, however, cares little for the true racists. His obsession to shield Israel's militant Zionist agenda trumped all other seemingly little irritants.

But the gambling mogul is not the exception among powerful Zionists in the United States.

Israeli commentator Gideon Levy agrees. In an article published by *Haaretz* on November 21, Levy wrote, "When friendship for Israel is judged solely on the basis of support for the occupation, Israel has no friends other than racists and nationalists."

Thus, it is no surprise that Adelson is funding a massively rich campaign and lavish conferences to combat the influence of the civil society–powered Boycott, Divestment and Sanctions (BDS) movement while plotting with American elements that consider the word "Jew" a swear word in their own social lexicon to support Zionist Israel.

By putting Israel and Zionism first, these rich individuals, powerful lobby groups, hundreds of think-tanks, thousands of networks across the country, and their allies among the religious right are now the main wheelers and dealers in any matter concerning US foreign policy in the Middle East and Israel's political and security interests.

Zionists often speak of a historical bond between the United States and the Jewish people, but nothing could be further from the truth.

On May 13, 1939, a boat carrying hundreds of German Jews was not allowed to reach American shores and was eventually sent back to Europe.

That was not a foreign policy fluke.

Three months earlier, in February 1939, members of Congress rejected a bill that would allow 20,000 German Jewish children to come to the United States to escape the war and possible extermination at the hands of the Nazis.

While these Jews were not always welcome, Zionists were already forging strong alliances in the government and applying pressure on the White House to establish a "Jewish state" in Palestine.

Indeed, the early days of Zionist lobbying go back to the early 20th century, but such lobbying became truly fruitful during the presidency of Harry S. Truman to pressure the White House to back the partition of Palestine.

Writing in his memoir, Truman noted, "The facts were that not only were there pressure movements around the United Nations unlike anything that had been seen there before, but that the White House, too, was subjected to a constant barrage."

"I do not think I ever had as much pressure and propaganda aimed at the White House as I had in this instance. The persistence of a few of the extreme Zionist leaders—actuated by political motives and engaging in political threats—disturbed and annoyed me."

In their seminal article, The Israel Lobby (which served as the thesis of their book) in the *London Review of Books*, two prominent American scholars John Mearsheimer and Stephen Walt took on the painstaking task of deconstructing the power of the "formal" and "informal" Israel lobby that has grown exponentially in recent years.

They argued that the power of the lobby is now so great to the point that it has largely orchestrated the US war on Iraq in 2003, only to shift following the war fiasco to advocate wars against Iran and Syria; in addition to ensuring that there can never be a balanced US foreign policy on Israel and Palestine.

"So, if neither strategic nor moral arguments can account for America's support for Israel, how are we to explain it?" they asked in their article, offering only one possible answer: "The explanation is the unmatched power of the Israel Lobby."

While certainly not all Jewish Americans are part of or even supporters of the lobby, the massive pro-Israel network managed to sell the idea to many US Jews that their fate is linked to supporting Israeli policy, no matter how destructive or self-defeating.

"Jewish Americans have set up an impressive array of organizations to influence American foreign policy, of which AIPAC is the most powerful and best known," the two American scholars wrote.

According to Fortune Magazine's 1997 issue, American Israeli Public Affairs Committee (AIPAC) is considered the second most powerful lobby in Washington, an assessment that was upheld by the National Journal Study in March 2005.

"The Lobby" also relies on Christian evangelicals who have long advocated the return of Jews to Palestine as to fulfill some biblical prophecy pertaining to the end of times. Historically, Zionists have had no quarrel working with such hate-peddling preachers as Jerry Falwell, Pat Robertson, and John Hagee.

When Israel attacked Lebanon in the summer of 2006, thousands of evangelicals descended on Washington to lobby Congress to support Israel unconditionally.

They arrived from all 50 states and, in one single day, they reportedly held 280 meetings on Capitol Hill.

But unlike the early days of Zionist lobbying, the lobby is no longer standing on the sidelines urging to the Congress and the executive branch to adopt a pro-Israel agenda.

In the last two decades, they have managed to infiltrate all aspects of government, thus formulating policy directly.

Mearsheimer and Walt, but also others discussed the evolution of the lobby in the form of the neoconservatives during the presidency of George W. Bush, which was coupled with the proliferation of "think-tanks" and policy forums, all with the ultimate aim of backing Israel, no matter the high cost for the United States and needless to say for Palestinians and the Middle East.

Moreover, the lobby is no longer satisfied with attempting to sway Washington, by pressuring the Congress and the executive branch—where being pro-Israel has been the expected natural state of mind for American lawmakers (save the few courageous ones)—but "It also strives to ensure that public discourse portrays Israel in a positive light, by repeating myths about its founding and by promoting its point of view in policy debates," according to The Israel Lobby.

"The goal is to prevent critical comments from getting a fair hearing in the political arena. Controlling the debate is essential to guaranteeing US support, because a candid discussion of US–Israeli relations might lead Americans to favor a different policy."

This is why the lobby is currently mobilizing to stop and even criminalize the BDS movement, for, even if it failed to nudge US foreign policy in a more sensible direction, BDS is relatively succeeding in creating more platforms for open discussions on many university campuses and some media.

Several US states have officially launched initiatives to defeat BDS and more are likely to follow. The fear of losing complete control over the narrative is frightening for the pro-Israel lobby. For them, only Israeli myth peddlers and fear-mongering preachers must be allowed to speak to Congress, media, and public.

Although recent polls have shown that younger Americans—especially among Democratic party supporters and young Jewish Americans—are losing their enthusiasm for Israel and its Zionist ideology—the battle for the United States to reclaim its foreign policy and a sense of morality regarding Palestine and the Middle East is likely to be long and arduous.

Only a better and more honest understanding of the rule of the lobby can serve as a first step toward its dismantlement.

RAMZY BAROUD has been writing about the Middle East for over 20 years. He is an internationally syndicated columnist, a media consultant, an author of several books, and the founder of PalestineChronicle.com. His latest book is *My Father Was a Freedom Fighter: Gaza's Untold Story* (Pluto Press, London).

Tamara Cofman Wittes and Daniel B. Shapiro

How Not to Measure Americans' Support for Israel

When the Pew Research Center released its findings this week on American views of the Israeli–Palestinian conflict, the traditional handwringing ensued. Many pundits and reporters read in the results that Republicans and Democrats are growing further and further apart in their support for Israel. Based on the findings, some Israeli pundits and politicians, and many on the American right, have been arguing that Israel and its supporters should give up on the Democratic Party and its elected representatives as supporters of Israel.

The Pew poll is a terrible foundation for such claims, and the claims themselves demand close scrutiny. Support for Israel is, in fact, becoming a politicized issue in the United States, and partisan divides on policy toward the Israeli–Palestinian conflict are indeed getting wider. But the wrong response risks making Israel's real problems in American public opinion worse.

Let's first understand the realities. This poll question, asked annually by Pew since 2001, is a very poor indicator of American attitudes toward Israel. The question reads, "In the dispute between Israel and the Palestinians, which side do you sympathize with more, Israel or the Palestinians?" The wording, quite obviously, asks the respondent to make a binary choice between two seemingly exclusive options. (The poll also records the number of those who volunteer an answer of "both" or "neither," but those options are not offered by the interviewer.)

The poll question is faulty because sympathy for Palestinians should not imply hostility to Israel, nor should sympathy for Israel require disregard for the fate of Palestinians. A solution to their conflict enshrining two states for two peoples is the outcome most preferred by Americans regardless of party, and administrations of both parties have sought to help both Israel and the Palestinians achieve their goals in a two-state solution. In fact, as the efforts of President Bill Clinton and President George W. Bush attest, successful U.S. mediation of the conflict requires empathy with both sides and understanding of their narratives.

Despite these realities, though, the strong push in the poll question's construction is toward dichotomy: Which side are you on? Thus the responses, by design, suggest greater polarization than perhaps exists in reality. In fact, the answers really don't show us how divided Americans are.

Even if you are among those who find the Pew survey valuable to the extent it shows *changes* in attitudes over time, it's important to understand what trend you're seeing. Looking at the underlying data from the survey responses, we see that 34 percent of this year's sample identify as independents—more than identify as Republicans (26 percent) or Democrats (33 percent). The gap between independents and Republicans remains large and trending larger, but the independents' trend tracks the Democratic trend—both moving toward less sympathy with Israel relative to the Palestinians in the conflict between them. That's the pattern that should worry Israelis, because independents and Democrats together represent more than ⊠ of Americans.

The deeper problem with the poll question is that the results are marketed by Pew, covered by the media, and used by political partisans to indicate American attitudes toward Israel, when what the question measures (albeit badly) is attitudes toward the Israeli–Palestinian conflict. This misleading framing reinforces an existing problem: that "Israel" is conflated in the public mind with "the Israeli–Palestinian conflict." Of course, the conflict is a major policy issue for the United States, although arguably less central to U.S. security interests, and less demanding of U.S. policy makers' time today, than it has been since the 1970s. But we think pro-Israel Republicans and Democrats should agree that the conflict is not, and should not be, the totality of what Israel means to Americans.

The reality of U.S. policy for years has reflected a broader understanding. President Barack Obama, like his predecessors, pushed hard for progress toward a two-state solution—an effort in which one of us was directly involved as a U.S. ambassador to Israel. Obama's push sometimes created tension or disagreements with Israel's leadership (although he hardly spared the Palestinians the same). At the same time, like other presidents of both parties, he celebrated the shared values at the heart of the U.S.–Israel partnership; encouraged U.S.–Israeli trade, investment, and scientific cooperation; and upheld U.S. commitments to Israel's security. He won praise from Israeli leaders for increased military assistance, investment in lifesaving missile defense technologies, and expanded intelligence cooperation to deal with regional threats. And he did all this with strong support from the American public.

Americans are far more divided on the Israeli–Palestinian conflict than they are on Israel or the U.S.–Israel relationship—and so when Israel advocates and Israelis themselves use this poll question as a proxy for American support for Israel, they are not doing themselves any favors. The organizations that have traditionally led on advocacy for Israel, like American Israeli Public Affairs Committee, have always prized bipartisanship, recognizing that the pendulum of American politics swings both ways and that Israel never benefits from being used as a partisan political football.

The Pew poll, though, does show real changes in attitudes toward the Israeli–Palestinian conflict among adherents of the two political parties, and a look at more detailed polling tells us why. In recent years, some Americans have come to look at the Israeli–Palestinian conflict through the lens of human rights—and this is especially true for younger Americans, African Americans, and Hispanic Americans. This makes them sensitive to the hardships faced by Palestinian civilians, and to certain Israeli practices, like housing demolitions. These groups form a larger proportion of the voting public than they have in the past, and a growing proportion of the Democratic Party's core constituency. And yes, there is some anti-Israel sentiment on the left end of the progressive political spectrum, just as there is some on the right end of the conservative camp.

These trends place a responsibility on Democrats like the two of us, who believe a U.S. commitment to Israel is a strategic and moral imperative, to continue educating others about why that is the case. We also believe, and will continue to explain, how such a commitment is fully consistent with working for a resolution to the Israeli–Palestinian conflict through a two-state outcome.

Likewise, Israeli leaders should take these underlying trends to heart, and act accordingly. The survey results point to how specific aspects of Israeli policy, such as the expansion of West Bank settlements that make a two-state solution more difficult, affect the way Israel is viewed in the United States. As American society becomes "majority–minority," with no group, including Americans of European origin, constituting a majority of the population, Israelis should consider what policies can best shore up the U.S.–Israeli relationship, and which might erode its foundations. Israelis don't have to take all the blame for the diplomatic stalemate—Palestinians bear plenty of their share, from failing to respond to negotiating proposals, to inciting and glorifying violence, to denying the historical Jewish connection to the land of Israel. But an Israeli government that does not seem committed at least to keeping the two-state solution alive and viable for the future will likely find there are some American supporters whose sympathy they will struggle to retain.

The sharp uptick this year in partisan divides over the Israeli–Palestinian conflict is also a consequence of the increased tribalism in American politics generally, and the readiness of American leaders to play into that tribalism, even on issues about which there used to be more consensus. In this fevered environment, anytime President Trump and his allies say "up," Republicans leap to agree and Democrats leap to say "down." Israeli leaders may find it difficult to resist the temptation to ride this wave, embracing one side in partisan U.S. political battles—as when Prime Minister Benjamin Netanyahu arranged his speech in Congress against the Iran deal solely with the Republican congressional leadership. But that approach comes at the cost of alienating even longtime allies across the aisle, and when the next crisis inevitably hits, Israel's leaders may regret having burned those bridges.

Indeed, Israelis of all stripes should beware of playing into partisanship in the United States. Israeli leaders would be wise not to allow the perception to take hold that they are writing off whole chunks of the Democratic camp, or disrespecting elected officials from the Democratic Party. And without weakening their own relationship with President Trump, Israeli leaders should find ways to demonstrate sensitivity to progressives' concerns, especially when those concerns touch on issues core to the values Israel and the United States share. One clear missed opportunity was Netanyahu's failure to speak out swiftly and strongly against the racism and anti-Semitism on display in Charlottesville last fall.

The bottom line is that a partisan divide over American support for Israel is neither natural nor inevitable.

Last year, polling data from the University of Maryland showed that ¾ of all Americans—including 70 percent of Democrats and 68 percent of Independents—see Israel as a strategic asset to the United States. That's a strong consensus, and one to hold onto.

TAMARA COFMAN WITTES is a senior fellow in the Center for Middle East Policy at the Brookings Institution. She directed the Center from March 2012 through March 2017. From November 2009 through January 2012, she was a Deputy Assistant Secretary for Near Eastern Affairs at the United States Department of State.

DANIEL B. "DAN" SHAPIRO is a diplomat and former Ambassador of the United States of America to the State of Israel. He was nominated by President Barack Obama on March 29, 2011, and confirmed by the Senate on May 29. He was sworn in as an ambassador by Secretary of State Hillary Clinton on July 8, 2011.

EXPLORING THE ISSUE

Is the United States Too Tied to Israel When Deciding Policy in the Middle East?

Critical Thinking and Reflection

1. Why do you believe the United States has always been linked so closely with Israel?
2. Do you believe a close relationship with Israel benefits American foreign policy? Why or why not?
3. How could America alter its relationship with Israel to improve its relationship with other Middle East nations?
4. What would the future of Israel look like in the Middle East with less American support?
5. Could a candidate win the American presidency without pledging full support to Israel? Why or why not?

Is There Common Ground?

Strategically, it is essential that the United States maintains solid allies throughout the Middle East. Yet, pressure remains on how heavily we should favor Israel in regional issues, including that of Palestine. This issue has remained a popular talking point on both the left and the right, while centrists of both parties are largely pushed to the sidelines. While the far left cries of an Israeli-committed genocide, the far right portrays Palestinians as backward people undeserving of statehood. Both sides hold and promote extreme views, leaving no room for the middle path many would prefer we walk. That middle path would require defending Israel to many liberals and Islam to many conservatives.

In reality, a true middle ground would acknowledge the flaws of both sides; it would not accept Islamophobia nor ignore human rights abuses. We need to allow for a political position that acknowledges two difficult truths: Israel is a flawed democracy—in which women, LGBT people, and others are well treated while ethnic minorities need defending—and Palestine is illiberal, undemocratic, and in need of much deeper reforms. This middle ground—which currently doesn't exist in American political discourse—is

the only rational path forward. Although I expect today's political polarization and extremism to continue, we can idealistically hope that Americans on both sides of the political spectrum will educate themselves and be ready to listen to centrist voices when we inevitably take on this conflict.

Additional Resources

John J. Mearsheimer and Stephen M. Walt, *The Israel Lobby and U.S. Foreign Policy* (Farrar, Straus and Giroux, 2008).

Robert O. Freedman, *Israel and the United States: Six Decades of US-Israeli Relations* (Routledge, 2012).

Dennis Ross, *Doomed to Succeed: The U.S.-Israel Relationship from Truman to Obama Paperback* (Farrar, Straus and Giroux, 2016).

Daniel Gordis, *Israel: A Concise History of a Nation Reborn* (Ecco, 2017).

David Lesch and Mark Haas, *The Middle East and the United States: History, Politics, and Ideologies* (Routledge, 2018).

Internet References . . .

AIPAC: America's Pro-Israel Lobby

https://www.aipac.org/

Fact Sheet U.S.–Israel Economic Relationship

https://il.usembassy.gov/our-relationship/
policy-history/fact-sheet-u-s-israel-economic-
relationship/

Israel–U.S. Relations

https://www.timesofisrael.com/topic/israel-
us-relations/

Repairing the U.S.–Israel Relationship

https://www.cfr.org/report/repairing-us-israel-
relationship

U.S. Relations with Israel

https://www.state.gov/r/pa/ei/bgn/3581.htm